Miraculous Realism

THE SUNY SERIES

HORIZONS OF CINEMA

MURRAY POMERANCE | EDITOR

Miraculous Realism

The French-Walloon Cinéma du Nord

Niels Niessen

Published by State University of New York Press, Albany

© 2020 State University of New York

All rights reserved

Printed in the United States of America

No part of this book may be used or reproduced in any manner whatsoever without written permission. No part of this book may be stored in a retrieval system or transmitted in any form or by any means including electronic, electrostatic, magnetic tape, mechanical, photocopying, recording, or otherwise without the prior permission in writing of the publisher.

For information, contact State University of New York Press, Albany, NY
www.sunypress.edu

Library of Congress Cataloging-in-Publication Data

Names: Niessen, Niels, 1980– author.
Title: Miraculous realism : the French-Walloon cinéma du Nord / Niels Niessen.
Description: Albany : State University of New York Press, [2020] | Series: SUNY series, horizons of cinema | Includes bibliographical references and index.
Identifiers: LCCN 2019036256 | ISBN 9781438477336 (hardcover : alk. paper) | ISBN 9781438477343 (pbk. : alk. paper) | ISBN 9781438477350 (ebook)
Subjects: LCSH: Borderlands in motion pictures. | Rosetta (Motion picture) | Humanité (Motion picture) | Nord-Pas-de-Calais (France)—In motion pictures. | Wallonia (Belgium)—In motion pictures.
Classification: LCC PN1995.9.B67 N54 2020 | DDC 791.43/658—dc23
LC record available at https://lccn.loc.gov/2019036256

10 9 8 7 6 5 4

To my parents

Ce n'est pas tant la Belgique ou la France qui ont gagné cette année à Cannes, que ce Nord rugueux et fier qui produit bon an mal an un cinéma régional dont la principale vertu est de veiller à maintenir une certaine flamme, ou à entretenir une vraie colère. (Not so much Belgium or France have won this year at Cannes, but this rough and proud Nord that with ups and downs produces a regional cinema, whose main virtue is to maintain a certain flame, or to entertain a true anger.)

—Serge Toubiana, "Le Cinéma retrouvé"

This is a fable, slightly wistful perhaps, but quietly optimistic within its poetic framework. If I might be allowed to give it such a name. Men and angels are to be found here, living on good terms together.

—Vittorio de Sica, "How I Direct My Films," preface to the English-language edition of the screenplay of *Miracle in Milan*

Contents

List of Illustrations	ix
A North Wind, or The Miracle of Cannes 1999	1
Introduction: A Critical Fairy Tale	5
1 Hunting for Easter Eggs in *Rosetta* and *L'humanité*	21

A Normal Life, 23 | humanity with a small *h*, 30 | The Acting/Acted Body, 35 | Of Little Flies and Burned-Out Priests, 47 | *a north wind*, 55 | Game Over, or The Moral of the Story, 62

2 Coal-Fired Dreams, the Cinéma du Nord	65

The Nord, 70 | From *Pays Noir* to Euroregion, 75 | Between Utopia and Dystopia: Wallonia in the Cinema, 95 | *Not* Paris: Nord-Pas-de-Calais in the Cinema, 107 | Conclusion, 122 | Of Giants, Angels, and Humans, 123

3 Cinéma du Nord, a Euregional Cinema	129

Transnational Coproduction, 133 | Argument, 135 | *Terre d'Images*: Northern French Cinema within French National Cinema, 136 | *Yes We Cannes*: Francophone-Belgian Cinema in Its Walloon Manifestation, 148 | At the Crossroads of Europe, 161 | Google, Van Gogh, the Louvre-Lens, and a *Terril* of Coats, 167

Excursion: From the Nord, with Love	175
4 New Realism after the Modern Cinema	189

What Is Realism?, 194 | Neorealism, 198 | From Neo to New: Miraculous Realism, 204 | The Modern Cinema, 211 | The Acting/Acted Image, 216 | The Question of Grace in Francophone European Film Philosophy, 224

Epilogue: Posthumanism   235

Acknowledgments   247

Notes   249

Films Referenced   281

Bibliography   289

Index   303

Illustrations

Figures

0.1	Front page of *La Voix du Nord*, May 25, 1999.	2
I.1	*Rosetta*.	7
I.2	*L'humanité*.	7
I.3	*Caché*.	14
I.4	*The Matrix*.	15
1.1–1.3	The opening scene of *Rosetta*.	22
1.4	Through a wooden gate she's not supposed to use.	24
1.5	Rosetta, carrying a heavy plastic bag, once again finds her way through the woods.	25
1.6–1.8	The opening scene of *L'humanité*.	31
1.9	*L'humanité* in reference to Georges Braque's *Landscape with Plow*.	32
1.10	Pharaon eating an apple in reference to René Magritte's *La Chambre d'Ecoute*.	33
1.11	One time, though, the camera catches Rosetta masturbating, perhaps.	39
1.12	A north wind creeping underneath the trailer window.	39
1.13	Rosetta holds the hair dryer just like a medic performing an ultrasound scan.	39

1.14	From the promotional trailer Jean-Luc Godard made for Bresson's *Mouchette*.	48
1.15	*Mouchette*.	49
1.16	*Sous le soleil de Satan*.	52
1.17	*Journal d'un curé de campagne*.	52
1.18	Rosetta bumps into the young woman whose job she has just been given.	58
1.19	The only thing Rosetta symbolically gives birth to is the hard-boiled egg.	58
1.20	Rosetta looks offscreen at her savior.	58
1.21	Pharaon looks offscreen at the diffuse white light.	59
1.22	Pharaon floating in the void.	61
2.1	The Rosetta Plan.	66
2.2	Ch'ti beer on display in the museum shop of the Louvre-Lens.	69
2.3	Official and unofficial language communities in Belgium and Nord-Pas-de-Calais.	71
2.4	Acquisition of territory by France along its northern frontier.	73
2.5	Geology of the French-Belgian border region.	76
2.6	Distribution of urban settlements in the French-Belgian border region.	77
2.7	Vincent van Gogh, *The Potato Eaters*.	80
2.8	*Lust for Life*.	81
2.9	Van Gogh (Kirk Douglas) in a coal mine.	81
2.10	"Every now and then . . ."	81
2.11	*Misère au Borinage*.	85
2.12	Workers parading with a portrait of Karl Marx.	85
2.13	The contradictions inherent to capitalism.	85
2.14	The Lille-Europe railway station as seen in *L'humanité*.	90

2.15	Pharaon waiting for the Eurostar to London.	90
2.16	The construction of the Liège-Guillemins railway station as seen in Thierry Michel's documentary *Métamorphoses d'une gare*.	90
2.17	*Métamorphoses d'une gare*.	90
2.18	EU funding in Nord-Pas-de-Calais.	91
2.19	The border-crossing metropolitan area around Lille as seen on Google Maps.	93
2.20	GDP per capita in 2000 in northern France, Belgium, Luxembourg, the southern Netherlands, and southwest Germany.	94
2.21	Unemployment rates at the end of 2004 in northern France, Belgium, and Luxembourg.	94
2.22	Unemployment among people under twenty-five at the end of 2004 in northern France, Belgium, and Luxembourg.	95
2.23–2.25	*Déjà s'envole la fleur maigre*.	99
2.26–2.28	*Enfants du hasard*.	104
2.29	*Les Convoyeurs attendent*.	106
2.30	*L'Enfance nue*.	114
2.31	*Les 400 coups*.	114
2.32	*L'Enfance nue*.	115
2.33	*Les 400 coups*.	115
2.34	*Hadewijch*.	116
2.35–2.38	*With Love from Calais*.	118
2.39–2.41	*La Vie rêvée des anges*.	126
3.1	*Rosetta*.	131
3.2	*L'humanité*.	133
3.3	Leader preceding francophone-Belgian films.	149

3.4	*Eldorado*.	157
3.5	*Les Géants*.	157
3.6	*Les Premiers, les derniers*.	157
3.7	Young filmmakers in francophone Belgium.	159
3.8	"It's in the Nord we make TransMedia foam."	166
3.9	The Van Gogh house in the Walloon town of Wasmes.	168
3.10	The *Galérie du temps* in the Louvre-Lens.	169
3.11	The Louvre-Lens addressing "those at a remove from culture."	170
3.12–3.14	Memorial of biscuit boxes. From Christian Boltanski's *La Salle des pendus* in the Musée des Arts Contemporains de la Fédération Wallonie-Bruxelles.	172
3.15	*Terril* of coats. From Christian Boltanski's *La Salle des pendus* in the Musée des Arts Contemporains de la Fédération Wallonie-Bruxelles.	173
i–ii	The Liège-Guillemins train station.	174
iii–iv	*Terril* in Wasmes, Wallonia.	176
v–viii	*fleurs du terril*.	177
ix	Maison Van Gogh de Colfontaine in Wasmes.	178
x	Brasserie Van Gogh in Boussu.	178
xi	Maison Van Gogh in Mons.	178
xii	Charbonnage de Frameries.	179
xiii	Charleroi.	180
xiv	Mons.	180
xv	Charleroi.	180
xvi	Marcinelle.	180
xvii–xviii	Lens.	181
xix	Liévin.	182
xx–xxii	Liévin.	183

xxiii–xxiv	Dunes de la Slack.	184
xxv–xxviii	*fleurs de la pierre*	185
xxix–xxx	Charleroi's phantom subway.	186
xxxi	Charleroi.	186
xxxii	Liège.	187
xxxiii	Borinage.	187
xxxiv	Valenciennes.	187
4.1	*Y'Aura-t'il de la neige à Noël?*	191
4.2	*Welcome.*	191
4.3	*Miracolo a Milano.*	205
4.4	*Still Life.*	205
4.5	*The World.*	205
4.6–4.8	*A Nos amours.*	221
4.9	"Amor Omnia Vincit."	231
4.10	"Je ne cherche pas, je trouve."	231
4.11	"Si vous vous moquez de Balzac, je vous tue."	231
4.12	*Le Silence de Lorna.*	232

Charts

3.1	Annual production of first and second feature-length French initiative films.	142
3.2	Coproductions with France in francophone-Belgian cinema, 2001–2017.	162
3.3	France's main coproducing partners, 2002–2015.	162

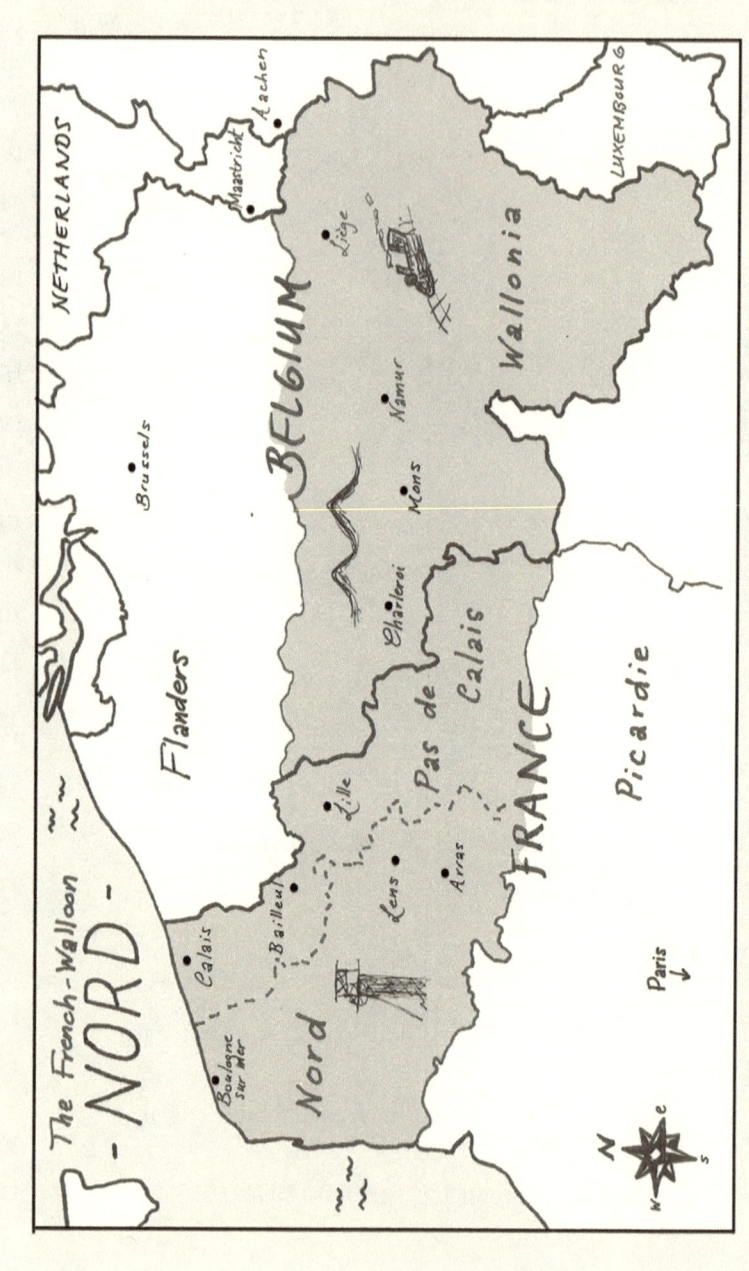

A North Wind, or The Miracle of Cannes 1999

Once upon a time in 1999 a miracle happened at the Cannes International Film Festival, when two films from the French-Belgian border region swept almost all main awards. *Rosetta* by the Walloon filmmakers Jean-Pierre Dardenne and Luc Dardenne won the Palme d'or, and *L'humanité* by the northern French Bruno Dumont won the Grand Prix, the festival's "second prize." Both films, moreover, remarkably received acting prizes for their first-time screen performances: Emmanuel Schotté (Pharaon in *L'humanité*) was chosen best male actor, and Séverine Caneele (Domino in *L'humanité*) and Émilie Dequenne (*Rosetta*) shared the award for best actress. "The battle of humanity has been won: the jury's big blow to the cinema professionals," headlines read the following Tuesday in the Walloon newspaper *Le Soir*. "*Vent du Nord*," A north wind, the northern French regional newspaper *La Voix du Nord* triumphed (fig. 0.1). And *Le Monde* dedicated its front page "to Rosetta, for Humanity."[1]

Not everyone was happy, however, with that night's course of events in the Lumière theater. That a jury led by David Cronenberg had lauded such seemingly bleak portraits of human struggle shot with largely nonprofessional casts stirred a controversy of the kind the festival had not seen since 1987, when the Golden Palm went to Maurice Pialat's *Sous le soleil de Satan / Under the Sun of Satan*, incidentally another tale of humanity from northern francophone Europe. Pialat's response that year to the boos and whistles: "If you don't like me, let me tell you, I don't like you either," while he raised his fist to the audience. Also in 1999 there was booing. Though most present in Cannes could live with

Figure 0.1. Front page of *La Voix du Nord* (May 25, 1999).

the jury's unanimous choice for *Rosetta* as best film, its embrace of *L'humanité*—and its implicit dismissal of festival favorites like David Lynch's *The Straight Story*, Jim Jarmusch's *Ghost Dog*, and Pedro Almodóvar's *Todo Sobre Mi Madre / All about My Mother*—created bad blood. "Clearly Cronenberg, following the Cannes furor over *Crash*, seemed determined to remain controversial," the *Guardian* commented. "La palme de l'exigence" (A demanding palm), *Le Monde* wrote in addition to its praise, as it lamented the jury's lack of consideration for the acting profession. And in his speech Almodóvar, chosen best director nonetheless, paid homage to Lynch, Jarmusch, and his other fellow nominees Atom Egoyan (*Felicia's Journey*) and Arturo Ripstein (*No One Writes to the Colonel*), this in implicit critique of the jury's antiestablishment statement.[2] That statement, by the way, had been in the air since the festival's opening night, when jury member Kristin Scott Thomas reminded the film world of the ongoing Balkan war: "This evening, I can't and don't want to forget that with what is going on two hours by plane from here, cinema is more precious to us than ever, like a counterpoison. . . . Cannes cannot be reduced to its shine and its glamour. We'll still need films to testify, and to fight forgetting and indifference."[3]

Clearly, *Rosetta* and *L'humanité* met the jury's desire for such a committed cinema. Leaving aside here whether the Dardennes and Dumont make a more political cinema than, say, Lynch or Jarmusch, it is certain that this heated Sunday in the French South meant a triumph for the cinemas of the French-Belgian border region and made felt a cross-border *Cinéma du Nord*. As Serge Toubiana, former president of the Cinémathèque Française, observed in *Cahiers du cinéma*: "Not so much Belgium or France won this year at Cannes, but this rough and proud Nord that with ups and downs produces a regional cinema that has the virtue to maintain a certain flame, and to entertain a true anger."[4] This interregional Cinéma du Nord is the topic of this book. The Cinéma du Nord is a new wind rather than a new wave. Whereas a wave manifests itself clearly as it washes over the land, a wind is only perceived in its effects, as a chill, or as a rustle in the trees, to call to mind the miraculous realism that amazed the first film audiences. The Cinéma du Nord exists, I have no doubt about that, but unlike, or at least much more, than is the case with cinematic movements tied to nation-states, the Cinéma du Nord requires a cross-border transregional perspective for its contours to materialize in the clouds.

Introduction

A Critical Fairy Tale

The Cinéma du Nord is a critical cinema, a cinema that at once expresses and emerges from crisis. The Cinéma du Nord brings, moreover, a marginal, northern perspective to longstanding debates in francophone European film and philosophy that, besides the Dardennes, Dumont, and Pialat, includes the texts and images of Blaise Pascal, Robert Bresson, André Bazin, François Truffaut, Jean-Luc Godard, Agnès Varda, Gilles Deleuze, Jacques Rancière, Alain Badiou, and, beyond francophone Europe, Vittorio de Sica, Antonio Hardt, Michael Negri, Lauren Berlant, and Baruch Spinoza, among others. The Nord after which this cinema from and of the North is named spans the French North (in particular Nord-Pas-de-Calais, France's northernmost administrative region until its 2016 merger with Picardy into Hauts-de-France) and Wallonia, the predominantly francophone south of Belgium. Other than the French language and their capricious climate, these bordering regions share a history of coal mining and heavy industry. Once, the Nord was a cradle of the first Industrial Revolution (and thus also of the era of fossil-fueled capitalism). In 1720, a coal mine in the Dardennes' hometown of Seraing, which is part of the Liège agglomeration, was first to operate the steam engine on the European continent, and subsequently the Belgian south and French north grew into economic superpowers. Over the course of the twentieth century this industrial golden age gradually gave way to structural economic crisis. At the turn of the twenty-first century—while only short train rides away, in the nearby cities of Brussels, Strasbourg, and Maastricht, political leaders founded the European Union—the French-Walloon Nord had become a rust belt, its coal mines depleted, its industries superannuated, while unemployment skyrocketed. After seven generations of life structured by the pace of heavy industry, that industry's decline created a generation in which many grew up without ever seeing their parents work, without an example of a "normal" life. In *Rosetta*, set and shot in Seraing, this crisis reality determines the protagonist's obstinate struggle for such a *vie normale*, starting with a job. Just across the border, *L'humanité*, which Dumont mainly filmed in his hometown of Bailleul near Lille, integrates socioeconomic crisis more obliquely and with a degree of caricature, turning the region's crisis reality into the backdrop for the film's carnal-spiritual quest for "humanity."

Rosetta and *L'humanité* have a lot in common, which is something that has also struck Jacques Rancière. Following Cannes 1999, in an essay titled "Le Bruit du peuple, l'image de l'art" (The noise of the people, the image of art) that was published in *Cahiers du cinéma*, Rancière asks:

> What is it exactly that unites *Rosetta* and *L'humanité*, other than the fact that at the latest Cannes festival they were both loaded with the jury's praise, and similarly dismissed by a large part of professionals and critics? What makes them a joined symbol or symptom, even though everything in the long shots, the distant gaze, and the aesthetic-spiritual discourse of Bruno Dumont seems to oppose itself to the panting camera, the lens glued to the protagonist, and the denunciatory tradition that characterizes *Rosetta*? That Bruno Dumont continues to film the small people of the North, and the Dardennes the slums and wastelands of Wallonia. . . . This all seems sufficient for certain people to locate—and generally lament—a new wave of "realism" and a new instance in which art compromises itself with the "social."[1]

I will return extensively to Rancière's own answer to his question of what unites *Rosetta* and *L'humanité*. But there are also a few parallels Rancière leaves unaddressed. The first is that *Rosetta* and *L'humanité* are both variations on films by Robert Bresson, namely, *Mouchette* (1967) and *Journal d'un curé de campagne / Diary of a Country Priest* (1951), respectively, which are in turn adaptations from novels by the French Catholic author Georges Bernanos. *L'humanité* cites, moreover, Pialat's aforementioned *Sous le soleil de Satan*, another Bernanos adaptation. Like these films by Bresson and Pialat, *Rosetta* and *L'humanité* are moral tales. They are fables, also, with humans instead of animals as their protagonists. Crucially, whereas Bresson's and Pialat's protagonists all die in the end, Rosetta and Pharaon (the protagonist of *L'humanité*) miraculously survive. Both films end on long close-ups of their main characters, looking offscreen, shots in which we at once see an acting face, an acted face, and an *idea* of a "human" face (figs. I.1 and I.2).

Figure I.1. *Rosetta* (Jean-Pierre Dardenne and Luc Dardenne, 1999).

Figure I.2. *L'humanité* (Bruno Dumont, 1999).

Second and directly related, both films owe their affective textures to the idiosyncratic ways the Dardennes and Dumont work with their predominantly amateur casts. Also in this respect, they clearly take inspiration from Bresson, who referred to his actors as "models." Yet whereas Bresson used his models as vessels for a disembodied speech, the Dardennes and Dumont are also very much concerned with bringing out the "humanity" of their nonexperienced actors. How comfortable are "we," critical viewers, with this whiff of humanity?

The third parallel between *Rosetta* and *L'humanité* is that they both employ a secular-Christian vocabulary for a world without God. Both films investigate what remains of humanity in a time and place where it is no longer clear what a normal everyday life looks like, as the power of traditional and modern, life-shaping institutions has waned—from mass-employment industries to the Church, and from the labor movement to the nuclear family. The Dardennes and Dumont ask this question in a way that integrates the universal with the particular. On the one hand, *Rosetta* and *L'humanité*, like all of the Dardennes' and Dumont's films, are secular-religious tales that self-consciously flirt with a human essence that binds people together in a single humanity. On the other hand, they are very contemporary stories rooted in the material-historical reality of the Nord. Other than being marked by economic crisis, this reality is one of tension between ethnic-cultural groups. Both Wallonia and the French North have a long history of migration, first from poverty-struck Flanders, and following World War II from southern Europe, Africa (in particular North Africa), and, more recently, the Middle East. In the recent past both regions have periodically made headlines in European and world news around issues of cultural tension. Liège and Charleroi, two of Wallonia's former coal belt cities with high rates of social exclusion, have been identified as breeding grounds for fundamentalist Islamic groups. At the other side of the border, the French North, long a socialist stronghold, was almost captured by Marine le Pen's Front National in the 2015 regional elections. Moreover, together with the Mediterranean and the Eastern borders of the EU Calais at the French northern Sea Coast is *the* place in northwestern Europe where the borders of and within the European Union are most tangible, as it has been "home" to encampments of migrants who wish to cross the Channel into the United Kingdom (which also before Brexit was not part of the Schengen Zone). The Dardennes and Dumont tend to address issues of migration and xenophobia only tangentially, but their work, and the Cinéma du Nord in general, does compel the viewer to think through the complex relations between cultural tension and economic crisis in this region where the transition from a mono-industrial economy to a more diversified and precarious, postindustrial socioeconomic structure has hit harder than anywhere else in Northwestern Europe.

The fourth major parallel between *Rosetta* and *L'humanité* is their "Egyptian connection," which is first of all present in their protagonists' names: Rosetta (whose name connotes the Rosetta stone) and Pharaon. Both films hide, in plain view, a hieroglyphic double meaning. At first sight *Rosetta* and *L'humanité* are rather straightforward quests of a young woman for a job and a policeman for a murderer. When watched more closely, though, these films turn out to be secular-religious mind games encrypted with the spirit: a north wind investing the image despite and because of its realism. That secular-Christian spirit only manifests itself to the obsessive viewer who, remote control in hand or glued to their laptop, commits to deciphering these films' secretly coded quests for grace.

So there are many parallels between *Rosetta* and *L'humanité*. In fact, the parallels are so many that I am tempted to speculate as to whether the Dardennes and Dumont did perhaps coordinate their 1999 Cannes releases. However, other than the visual evidence cited here, I don't have any proof for such a *com*plot. That said, I find it hard to believe Dumont's claim in a 2009 interview that he never saw *Rosetta*.[2] Speculation aside, it is certain that the joint victory of *Rosetta* and *L'humanité* cast the spotlight on the intricate web of parallels between these two films: the "miracle" of Cannes '99.

What, actually, is a miracle? A miracle is impossible, per definition, or more precisely, a miracle is *the* impossible. A miracle remains impossible even though its very occurrence has just demonstrated the opposite. And strictly speaking, a miracle does not *occur*, that is to say, it does not occur in the present tense. A miracle knows no presence, because its occurrence changes, or would change, the very notion of what it means to be present. There is no point in hoping for a miracle; a miracle can only be the object of belief. Whereas hope is oriented at a potential event, belief orients itself at that "event which surpasses, or is thought to surpass, human comprehension,"[3] the definition of miracle Baruch Spinoza gives in his *Theologico-Political Treatise* (1670). Like Spinoza, I do not believe in miracles, because I also agree with Spinoza that there are no potentialities that remain unactualized, or events that surpass comprehension. So if a miracle seems to have happened anyway, like at Cannes '99, one better reminds oneself that such a miracle exists in the gaze of its beholder and take the invitation to dwell in wonder, for as Spinoza writes, "most people think they sufficiently understand a thing when they have ceased to wonder at it."[4]

This book therefore explores the extraordinary coincidence of *Rosetta* and *L'humanité*. It seeks to explain why and how these two films with such similar narratives, vocabularies, and inspirations saw the light at the place (the French-Walloon Nord), and at the moment in history (the end of the twentieth century, and of cinema's long first century) they did. The book does so by situating both films within the French-Walloon Cinéma du Nord, understood as both an artistic-cultural movement and an industry. As stated, my overarching argument is that this cross-border Cinéma du Nord at once expresses and emerges from crisis. The Cinéma du Nord expresses crisis in that it asks how the Nord's uneven transition from a heavy-industrial to a precarious, postindustrial economy has affected the social fabric, down to the structures of people's quotidian lives. The Cinéma du Nord emerges from crisis in that the development of Wallonia and the French North into major Euregional hubs of cinema and media production has been part of these regions' more general endeavors to reinvent themselves economically and culturally after decades of recession.

Let me briefly situate my analysis of the Cinéma du Nord within a broader discourse of national and transnational cinemas. For long, the study of cinematic movements has been dominated by a nation-state-based approach that goes as far back as Siegfried Kracauer's *From Caligari to Hitler: A Psychological History of the German Film* (1947). As Dudley Andrew writes in "An Atlas of World Cinema" (2006), "national cinema studies have by and large been genealogical trees, one tree per country.... Their elaborate root and branch structures are seldom shown as intermingled."[5] In the globalized era, Andrew observes that this nation-based approach continues to remain the dominant model, but he also observes tendencies that call this approach into question:

> Let me not be coy. We still parse the world by nations. Film festivals identify entries by country, college courses are labeled "Japanese Cinema," "French Film," and textbooks are coming off the presses with titles such as *Screening Ireland*, *Screening China*, *Italian National Cinema*, and so on. But a wider conception of national image culture is around the corner, prophesied by phrases like "rooted cosmopolitanism" and "critical regionalism." ... Such terms insist upon the centrifugal dynamic of images, yet without surrendering the special cohesion that films bring to specific cultures.[6]

So even though the nation-state remains the most common label to identify new waves and film cultures, the consensus is that as a concept "national cinema" falls short. This is now also the opinion of Andrew Higson, who a decade after his "The Concept of National Cinema" (1989) writes that "the contingent communities that cinema imagines are much more likely to be either local or transnational than national."[7] In recent years, cinema studies has seen a surge of publications that adopt a transnational perspective. Here it is important to distinguish "transnational" from "international" and "global." As Nataša Ďurovičová writes in *World Cinemas, Transnational Perspectives* (2010), whereas the term "international" is predicated on relations of parity between nation-states and "global" is predicated on the category of totality, "the intermediate and open term 'transnational'" "acknowledges the persistent agency of the State" and thus implies "relations of unevenness and mobility."[8]

Intertwined with this transnational turn, but also partially in opposition to it, cinema studies has equally seen an increased attention for local, regional, and small national cinemas, which often are inherently transnational cinemas. As Mette Hjort and Duncan Petrie write in *The Cinema of Small Nations* (2007), many small countries have limited domestic markets for the goods and services they produce. As a result, their cinema industries face relatively strong pressure to integrate themselves into transnational structures, if only because with their small domestic markets it is very difficult to raise the funds necessary for feature-length fiction production.[9] In the case of Europe, so Janelle Blankenship and Tobias Nagl argue in their collection *European Visions: Small Cinemas in Transition* (2015), this integration of small national cinemas into transnational networks has been stimulated by EU funding initiatives like Eurimages, the MEDIA program, and the Convention on Cinematographic Co-Production, as well as by the European Film Academy and the Europa Cinemas Network.[10] Also the Cinéma du Nord is a small cinema integrated into transnational and European structures. But the Cinéma du Nord is not a small *national* cinema. It is the cinema of a geopolitical, socioeconomic, and cultural region—the Nord—that itself exists across a national border.

This book thus adopts at once a transnational and regional perspective, and in doing so proposes to think transregionally, which is the slanted perspective from which the Nord and its cinema are seen. Much more than cinematic movements tied to geopolitical spaces firmly entrenched in international law and power relations, the Cinéma du Nord is largely immanent to the researcher's efforts to trace the contours of the border-crossing space it is named after. And let me state from the outset here that my thinking about space and territory has been inspired by Spinoza's equation of right and power, which in this context implies, for example, a perspective according to which France has the borders it has simply because the structures that keep these borders in place outweigh the powers that may have an interest in challenging them, like the Basque National Liberation Movement (Basque Country being a region that, like the Nord, exists transnationally, albeit in a very different way).

The Cinéma du Nord is at once a cultural-aesthetic movement—a "north wind"—and an industry. On the one hand, "Cinéma du Nord" thus refers to a body of films that at once emerge from and that express the Nord as a transnational reality. On the other hand, it is the infrastructure of film production in Wallonia and the French North. Defined more precisely, in its connotation of cinematic movement, Cinéma du Nord is a body of fiction features, shorts, and documentaries, including TV productions, that 1) have a narrative set or partly set in either Wallonia or Nord-Pas-de-Calais; 2) have a production connection to either Wallonia or Nord-Pas-de-Calais, either because they were shot or partly shot in one or both of these regions, or because they were produced or coproduced by an organization established in these regions; and 3) contribute to a definition of the Nord as a cross-border region. In its connotation of a cinematic infrastructure, Cinéma du Nord refers to the network of organizations involved in the production and financing of cinema in Wallonia and the French North, including collaborations between both regions.

As far as the criterion that films *du Nord* have a production connection to Wallonia or Nord-Pas-de-Calais is concerned, here I follow the funding criteria used by Wallimage and the northern French Pictanova (formerly Centre Régional de Ressources Audiovisuelles du Nord-Pas-de-Calais), which have promoted film production in Wallonia and the French North since 1999 and 1985, respectively. Both these organizations almost exclusively support films that have a connection to their regions, both in terms of content and production. Here it is important to emphasize, though, that my definition of the Cinéma du Nord is also inclusive of films that engage the region even though they were *not* produced or coproduced regionally. For example, *Nord* (1991) by Xavier Beauvois was shot in Nord-Pas-de-Calais but without regional funding, while *Rosetta* was coproduced by the Walloon region only *after* the film's success in Cannes (a story to which I will return in chapter 3).

Because the Nord is not an official administrative region, integral to my investigation of the Cinéma du Nord is a mapping of the Nord as a geopolitical, socioeconomic, and cultural region. I thus define the Cinéma du Nord recursively, as a cinema that allows me to define this region immanent to the material and discursive realities that cross the French-Belgian border. Films play a double role in my analysis. Insofar as that analysis is a transdiscursive mapping of the Nord, I discuss films as cultural objects among other cultural objects that allow me to identify the Nord in discourse, including literary texts (e.g., Émile Zola's *Germinal*), painting (Van Gogh, Magritte), architecture (the new international railway stations of Lille and Liège), but also folklore, interregional maps, political documents, reportage, and economic analyses. In this endeavor to identify the Nord as a truly transregional space and to at points invite the reader to forget that that space is cut through by an international border, the main challenge has been that also in an increasingly transnational world most regional discourses are still written from within an intranational perspective. Insofar as my analysis is an argument *about* the Cinéma du Nord, I simply assume the Nord exists, like most studies of French national cinema assume that France exists.

As a final note on method: my analysis of the Cinéma du Nord is not bound by a historical period, at least not directly, because of course the Nord, like any space and community, is also a product of history. The following pages therefore do not tell the story of the Cinéma du Nord from its beginning—say André Capellani's 1913 screen adaptation of *Germinal*—to its transmedia future. Instead, my organization of argument gravitates around the moment that the Cinéma du Nord manifested itself most clearly to an international audience for the first time: the joint victory of *Rosetta* and *L'humanité* at Cannes 1999. Formulated differently, were this project a museum exhibition, it would commence in an auditorium where *Rosetta* and *L'humanité* are screened back to back. From there, the exhibition continues in four connected gallery spaces, each of which corresponds to a different methodological approach. While the first space contains a lot of clips and frame grabs, in the second the walls are covered with maps, and while at some moments my analytical gaze may seem as obstinate as Rosetta's battle for employment and Pharaon's investigation, at other moments I paint in broader strokes. What unites these four spaces is their combined endeavor to explain why the two films, whose sounds and images resonate throughout the rooms, were made at the time and place they were.

Metaphor aside, the book has four chapters, over the course of which it integrates methods and perspectives of textual analysis, discourse analysis, film history, theory, industry studies, and film philosophy. While the first and last chapters are conceptually driven, the two middle chapters are historical in their orientation and are largely based on the research I did at the Cinémathèque Française and the Bibliothèque National de France in Paris (which also houses the Inathèque of the French Institut National de l'Audiovisuel) as well as the Cinematek in Brussels. At those archives I substantiated my idea of the Nord, and I analyzed films unavailable through North American academic libraries, the web, or P2P file-sharing programs.

The first chapter, "Hunting for Easter Eggs in *Rosetta* and *L'humanité*," presents a *very* close analysis of the films whose coincidence forms the starting point of my exploration of the Cinéma du Nord. The chapter opens with a *play* button, this in emphasis of the chapter's reenactment, in writing, of my process of decoding of the affective mind games both films cast their viewers into. As the chapter title indicates, over the course of that analysis I discover a number of Easter eggs, including the very hard-boiled egg Rosetta knocks against her head and eats before she attempts suicide in the final scene. In computing, an Easter egg is a program's coded response to an undocumented user command, like a secret level in a computer game or the tilted interface upon googling the word "askew." In cinema, an Easter egg is an element easily missed by the first-time spectator but that may aid in unlocking the narrative code. Consider, for instance, Alfred Hitchcock's cameos, the shadow of Michael Haneke's camera in *Caché* (2005) (which proves it's the filmmaker himself who did it; fig. I.3), the mirroring scars in Bernardo Bertolucci's *The Dreamers* (2003) (which confirm that Isabelle and Théo are really two sides of the same fantasy), or the password at the end of the final credits in *The Matrix* (Lana Wachowski and Lilly Wachowski, 1999) (which allows the spectator to "hack" into whatisthematrix.com, until Warner Bros. suspended the website in 2011; fig. I.4). In Christianity, the originally pagan association of the egg with fertility was baptized as a symbol of Christ's resurrection. Combining these three connotations, in the spiritual mind games that play out in *Rosetta* and *L'humanité*, these hidden plot elements lead the close viewer to reveal the well-hidden yet unmistakably coded passion stories— with a lowercase *p*—that both films hide in their plot spaces, like a secret level in a computer game. Mind-game films, Thomas Elsaesser writes, are "indicative of a 'crisis' in the spectator-film relation, in the sense that the traditional 'suspension of disbelief' [is] . . . no longer deemed appropriate, compelling, or challenging enough."[11] *Rosetta* and *L'humanité* indeed subtly challenge that suspension of disbelief, as both films tease the viewer into a concealed postsecular vocabulary, much like *The Matrix*, also from 1999, and an equally postsecular *neo*-Christian tale for a disenchanted world.

Figure I.3. *Caché* (Michael Haneke, 2005).

Figure I.4. *The Matrix* (Lana Wachowski and Lilly Wachowski, 1999).

But chapter 1 does not merely play along with *Rosetta* and *L'humanité*; it is also a critique. However self-reflexive these films may show themselves in their flirtations with Christian humanist tropes, their narratives are modeled on classical quest structures in which the male protagonists (Pharaon, Rosetta's friend Riquet) operate as the humanizing agents, while the female protagonists (Rosetta and Domino) are the passive recipients of a rather vague notion of "humanity." We here have yet another parallel between *Rosetta* and *L'humanité*: both their self-reflexive passion stories are driven by a conventional and somewhat patronizing Oedipal logic on its ceaselessly problematic quest for narrative closure.

Chapter 2, "Coal-Fired Dreams: The Cinéma du Nord," maps the Nord as a geopolitical, socioeconomic, and cultural-linguistic space. As stated, this transdiscursive mapping integrates the analysis of a variety of objects, including many films: from Henri Storck and Joris Ivens's 1933 pamphlet documentary *Misère au Borinage* (praised by Walter Benjamin as a film that turns any man into a movie extra) to the northern French blockbuster *Bienvenue chez les Ch'tis / Welcome to the Sticks* (Dany Boon, 2008). Following my construction of the Nord as a material and discursive space that fades out the French-Belgian border, I reintroduce that border in order to articulate the similarities and differences in the ways films from either side of the border engage a similar crisis reality. As one may expect from a coal-fired cinema, in both its Walloon and northern French manifestations the Cinéma du Nord displays a tendency toward socially critical and stylistically austere forms of realism. The Cinéma du Nord is highly affective but rarely becomes sentimental. It's often a cinema of silence (e.g., *L'humanité*) or terseness (e.g., *Rosetta*), but also of audiovisual poetry, as the folklore fairy tale *Quand la mer monte / When the Sea Rises* (Yolande Moreau and Gilles Portes, 2004), or Paul Meyer's 1963 *Déjà s'envole la fleur maigre* (The scrawny flower has already flown), the most Italian non-Italian neorealist film ever made. But there are also some important differences between the two halves of the Cinéma du Nord. Most crucially, northern French cinema, much more than its Walloon counterpart, is also a regional*ist* cinema that tends toward social caricature. This difference is explained by the difference in cinematic history between the French North and the Belgian South. As I will demonstrate, whereas Walloon cinema dates far back and emerged gradually from its 1930s documentary origins (even though for decades a Walloon *fiction* feature seemed a financial impossibility), a truly regionally rooted northern French cinema did not see the light until the mid-1980s (even though films have been made in Nord-Pas-de-Calais since the early decades of cinema).

Chapter 3, "Cinéma du Nord, a Euregional Cinema," continues the analysis started in chapter 2. Whereas the second chapter discusses the Cinéma du Nord as a cinematic movement, the third chapter looks at it as an infrastructure of film and digital media production. The chapter explains the remarkable stream of cinematic productions that have emerged from Wallonia and Nord-Pas-de-Calais since the early 1990s. I examine the emergence of northern French and Walloon regional cinemas within their French and Belgian national contexts. Whereas northern French cinema for the last three decades has been a forerunner region in France's traditionally very centralized national cinema, Walloon cinema is part of francophone-Belgian cinema at large, which further includes films from the Brussels region (e.g., Chantal Akerman's *Jeanne Dielman, 23 Quai du Commerce, 1080 Bruxelles*). On its turn, that francophone-Belgian cinema operates as a small national cinema within Belgium's internally split "federal" cinema (which further includes Flemish cinema). This structural difference between Walloon and northern French cinema manifests itself especially in the production of feature-length films. Whereas almost all Walloon (and more broadly francophone-Belgian) fiction features are coproductions with France, most films set and shot in Nord-Pas-de-Calais are entirely French productions. The chapter demonstrates that the development of distinct Walloon and northern French cinematic identities has been spurred by the active, and occasionally collaborative, efforts by these regions to resituate themselves at the crossroads of Europe after decades of recession. As a Walloon commentator observes: "Cinema is good for the economy."[12] The chapter ends on an excursus that cuts back and forth across the French-Belgian border, from Van Gogh's house and Google's datacenters near Mons to the Louvre museum in Lens, and back to Wallonia for a breathtaking art exhibition whose site-specific spirit is also found in the Cinéma du Nord.

Following a continuation of that excursus through the Nord in all its colors captured in black-and-white, chapter 4, "New Realism after the Modern Cinema," situates the Cinéma du Nord within a wider wave of new realism in francophone-European and, more broadly, world cinema of the last three decades. I understand new realism as an ethics and aesthetics of filmmaking that reinvents earlier realist, and in particular neorealist, perspectives on the everyday lives of ordinary people for the age of global capitalism, often in an austere documentary-like fashion. New realism, in the words of Anthony Scott, is "less a style than an impulse that surfaces, with local variations"[13] all over the world, from postcommunist Romanian cinema (e.g., Christian Mungiu's *4 Months, 3 Weeks, 2 Days*) to sixth-generation Chinese film (e.g., Jia Zhangke's *Still Life*), from Naples (Matteo Garrone's *Gomorrah*) to Alaska (Kelly Reichardt's *Wendy and Lucy*). New realism is, according to Lauren Berlant, a "cinema of precarity" that witnesses the fraying of socioeconomic structures all over the globe and across classes.[14] To this, one can add that new realism produces an explicitly *humanist* cinema. *Humanism*, in this context, refers to a belief system according to which people have an innate moral drive toward community. Such humanism has been rightfully critiqued for its male, heteronormative, white, and European-centered gaze. For these same reasons, we need to be very critical, even vigilant, about new realism's flirtations with humanist understandings of life, as for example through its frequent close-ups of human faces. Above all, new realism marks a return of belief in representation and realism in the wake of what Gilles Deleuze in his *Cinema* books (1983, 1985) has called "the modern cinema." In contrast to that modern cinema, new realism resorts to rather classical modes of storytelling less conscious of the camera and the viewer. From the perspective of Deleuze's film philosophy, new realism's return to a plot-driven and often overtly humanist cinema can only be seen as a regression. It often is indeed, but in its most self-conscious forms new realism also urges critical posthumanist viewers to think through the vestiges of humanism in their outlook on the contemporary world, in their desire for a "human" face in a reality in which it is no longer clear what a life looks like.

This minimal humanism is also found in the posthuman tradition to which Deleuze belongs, because I would argue that that tradition has not always been as "anti-humanist" as Rosi Braidotti claims it to be in *The Posthuman* (2013). Braidotti writes that the "radical thinkers of the post-1968 generation rejected Humanism both in its classical and its socialist version."[15] I largely agree. But why then does Deleuze mourn cinema's "Catholic quality" to restore the belief in "love or life," while he leaves unaddressed the patriarchal structures this belief in the world is tied up with?[16] Similarly, why do Michael Hardt and Antonio Negri at the end of their otherwise immanentist *Empire* bring to stage Saint Francis, the *alter Christus*? And why do they list the utopian ending of *Miracolo a Milano / Miracle in Milan* (1951) as an inspiration for their "posthumanist humanism," while they leave unacknowledged the male quest structure of De Sica's fairy tale (whose hero Toto was found, "once upon a time," in a cabbage patch)?[17] Addressing these questions, I argue that post-structural critiques of humanism form a discourse of belief that is not fully prepared to do away with classically humanist assumptions about what drives people to community. This minimal humanism is not a problem per se. The problem is that these thinkers leave their secular-religious vocabulary undertheorized. That vocabulary takes very different forms than it does in *Rosetta* and *L'humanité*, but like Dumont and the Dardennes, Deleuze, Hardt and Negri, as well as Godard and Badiou inherit the same tradition of socialist-Catholic humanism in French film and philosophy. This book critiques these humanist vestiges, which remain too much of an afterthought in that tradition itself.

Miraculous Realism is thus not only an analysis of the Cinéma du Nord but also an analysis of francophone-European film and philosophy more broadly. Throughout its four chapters, the book traces—from a northern perspective—a secular-religious tradition from Pascal, via Bernanos, Bresson, Bazin, Pialat, and Deleuze to the Dardennes, Dumont, and Godard. In tracing this tradition, *Miraculous Realism* intervenes in a broader debate about the postsecular turn. Much like postmodernism presupposes a process of modernization, the postsecular turn presupposes a secular moment, "secular" understood as in Charles Taylor's definition of it as a worldview that distinguishes between an immanent and a transcendent domain.[18] As Jürgen Habermas writes, "a '*post*-secular' society must at some point have been in a 'secular condition,' after which it has gone through "a change of consciousness" about its secularity."[19] Or as John Caruana and Mark Cauchi write in *Immanent Frames: Postsecular Cinema between Malick and Von Trier* (2018), "in homology with the classic definition of postmodernism given by Lyotard—that it is an 'incredulity toward metanarratives'—we could thus say that postsecularism is an incredulity toward the secularist narrative" (to which one could add that postsecularism may be also understood as a response to the postmodern incredulity toward overarching stories of humanity).[20] Citing Taylor's characterization of the postsecular as an "open space" where "you can feel the winds pulling you, now to belief, now to unbelief,"[21] *Immanent Frames* identifies a body films that "inhabit" that space, from Lars von Trier to Terrence Malick, from Alejandro González Iñárritu to Jean-Luc Godard, and from Dumont to the Dardennes.

Miraculous Realism critiques the postsecular tradition and its move away from immanence, especially insofar as that tradition takes on secular-Christian forms, like in the films of the Dardennes, Dumont, and Godard (in whose disillusion with Representation and his concomitant montage of Grace the postmodern and the postsecular meet). They are films that employ a Christian vocabulary for a world without God. As stated, I situate the Dardennes and Dumont in a new realist tendency in world cinema that also includes strictly immanentist films like those of Jia Zhangke (e.g., *Still Life*, 2006) and Laurent Cantet (*Entre les murs / The Class*, 2008). I critique new realism for its postsecular tendency, its problematic humanism, its obsession with a human face in times of crisis, its obsession with grace also, regardless of whether the viewer is actually granted that grace, because as I will argue in chapter 1, to speak the vocabulary of redemption in order to say that "God does not exist" (as do the Dardennes, Dumont, and Godard) is still to confirm God. As I argue in chapter 4, whereas the Dardennes and Dumont make a cinema of affect and Godard a cinema of thought, they share a Bressonian inheritance, namely, the Question of what remains of grace in a world without God. Even more than in the answers their films formulate to this question of grace, I am interested in the fact that they ask it in the first place, without acknowledging that the terms of the question are not neutral but embedded in a parochial patriarchal tradition.

The question of grace is a recurring problem in francophone-European film and philosophy, as it stands in the way of a truly non-normative ethics. To think such an ethics is the drive behind this critical fairy tale of the Cinéma du Nord, which, inspired by that cinema itself, integrates an emphasis on the particular (my transregional focus on a small part of northwestern Europe) with a broader film philosophical reflection on questions that move beyond, but at once emerge organically from, that focus on the particular, which functions as a crystal ball onto the more universal outlook its sparkle is immanent to. That tale started, *once upon a time*, with a miracle, the extraordinary coincidence of *Rosetta* and *L'humanité*, while the final chapter ends on a *happily ever after*. In the pages in between there will be dragons, angels, burned-out priests, a magic mountain, flying broomsticks, a UFO, some monsters, several giants, and many christs (with a lowercase *c*). As in the best fairy tales there won't be a moral to the story.

1

Hunting for Easter Eggs in *Rosetta* and *L'humanité*

▷ A DOOR SLAMS. A YOUNG woman agitatedly walks down a corridor, the handheld camera on her heels. She's wearing a white overcoat and a hair net. We don't see her face. She turns right, right, left. A second door. *Slam!* She moves down the stairs into a factory hall, which remains blurry as the camera maintains focus on her back. We hear the noise of machines. "Entrez dans mon bureau!" [Come back to my office!] calls a man, in shirt and tie, as he obstructs her way, "Entrez dans mon bureau, je vous dis!" She evades him and slides underneath the assembly line, while the camera struggles to keep up with her and to keep her in focus. "C'est vrai que t'as dit que je suis souvent en retard!?" [Is it true you've said I'm often late!?], she asks angrily, out of breath, to a female coworker. She has been fired, we realize.[1]

Inevitably, this transcription of the opening scene of Jean-Pierre Dardenne and Luc Dardenne's *Rosetta* (1999) remains insufficiently expressive, of the film's texture, of its color, and of its rapid pace. Figures 1.1 1.3 capture the close range at which the camera follows Rosetta (Émilie Dequenne), the film's seventeen-year-old protagonist. The scene is characteristic of the Dardennes' realism: the protagonist's obstinacy, the close-up shots of the back of her head, the direct sound, the elliptical editing, and the camera's refusal to leave her alone. The camera is determined to follow Rosetta and to make felt her struggle for a human life, her small war.

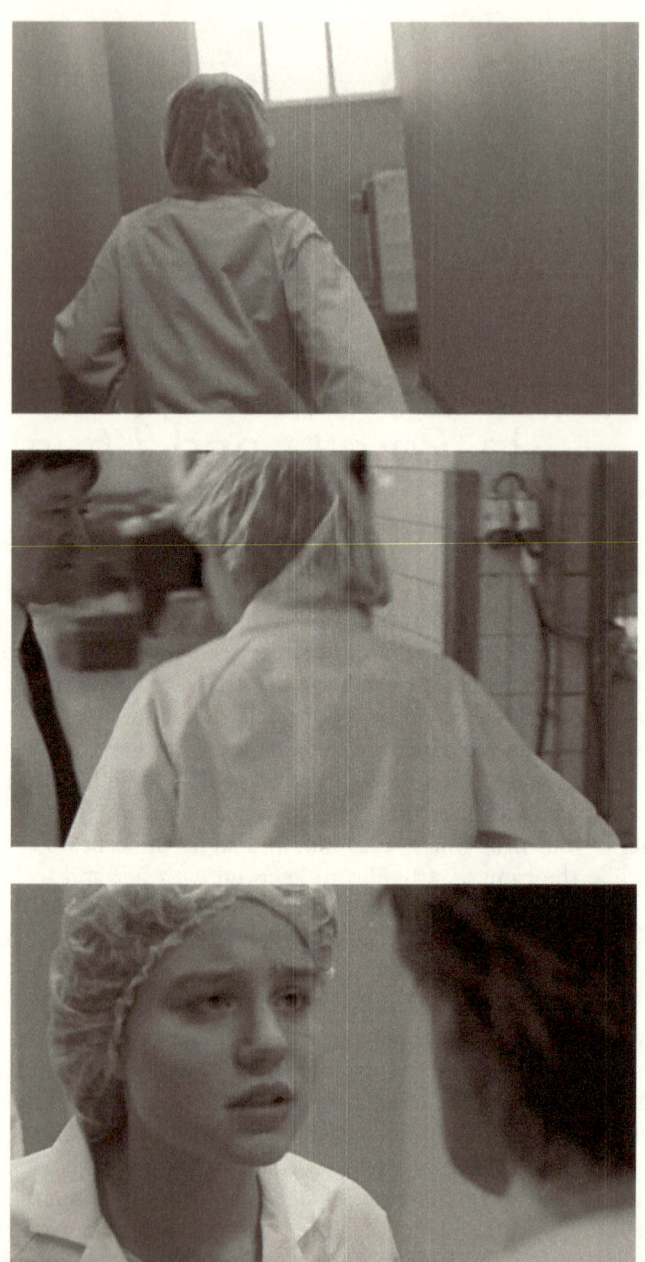

Figures 1.1–1.3. The opening scene of Rosetta (Jean-Pierre Dardenne and Luc Dardenne, 1999).

Other than *Rosetta*, the film that stands central in this chapter is *L'humanité* by Bruno Dumont, also from 1999, and which like *Rosetta* is a story rooted in the French-Walloon Nord. The question that guides my argument is the same Rancière asks in his *Cahiers du cinéma* essay about these two films: "What unites *Rosetta* and *L'humanité*?" As stated in the introduction, one of the parallels Rancière leaves unmentioned is that both *Rosetta* and *L'humanité* are variations on films by Robert Bresson, namely, *Mouchette* (1967) and *Journal d'un curé de champagne* (1951), stories Bresson in turn adapted from novels by Georges Bernanos. *L'humanité* cites, moreover, Maurice Pialat's film *Sous le soleil de Satan* (1987), another Bernanos adaptation and like *L'humanité* a film set and shot in the French North. Like Bresson, the Dardennes and Dumont create moral tales for a world abandoned by God and lacking in solidarity. Unlike, or at least much more openly than Bresson, the Dardennes and Dumont also flirt with a belief in an innate human essence. I do not share this minimal humanism, at least not in the form it presents itself in these films. However self-conscious *Rosetta* and *L'humanité* may show themselves in their play with dominant understandings of sexuality, gender, race, and class, ultimately they model their notion of "human" on a male, heterosexual, white subject position. At the same time, these films are also smart, teasing their viewer into spiritual mind games from which there seems to be no way out. Upon *very* close analysis *Rosetta* and *L'humanité* turn out to share a hieroglyphic double nature, in that their seemingly straightforward quest stories are encrypted with the spirit, hiding in plain sight, like an Easter egg painted in the colors of the field.

But let me not reveal too much at this point. Inasmuch as this chapter is an argument about and critique of *Rosetta* and *L'humanité*, it is also a reenactment, in writing, of my comparative analysis of these two films, playing, pausing, and replaying them over and again, while piecing together their secret codes. To fast-forward to the end of this chapter to find out *whodunit* would really spoil the analysis.

A Normal Life

Let's press *play* again. Following the opening scene, which ends with the police dragging Rosetta out of the factory, we see her eating a waffle. The camera then follows Rosetta—on the bus, through a wooden gate the viewer infers she's not supposed to use (fig. 1.4), across a busy road, down the road's shoulder, through the forest, underneath a fence—to her home at the "Grand Canyon," the trailer park where she lives with her alcoholic mother (Anne Yernaux). By trailing Rosetta's trespasses and shortcuts, the camera maps her small world at the margins of society.

As Luc Dardenne observes, Rosetta "is in a state of war."[2] Her radius of action is small: other than the forest and the trailer park, the main hubs in her life are the thrift store to which she sells the clothes mended by her and her mother, the apartment of her new friend Riquet (Fabrizio Rongione), and the waffle stand where Riquet works until Rosetta denounces him to get his job. As she travels between these places, in scenes that are very similar to one another in terms of framing and editing, the film familiarizes the viewer with her habits and hiding spots, including the drainpipe in which she keeps her rubber boots. Having exchanged her shoes for her boots, Rosetta, carrying a heavy plastic bag and with the camera in close pursuit, once again finds her way through the forest, changes into her shoes, and disappears underneath the fence that encloses the trailer park (fig. 1.5).

The Dardennes shot *Rosetta* in Seraing near Liège. Liège is the largest metropolitan area in Wallonia, which at the turn of the millennium had unemployment rates among the highest in Europe. The film engages this crisis through Rosetta's desperate quest for a job. Rosetta expresses her desire to become a member of the working class and to *belong* in a more general sense; at the end of the day, after her painstaking efforts have finally paid off: she has found a job. Lying in bed in Riquet's apartment, Rosetta assures herself of her normalcy:

Figure 1.4. Through a wooden gate she's not supposed to use.

Figure 1.5. Rosetta, carrying a heavy plastic bag, once again finds her way through the woods.

Tu t'appelles Rosetta. Je m'appelle Rosetta. Tu as trouvé un travail. J'ai trouvé un travail. Tu as trouvé un ami. J'ai trouvé un ami. T'as une vie normale. J'ai une vie normale. Tu ne tomberas pas dans le trou. Je ne tomberai pas dans le trou. Bonne nuit. Bonne nuit. (Your name is Rosetta. My name is Rosetta. You've found a job. I've found a job. You've found a friend. I've found a friend. You have a normal life. I have a normal life. You won't fall in a rut. I won't fall in a rut. Good night. Good night.)

The day following this self-subjectifying prayer, however, Rosetta is laid off again and finds herself back at square one of her flight forward.

Rosetta's pursuit of a normal human life is characteristic of the Dardennes' practice and philosophy, which can be situated in a broader wave of new realism, especially in northwestern European cinema that expresses life in a postindustrial society. As Philip Mosley writes, the Dardennes share with other filmmakers from Wallonia (Lucas Belvaux, Benoît Mariage) as well as neighboring regions in France (e.g., Laurent Cantet, Dumont) and the United Kingdom (Mike Leigh, Ken Loach) "a preoccupation with the lives of working-class individuals struggling to survive with a measure of dignity." Mosley refers to the Dardennes' practice as a "responsible realism" that displays an "acute awareness of a need for both individual and collective responsibility in human relations."[3] To this one can add that the Dardennes' films are moral tales that test their protagonists' "humanity." At first sight the Dardennes' universe appears strictly immanent, yet all of the Dardennes' films disallow the viewer to understand character action as being fully motivated by the precarious material conditions these protagonists often find themselves in. From *La Promesse / The Promise* (1996), via *L'Enfant / The Child* (2005), to *Deux jours, une nuit / Two Days, One Night* (2014), ultimately plot progression also transcends the material dimension of the quest for a "normal" life, as that quest is connected to a moral stake (while in their most recent films *La Fille inconnue / The Unknown Girl* [2016] and *Le Jeune Ahmed / Young Ahmed* [2019] the economic dimension has moved to the background altogether). Also *Rosetta* connects its protagonist's quest to a moral struggle, leaving space for a minimum of agency on the young woman's part to do the right thing despite everything. How far will Rosetta go to pursue her modest dreams? Is she willing to sacrifice her humanity? This testing of her moral character becomes most explicit in the scene in which Rosetta stands by passively for forty seconds after Riquet, the waffle maker, has fallen into a muddy stream. Only after a sustained inner debate does Rosetta grab a stick to pull her friend out of the water, even though she wants his job.

What are we to make of this spark of compassion that interrupts Rosetta's painfully long moral struggle? Does it demonstrate "the possibility of human agency in a time when we have lost faith in that possibility," as Thorn Andersen argues in relation to the Dardennes' *Le silence de Lorna* (2008)?[4] Andersen distinguishes Lorna (Arta Dobroshi) from the wandering protagonists of Italian neorealist cinema. "[Lorna's] perceptions," he writes, "lead immediately to actions, there is no dissociation between them. Against the tide of neorealism, the Dardennes continue to insist that action is character."[5] Like nearly all of their protagonists, Lorna and Rosetta are always moving. They are always acting, and in that respect they differ from the neorealist wanderer. But when perceptions immediately lead to actions and are inseparable from the actions they trigger, what is the role of agency, if agency is understood as the locus of indeterminacy between perception and action? If Rosetta acts, it is because she is acted *upon*—she is acted upon by a society that chases, confines, excludes, exploits, and dehumanizes her. Most of the time, she's depicted as acting out of instinct, the near elimination of the interval between perception and action, rather than agency. The forest Rosetta cuts through and where she fishes, for food rather than fun, is an urban wilderness where she needs to be continuously on her guard, especially for the park manager. If she does not wander, it is not because she is less desperate than her neorealist predecessors. She simply does not have time to wander.

To understand the temporal structure of Rosetta's subjectivity, it is instructive to compare her to another Dardennes protagonist, Bruno (Jérémie Renier) from *L'Enfant*. Slightly older than Rosetta, Bruno is the leader of a small gang of petty thieves. Assuring himself that he will always "find" money, he is only interested in the current rate at which things are going, from a stolen camera and the hat that looks so good on him (and that gives him the air of a French New Wave hero) to his own child, whom he sells to a black market adoption ring for some quick cash. He lives strictly in the present, which makes him seem somewhat psychotic. Rosetta, in contrast, refuses a reality without future orientation. She struggles to survive, but she also has her pride and persistence, her humanity. Whereas Bruno seems to have accepted his life at the margins and survives day to day until reality decides otherwise, Rosetta wants a normal life, starting with a job. Unlike Bruno, she is obsessed with her future, with making a quantum leap into normalcy, a desire for which she's willing to sacrifice the present. She rejects Riquet's offer to assist him in swindling his boss by selling his own homemade waffles at the stand because she wants "un vrai travail," a real job. Rosetta refuses to dehumanize herself in the face of a dehumanizing society. That's why she throws out the salmon her mother has been given for free: "On n'est pas des mendiants" (We're not beggars). Rosetta catches her own fish with her own homemade traps. And that's why she pulls out the plants her mother has planted near the trailer because she refuses to accept the trailer as her home: "Pourquoi tu plantes tous ces trucs? On va pas quand-même rester ici hein?" (Why are you planting all these? We will not stay here anyway?). But Rosetta is also ashamed of her current situation, which leads her to lie that she's living at a "manège" (a horse-riding school) to a social security officer. She wants a job, but, more than that, she wants to be normal and human, in her own eyes and those of society, whose gaze she ventriloquizes before going to sleep: "Tu t'appelle Rosetta" (Your name is Rosetta).

Rosetta's fight to integrate herself into a fraying postindustrial social tissue attests to the waning of parochial power structures—including the nuclear family, the church, trade unions, and the welfare state—that seek to define a "normal," "human" life, attaching people to a stable set of subject positions from cradle to grave. In his late essay "The Subject and Power" (1982), Michel Foucault describes parochial power as a form of power, or a "power technique," that originated in Christian institutions and subsequently became integrated into the modern Western state.

Christianity, Foucault explains, introduced a code of ethics that spread new power relations throughout the ancient world. By organizing itself as a church, Christianity postulated "in principle that certain individuals can, by their religious quality, serve others not as princes, magistrates, prophets, fortune-tellers, benefactors, educationalists, and so on, but as pastors."[6] Foucault outlines four characteristics of pastoral power: first, pastoral power is salvation oriented in that it aims to assure the individual's place in heaven; second, it's an oblative power willing to sacrifice itself for the well-being of the flock (this in difference with sovereign power); third, it is a life-shaping power at once invested in the community as a whole and in individual life in particular; and fourth, pastoral power produces truth, the truth of the individual. With the spread of early-modern capitalism, pastoral power lost its vitality. At the same time, the pastoral function was redistributed beyond the church and became incorporated by the modern state in a secular form. Foucault writes:

> I don't think that we should consider the "modern state" as an entity which was developed above individuals, ignoring what they are and even their very existence, but on the contrary, as a very sophisticated structure, in which individuals can be integrated, under one condition: that this individuality would be shaped in a new form and submitted to a set of very specific patterns. In a way, we can see the state as a modern matrix of individualization, or a new form of pastoral power.[7]

This modern pastoral power is no longer salvation oriented but instead seeks to protect people in *this* world through, for instance, public health care, social security, and a police system (which, Foucault emphasizes, not only was invented to maintain law and order but also operated in the eighteenth century as a distributive infrastructure for urban supplies). Modern pastoral power *subjects* the individual considered human: It disciplines the subject with carrot and stick, and, in the same movement, creates the subject as an agent capable of speech, action, and partaking in discursive and material exchange.

Moreover—and this is the crux of Foucault's argument—modern pastoral power creates the individual as a potentially resistant subject who can challenge, individually and collectively, those very subjectifying structures. In her essay "Bodies and Power Revisited" (1990), Judith Butler refers to this line of argument in order to defend Foucault against the critique that he did not sufficiently theorize resistance. She argues that Foucault develops, in "The Subject and Power" and the last two volumes of *The History of Sexuality* (1984), a dialectical understanding of subjectivity that defines the subject as both the product of power and a form of resistance against the ways power attaches the subject to its own identity. Butler observes in Foucault an "implicit theorization of passion," with "passion" understood as the attachment to the norms through which subjects relate to themselves. But Butler also signals in the late Foucault a tendency to think of passion as a persistence in being that seeks to detach itself from the norms that bind it, which brings this passion close to Freud's notion of the drive or Baruch Spinoza's concept of *conatus* (inclination). Combining these two lines of thought at work in Foucault, Butler writes:

> Perhaps we can speculate that the moment of resistance, of opposition, emerges precisely when we find ourselves attached to our constraint, and so constrained in our very attachment. To the extent that we question the promise of those norms that constrain our recognizability, we open the way for attachment itself to live in some less constrained way. But for attachment to live in a less constrained way is for it to risk unrecognizability and the various punishments that await those who do not conform to the social order.[8]

To detach oneself from social norms, and to detach oneself from oneself, is to risk one's life, discursively and materially. To do so is dangerous, but it is also potentially transformative. I fully agree with this reading of Foucault. However, and to return to *Rosetta*, what happens at the state's margins, where pastoral-disciplinary power disintegrates and the social tissue frays, leaving life more formless and precarious, less "human" also? What resistance remains when there is no "normal life" for the subject to relate to? Such is Rosetta's dilemma. She is all resistance, but instead of detaching herself from a norm, her struggle for recognition is driven by precisely her attachment to the idea of a normal, working-class life. As Lauren Berlant argues, what matters most for Rosetta is the *feeling* of normativity, of being confirmed in her existence by reality. "The ongoing prospect of low-waged and uninteresting labor," Berlant writes, "is for Rosetta nearly utopian, and it makes possible imagining living the *proper* life that capitalism offers as a route to the *good* life."[9] However, Rosetta is thwarted time and again in her feeling of belonging. Her character testifies to a postindustrial precariat scraping by through underpaid labor or who find themselves excluded from the work process altogether. They are subjects deemed by that process as "unexploitable" and typically lack the social mobility to escape their small worlds. Because where would Rosetta go, without much of an education or transferable labor skills and with her mother to take care of? Rosetta lacks a support system. Her family is broken, if she ever really had a traditional family situation at all. (We never hear about her father, but the film leads us to infer that she and her mother lived elsewhere before moving to the trailer park.) And with the exception of the repressive police intervention in the opening scene, the state is only present in its absence. As a young person lacking job security, Rosetta is fired twice for no good reason, and her application for unemployment benefits is rejected because she hasn't worked "long enough." Rosetta is highly aware of this position a society with few unskilled labor opportunities has cast her into, and she resists her less-than-human nonsubjectivity with all her life force.

Rosetta does not merely narrate this struggle for humanity, it also makes it felt. The film stays literally close to its protagonist, mimicking her movements and revealing the corporeality of her struggle—her sweat, her breath, her pain. Such elements of what Joseph Mai identifies as the "sensuous realism" of the Dardennes' aesthetic include the extreme close-ups, the sheer absence of establishing shots, the fast-paced editing, the direct sound, and, above all, the haptic cinematography.[10] Like all the Dardennes' early works, *Rosetta* was shot with a lightweight sixteen-millimeter handheld camera, allowing the camera operator Benoît Dervaux to follow actress Émilie Dequenne from a very close range. For most of the film, Rosetta's body, most often her back or the back of her head, fills the entire frame. Shots are often bouncy and out of focus, as when she suddenly turns and surprises both camera and viewer. As Mai writes, "Sensuous realism demands a good amount of effort on the part of viewers. Objects and bodies become more important but less coded, and we tend to look at them as we do to real objects and bodies, as shapes, textures, weights, smells, and relations we investigate."[11]

The Dardennes' "punch camera" (Rancière) is certainly affective and makes the viewer part of its own obsession with its protagonist. *Rosetta* shares this obsessive gaze with *L'humanité*, but in difference with *Rosetta*, Dumont's "entomologist camera" (also Rancière) maintains much more distance. As Luc Dardenne observes: "we don't film bodies the same way and Dumont shows more sky than we do."[12]

humanity with a small *h*

L'humanité—which Dumont insists on spelling with a lowercase *h*[13]—opens with an extremely long shot of a sloping landscape that leaves a little over half of its CinemaScope frame green and the rest of it in various shades of light blue, except for four trees in the top-left corner. Earth and sky. First we hear a sound close up of heavy breathing, then we see a human figure tracing the horizon, traveling across the image, their head bent forward, in a hurry it seems. The breathing continues also after this figure has left the frame, who—cut to a medium-long shot—turns out to be male. His face tormented, the man now climbs across a barbed-wired fence and makes his way through the recently plowed field. With his breathing still in our ears, he walks away from us, followed by a close-up of his feet plowing through the mud, followed by a medium close-up of the upper part of his body, his sloping shoulders, his washed-out jacket, his empty gaze. The man falls flat, forward into the mud, where he lies as if dead for over half a minute, after which his breathing resumes (figs. 1.6–1.8).[14]

Figures 1.6–1.8 The opening scene of *L'humanité* (Bruno Dumont, 1999).

This man is Pharaon de Winter (Emmanuel Schotté), a police lieutenant in Bailleul, a small rural town about thirty kilometers northeast of Lille. It's the part of the world of *Germinal* (1885), and it's with the same clinical gaze as that of Zola's novel that *L'humanité* captures this part of the world. On the one hand, *L'humanité* is an unmistakable product of the French North, of its landscape, its architecture, its diffuse light, and of the physiognomy of its people. On the other hand, from the first scene onward it is clear that the film's world is not "real" but a staged setting. In reality, Bailleul (population eighteen thousand) is certainly not as emptied out as it appears in *L'humanité*. A commentator describes the town as "a small, pleasantly commercial village, reconstructed after World War I, where the red of the bricks fights the gray of the dust and the sky. The alimentation and textile industries have declined, and many people go work in Lille."[15] In *L'humanité* Bailleul is a naturalist laboratory setting for the film's quest for its title concept. This quest for humanity coincides with Pharaon's investigation of a young girl's murder. The viewer doesn't yet know of this crime, but Pharaon already does. While he is still facedown in the mud, we hear a signaling sound from a parked car in the distance. In the next shot, Pharaon is sitting in the car. "J'arrive" (I'll be right there), he speaks through the intercom. Before he starts the engine, Pharaon turns on the cassette player, leaving his dirt-covered finger motionless on the *play* button. For more than a minute, Pharaon—his head tilted backward, his gaze blank—listens to the harpsichord piece that will also accompany the film's closing titles.[16] This close-up is followed by a point-of-view shot that captures Pharaon staring at the rural landscape, in reference to Georges Braque's *Landscape with Plow* (fig. 1.9). Pharaon knows what he's about to see, and it is this *pre*-sense that Dumont's camera captures in the landscape. As James Williams observes, in Dumont's cinematic world "landscapes are *always*

Figure 1.9. *L'humanité* in reference to Georges Braque's *Landscape with Plow*.

interior states."[17] Cut to a close-up of the girl's corpse, framed headless in citation of Marcel Duchamp's *Etant donnés* (1946–1966). The body is yellow-gray from cold and decay; an ant crawls up and down its leg.

L'humanité proceeds by a continuous juxtaposition of extremes: horror versus art, earth versus heaven, nature versus culture, flesh versus spirit, darkness versus light. These binary oppositions seem banal, but what makes the film so compelling is the absurdism with which it portrays its characters, Pharaon in particular. In many respects Pharaon leads the normal life Rosetta is so obsessed with. He has a home (which like Rosetta he shares with his mother), a stable job, and a few friends. In his free time Pharaon takes care of the flowers in his garden, drives to the coast with his neighbor Domino and her partner Joseph, or goes for a bike ride in the country. Back from the ride, he eats an apple and helps his mother peel potatoes. This all seems very normal, but Pharaon often acts far from normal. Take his eating of the apple (fig. 1.10). Even before the film shows him gagging above the sink, this activity already appears as slightly perverted, because of the deliberation with which Pharaon places his teeth in the fruit, and because of the sound close-up of the spit collecting in his mouth. Pharaon is difficult to read. His monotonous voice and incapacity to respond spontaneously reveal him to be emotionally blocked and probably also somewhat autistic. The film frames him as a little slow, yet sharp and sensitive, nonetheless. As stated, Pharaon lives, still or again, with his mother, and as we also come to learn, he has recently lost his fiancée and child. Strangely, the film provides the viewer with this seemingly crucial information only halfway through the narrative, and only very offhandedly. Whereas a more conventional psychological thriller would relay this prediegetic information at least two times, *L'humanité* presents it in a way as if it almost *wants* the viewer to miss it.

Figure 1.10. Pharaon eating an apple in reference to René Magritte's *La Chambre d'Ecoute*.

This does not mean that Pharaon's traumatic prehistory forms the key to his psychology. Even though Pharaon's loss may explain his massive sadness, it does not explain his fits of anger, or his sexual inclinations. At first Pharaon's desire seems straightforward: he has a crush on Domino, who is in a relationship with Joseph. As the film unfolds, however, Pharaon's sexuality becomes more and more complex. When he is in the car with his chief, the camera registers him staring at the other man's crotch, captured in close-up. Later, when he disperses a small mob of striking factory workers, Pharaon aggressively shoves Domino, who is among the protestors, upon which he gives her a long, intimidating stare. And during a work visit to the psychiatric clinic, he all of a sudden embraces a male nurse. Even more puzzling is Pharaon's behavior in the police office toward a French Algerian man who has been arrested for dealing drugs. After his colleague has left the office, Pharaon sits down across from the arrestee, pulls the man's head toward his own, and caresses his face. In the next shot, while sitting alone at his desk, Pharaon sniffs the hand with which he has just touched "the dealer" (as the closing titles find the man guilty before trial). At the end of the film Pharaon will repeat this same behavior toward Joseph, who turns out to be the murderer of the little girl. While some of these scenes have a clear homoerotic charge, Pharaon's caressing of the French Algerian man seems mostly an act of pity in response to his broken life story. As far as Pharaon's overreaction toward Domino is concerned, Pharaon was just "doing [his] job," as he defends himself to her later. In fact, *all* of these events occur while Pharaon is on duty, which gives his behavior an inappropriate and, in the case of the arrestee and Joseph, even abusive side. Surprisingly and perhaps also shockingly, however, *L'humanité* does not make Pharaon seem inappropriate, as both the dealer and Joseph react as if his behavior were in fact very normal.

Like *Rosetta*, *L'humanité* is a moral tale, though of a different kind. Whereas *Rosetta* situates its protagonist's quest in the context of socioeconomic crisis, *L'humanité* only makes reference to crisis at the margins of its narrative, especially through the subplot of the factory strike. Domino and her colleagues strike because of the imminent relocation of the production process. Their attempt at collective action falls through almost immediately, however, because the workers are "not very courageous," as Domino says to Pharaon. Pharaon is from a working-class background himself, but his job is to maintain the social order. It's a patriarchal social order, so *L'humanité* emphasizes. The film establishes a poignant parallel between the aforementioned scene in which Pharaon, in his role as a police officer, confronts Domino, and a subsequent scene in which Domino passes by the local church while chewing gum and listening to loud music on her earphones. As she turns her head and looks through the open church doors, the camera captures her confrontation with the crucifix above the altar, upon which she turns off her music. In both scenes Domino stands corrected by the male gaze of the law.

I will return to this parallel *L'humanité* draws between the male gazes of Church and State, as well as to the film's association of Pharaon with Christ. What matters for now is that the universe of Dumont's film is not determined by socioeconomic reality, but by a Manichean battle between a carnal *bête humaine* and a more spiritual, secular-Catholic idea of humanity. *L'humanité*'s realism is explicitly *anti-social*, this in difference with Dumont's first feature, *La Vie de Jésus / The Life of Jesus* (1997), which defines its characters along socioeconomic lines. On the one hand, *L'humanité* maps Bailleul's social infrastructure, in that Pharaon's investigation leads us from the police office to the psychiatric clinic, and from Hôtel de Ville to the surrounding farmland. Moreover, through repeated references to Paris and scenes in Lille, Boulogne-sur-Mer, and London, the film situates Bailleul in its interregional and transnational contexts. On the other hand, the film strips the town of its particularity and transforms it into the setting for a more universal reflection on human nature. It's a violent nature, so *L'humanité* tells us, as through the news images of an unspecified armed struggle playing on Pharaon's television set. With the TV on mute, Pharaon hums along with a canned melody on his electronic piano, as if seeking to redeem what he's forcing his eyes to see. His blank gaze, here and in other scenes, registers the muteness of things, a sight that often leaves him speechless. Occasionally, though, Pharaon lets it all out. Right after he has visited the improvised memorial for the murdered girl, he starts running through the fields. He utters a scream, in reference to Munch, until he hits a fence. Caged by his simultaneous sensitivity and impassivity, Pharaon utters a second scream, which is smothered by the bypassing Eurostar, a railed monster connecting Paris and London cutting through the French North like once did the steam train in Émile Zola's *La Bête humaine*.

The Acting/Acted Body

As stated, both the Dardennes and Dumont are inspired by Bresson's idiosyncratic way of working with his amateur casts. Bresson's abhorrence of professional actors was almost proverbial, which is why he referred to his screen performers as "models," equating himself to a painter rather than a *metteur-en-scène*. As Bresson explains in a 1966 conversation with Jean-Luc Godard and Michel Delahaye, titled "The Question," he wanted the model to be a "virgin" of cinema, "crude matter that does not even know what it is and that surrenders to [the director] what it did not intend to surrender to anyone." Godard does not understand:

"When you say 'virgin of all experience,' but as soon . . . as [the actor] has filmed one twenty-fourth of a second, he is less virgin by that one twenty-fourth. . . . He is a little like a non-Christian who, once plunged into the water, will be baptized, and theoretically Christian." "No, not at all," Bresson responds, and he continues to explain that an actor is always acting, that nothing can destroy the habit of acting, and that the actor continues to exteriorize "himself" (male pronoun Bresson's) even in life. Instead, Bresson wants his "non-actor character . . . absolutely closed, like a container with a lid."[18] In the same vein, in *Notes sur le cinématographe* from 1975 (so almost a decade after this interview) Bresson writes that "it would not be ridiculous to say to your models: 'I invent you like you are.'"[19] As Steven Shaviro argues, by this Bresson means that the "models do not act; they are neither themselves nor somebody else. . . . The models *are* exactly as, and only as, they *appear*."[20]

Dumont too has repeatedly expressed his aversion of professional actors: "I immediately see their game, their tics, their falsity, I need *crude material* [*matière brute*] in order to sculpt my characters."[21] Similarly, Jean-Pierre Dardenne states about the casting for the role of Sonia in *L'Enfant*: "We were looking for someone who was the most flexible, who in a way was like *clay*, who we could work with."[22] To stay with the Dardennes: like Bresson the brothers require their actors to repeat gestures and dialogue until all semblance of performance has been eliminated. Unlike Bresson, who did not recast his models, and who after *Les Dames du Bois de Boulogne* (1945) strictly worked with nonprofessionals, the Dardennes have built career-long relationships with some of their male actors (Jérémie Renier, Olivier Gourmet, Fabrizio Rongione), while they have also worked with the art cinema stars Cécile de France (*Le Gamin au vélo*) and Marion Cotillard (*Deux jours, une nuit*). The other main difference between the Dardennes and Bresson is that whereas Bresson saw his models as "all face," as "two mobile eyes in a mobile head, the latter itself on a mobile body,"[23] the Dardennes are much concerned with bringing out their actors' *humanity*.

How does this dialectic between the profilmic acting body and the fictional acted body play out in *Rosetta*? The Dardennes selected Dequenne out of a group of two thousand young women who responded to a call printed in the Walloon press and aired on the Walloon radio. From this group, the Dardennes invited three hundred young women for a screen test. Because Rosetta's accent was crucial for the brothers, they did not cast in France. As Luc Dardenne explains, Rosetta "had to speak French without a Parisian accent, given the fact that in the script—and even more in the script than in the film—there are '*belgicismes*.' We also looked for a way of speaking, for [a young woman] which had the same accent as we, because we do not really speak like you [the interviewers]."[24] Having been offered the part, Dequenne still had to become Rosetta. The brothers asked Dequenne to dye her hair and let her plucked eyebrows grow back, and during a period of two months they practiced gestures and actions, such as fishing, waffle making, and fighting, with her. At the same time, Dequenne also had to "unlearn" certain traits, like dancing, because Rosetta does not know how to dance.[25]

On the set, the Dardennes continued to challenge Dequenne's physique. The film was shot in late fall and early winter, but Rosetta wears only a skirt and thin red jacket. So when Rosetta's cheeks look rosy and her fingers numb, and when she shivers all over after her mother has thrown her into the stream, this is because Dequenne herself—who was not wearing any makeup—was actually freezing. Similarly, the scenes in which Rosetta becomes exhausted by dragging her drunk mother up a flight of stairs or carrying heavy bags of flour owe their poignancy to Dequenne's actual fatigue. Luc Dardenne describes the shooting of the final scene, in which Rosetta struggles with a gas canister: "We did maybe ten takes and chose the last one, because the more the actress did it, the more tired she got. And the moment when she falls is the moment where we improvised in the frame."[26]

As much as *Rosetta* exploits Dequenne's physique, the film refrains from sexualizing her, even if Rosetta frequently appears in positions and situations that, had they been framed slightly differently, would have likely obtained an erotic charge. Consider the scene in which she and Riquet are fighting in the grass when the camera reveals her underwear and stockings. Like Rosetta herself, who expresses no sexual interest in the sympathetic Riquet (even though he is clearly attracted to her), the camera is sexually uninterested in Rosetta. She is too closed off to enter into an intimate relationship, caught up as she is in her survival mode. "Je peux avoir les bottes?" (Can I have the boots?), she asks Riquet only minutes after arriving at his place for what he presumes is their first date. But Rosetta is not ready for love, even though she gradually loosens up, and even smiles, when Riquet demonstrates his poor gymnastics skills. After their supper of Jupiler beer (like waffles, another Liège specialty) and *pain perdu* ("lost bread," better known as French toast), Riquet asks her to dance. But Riquet is moving too fast: Rosetta cannot dance, she tells him, and when he insists she dance with him anyway, she is struck with stomach cramps.

At one point, however, the camera catches Rosetta masturbating, *perhaps*, because the scene, on a deliberate play with the viewer's attentiveness, seeks to go unnoticed. Let's *rewind* to the conversation Rosetta has with her mother inside their cramped trailer. It's a key scene, "key" in the sense that this *triptych* of shots contains crucial information about Rosetta's cramps and, directly related, her relationship with her mother. The scene occurs about fifteen minutes into the film, when Rosetta has just arrived home:

Close-up of Rosetta sitting on the edge of her bed. She's in pain and presses her knee into her chest. The shot feels cramped because of the thick curtain that covers almost half the frame. "Give me a glass of water," she asks her mother. Her mother tries to help: "When that happened to me . . ." Rosetta interrupts her: "I don't care." (Je m'en fous.) Her mother: "I can at least tell you." Rosetta (annoyed): "You tell me each time. I'm not you." (Moi c'est pas toi.) Rosetta swallows a painkiller. She's still on the bed, her clothes disheveled. With her hand, she applies pressure to her lower belly and pelvic area to relieve her pain. Meanwhile, her mother reaches for the bag with beers Rosetta has bought at the waffle stand. Rosetta, as if bitten by a snake, jumps up, too fast for the camera: "It's not yet six!" Her mother: "So what, you're here." Rosetta: "I'm here because I got fired, not so that you can drink." Rosetta is getting really angry now and pulls the bag out of her mother's hands. "You only think of drinking and fucking!" she yells as she disappears behind the curtain that she draws in front of the frame. *Cut*: In the next shot, the camera is with Rosetta behind the curtain. She's sitting on the bed, her body still contorted from pain. She lies down. While we get a close-up of her face, she presumably comforts either her lower belly or pelvic area, outside the camera's field of vision. She closes her eyes. Her facial muscles relax a little, and for an instant her mouth curls up in a way that suggests pain relief yields to sexual pleasure (fig. 1.11). Almost immediately, though, Rosetta is distracted by a cold *north wind* creeping underneath the trailer window (fig. 1.12). She gets up and, somewhat neurotically, stuffs the window frame with toilet paper to shut out the draft. (As we have learned in an earlier scene on the city bus in which she sneezes and then decisively shuts the window, Rosetta has an intolerance for drafts.) We hear her mother's offscreen voice: "Let me drink one." "Leave!" is Rosetta's only response. *Cut*: Rosetta grabs a hair dryer from underneath her bed, lays down, and turns it on. From a close-up of the side of her face, the camera pans right—down her body, to her uncovered belly—as she comforts herself with the hot air. Rosetta moves the hair dryer back and forth just above her navel, holding the tool very close to her skin in a fashion that calls to mind the gestures of a medic performing an ultrasound scan (fig. 1.13). The camera pans back up her body, but the scene ends before the camera reaches her face.

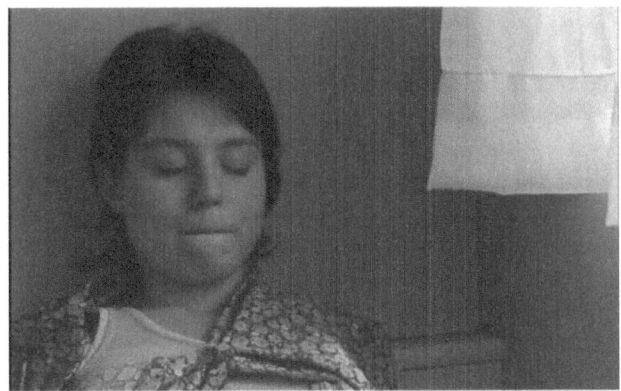

Figure 1.11. One time, though, the camera catches Rosetta masturbating, perhaps.

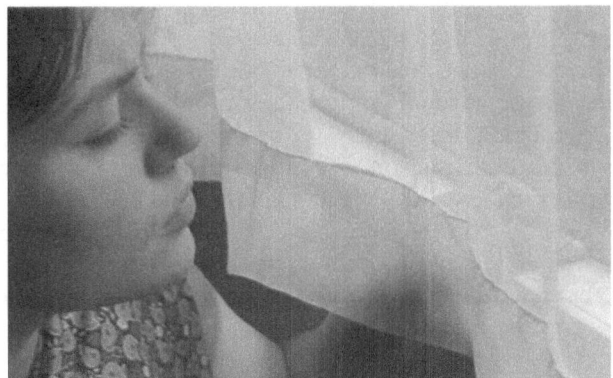

Figure 1.12. A north wind creeping underneath the trailer window.

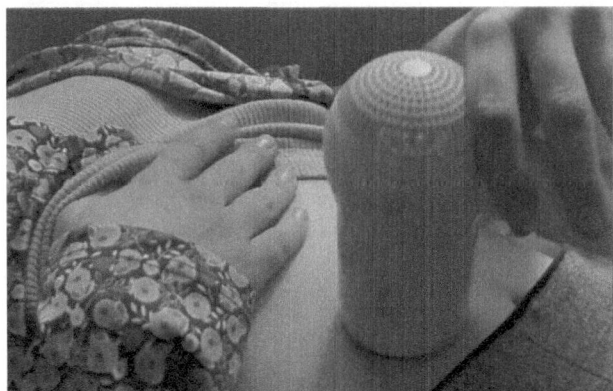

Figure 1.13. Rosetta holds the hair dryer just like a medic performing an ultrasound scan.

The exact cause of Rosetta's cramps remains ambiguous. They could be menstrual cramps; they could be symptoms of psychosomatic stress. Or is Rosetta expecting? No, that last scenario seems unlikely, given the conversation she has with her mother, who tells her daughter "each time" how she used to deal with the cramps when she was Rosetta's age. What becomes clear from this conversation, though, is that Rosetta's cramps are connected to her femininity (as depicted by the film), because she has inherited the cramps from her mother. This last observation is crucial. Rosetta is female, a fact that contrasts ironically with Luc Dardenne's confession that "on the set [he and his brother] called Rosetta Rosetto," doubtful as they were about their ability to create a convincing female protagonist.[27] But Rosetta needs to be Rosetta, not necessarily because of her struggle but because of the film's *depiction* of that struggle, for a number of reasons. First of all, whereas now sexual repression—if that's the right term—is an important part of Rosetta's survival mode, had she been a young man, the film's depiction of that repression would have been much less explicit. Second, the mother-daughter relationship is essential to the narrative: Rosetta refuses to inherit her mother's position, and she expresses that refusal, in part, by denying the fact that she is in many respects like her mother: "Moi c'est pas toi" (I'm not you). Third, the film's depiction of Rosetta's fighting and her carrying of heavy objects relies heavily on the stereotypically "unwomanly" nature of such actions, as well as the fact that these actions stretch the limits of what both Rosetta and Dequenne are physically capable of. Had she been a young man of the same age, this physical struggle would have seemed much more traditional. Fourth, had Rosetta been male, we would not have been able to speculate whether she's pregnant. To these reflections about Rosetta's gender identity one can add the fact that the film leaves Rosetta's ethnic descent somewhat ambiguous. Her name invites us to wonder, though, whether her father was—or is, if he's still alive—part of Wallonia's large Italian immigrant community. And here it does not really matter that Dequenne is not Italian Walloon, if only because the Dardennes also cast the Italian Walloon Patrizio Rongione for the role of the non–Italian Walloon Riquet (for *Le silence de Lorna*, the Dardennes cast Rongione more stereotypically as the gangster Fabio, while in *Deux jours, une nuit* [2014], Rongione stars as Manu, short for either Manuel or Manuelo).

To return to gender: however complex Rosetta may be as a character, there is also an uncomfortable, moralistic side about the film's depiction of her female identity. The film suggests a connection between Rosetta's sexual and emotional repression, on the one hand, and her struggle for a "normal life," on the other (a connection equally found in *Deux jours, une nuit*). In a Catholic spirit, the film associates "a normal life" with the holy Oedipal triangle of "mommy-daddy-me" (per Gilles Deleuze and Félix Guattari), restricting female sexuality to the confines of romantic, heterosexual union.[28] Moreover, Rosetta's explicitly desexualized survival mode contrasts with the reality that many young women who find themselves in a precarious position similar to Rosetta's end up working in the sex industry, whether or not of their own consent. Even though *Rosetta* never explicitly identifies its protagonist's sexual orientation, the film does not allow for a reading in which she's queer: as it turns out in the final scene, Rosetta's journey down her own *Via Dolorosa* has been structured on a male quest motif all along. Moreover, Rosetta and Riquet ultimately do end up together, not in a kiss or in romantic union (as would have been the case in traditional melodrama) but face to face before the image cuts to black.

The narrative thus follows a heteronormative logic in which "the male protagonist is free to command the stage" while female sexuality is represented as a mystery.[29] As Teresa de Lauretis writes, in the case of melodrama, this logic usually entails an inward or outward journey of the female protagonist that ends with her reaching the place where "a modern Oedipus will find her and fulfill the promise of his (off-screen) journey."[30] This is exactly what happens in *Rosetta*: she is saved last minute by Riquet. As the credits start to roll, we still don't know what will become of her or whether something will happen between her and Riquet. Yet despite this open ending, the film provides some sense of closure by suggesting that Riquet's intervention will lead Rosetta to drop her emotional shield.

In the preceding hour and a half, the film makes felt that emotional shield through the many times Rosetta appears out of focus or slips out of the frame—aesthetic choices that contribute to the film's frayed, documentary texture. Despite this documentary feel, *Rosetta* is a very dense, highly coded narrative. Almost everything Rosetta says or does has an unambiguous significance within the film's narrative structure. That significance, and even the fact that a plot element is a coded sign in the first place, is not always immediately clear, like Rosetta's sneezing in the bus (which implies her intolerance for drafts), or her chugging of a bottle of beer (which suggests that she might have inherited her mother's alcohol issues). And even if we can situate such seemingly insignificant details within a larger web of meaning, they retain a contingent quality that the Dardennes construct very deliberately. "In a documentary," Luc Dardenne remarks, "if the person makes an unexpected movement, you try to follow them but you don't always succeed. The person goes in and out of shot. What takes a lot of time in our rehearsals is constructing scenes or shots as if we couldn't manage to be in the right spot with our camera."[31]

This is a good point to turn again to *L'humanité*. In contrast to the Dardennes' carefully contrived documentary texture, the affect of Dumont's staged realism is more composed and painterly. The film roots itself in the "real" inasmuch as it exposes itself as art, for example, through its many references to iconic paintings such as Cézanne's or Magritte's apples, or Rembrandt's urinating woman. As Rancière writes, Dumont "affirms to make art and art only," an affirmation that

> ... passes through a double road. On the one hand it borrows the classical forms of the citation and the self-demonstration. The body of the young girl, turned in the same posture as the mannequin in [Duchamp's] *Etant donné[s]* ... seen through the door opening of the Museum of Philadelphia, warns us—through its celluloid aspect, the very "made-up" red of its blood, and the very pictorial ant—that "this is art."[32]

A crucial tactic of *L'humanité*'s self-conscious aesthetics is the static long take, whether in combination with an extreme long shot that reduces the human figure to an insect in a landscape, or in combination with an extreme close-up, creating "screenscapes" of objects and body parts: the murdered girl's genitals, a sweat-stained collar, the flowers in Pharaon's garden, and, in citation of Courbet's *L'Origine du monde* (1866), Domino's genitals as she invites Pharaon to touch her, which he refuses: "Not like that." As Martine Beugnet argues:

> Dumont's filmmaking pushes banality, and the banality of horror, to its limits; his camera investigates the concrete surface of things relentlessly, the long take extending the possible meaning of the images well beyond their denotative and connotative functions, to the point of total defamiliarization, where the categories are upturned and the banal turns into the repulsive and the uncanny, and, more rarely, the repulsive into the absorbing and moving.[33]

In *L'humanité*, this banalizing effect operates primarily through Pharaon's gaze. Often Pharaon just stands, motionless, staring at things and people, seemingly without understanding what his eyes are seeing. One commentator remarks that "the reason Pharaon de Winter is a cop is simply that it gives him a license to stare at people and things."[34] Sure, but Pharaon's gaze also has an obsessive, perhaps even psychopathic side.

As Beugnet continues, "The intense stare of Pharaon betrays his incapacity to distance himself from the world's meaningless, organic obscenity."[35] Moreover, Pharaon is the grandson of the painter Pharaon de Winter (1849–1924), also from Bailleul. Pharaon knows little about painting. "Il est beau ce bleu" (the blue is beautiful), he comments on one of his grandfather's works in the Lille art gallery. "Il est unique," the curator politely outbids him. No, if Pharaon, like the donkey in Bresson's *Au hasard Balthazar* (1966), gazes at the world, it's because the world gazes at him. The ant, the apple, the flowers, the violated girl: Pharaon does not understand, but simultaneously he understands too well. Pharaon is paralyzed by the banality of things, not in a philosophical, existentialist way, but in a very banal way. His mode of behavior is pensive or even slow, he weighs every syllable, and he gives great deliberation to every action. To a degree we can ascribe Pharaon's appearance to that of his actor, Emmanuel Schotté, to his physiognomy, his face, motor system, and manner of speaking. At the time of his casting, Schotté was an air force soldier from the Lille area who had never acted before (and neither had Séverine Caneele who, like the character of Domino she performs, worked in a factory). In an interview Dumont says the following about the casting process for *L'humanité*: "I spent a year finding my Pharaon. I needed someone who was massive and very sensitive at the same time, and with somewhat bulging eyes. Someone older, and also more cultivated, than the guys from *La Vie de Jésus*: someone who expresses kindness and is receptive to all emotions. Someone porous."[36] Dumont could have added, "someone like the priest in Bresson's *Journal d'un curé de campagne*," because Schotté's appearance in *L'humanité* strongly resembles that of Claude Laydu modeling for Bresson.

Before and during the shooting Dumont, like the Dardennes, invests a lot of time in building a personal relationship with his actors. He does so not in order to become their friends, but to be able to bring out elements of their real-life personalities, and "steal" their emotions:

> You cannot make someone cry by saying: "Come on, cry." If you want it to be powerful, you need a tension. . . . I am not a torturer, but I am demanding. . . . In order to make an actress cry, I will remind her in her ear of things that she has told me. I will try to make her recall personal situations that get [the crying] started. . . . I can only direct actors on the basis of what I know of them.[37]

As this example illustrates, in his filmmaking practice Dumont thus seeks the limits of his actors' consent in his unequal power relationship with them. The most complex example in this regard is *Camille Claudel 1915* (2013), for which Dumont worked with the real-life patients and nurses in a psychiatric hospital in the south of France. Many of these patients were not even aware that they were going to be in a film, let alone capable of consenting to a "normal" actor-director contract. At the same time, this film stars Juliette Binoche in the role of Camille Claudel. After Binoche had approached Dumont with the proposal to make a film together, Dumont wrote this biopic about a famous French female artist who is hospitalized by a patriarchal system, thus negotiating Binoche's stardom with his principle to strictly work with amateurs (a principle Dumont fully deviated from for his farcical comedy *Ma Loute* [2016], which has a cast of stars—including again Binoche—and Ch'tis, that is, those inhabitants of the French North associated with the Ch'ti language, also known as Picard).

Also *L'humanité* is the result of a dialogue between director and actor. Significantly, Dumont changed the ending of the film after Schotté had expressed his discomfort with the sex scene he was supposed to be in:

> It was planned that Pharaon de Winter fucks Domino at the end of the film. When I asked [Schotté], he refused. I could have very well told him: "Listen, *mon petit père*, if that's the case, I'll take someone else." But I wanted him, and I accepted it. The moment the actor says "no," I revise, and from time to time I realize that what I'm asking is not really justified. It is good to have a reaction from someone calling into question the principle of a scene. Pharaon, Emmanuel Schotté, has given a lot of spirituality to the character, while mine was hypersexual. . . . It is up to me to know what I want or what I don't want. But I stay convinced that I don't know what I want: I want to realize what occurs.[38]

In his "exploitation" of actors' physique and emotions, Dumont goes a step further than the Dardennes. Dumont, like the Dardennes and unlike Bresson, integrates his actors' real bodily affects into his art. Unlike, or at least much more than the Dardennes, and definitely unlike Bresson, he uses, and some will say abuses, their emotional histories and personalities. Largely in difference with the Dardennes, Dumont typecasts many of his actors, in that he looks for actors whose real-life personas and social subjectivities correspond to the characters he has in mind. This may sound like social realism, but certainly after *La Vie de Jésus* Dumont has explicitly moved away from the social. He does not simply have his working-class actors play themselves; he has them play explicit stereotypes and even caricatures of working-class subjects. Similarly, for all of his works that are set in the French North (*La Vie de Jésus, Flandres, Hadewijch, Hors Satan, Jeannette: l'enfance de Jeanne d'Arc*, and the TV miniseries *P'tit Quinquin* and *Coincoin et les z'inhumains*), Dumont used actors from the region in a way that self-consciously plays into dominant stereotypes of the French northerner as being more rough and less cultivated than people from more southern parts of the hexagon.

In the case of *L'humanité*, this play with northern French, working-class identity manifests itself most clearly in the "white trash" characters of Domino and Joseph: their curses, their sports clothing and techno music, their discomfort in explicitly bourgeois situations like eating in a nice restaurant, their loud sex (for which Dumont used stand-ins). Other than with essentialist understandings of class and regional identity, *L'humanité* plays with stereotypes of gender and racial identity. As far as its play with gender is concerned, the film demonstrates a degree of awareness about the patriarchal binaries it ventriloquizes, especially through its recurring thematization of a male, Catholic, small-town gaze. The film's play with racial stereotypes, in contrast, and in particular with existing stereotypes about French Algerian men, is less integrated into the narrative. I am thinking in particular about the scene in which Pharaon caresses "the dealer." The fact that Malik Haquem's character is never named is not a problem per se, nor is it a problem that Dumont typecast a French Algerian man into a clichéd image of a petty French Algerian criminal. After all, such caricature is fundamental to Dumont's strategy. My critique is that the *fictional* French Algerian identity of Haquem's character is only very loosely justified by the story, in that for the narrative it is not really important that this man is French Algerian. For the narrative it only matters that the character is male, because had he been female the scene in which Pharaon intimately touches his face would have much less unambiguously appeared as an act of harassment (which it is, even though the film does not necessarily portray it that way). What matters further is that the arrestee is from the city, perhaps the nearby Roubaix, as Pharaon's colleague accuses the "dealer" of having come "down here to ruin our kids."

Having analyzed *Rosetta* and *L'humanité* in some detail, we can formulate a preliminary answer to the guiding question, "What unites both films?" As we have seen in the previous two sections, both films are concerned with the dichotomy "human" versus "nonhuman." And as we have seen in this section, both films explore this dichotomy by integrating the "real" affects, and in the case of Dumont also personalities, of their actors into the fictional characters. Now, when we try to forget for a moment what we've learned about *Rosetta* and *L'humanité* through behind-the-scenes sources like interviews or Luc Dardenne's journal—and instead concentrate strictly on Rosetta's and Pharaon's two-dimensional acting/acted presence flickering over the screen—how can we distinguish between what is "acted" and what is not? How can we isolate those aspects of the on-screen body that are not actively acted but are "real," in that they are gestures acting through the body of the actor who is hiding themselves in the act? Giorgio Agamben discusses this nonacted excess, or remainder, perceptible in the screen actor's performance as "cinema's essence." That essence, he argues, lies not in the image but in the gesture. For Agamben, "what characterizes gesture is that in it nothing is being produced or acted, but rather something is being endured and supported. The gesture, in other words, opens the sphere of *ethos* as the more proper sphere of that which is human."[39] Gesture is where acting breaks down. It is the action in a person's acting that happens inadvertently, that accompanies acting but also happens despite it: a nervous tic, a way of doing, an unfeigned blush. Gesture escapes meaning and reminds us of the fact that we're human only insofar as we exist in discourse. Agamben writes: "Cinema's essential 'silence' is, just like the silence of philosophy, exposure of the being-in-language of human beings, pure gesturality."[40]

Is Agamben's concept of *gesture* useful for our analysis of *Rosetta* and *L'humanité*? Yes and no, because now the question becomes: How can the viewer determine when and where acting yields to gesture, especially when a film integrates an actor's real-life presence into their on-screen performance? We know that the Dardennes extensively practice gestures with their actors, like Dequenne selling waffles, in order for those activities to look natural. At the same time, they cast Dequenne in the first place precisely because "she made the stand exist." "We went to buy waffles," Luc Dardenne recalls, "and we really felt it was her stand."[41] Based on this anecdotal evidence, we can speculate that, especially in those few moments when Rosetta appears most "human" and "normal," like in the waffle-selling scene or the last supper with Riquet, the gestures are essentially Dequenne's own. Had the Dardennes practiced them with a different actress, Rosetta's on-screen presence would have felt very different. In *L'humanité* the situation is different yet equally complex. We can only agree with Dumont that Pharaon could not have been played by a different actor. At the same time, we are aware of the fact that Schotté's real-life appearance only became Pharaon's meaningful muteness in the context of the film's banalizing aesthetics. In sum, both films thus encourage their viewer to conflate character and actor, transferring, through the screen as it were, the tension internal to the acting/acted body. This tension is not a fine line separating the performing real from the performed nonreal. Rather, it is immanent to the on-screen presence of a performing/performed life.

Of Little Flies and Burned-Out Priests

Screen acting is only one dimension of the conversations *L'humanité* and *Rosetta* initiate with Bresson. Also in terms of story, these films are inspired by the filmmaker whose work helped shape the cinematic imagination of the French North. *Rosetta* is as stated a variation on Bresson's *Mouchette* (1967), which in turn is an adaptation of the 1937 novel *Nouvelle histoire de Mouchette* (New history of Mouchette) by Georges Bernanos. Similarly, *L'humanité* quotes *Journal d'un curé de campagne* (1951), which Bresson based on Bernanos's 1936 novel of the same title. *L'humanité* contains, moreover, visual and narrative references to Maurice Pialat's *Sous le soleil de Satan* (1987), yet another Bernanos adaptation.

One aspect that all these novels, adaptations, and variations on adaptations share is that their stories include a Mouchette or a Mouchette-like character. Bernanos first introduced Mouchette—whose name literally means "little fly"—in *Sous le soleil de Satan* (1926), which opens with the "Histoire de Mouchette." This story ends with Mouchette's suicide, after which she reappears as an angel. A decade later, Bernanos reincarnated Mouchette's spirit into the "new Mouchette." Bernanos begins this *Nouvelle histoire de Mouchette* by explaining himself to the reader:

> From the first pages of this tale the familiar name of Mouchette has imposed itself upon me so naturally that from then on it was impossible for me to change it.
>
> The Mouchette of the *Nouvelle Histoire* has nothing in common with that of *Soleil de Satan* besides the same tragic loneliness in which I have both of them seen live and die.
>
> May God have mercy on both of them![42]

The two Mouchettes *do* have more in common, starting with the fact that they both live and die in the Pas-de-Calais region in the French North. The French North has traditionally been prone to imaginations of lonely human struggle, due to its coal industry and history of crisis as well as the region's open fields and cold and wet climate. Ironically, this unpredictable climate is why many films set in Nord-Pas-de-Calais were shot elsewhere. Bresson's *Mouchette*, for example, was shot in the sunnier Vaucluse region, while the film only makes offhand reference to the French North. Moreover, whereas Bernanos has his tragic heroine speak "in that awful Picard accent,"[43] the voice actress of Bresson's Mouchette speaks a more standard French.

As Godard states in voice-over in the promotional trailer he made for Bresson's film, *Mouchette* is at once "Christian and sadistic" (fig. 1.14). The New Mouchette is about thirteen and lives in a dark one-room apartment together with her terminally ill mother, her baby brother, and her father and older brother who are both heavy alcoholics. At home, most chores fall on her. At school, her bourgeois classmates ridicule Mouchette for her poor dress, and her female teacher treats her harshly for failing to hold key while singing religious cantatas. Mouchette rebels, but she only has her curses and the mud she throws at her classmates and stampedes into the church. She finds some relief in the woods, but also there she is not safe. The film draws a poignant parallel between Mouchette and the rabbits running for both the licensed hunters and the poacher. That poacher, Arsène, is a social outcast like Mouchette. When one night in the forest Mouchette is caught by a rainstorm, Arsène helps her find her clog. When he asks her to provide him with an alibi for a murder he fears having committed, she agrees. When he is sick from drinking, she wipes the vomit off his mouth, while singing, in key this time, the cantata she has learned at school. Mouchette is an angel, a truly human being in a world deprived of humanity, who despite her misery keeps

Figure 1.14. From the promotional trailer Jean-Luc Godard made for Bresson's *Mouchette*.

humming while preparing coffee for her family (with reference to the maid Maria in Vittorio de Sica's *Umberto D* [1952]). That same night, however, Arsène sexually assaults Mouchette; the next morning her mother dies; and meanwhile the people in the village call her a *salope*, a slut. The film ends with Mouchette drowning herself in a stream. At her first attempt Mouchette fails, but at her second attempt she succeeds.

Also Rosetta at one point finds herself drowning in the water, with the difference that she has been pushed into it by her mother, and unlike Mouchette, Rosetta fights for her life. *Rosetta* contains many references to *Mouchette*: the shortcuts through the woods (fig. 1.15, cf. fig. 1.5), the mother-daughter relationship, the absent father, the male friend who involves the heroine in his illicit affairs, the lost footwear, the alcohol, the mud, the fighting, and the two suicide attempts. Even the *s* and *t* sounds in "Rosetta" echo "Mouchette." Equally crucial are the Dardennes' deviations from Bresson (and from Bernanos). Whereas Mouchette's struggle is one of sexual awakening, Rosetta's is explicitly desexualized. Second, whereas the Dardennes' camera is almost glued to its protagonist, Bresson keeps much more distance, literally, in terms of shot length, and figuratively, in terms of emotional investment. Third, while Mouchette dies, *Rosetta* ends on an open, hopeful note.

Like *Rosetta*, *L'humanité* also inserts itself into the Mouchette mythology, by referencing, and in that act of quotation deviating from,

Figure 1.15. *Mouchette* (Robert Bresson, 1967). Compare to figure 1.5.

both Bresson's *Journal d'un curé de campagne* and, though more indirectly, Pialat's *Sous le soleil de Satan*. Like Pharaon, the priests of *Journal d'un curé* and *Sous le soleil* represent the Law for the members of their rural, northern French communities, the towns of Ambricourt and Campagne, respectively. And as is the case with Pharaon, this responsibility weighs heavily on their seemingly strong shoulders, as their pains and temptations lead them to question the authority they have vowed to emobody. The priests are burned-out, physically and spiritually. Bresson's never-named *curé* is tortured by terrible pains in his stomach that contribute to his sense of lacking the grace he has committed to pass on to others. Similarly, Donissan in *Sous le soleil* (Gérard Depardieu) confesses to his superior (performed *à l'improviste* by Pialat himself) that he feels that he is "spending his life seeing God humiliated."

So far so good. After all, such doubts are very "normal" and even necessary in the constitution of a true believer, certainly in the Jansenism in which Bernanos steeped his stories. Jansenism, named after the Dutch theologian Cornelius Jansen, was an almost Calvinist movement in the Catholic Church that especially gained popularity in seventeenth-century France. The Jansenist life was austere, torn between fear and hope: fear of original sin, hope of having been divinely predestined to partake in God's infinite grace. "If there is a God," as Blaise Pascal (1623–1662) rationalized the doubt fundamental to belief, "He is infinitely incomprehensible, since, having neither parts nor limits, He has no affinity to us. We are then incapable of knowing either what He is or if He is." This existential doubt requires that humanity play a game. "You must wager," Pascal writes, "It is not optional. You are embarked. Which will you choose then?"[44] As Gilles Deleuze writes in *Cinema 2*, the dilemma is not "that of choosing between the existence or non-existence of God, but between the mode of existence of one who believes in God, and the mode of existence of the one who does not."[45] Pascal's wager, in other words, is a game of heads and tails in which mankind has an Infinity to gain and a finite nothing to lose. So "wager, then," Pascal urges his reader, "without Hesitation that He is."[46] But what if the existential anxiety consumes body and soul? The *curé* and Donissan are too fatigued and oversensitive to wager much longer, a condition that frustrates them in their professional right and duty to ventriloquize the Law. They are no longer able to subjugate the signs of the senses to the self-referential Sign that is God's word.

In both the novels and the screen adaptations of *Sous le soleil* and *Journal d'un curé* this religious struggle is tied to the physical surroundings of the *enfer du Nord*, the northern hell, in which it is set. In *Le Nord et le cinéma* (an edited volume on cinema and the French North) Paul Renard paints the following picture of these films:

> The places [in *Journal d'un curé de campagne* and *Sous le soleil de Satan*] do not only provide a realist framework. As a result of the lighting and the framing, they also obtain a supernatural dimension.
>
> Bresson, in a black-and-white film, insists on the black. Cassocks of priests, the presbytery's interior during the night, undergrowth cast in darkness. In contrast with this black, we have the white pages of the journal in which the *curé* is constantly seen writing. Those contrasts reflect the battle between good and evil, between grace and sin, but in a way that refuses univocal Manichaeism. In fact, the darkness springs to mind [*jaillit*] because of and in the light: the lamp lighting the priest's desk symbolizes conscience seeking to open itself up to grace, but, on the other hand, the whiteness of the notebook's pages covered by the black ink of the *curé*'s words correspond to the ambiguity of an undertaking that yields analysis as much as narcissism.
>
> Pialat often presents Donissan as a remote silhouette crushed by the immensity of a nature whose green grass and gray sky take on cold nuances; the "temptation of despair" (as one of the sections of Bernanos's novel is titled) thus emanates from the landscape. This is the same in the numerous nocturnal scenes, in particular during the confrontation of the lost priest with the diabolic horse tradesman. Nevertheless, during those same moments the cinematographic process of the "nuit américaine," through its bluish colors, also gives a *pre-sense* of the irruption of the grace that will manifest itself not long after it, by Donissan's encounter with the carrier who helps him and puts him back on track.
>
> In an unexpected way, Bresson and Pialat insist much less than Bernanos on the rain and the humidity of a region that is not devoid of it.[47]

Also in *L'humanité* the weather stays dry, while the wind never grows much stronger than a breeze in Pharaon's jacket and the viewer's ears. The film's clearest visual references to *Journal d'un curé* and *Sous le soleil* are found in its opening scene, in which Pharaon carries the priests' nocturnal journeys to the light of day. Like Donissan, Pharaon is framed as "a remote silhouette" tracing the horizon (fig. 1.16, cf. fig. 1.7); and like the *curé* Pharaon falls flat forward into the mud (fig. 1.17, cf. fig. 1.8). While they thus recall Christ's journey through the desert, both priests and Pharaon run into an incarnation of Mouchette, whose character references Mary Magdalene, described by Luke as the "sinful woman" (7:36–50).

Figure 1.16. *Sous le soleil de Satan* (Maurice Pialat, 1987).

Figure 1.17. *Journal d'un curé de campagne* (Robert Bresson, 1951).

To start with Bresson's *curé*: facedown in the mud and contorted by terrible pains, he yearns for the Holy Virgin, not only "the mother of mankind" as his superior described her earlier that day, but also her daughter, "a little girl, this queen of angels." The Virgin never shows, but who does appear to his delirious vision is the poor Séraphita, a pupil in his Eucharist class. Earlier that day, the flirtatious Séraphita deliberately had embarrassed him in front of her classmates by attributing her excellent performances to the his "beaux yeux," his beautiful eyes. Now, at this nightly hour, Séraphita helps the *curé* back on his feet and wipes the vomit of his face, like Mouchette does to Arsène, and like Mary Magdalene washed and kissed the feet of Christ. Séraphita is Mouchette: a young woman who would have been an angel had there been a God, but who now, in the stern gaze of her community, is nothing but a sinful little fly. As we have seen, Mouchette's original incarnation is found in *Sous le soleil de Satan*. In this story, Germaine ("dite Mouchette") is the sixteen-year-old daughter of a wealthy brewer. She has slept with multiple married men and early in the story she kills the one she is pregnant by. Donissan blames her sins on Satan, which is the reason for his journey through the northern desert. When in the middle of the night the devil disguised as a horse tradesman offers him "a gaze that traverses all things," Donissan still finds the power to quote Christ: "Retire-toi Satan!" (Matthew 4:10). However, the sexually forward Mouchette (in Pialat's adaptation performed by Sandrine Bonnaire) does not want to be saved. "What gives you the right?!" she tells Donissan upon his return, "God, what a joke, 'God' doesn't mean anything." In the next scene, Mouchette slits her throat, upon which Donissan carries her corpse to the altar, an act of blasphemy that forces him to temporarily retreat in a monastery. Only there does Donissan become the savior he always already was predestined to be. First, he receives a visitation from Mouchette, an angel now. Soon after, Donissan resurrects a little boy in the hamlet of Lumbres, near Calais.

In *L'humanité*, in contrast, any hope for visions and miracles is crushed from the onset. The landscape Pharaon crosses is really deprived of grace, and Pharaon's only encounter is with the already decomposing, faceless corpse of the murdered girl, a *mouchette* clipped of her wings. It's a vision that leaves Pharaon gazing, speechless. In this muteness, Pharaon differs from his clerical predecessors who both have the gift of the word, in two respects. Donissan and the *curé* have the word of God on which they base their authorities. Second, they have their journals to which they confide their pains and doubts. The difference with Pharaon is only an apparent one, though. The priests may have the *written* word, but in the end the *curé* and Donissan, like Pharaon, often stand speechless in the face of things. Initially the *curé* still manages to reassure himself that "the desire to pray already is a prayer, and that God would not desire more." As time passes, though, and as his pains grow more severe, he needs to admit that his suffering is killing his spiritual appetite. Similarly, Donissan confesses that he can only "absolve or cry," which is why he flagellates himself until he bleeds. Crucially, unlike Pharaon, both the *curé* and Donissan die in the end. In its final scene *Journal d'un curé* confides to the spectator the *curé*'s last moments as written down by his friend, a former *confrère*, now a pharmacist in Lille:

> Then he seemed to regain some force, and in an almost inaudible voice asked me for absolution. His face was calmer, he even smiled. Neither humanity nor friendship would permit me to refuse, though while discharging my duties I explained to my unfortunate comrade my hesitation against granting his request. He didn't seem to hear me. But a few moments later he laid his hands on mine while he entreated me to draw closer to him. He then said very distinctly, if extremely slowly, these exact words: "What does it all matter? All is grace." [*Qu-est-ce que cela fait? Tout est grâce.*] I believe he died just then.

As the voice-over reads the letter, the typed words dissolve into a black crucifix on a white wall. In his essay on the film André Bazin, at his most Catholic, hailed the film's conclusion on a "screen, free of images and handed back to literature" as a "triumph of cinematographic realism," while he called "the black cross on the white screen . . . the only visible trace left by the assumption of the image, *témoigne de ce dont sa réalité n'était qu'un signe.*"[48] I'm most interested here in the part of Bazin's interpretation of the crucifix that I left untranslated. Bazin writes that the crucifix is witness of (*témoigne de*) that (*ce*) whose reality (*dont sa réalité*) was but a sign (*n'était qu'un signe*). Does Bazin mean here that the crucifix bears witness to Christ (*ce*), whose miracle (*dont sa réalité*) was "but a sign" of God's infinite grace, thus interpreting *Journal d'un curé* as a religious film? Or does *ce* refer to the *curé*'s uneventful death in a world *without* God in which *all* is grace, an interpretation that would imply that the crucifix—also the final image of *Sous le soleil de Satan*—has lost its intrinsic, testimonial value and become "just an" (*qu'un*) iconic sign ("†") like any other? The ambiguity is the point, both Bresson's and Bazin's. Both film philosophers employ a Christian audiovisual vocabulary in order to express a disenchanted world. Essentially, their critical and cinematographic writings keep saying over and again that "there is no God." But precisely in that speech act, they keep the memory of the

Christian God very much alive. I am critical of this secular-Christian position that wants to have its cake and eat it too, because by explicitly denying God in a Christian vocabulary in his Word and Image, Bazin, Bresson, and also Pialat self-consciously place themselves in the legacy of Pascal's wager, according to which doubt is essential for true belief. Regardless of their answers to the Question of grace, what matters is that these film philosophers ask this question in the first place. In the words of the *curé*, the desire to pray already is a prayer, and God would not desire more. To think about God in his own terms is to affirm his existence, because there never has been a Christian God outside of people's inner and outer speculations surrounding the question and terms of his existence. "God" has always been nothing but a memory, a collective, transindividual cloud of associations in word and image.

One encounters the same memory of God in *L'humanité*. Like Bazin, Bresson, and Pialat, Dumont uses the textual-visual vocabulary from a time in which people still massively believed in a Christian God in order to say that "God does not exist." And like the *curé* and Donissan, Pharaon, who is all gaze, registers the intrinsic muteness of signs, hence his own muteness, which without words expresses the lack of humanity essential to the nonexistence of God. In the universe of *L'humanité*, the human figure is nothing but an insect in a deserted landscape and the human body nothing but mere flesh. It's a vision in need of redemption, the resurrection of "humanity." The only one capable of such a miracle is, of course, Pharaon, the mute Christ.

And what about Rosetta? What is her relation to Christ?

a north wind

While this chapter is slowly homing in on the answer to the question, "What unites *Rosetta* and *L'humanité*?" let's walk through Rancière's answer. Rancière begins by evaluating the degree to which *Rosetta* and *L'humanité* partake in the "Bovary effect." By that effect, witnessed par excellence in Flaubert's 1856 novel, Rancière understands the phenomenon that a text becomes "art" "not *in spite* but precisely *because of* the nullity of the action and the stupidity [*bêtise*] of the characters."[49] According to Rancière, this Bovary effect is indeed present in *Rosetta* and *L'humanité*. He writes:

> Rosetta is not a subproletarian representative who, defined by close-ups, moves us in her misery and alerts us about the condition of her equals. The close-ups of faces in *Rosetta* and *L'humanité* do not bring us closer to human suffering and the human face. On the contrary, they perform the function

superbly described by Jean Epstein and commented on by Gilles Deleuze: to transform one part of the human body into a strange relief or a monstrous animal. Rosetta's goal-oriented obstinacy, her clenching fists or her stomach contracted by pain, like the fatigued blush on Domino's face when she is having an orgasm, or the sweat on the police chief's greasy face: they are not the revealing properties of a social state to be known in its cruelty. They are precisely the *subject* of art, the brute presence, the *"bêtise"* [stupidity and animality] in which the will of art realizes itself as art by annulling itself as will.[50]

In other words, in Rancière's understanding *Rosetta* and *L'humanité* are not allegorical narratives whose characters stand in for a social group. Instead, these films take as their subject, their subject of art, precisely the *lack* of sense Rosetta and Pharaon make as characters. At the same time, though, *Rosetta* and *L'humanité* drive the *bêtise* of their characters to a point of excess, where the "art effect" turns over into its opposite and an element of social caricature is reintroduced. As far as Rosetta is concerned, Rancière argues that, on the one hand, she appears as a "wild child" (*sauvageonne*) fighting for mere survival. On the other hand, Rosetta's pride and her desire for a "real job" make her a Brechtian *fille courage*, who attests to a dehumanizing society. In sum:

> The perpetual movement through which the film glues us to her body exacerbates the classical gesture of the militant or sociologist, and obliges us to share in the sensory experience of the inhabitant of this world so close that we would rather not see it. *Rosetta* thus cumulates the power of art of what doesn't want to say anything and the overwhelming force of the testimony that does not need words.[51]

I agree with this reading. Rosetta's affective screen presence is at once allegorical and nonallegorical. Rosetta is on her own in her struggle, but she's not alone *in it*, as the film subtly reminds us by having her bump into the young woman whose job she has been given (fig. 1.18). She is both brute presence and representative of a heterogeneous, precarious class in an era in which traditional class categories have become blurry and in which it is difficult, if not impossible, to represent, politically and aesthetically. This precariat figure emerges from the crisis of parochial power, a crisis that has left it unclear for many what a normal life looks like. We shouldn't feel too nostalgic about those power structures, at least not insofar as their ideal of a normal, human life was—and continues to be—modeled on a male, white, heterosexual, able-bodied European subject. Moreover, we should be equally wary of the inclusive and diverse, "mindful" faces with which the post-state life-shaping platforms of Google, Facebook, Airbnb, and the like challenge and supersede the old modern structures. This disruptive movement is used, after all, to enhance corporations' profit-driven activities that contribute to socioeconomic segregation within and between societies, often along lines of gender and race.

To return to Rosetta, Rancière also misses something crucial about her cramps: these cramps are not just instances of her "brute presence, her animality." They're also an allegorical device that positions Rosetta in a relation of inheritance with her mother. Rosetta is emphatically *not* like her mother, yet in her refusal to inherit her mother's social position, she attempts to deny the fact that in many respects she *is* like her mother. Rosetta refuses to dehumanize herself in the face of a dehumanizing society, but this desperate obstinacy to affirm her humanity, her refusal to inherit, leads her to lose her humanity and bring out her *bêtise*, what the film presents as her animality and stupidity. Rosetta simultaneously does and does not know what makes or would make her human. That's why she almost lets Riquet drown, and why she betrays him to get his job. The following day, however, Rosetta realizes that, having exchanged a friend for a job, she has stripped the latter of its normalizing quality. "Laisse-moi passer" (Let me through), she says while evading Riquet when he tries to hold her accountable for her betrayal. Rosetta's only answer to the world is her flight forward—across the road, back to the trailer park, where she finds her mother drunk again. She drags her mother into the trailer, boils an egg, walks to the outside pay phone, quits her job, returns, cools the egg in a bowl of water (fig. 1.19), turns on the gas, shuts the curtain in front of her bed, lies down, and eats the overboiled egg—all in one interrupted movement. Over a long take, the gas fills up the screen until the soundtrack swells and dies out. Rosetta gets up again, disconnects the gas canister, and goes to buy a new one. While she's on her way back to the trailer, struggling with the canister like Christ with his cross, we are reminded of Mouchette, who did succeed in her second suicide attempt, and whose tragedy Rosetta is about to repeat. Then Riquet arrives on his moped, aggressively circling around her, the camera, and the viewer (recalling the ending of Fellini's *Le Notti di Cabiria*) until Rosetta stumbles and breaks into tears, her head on the canister. Riquet helps her up, and Rosetta, in a rare close-up of her face, just looks, not at the camera—which rests momentarily, panting from exhaustion as she does—but at her savior (fig. 1.20). Somewhere in the middle of this long close-up, the film cuts to black. No music.

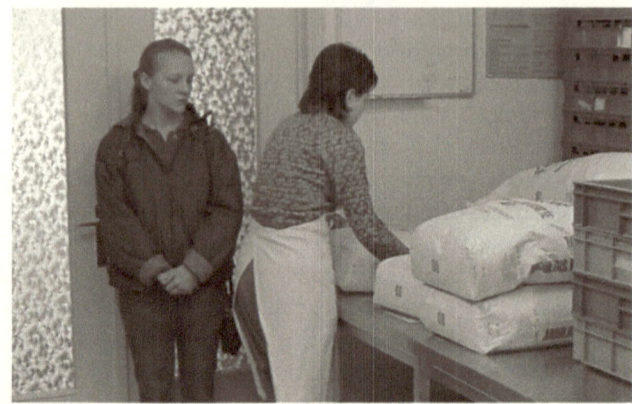

Figure 1.18. Rosetta bumps into the young woman whose job she has just been given.

Figure 1.19. The only thing Rosetta symbolically gives birth to is the hard-boiled egg.

Figure 1.20. Rosetta looks offscreen at her savior.

In *L'humanité* there *is* music at the end. Other than that, the film's ending is very similar to that of *Rosetta*: a long close-up of the heavily breathing protagonist looking into a direction that lies behind the camera's field of vision. Pharaon slightly raises his blank blue eyes (fig. 1.21). As we know from the previous shot, he is staring at the diffuse white light that shines through the windows of the police office. Pharaon is sitting in a chair. For an instant, his mouth curls up, as if acknowledging someone. We see and hear him swallow and inhale through his nose. Other than that Pharaon's face is calm, he perhaps even smiles, this in paraphrasis of Bresson's *curé*. What we also know from the previous shot is that Pharaon is wearing handcuffs. Pharaon is guilty, but of what? Is not Joseph but Pharaon himself the murderer after all? Has Pharaon all this time been the object of his own investigation? Several commentators have suggested this reading. Kent Jones, for example, argues that "Pharaon's behavior (his glassy-eyed demeanor; his fixation on crotches and folds of flesh; his semi-autistic moments of upset . . .), his emotional specifics . . ." proves that he "is the murderer in the first place."[52] The problem with this straightforward typecasting of Pharaon into a psychopath profile is that it fails to account for the film's self-consciously Catholic vocabulary. Pharaon *is* in the police station and he *is* handcuffed, but it is also possible that he has taken Joseph's guilt upon himself, either literally, by having made a false confession out of pity for Joseph and Domino, or spiritually, revealing himself as the Christ figure we always already suspected him to be. As Rancière argues about the resolution of Pharaon's quest:

> The march in place of the atypical policeman, whose difficult speech, static voyeurism, and derisory inquiries have as their only goal to show that there is nothing to look for. Because

Figure 1.21. Pharaon looks offscreen at the diffuse white light.

> the criminal and the victim, the lawman and the witness are one and the same person: this suffering and savoring [*jouissante*] "humanity." ... This Schopenhauerian humanity of which Pharaon is simultaneously representative and witness: a criminal underneath his police uniform, an innocent idiot [*idiot-innocent*] who carries on his back the misery and cruelty of the world, Christ or Muychkine [the prince of Dostoevsky's *The Idiots* who is unable to face the evil in the world] offering the guilty victims [*victimes-coupables*] of this perpetually innocent game the only possible cure: the gesture of compassion.[53]

I largely agree with Rancière. Pharaon is the mute Christ, the word become flesh that redeems humanity from its sins, and simultaneously a rather slow man, perhaps even an idiot lacking the word, unable as he is to express himself "humanly." Less-than-human and more-than-human at once, Pharaon is his lack, his expressive inability to express himself. It is this speaking muteness of his gaze that Pharaon acknowledges in the blissful light filtered by the curtains. *All is grace*. The ontological gap between the realism of the film's first 138 minutes and the Christianity of its final scene is in fact always already present *within* each of the film's images, invisibly expressive of its protagonist's double, miraculously normal nature.

Moreover, in some scenes the Spirit actually *does* manifest itself as a visibly coded element in or in between its images. *L'humanité* contains a number of hidden plot elements, or *Easter eggs*, some of which more difficult to spot than others. As stated in the introduction, in computing, an Easter egg is a program's coded response to an undocumented user command. In cinema, where the code is immanent to the screen interface, an Easter egg is a plot element easily missed by the first-time spectator but that may be a "key" to the narrative. In Christianity, the originally pagan association of the egg with fertility came to symbolize Christ's resurrection. The first Easter egg in *L'humanité* is Pharaon's levitation while he is standing amid the flowers in his garden, first in a shot in which his head slowly rises into the frame, followed by a long objective shot of him that proves that Pharaon is not only gazing into but also floating in the void (fig. 1.22). The second plot element that is easily missed on first viewing is found two scenes before the end, when Pharaon learns of Joseph's arrest. "Joseph, it wasn't you was it?" "Yes," his friend nods. Then *L'humanité* reveals something about Pharaon that the film, through an elliptical cut that passes as a continuity cut, explicitly hid from the viewer in the earlier scene in which Pharaon caresses the

Figure 1.22. Pharaon floating in the void.

French-Algerian arrestee. First Pharaon caresses Joseph's face like he did with the "dealer." Then he presses his mouth firmly against Joseph's, sucks out the evil, exhales loudly, throws his former friend back into the chair, and leaves the room without a word. Pharaon is not an idiot. He is a beast, a northern *bête humaine*, and at the same time he's christ, with a lowercase *c*, who is here on earth to redeem humanity and exorcize its evil.

Rosetta too is a twisted variation on the Passion narrative, as I have made already more or less explicit throughout this chapter: the sacramental waffles, Rosetta's bedtime prayer ("Your name is Rosetta"), the last supper with beer and "lost bread," the fish, the betrayal, her stumbling with the gas canister, the "revivifying hard-boiled egg,"[54] the baptisms of both Rosetta and Riquet in the stream, and, hidden in plain sight in the trailer, fifteen minutes into the film, the triptych of shots that cracks the mystery of Rosetta's immaculate impregnation, the Rosetta stone. First, we have Rosetta's split second of sexual self-pleasure (which is not so ambiguous after all); second, her inspiration by the holy spirit in the guise of a "cold north wind creeping underneath the trailer window"; and third, the close-up of Rosetta using the hair dryer to perform an ultrasound scan of her empty womb (figs. 1.11–1.13). Now, we finally understand her cramps, which Luc Dardenne describes as "birthing pains that deliver no child."[55] The only thing Rosetta symbolically gives birth to is the hard-boiled egg, which she baptizes in the bowl before knocking it against her head. In sum, Rosetta is all at once the unholy Virgin Mother of her own resurrection and the daughter of an absent father, a female christ in a world without God.

Game Over, or The Moral of the Story

So what unites *Rosetta* and *L'humanité* above all is that both their strange yet straight narratives hide passion stories that, much like a secret level in a computer game, only reveal themselves upon very close viewing. *Rosetta* demands an active, pensive, even obsessive spectator who "return[s] to and repeat[s] certain moments and break[s] down the linearity of narrative continuity," as Laura Mulvey defines the pensive spectator.[56] *Rosetta* and *L'humanité* are mind-game films that "imply and implicate spectators in a manner not covered by the classical theories of identification," as Thomas Elsaesser defines this category of narrative-driven cinema especially popular in the 1990s and 2000s.[57] Think of *Donnie Darko* (Richard Kelly, US, 2001), *Memento* (Christopher Nolan, US, 2000), and *The Matrix* (like *Rosetta* a secular-Christian mind game from 1999). As is the case with these films, *Rosetta* and *L'humanité* reveal their complete diegesis only to the spectator willing to search for and piece together fragmentary plot elements, thus integrating the act of watching into their plot (and hence their diegesis). On first viewing, however, based on their documentary-like and painterly textures, *Rosetta* and *L'humanité* don't appear to be mind-game films at all but goal-oriented quests that *touch* the viewer, playing on their emotions and senses in a way that, as Laura Marks writes, "vision itself can be tactile,"[58] and that sound can be tactile, one can add. Think of Rosetta running out of focus, dragging the camera with her through the woods, or of Pharaon eating his apple, his spit in our ears. But *Rosetta* and *L'humanité* don't just play on the senses, their mind games also have a spiritual dimension. *Rosetta* and *L'humanité* tease their viewer into their excavated Christian vocabularies, thus inviting the viewer to play along in their flirtations with grace. Both films signal a bleak world lacking in "humanity"—whether in terms of parochial care, working-class solidarity, or compassion—and respond to this lack with critical fairy tales, fairy tales made of crisis, in which the normal and the miraculous are two sides of the same self-referential coin. Studying the combined afterimage that the concluding close-ups of *Rosetta* and *L'humanité* have left in our mind, one sees at once the affective presence of a particular acting/acted human face and the universal notion of a human face. Like Rosetta's hieroglyphic egg and Pharaon's light in the curtains, these faces are simultaneously what they are and, through these films' evangelical subtexts, what they are associated with, namely, christ with a lowercase *c*.

The question is, how comfortable are we with this Christian vocabulary? In conclusion to his argument, Rancière formulates a critique of *L'humanité* that equally applies to *Rosetta*, namely, that both films, by having "the Spirit blowing in [their] voids," end up "being a bit too much in consonance with [their] time, which substitutes politics with 'the humanitarian.'"[59] This does not mean that *Rosetta* and *L'humanité* are explicitly humanist films that reinvest the word *human* with inherent meaning. Nor do their fairy tales contain outspoken morals about friendship or forgiveness. For that the Dardennes' and Dumont's flirtations with the Word-become-flesh are too self-conscious and smart. Instead, the humanism of *Rosetta* and *L'humanité* lies in their narrative structures. These films only implicitly define *human* by integrating their perverted Passion stories into overarching, binary confines of a heteronormative narrative structure. Neither of the films ends on romantic union, as male quest narratives classically do, but both stories *do* end on a miraculous twist brought about by the male protagonist who operates as the humanizing agent while the female protagonist, face to face with her compassionate savior, appears as the passive recipient of that humanity (the final shot of *Rosetta*, the second-to-last shot of *L'humanité*, which frames Domino as she is being consoled by Pharaon right after having found out that Joseph is the murderer). Here the game ends, with the moral of the story. *Rosetta* and *L'humanité* ultimately affirm the patriarchal binaries their secular passion stories challenge at other points. As it turns out, even God's absence cannot prevent that the spirit chasing these films' postsecular plot spaces, blowing across the northern fields, sneaking underneath Rosetta's window and into our ears, is modeled on an old-fashioned Oedipal logic on its quest for narrative closure.

2

Coal-Fired Dreams, the Cinéma du Nord

> Vu du ciel, il n'y a pas de frontière. (Seen from heaven, there is no border.)
>
> —From a 1998 EU brochure about the "Interreg" program between Wallonia and Nord-Pas-de-Calais

∽

Having answered the question, "What unites *Rosetta* and *L'humanité*," the next question is: How can we explain that these two, in many respects so similar, secular-Christian portrayals of "humanity" in the face of crisis emerged at the same place and time? This second chapter, in combination with the next, addresses that question by situating the films of the Dardennes and Dumont in a broader Cinéma du Nord, understood as a cinematic movement and industry that at once expresses and emerges from the long history of socioeconomic crisis in the former coal-mining region traversing the French-Walloon border.

I will start my mapping of this Cinéma du Nord with two anecdotes in which fact and fiction, reality and cinema enter into a short circuit. The first anecdote is from Wallonia. On November 12, 1999, half a year after the Cannes festival, the Belgian federal government accepted a "youth unemployment plan" that soon became known as the Rosetta

Plan (fig. 2.1). Unlike this plan's unofficial name suggests, however, the Dardennes' film was not the effective cause of the law, which went into effect on December 24, so on the eve of Rosetta's birthday. "It was pure

Figure 2.1. The Rosetta Plan (http://www.perwez.be/actualites/avis-emploi-pour-les-jeunes-de-moins-de-26-ans).

chance . . . ," Jean-Pierre Dardenne explains, "There was already a bill going through, and the minister took advantage of our award to call it the Rosetta Law. But we never intended to get laws changed." To which his brother adds: "Of course, we always hope our films will speak to people, disturb them, but it was never our hope to change the world."[1] The fact is, though, that "Rosetta" has become a household name in Belgian popular discourse. While Rosetta's struggle for a normal life was instantly received as an allegory of a turn-of-the-twenty-first-century Wallonia in which for many young people unemployment had become the new normal, the film's international success became a symbol for the region's efforts to reinvent itself. In a regional history published in 2004 the Dardennes' Golden Palm is even listed as a "major stimulant" of a renewed Walloon self-image, alongside Justine Henin's tennis successes and UNESCO's recognition of the Carnival of Binche as a "world heritage event."[2] For politicians invested in the narrative of a "Wallonie qui gagne" (a Wallonia that wins), *Rosetta* has posed a somewhat uncomfortable paradox, though. As the Flemish journalist Pascal Verbeken writes in his 2007 travelogue *Arm Wallonië: Een Reis door het Beloofde Land* (Poor Wallonia: A journey to the promised land): "For many Walloon politicians, the Dardennes . . . are the most successful and well-known Walloons abroad, but at the same time they have been accused of painting a one-sided, somber image of their region. The Brothers Grimm. Supposedly their films would not show the 'true Wallonia.' "[3] Let's say for now that that true Wallonia is a region torn between the ruins of its glorious industrial past and the future visions of those who continue to believe in the Walloon Dream. This internal tension is felt throughout Wallonia. As Verbeken reports: "The Science Quarter [in Louvain-la-Neuve] is light-years removed from *trailer country*, where Rosettas and Brunos seek to scrape together their daily meals."[4]

The second anecdote is from the other side of the French-Belgian border. On February 18, 2008, a specially chartered TGV pulled into the Lille Flandres railway station. Onboard this train was the production team of the film *Bienvenue chez les Ch'tis / Welcome to the Sticks*, which that night had its festive *avant-première* in the local Pathé movie theater. The party was hosted by the Conseil Régional du Nord-Pas-de-Calais, which embraced the presentation of this comedy written by Dany Boon—who was born as Daniel Hamidou to an Algerian father and a northern French mother—as the start of a promotional campaign for its region. As then president of the Council Daniel Percheron motivated this choice: "Given the fact that the region annually spends €400,000 on [the] Paris-Roubaix [road cycling race] that valorizes the 'Hell of the North,' why not an occasional €600,000 for a film that promotes it?"[5] *Bienvenue chez les*

Ch'tis challenges the stereotypical image of the French North as a cold and inhospitable place clouded by its coal mining past. The film tells the story of Philippe Abrams, a post office manager who is transferred from the sunny French South to Nord-Pas-de-Calais. To prepare himself for this culture shock, Philippe pays a visit to a distant relative who spent his early childhood in the North. The ominously framed old man responds frankly to Philippe's inquiry about what life is like up there: "*Dur, dur, dur*, very, very tough. Only those who work in the mines live well. The others are miserable. They die young, *very* young." The old man also informs Philippe—and with him the viewer—about *Ch'ti* culture. Ch'tis are those in the French North who culturally identify themselves with Ch'ti or Ch'timi, a regional language largely identical to Picard, and which, other than in Picardy, is also spoken in the Walloon province of Hainaut.[6] Ironically, though, the picturesque town of Bergues where *Bienvenue chez les Ch'tis* was largely shot belongs to a part of French Flanders where Picard is actually *not* that commonly spoken, an *anatopism* (the spatial equivalent of an anachronism) that may be understood as part of the film's strategy to counter a negative cliché with a positive one. According to that countercliché, Nord-Pas-de-Calais is a hospitable place full of bell towers, *baraques à frites*, and men who pat each other on the shoulder. Whatever one thinks of this strategy, *Bienvenue chez les Ch'tis* has certainly put Nord-Pas-de-Calais on the map. With over twenty million visitors, the film became the second-biggest box office hit in France ever, after *Titanic* (and thus the best-visited French film in France ever). The film unleashed, moreover, a veritable Ch'timania. In the film's opening week, Ch'ti beer ran out of stock all across France (fig. 2.2); the greeting "Ça va biloute!?" (which means something like "What's up dude?") was heard all over France;[7] and almost a decade later the "Ch'ti tour" in the town of Bergues continues to bring the film to life.

The reason I start my analysis of the Cinéma du Nord with these two short circuits between cinema and reality is that the Cinéma du Nord itself is a short circuit. The Cinéma du Nord exists, but it does so above all in discourses and stories, including the ones it has created itself. The reason for this somewhat spectral nature of the Cinéma du Nord is that it is tied to a region that does not exist, at least not officially as an administrative geographic entity like Wallonia or France. The Nord is not a region by definition, but one in need of definition, and one of the main discourses in which it has found definition is cinema. As stated in the introduction, I define the Cinéma du Nord self-referentially, as a cinema that allows me to identify the Nord as a geopolitical, socio-economic, and cultural-historical reality. Films therefore hold a double place in this chapter. Insofar as the chapter is a transdiscursive mapping

Figure 2.2. Ch'ti beer on display in the museum shop of the Louvre-Lens (author's photo).

of the Nord, films are texts among other texts, images, and objects through which I trace the contours of the Nord. Insofar as this chapter is an argument *about* the Cinéma du Nord, I discuss films as the cultural products of a border-crossing region whose existence I postulate. While my mapping of the Nord cuts back and forth across—and in that act of crossing somewhat erases—the French-Belgian border, subsequently I will reintroduce that border, as if by a click on Google Maps, in order to turn productive the unique experimental setup the Nord offers to the film researcher. On the one hand, we have a transborder reality of socio-economic crisis. On the other hand, the French-Belgian border separates two regional cinemas with very different histories and origins, and with very different production and funding infrastructures. Whereas Walloon cinema is a small and inherently transnational cinema that has grown gradually out of its documentary origins, the northern French cinema is a still relatively young frontrunner in Europe's largest, and still very centralized, national cinema. This chapter presents a comparative analysis of the ways filmmakers at each side of the Nord's internal border have given expression to a shared interregional crisis reality. The first major difference between the two "halves" of the Cinéma du Nord I have in fact already touched on, through the two anecdotes with which I started this second chapter, as well as through my earlier analysis in the first chapter of *Rosetta* and *L'humanité*: Whereas Walloon cinema is known for its political engagement and documentary-like aesthetics (e.g., *Rosetta*), northern French cinema tends to turn economic crisis into a *couleur locale*, or rather the grayish absence thereof, in tales that treat the French North with a degree of social caricature (as is the case in *Bienvenu chez les Ch'tis* and, though in a very different way, *L'humanité*).

The Nord

Throughout most of my analysis of the Cinéma du Nord I refer to "the Nord" as Wallonia "plus" Nord-Pas-de-Calais (which in 2016 was merged with Picardy into the new administrative region of Hauts-de-France). The reason I leave "Nord" untranslated is that its location in northern-francophone Europe is a crucial element of what defines this region as a border-crossing reality. More precisely, the Nord corresponds to that area of the French North and the Belgian South where French is the primary official language. This added precision is necessary not only because there are of course people in these parts of Belgium and France who do not speak French, or who identify themselves with other major or minor languages (e.g., Ch'ti, Italian, Arabic), but also because there is a small part of Wallonia where German is the primary official language. Moreover, the Nord does not include the Brussels-Capital region, where French is the official language alongside Dutch.

The French-Belgian border across which the Nord exists is 620 kilometers in length and runs from the North Sea coast, about fifty kilometers northwest of the Channel (the Pas-de-Calais), to the tripoint between Belgium, France, and Luxembourg. The border is a purely political construct. At hardly any part of its trajectory does it coincide with major physical delimitations such as mountains or rivers, while it only partially coincides with the demarcation lines between linguistic communities. As the French geographer Firmin Lentacker writes: "Implanted almost three centuries ago and the result of contingencies of the politics of the European powers, the French-Belgian border, much like a pastry cutter, cuts up natural and human environments that at first sight cannot be distinguished from each other without its presence."[8]

On the south side, Nord-Pas-de-Calais was, until its merger with Picardy, France's northernmost administrative region, subdivided into the departments Nord and Pas-de-Calais (which existed independently until 1956). At the time of its merger in 2016, Nord-Pas-de-Calais had little over four million inhabitants. Its capital was Lille, which is also the capital of the newly formed Hauts-de-France. As in all French regions, the official language is French, but in the rural areas around Dunkirk in French Flanders parts of the population also speak Flemish or variations thereof. The current French-Belgian border thus not only divides the northern European francophone community, but also the Flemish community (fig. 2.3).

North of the border, Wallonia (Wallonie) is the predominantly francophone, southern region of Belgium. The region has a population

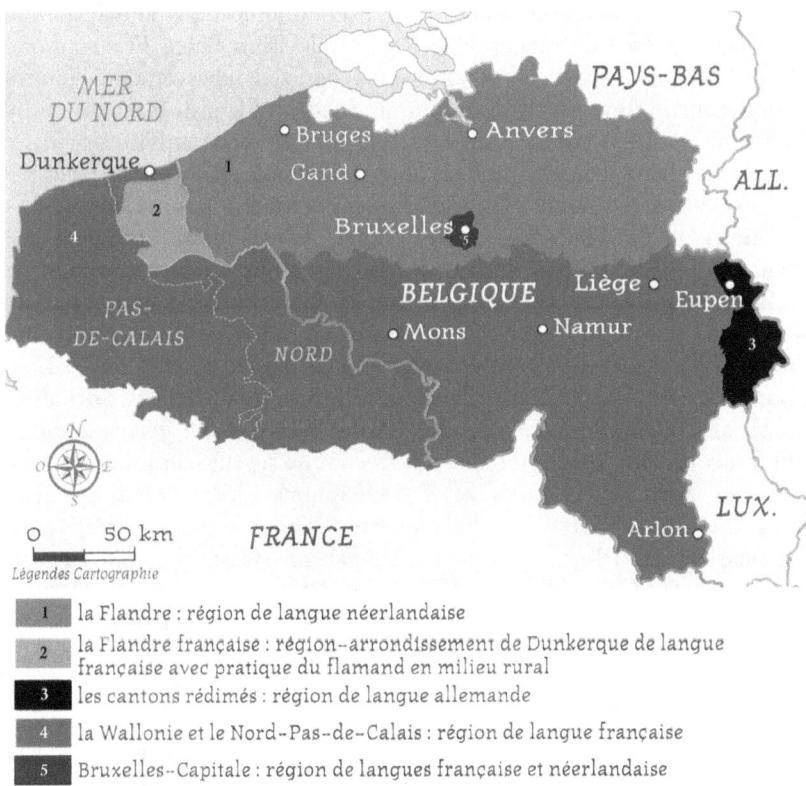

Figure 2.3. Official and unofficial language communities in Belgium and Nord-Pas-de-Calais. *Source:* Popelier, *Belges et Français du Nord*, 10.

of around 3.5 million distributed over five provinces: Walloon Brabant, Hainaut, Liège, Luxembourg, and Namur. Crucially, Wallonia is not the same as the French Community of Belgium (Communauté Française de Belgique), even though their geographical areas of influence largely overlap. Whereas Belgium's federal regions (Wallonia, Flanders, Brussels-Capital) are primarily political-economic entities, its communities (francophone, Flemish, and germanophone) are defined along linguistic lines and have a primarily cultural mission. In contrast to the Flemish Region and the Flemish Community (Vlaamse Gemeenschap), which have unified their competences, the Walloon Region and the French Community each have their own parliaments, seated in Namur and Brussels, respectively. To make matters even more complex: in 2011, the parliament of the French Community accepted a resolution to change the community's name into "Fédération Wallonie-Bruxelles" (Wallonia-Brussels Federation), which now appears in the community's official communications and in public broadcastings by the francophone Radio Télévision Belge Francophone (RTBF). The name change has not been recognized, however, by Belgium's federal constitution, nor is it commonly used by Flemish Belgians or by the Flemish VRT (Vlaamse Radio- en Televisieomroeporganisatie), as many in Flanders have seen this unilateral as a Walloon claim on Brussels.[9]

As far as the name "Wallonia" is concerned, it has its etymological origins in the Germanic word "Walha," which means strangers and from which also "Wales" derives. Following Julius Caesar's conquest in 57 BC of the western European region of Gaul, these Walha gradually abandoned their Celtic dialects and started speaking Vulgar Latin. In the early Middle Ages, as the Merovingian Franks gained control of the Low Countries, this Vulgar Latin developed into several dialects, including Picard and Walloon. The language border between the germanophone and francophone world crystallized between the seventh and the eleventh centuries, with the emergence of francophone cities including Liège along the Meuse River, on the one hand, and the germanification of the nearby Gallo-Roman cities of Tongeren, Maastricht, and Aachen on the other.[10] Originally the Walloon provinces were—like the largest part of the region that is now the French North—part of the historical southern Netherlands. In the fifteenth century these provinces, together with what would become the northern Netherlands, fell under control of the Dukes of Burgundy, who referred to this territory as the *pays de par deça*, "lands over here." From the Burgundian Netherlands arose the seventeen provinces of the Low Countries, which roughly included what is now the Netherlands, Belgium (with the exception of, among other territories, the Prince-Bishopric of Liège), Luxembourg, and the provinces of Artois, French Flanders, and French Hainaut in what is now the French North. In 1482, the House of Habsburg inherited the seventeen provinces, which became subsequently known as the *Pays d'embas*, "lands down here," from which the name *Neder-landen* (nether-lands) derives. In 1556, with the abdication of Emperor Charles V, these provinces fell to the Spanish Empire of his son Philip II. Whereas the northern, predominantly Protestant provinces rebelled against this Spanish rule, the southern and predominantly Catholic provinces rallied behind Spain, leading in 1579 to the Union of Arras. In this accord several provinces of what would later become Nord-Pas-de-Calais and Wallonia expressed their loyalty to the Spanish king, recognizing Catholicism as the only religion. This precursor of the northern French-Walloon Nord was eroded, however, when during the Thirty Years' Wars (1618–1648) France gradually annexed the territory that later, in 1790, would become the departments of Nord and Pas-de-Calais, when the newly installed revolutionary government abolished the provincial structure of the ancien régime.

The northern French border predates the Belgian nation-state and was approximately fixed in its current course by the 1713 Treaty of Utrecht, which ended the War of the Spanish Succession between, among other nations, the France of Louis XIV and the Spanish Empire of Philip V. As illustrated by figure 2.4, up until this treaty the border had shifted many times. Much of the territory that is now Hauts-de-France only became French over the course of the seventeenth century, while significant parts of what is now Belgium once belonged to France. In 1794, the Low Countries, including the Belgian provinces, were annexed by Napoleon,

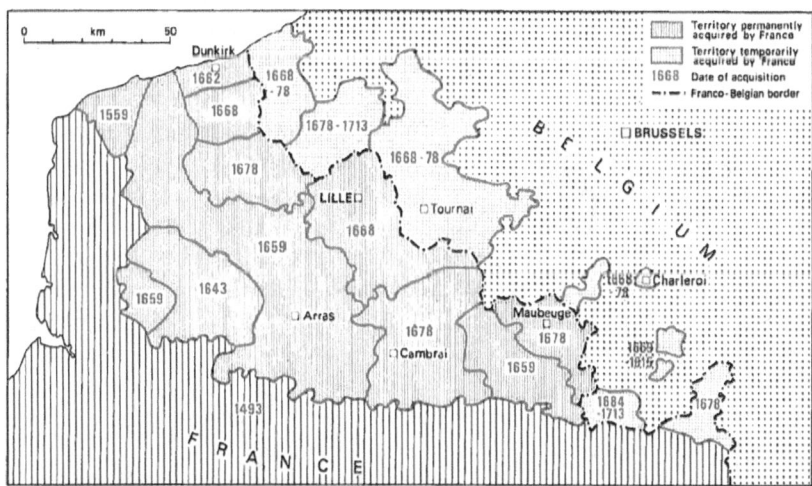

Figure 2.4. Acquisition of territory by France along its northern frontier. *Source:* Clout, *The Franco-Belgian Border Region.*

a situation that lasted until Napoleon's defeat during the 1815 Battle of Waterloo in Walloon Brabant, following which the Walloon provinces became part of the newly formed Kingdom of the Netherlands. The recognition of this monarchy by the 1815 Treaty of Vienna also meant a reconfirmation of the 1713 northern French border. In 1830, the predominantly francophone and Catholic population of the southern parts of the Netherlands rebelled against the Dutch king Willem I, a Belgian revolution that in 1830 led to the creation of a predominantly Catholic and, at that time, officially francophone Belgian nation-state. This state was fully recognized in 1839 and included the pre-1794 Belgian provinces (with the exception of parts of Flanders and Limburg, as well as the area that would later become the Grand Duchy of Luxembourg). During World War I, Belgium was almost entirely occupied by German troops, while Nord-Pas-de-Calais, at the moment of Germany's farthest advance in 1918, was over two-thirds occupied. In the aftermath of World War I, which left the Nord in ruins—German troops had even burned down trees along the roads—the formerly Prussian districts of Eupen and Malmedy were annexed by Belgium. During World War II, Belgium and Nord-Pas-de-Calais fell entirely into German hands, and, for strategic reasons, were united into a single zone that fell directly under the rule of the German military administration located in Brussels.[11] This temporary secession of Nord-Pas-de-Calais from France did, however, not leave lasting traces in the course of the French-Belgian border.

As far as the emergence of a distinct Walloon self-identity is concerned, this started to take firmer shape over the course of the first Industrial Revolution. The oldest known reference to "Wallonia" as a noun has been attributed to the poet Joseph Grandgagnage, who in 1844 urged his fellow Walloons to "be themselves by all Saints of wallonia [*par tous les Saints de wallonie*]."[12] It would not be until 1970, however, that, under pressure of the Walloon Popular Movement, the region became officially recognized by the Belgian constitution as La Région Wallonne. In 1980, Wallonia acquired decretal power and an executive government. In 1992, the name "Wallonie" was entered into the Belgian constitution.[13] Following Belgium's federalization in 1993, the Belgian regions could enter treaties with foreign regions and nations, allowing them a greater degree of autonomy in their participation in Euregional collaboration structures (including cinematic coproductions). Similarly, across the border, since the passing in 1982 by the French parliament of a Decentralization Law, Nord-Pas-de-Calais and now Hauts-de-France holds autonomy in the domains of infrastructure, education, and culture.

While it becomes clear from these genealogies of Wallonia and Nord-Pas-de-Calais that these regions have strong historical connections, in themselves these connections do not justify my definition of the Nord as the combination of Wallonia and Nord-Pas-de-Calais. The Nord resists, per definition, a single unambiguous definition in terms of existing geographical territories. The Nord is not a territory, but an idea of a space immanent to the border-crossing realities that define it. That said, I do have a few good reasons for congealing the Nord into Nord-Pas-de-Calais and Wallonia. First, and the reason I tie the Nord to a geographic space to begin with, is that I think of the Nord primarily as an idea immanent to the shared socioeconomic reality of the French North and the Belgian South. Given the role that the administrative entities of Nord-Pas-de-Calais and Wallonia have played in the shaping of this socioeconomic reality, it is difficult to think of the Nord other than by reference to these official regions. The second reason for my definition of the Nord is that it reflects the increasing collaboration between Wallonia and Nord-Pas-de-Calais (and now Hauts-de-France) in domains such as city planning, healthcare, and pollution control. Third and most crucially, the reason I define the Nord as Wallonia plus Nord-Pas-de-Calais is that the development of their regional cinemas is largely the result of the fact that, especially from the early 1990s onward, both regions have actively promoted film production within their borders, both for economic and cultural reasons (this in difference with their bordering French regions of Picardy and Champagne-Ardenne). As a result, the Cinéma du Nord as it has taken shape over the last three decades at once expresses and is the product of these regions as geopolitical realities.

From *Pays Noir* to Euroregion

As stated, the French-Belgian border does not coincide with any major geophysical barriers. The border cuts up a geological area of transition between the physical provinces of the Paris basin and the Rhine delta lands and it traverses the clays of the Flanders plain and the old hard rocks of the Ardennes (fig. 2.5).[14] The border intersects, moreover, with several rivers, including the Lys, Scheldt, Sambre, and Meuse, which all originate in France and, via the estuaries of the Scheldt and the Dutch Maas, drain into the North Sea.[15] Crucially, the French-Belgian border divides into two almost equal parts the carboniferous layers that have been found in a strip that runs from the Lys in central Nord-Pas-de-Calais to Liège in northeast Wallonia, with an interruption around the Walloon city of Namur, where the coal has been eroded. This coal strip, which at its widest point measures fifteen kilometers, is the western segment of the Austrasian field, which further extends to Dutch Limburg, the Aachen area, and the German Ruhr district.

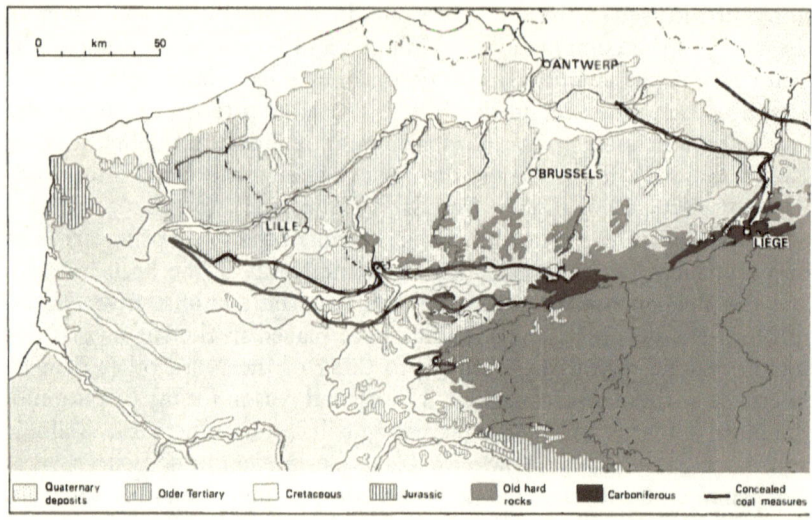

Figure 2.5. Geology of the French-Belgian border region. *Source:* Clout, *The Franco-Belgian Border Region.*

Between the early seventeenth and the late twentieth centuries, this subterranean fossil mass has found expression, quite literally, in an urban strip that runs from the French cities of Béthune, Lens, Douai, and Valenciennes to the Walloon cities of Mons, La Louvière, Charleroi, Namur, and Liège (fig. 2.6). In the Walloon regions, the exploitation of coal goes back to at least the Middle Ages, as in certain parts of Hainaut and Liège the coal layers reached the terrestrial surface. The industrial exploitation of coal began in the early eighteenth century. In 1720, the first steam engine on the European continent was installed at the mine of Jemeppe-sur-Meuse in Seraing (Rosetta's town), and Seraing was also the first place on the European continent to witness the construction of a coke-fired blast furnace, iron ore being one of Wallonia's other mineral treasures. The investor behind this furnace was John Cockerill, a Brit whose family at that moment had already been involved for some thirty years in the Verviers textile industry. In 1817, when the Walloon provinces were still part of the Netherlands, Cockerill convinced King Willem I, a fellow Protestant, to sell him the former palace of the Prince Bishops of Liège, which he subsequently turned into the headquarters for his enterprise. On the ground behind the palace he constructed a hypermodern, vertically integrated iron foundry and manufacturing factory that, as narrated by the RTBF documentary *John Cockerill, toute*

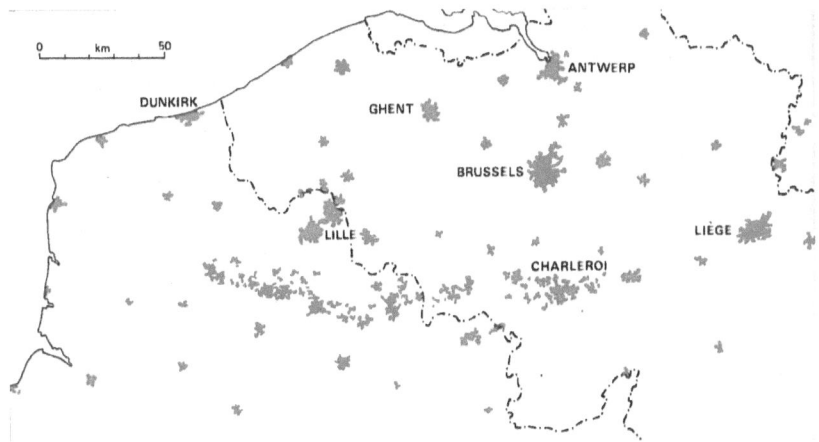

Figure 2.6. Distribution of urban settlements in the French-Belgian border region. Source: Clout, *The Franco-Belgian Border Region*, 12.

une histoire (Bernard Balteau, 2017), attracted journalists, writers, and politicians from all over Europe as they wanted to witness this "temple du métamorphose du fer." Soon, similar furnaces started popping up like mushrooms, not only in the Liège area, but also in Charleroi and in the Borinage region around Mons. On the eve of the creation of the Belgian nation-state in 1830, Wallonia thus laid the foundations for its industrial heydays, which other than coal and steel had glass and textile as its main pillars.[16] During the first half of the nineteenth century, the Walloon regions remained far in advance of nearby industrial areas, including the French North and the German Ruhr area. In the 1830s, the Walloon regions even constituted, in relative terms, the world's second industrial power in terms of industrial development, after England, tied with the United States, and before Prussia and France.[17] Together with Manchester and Liverpool, the Walloon industrialized regions were among the cradles of the modern industrial society in which a small elite dominated the major industries. In this context, halfway through the nineteenth century, the Walloon labor movement also started to take shape. In 1851, the first *sociétés mutualistes* (cooperatives) emerged; toward the end of the nineteenth century the first Walloon labor unions were founded; and in 1885, in Café Le Cygne in Brussels, the Parti Ouvrier Belge held its inaugural congress.

On the other side of the border, in the French North, digging for coal started in the early eighteenth century, after France had lost control in 1713 of the coal basins around the now-Walloon city of Mons. The first coal was discovered in 1716, north of Valenciennes, but only after the discovery in 1734 of the Anzin deposits, also north of Valenciennes, the northern French coal industry really took off.[18] A century later, the first coke furnace started operating in Ferrière-la-Grande, near the border.[19] In 1850, the coalfield in the Nord department had an annual output of one million tons, still modest in comparison to the annual six million tons the Walloon fields of Hainaut and Liège produced in that same era.[20] During the second half of the nineteenth century, the northern French exploitation area was extended westward, into the Pas-de-Calais department. By 1900, the joint coal production of the Nord and Pas-de-Calais districts had risen to twenty million tons per year, an amount close to that of the Walloon regions.[21] On the eve of World War I, Nord and Pas-de-Calais were responsible for two-thirds of the French national coal production.[22] Like in the Walloon regions, other than coal and steel, also textiles formed a thriving industry, as the steam engine allowed Lille, Roubaix, and Tourcoing to develop into cloth capitals.

Economic superpowers of their era, the French North and Belgian South attracted large streams of migrant workers, first of all from poverty-struck rural Flanders. In 1886, the French census counted 320,000 Belgian immigrants in Nord and Pas-de-Calais, which amounted to 10 percent of these districts' total populations.[23] Exact statistics about Flemish migration to the Walloon industrial basins are not available, also because technically these Flemish did not *e*migrate. It is certain, though, that from the mid-nineteenth century onward, following a famine in rural Flanders, the migration of a nation within a nation commenced. This population movement reached a second peak between 1880 and the beginning of World War I, and only really ended in the 1960s, when Flanders surpassed Wallonia economically. In 1967, Wallonia for the first time had a higher unemployment rate than Flanders. Wallonia had ceased to be the Promised Land, at least for Flemish workers.[24] Other than from Flanders, over the course of the twentieth century these regions received large migratory streams from eastern and southern Europe, and later also from North Africa. Especially in the period directly following World War II, many Italians and Polish were recruited for the *bataille du charbon*, the coal battle. In 1946, Belgium and Italy signed an agreement that involved the migration of fifty thousand *operai* (workers) from rural Italy to industrial Wallonia. The agreement stipulated that Italian immigrants had to work *du fond* (underground) for five years before they were given full work permits. In return, Wallonia promised the annual transport of two to three million tons of coal into the opposite direction, a deal that gave many Italian Walloons the feeling of having been sold for a few bags of coal.[25] The Italian migration stream largely halted in 1956, when the Italian government abruptly terminated its supply of manpower, this in response to the mine catastrophe of Marcinelle, near Charleroi, with over half of the 262 victims of Italian origin. This required Belgium to shift its recruitment efforts to other countries, especially Spain, Greece, Turkey, and Morocco. According to statistics of the Fédération Charbonnière de Belgique, in 1959 almost half of the seventeen thousand people employed in the Borinage basin were foreign, with a staggering 97 percent of that group working underground.

In this era of mass immigration, Wallonia and Nord-Pas-de-Calais had already begun down their long paths of economic decline. Following the end of World War I, both regions gradually fell victim to their one-dimensional economic structures. One economic study describes interwar Wallonia as a "colosse au pied d'argile," a clay-foot giant, a characterization that equally applies to the French North of that era.[26] Between 1918 and 1939, the northern French and the Walloon coal industries saw their competitive positions wane, as their coal reserves had become more expensive to exploit in comparison to those of Dutch Limburg and the German Saar and Ruhr regions.[27] The Walloon regions proved especially vulnerable, as from the 1920s onward they faced competition from the newly discovered coal basins in the Flemish De Kempen region (Campine).[28] Across the border, in the French North, the economic situation was less grim during the early interwar years, but the northern French economy showed the same structural weaknesses as that of Wallonia. Both regions were economic monocultures with little to no industrial diversification and innovation, as they continued to concentrate on the industrial processing of raw materials increasingly more difficult to extract. While the neighboring Flanders, Netherlands, Germany, Ile-de-France, and England saw the development of electronics, chemical, and automobile industries, the French Belgian Nord continued to live in its nineteenth-century past. As a Walloon historian observes, right after World War II "the industrial areas of Wallonia [and the same holds true for Nord-Pas-de-Calais] had an outdated industrial structure, almost identical to that at the beginning of the century."[29]

Life was hard in the Nord, a reality that has found expression in art of all media and from throughout the centuries. "Caves de Lille! On meurt sous vos plafonds de pierre!" (Caverns of Lille! People are dying under your stone ceilings!), Victor Hugo wrote in the mid-nineteenth century in the poem "Happy Life."[30] And a few decades later, a stay in the Walloon Borinage region inspired Vincent van Gogh in his first major painting, *The Potato Eaters* (*De Aardappeleters*, 1885; fig. 2.7), which he painted upon his return in the Netherlands, using coarse Dutch models in a neorealist fashion avant la lettre. Van Gogh lived in the Borinage for almost two years, in the town of Wasmes where he worked as a Protestant priest. This episode in Van Gogh's life forms the start of the 1956 MGM production *Lust for Life* (dir. Vincente Minnelli and George Cukor), based on the novel by Irving Stone. In the film we see Van Gogh, played by Kirk Douglas, paying a visit down a coal mine, where he is shocked at the sight of an eleven-year-old girl working *du fond*. Back in his modest residence, while rinsing the dirt off his face, Van Gogh hears again the voice of a worker who that Sunday had walked out of his sermon: "Let's understand, every now and then someone comes here from the outside and tries to help us. They mean well, so do you probably, but that doesn't help us at all, does it?" (figs. 2.8–2.10).

In the Borinage, Van Gogh developed his painter's gaze, which in these early years, and again in a neorealist fashion, sought sparks of redemption in the harsh human condition. Early in his stay, on the day after Christmas 1878, Van Gogh wrote to his brother Theo:

Figure 2.7. Vincent van Gogh, *The Potato Eaters* (*De Aardappeleters*, 1885, oil on canvas, Van Gogh Museum, Amsterdam, the Netherlands).

Figure 2.8. *Lust for Life* (Vincente Minnelli, 1956).

Figure 2.9. Van Gogh (Kirk Douglas) in a coal mine (*Lust for Life*).

Figure 2.10. "Every now and then someone comes here from the outside and tries to help us. They mean well, so do you probably, but that doesn't help us at all, does it?" (*Lust for Life*).

As far as I'm concerned, you surely understand that there are no paintings here in the Borinage, that in general they haven't the slightest idea of what a painting is, so it goes without saying that I've seen absolutely nothing in the way of art since my departure from Brussels. But this doesn't mean that this isn't a very special and very picturesque country, everything speaks, as it were, and is full of character.

These last few days . . . it was an extraordinary sight, with the white snow in the evening around the twilight hour, seeing the workers returning home from the mines. These people are completely black when they come out of the dark mines into the daylight again, they look just like chimney sweeps. Their houses are usually small and could better be called huts, scattered along the sunken roads and in the wood and against the slopes of the hills.[31]

Half a century later, despite social legislature like the eight-hour working day (1919 France, 1921 Belgium), little had changed in the Nord's grim picture. In the early 1930s, during the Great Depression, industrial production saw a vehement decline, forcing numerous factories to shut down and leading tens of thousands to lose their jobs. We find a poignant account of these crisis years in the 1933 novel *Quand les sirènes se taisent* (*When the Looms Are Silent*) by the French Flemish author Maxence van der Meersch, also known as the "Christian Zola." The novel is set in Roubaix during the strikes of 1931 and describes, through the third-person perspective of Laure, the *courées*, the small cottages built around a courtyard typical for the region:

> Elle regardait maintenant la "cour," sa "cour," où elle avait toujours vécu. Deux rangées de maisons basses se faisaient face, six de chaque côté. Peintes à la chaux, avec des soubassements vernis au goudron, elles eussent paru uniformes, identiquement sales, vétustes et branlantes, aux yeux d'un étranger. Mais Laure les conaissait depuis toujours, et l'habitude les faisait dissemblables à ses yeux. . . . Des fils de fer, en réseau dense, formaient à travers toute la courée, à deux mètres du sol, comme une nappe serrée. La lessive du samedi y pendait, un étalage de hardes pauvres et multicolores que gonflait le vent . . . (She now looked at the court, her court, where she had always lived. Two rows of low buildings faced one another, six on each side. Whitewashed and with their foundation walls tarred with black pitch, they would all have looked alike to

a stranger, all identically dirty, old, and tumbled down, but Laure had known them all her life and long familiarity gave each of them an individuality in her eyes. . . . A close network of wires made a sort of awning over the entire court, six feet above the ground. The Saturday laundry was hanging there, a display of miserable garments of many colors, puffed out by the wind . . .]³²

Laure's impression of the *courées* continues in a later chapter, right after she has found out she's pregnant:

Il semblait que pour la première fois elle vît l'infamie du quartier, toute la misère de ces maisons surpeuplées, de ces cabarets de débauche, de ces garnis envahis de Tchèques, de Polonais et d'Italiens, de ces courées pullulantes et empestées. Les gens, tous, lui paraissaient blêmes et sales, les gosses minables et dépenaillés, les bêtes même affamées et misérables. Qu'importe tout cela, tant qu'on est jeune, et qu'on attend. . . . Qu'importe, quand, plus tard, l'amour vient transfigurer ces laideurs, et vous apporte la sereine indifférence pour tout ce qui n'est pas l'être aimé. Mais après, le songe dissipé, combien douloureux le réveil, combien sinistre la réalité! (She seemed to take in all the sordidness of the district for the first time—the wretchedness of the overpopulated buildings, the drinking dives, the rooming houses invaded by Czechs, Poles, and Italians, the swarming, foul-smelling inner courts. All the people looked sallow-faced and dirty, the children ill-kept and ragged, even the dogs and cats starving and miserable. What matters all that when one is young and full of hope? And what does it matter when, later, love comes along, transfiguring all the ugliness and bringing serene indifference to everything except the loved one? But afterward, when the dream had been shattered, how painful is the awakening, how sinister the reality!)³³

The novel ends with the return of Laure's lover and the birth of her child. This family idyll is offset, however, by the fact of it taking place amid conditions in which child mortality is extreme and most people end up in communal graves.

In the same year that Van der Meersch published his novel, a very similar testimony to misery and class struggle saw the light right across the border: the documentary film *Borinage*, which in 1963 was renamed *Misère au Borinage*.³⁴ A film by the Flemish Henri Storck and the Dutch

Joris Ivens, *Borinage* is generally considered to mark the birth of Walloon cinema. The film was initiated by the Club de l'Ecran, a left-wing cineclub in Brussels that mainly screened Soviet films. Inspired by a pamphlet about "how people are starving to death east of Mons," the cineclub asked Storck and Ivens to make a documentary film on the subject. With a budget of BEF 35,000 (US$6,250[35])—25,000 of which had been provided by an anonymous patron, the rest by the club members themselves—and an extremely compact thirty-five-millimeter Kinamo camera and a petrol lamp as their only equipment, Storck and Ivens spent three weeks in the *pays noir*, where they sought to stay under the radar of the suspicious coal mine management and the police.[36] The result is a partly staged, partly newsreel-like pamphlet documentary that reveals the influences of Anglo-Saxon social realism (Flaherty, Grierson, Wright), Russian montage (Eisenstein, Vertov), and also Van Gogh. As Joris Ivens writes about the painter in his memoirs: "Somehow, I could understand why after living in the Borinage Van Gogh stopped preaching and began to paint. My first impression of the district was its dark and colorless uniformity—no bright thing, no happy thing. Black, dusty—no whites. The lightest tone is gray. Even nature seems saddened by the district's misery."[37]

As it captured the 1932 strike (fig. 2.11), Borinage gave face to a people, reason for Walter Benjamin to praise the film in his "Work of Art" essay as an example of cinema's potential to transform "any man" into a "movie extra."[38] The film opens with a montage sequence that depicts the "crise dans le monde capitaliste," as the later-added voice-over states: "Factories have been closed, abandoned. Millions of proletarians are hungry. Production is no longer yielding enough . . ." The film ends with a march of workers who carry with them a portrait of Karl Marx (fig. 2.12). This march, which was met with real police intervention, unleashes a montage sequence that sums up the contradictions inherent to capitalism in general and those in the Borinage in particular: a worker who has been on strike for fourteen weeks and whose six children are hungry and sick while elsewhere in the world people are throwing out surplus of food; and people who "in the heart of the coal region" are forced to glean substandard coal from the *terrils*, or slag heaps, in order to heat their homes (fig. 2.13).

Although the strikes did not lead to the "dictatorship of the proletariat" called for by *Borinage*, in 1936 the Belgian and French labor movements did manage to wrest structural reforms, through new waves of massive strikes. In June 1936, representatives of Léon Blum's newly installed Front Populaire government (an alliance of France's three main left-wing parties) convened with the employers trade union confederation and the general confederation of labor.[39] On June 8, Roger Salengro, minister of internal affairs and former mayor of Lille, announced a

Figure 2.11. *Misère au Borinage* (Joris Ivens and Henri Storck, 1933).

Figure 2.12. Workers parading with a portrait of Karl Marx (*Misère au Borinage*).

Figure 2.13. The contradictions inherent to capitalism (*Misère au Borinage*).

package of legislation known as the Matignon Agreements, stipulating the forty-hour work week, paid vacations, the right to strike, collective bargaining, and mandatory education until the age of fourteen.[40] These developments in France accelerated similar developments north of the border. At Belgium's first National Labor Conference, tripartite negotiations between employers, employees, and the Belgian government (a mixed coalition of socialists, Catholics, and liberals) resulted in a set of legislative measures similar to those in France. After World War II, social conditions ameliorated rapidly for many in France and Belgium, as the postwar economic boom went hand in hand with the gradual rolling out of the welfare state.

For both the Walloon regions and the departments of Nord and Pas-de-Calais these so-called "thirty glorious years" after World War II were a mixed blessing. Major fossil reservoirs and producers of final and intermediary industrial products, both regions had a crucial role in the postwar reconstruction of their countries. Industrial processes were mechanized and rationalized, and production levels of coal, steel, and glass skyrocketed. In the years directly following the war, Belgium even had the highest growth levels of all European countries, while the Nord and Pas-de-Calais departments combined formed France's second economic pole, after Ile-de-France.[41] In this same postwar era, however, and precisely because of the short-run indispensability of their industrial resources, little was done to diversify these regions' economies. Even though the aftermath of the second German occupation may have meant a new golden age for the French-Belgian Nord, its economy was bound to collapse.

Coal played the lead part in this postwar industrial revival and decline of Wallonia and Nord-Pas-de-Calais. The Walloon mines had withstood the occupation relatively well and experienced a last boom in the years directly after the war. In France, where the pits had suffered more, the mines were nationalized in 1946, because the *bataille du charbon* exceeded regional and also national proportions. As a French economist stated in 1954 about the Nord department, the region's coalfields "will be indispensable not only to the national economy but also to the economy of Western Europe."[42] Two years earlier, France, Belgium, the Netherlands, Luxembourg, West Germany, and Italy had created the European Coal and Steel Community (ECSC), a forerunner of the European Union whose main goal was to "make war not merely unthinkable, but materially impossible," as the 1950 Schuman Declaration reads.[43] For the northern French and Walloon coal industries this common market was mostly a threat, as it confronted them with their relatively high production costs. On top of that, northern French and Walloon coal increasingly faced competition in the fossil energy market from imported American coking coal, oil, and later also Dutch natural gas. During the 1950s and 1960s coal output remained relatively stable in the North due to the modernization of the production process. In 1968, however, the French government decided to halve national production. By 1971, the region's production had gone down to fifteen million tons, compared to twenty-nine million in the 1950s, while employment in the northern French mines dropped even faster, from about 220 thousand positions in 1947 to sixty-two thousand in 1971. Also in Wallonia coal production plummeted during the same era, despite ECSC subsidies. In the period between 1955 and 1968, the annual production of the southern Belgian mines dropped from twenty to six million tons, while the number of people employed by the Walloon mines went down from one hundred to twenty thousand. By 1973, on the eve of the international oil crisis, these figures had dropped further to around three million and nine thousand, respectively.[44] On both sides of the border, the coal battle was thus marching toward its ineluctable end: the shutting down of an industry that had determined this region since early modern history. In Wallonia, coal mining ended in 1984, with the closure of the Roton de Farciennes east of Charleroi. Eight years later—in the same year as the Maastricht Treaty on European Union—France liquidated the Houillères du Bassin Nord-Pas-de-Calais. In the context of this concluding chapter of coal mining in the Nord, a noteworthy document is the 1982 Walloon film *Hay Po l'jou* by Manu Bonmariage, which captures the closing of one of Wallonia's last mines and whose title in Walloon dialect translates as "to the daylight."

For a while, the Nord's industrial decline had relatively little impact on employment rates. This drastically changed in the early 1970s, when the global economic recession connected to the energy crisis laid bare the Nord's vulnerability. Nord-Pas-de-Calais was hit harder than any other region in France, and between 1973 and 1998 the region lost half of its 550,000 industrial jobs.[45] In Wallonia, unemployment exploded from 5 percent in 1971 to 23 percent in 1985, with peaks of 30 percent in former coal centers like Charleroi.[46] On both sides of the border, people were thwarted in their hope that the conversion from an economic structure inherited from the nineteenth century to one that combines high-technological industry with a strong tertiary sector would happen smoothly. This conversion only really took off in the 1960s and is still ongoing. Nord-Pas-de-Calais, aided by the French government, initiated new large-scale industries. Dunkirk grew out to one of the country's main seaport cities, as the result of the construction of a new production site by the French steel group Usinor. In 1970, Renault opened a car factory in Douai, followed by Peugeot and Toyota factories near Valenciennes in subsequent decades. This introduction of the automotive industry in the French North was actively promoted by the French national government and helped alleviate the impact of the coal mining decline.

Wallonia, in contrast, never saw such grand-scale, low-skilled mass employment industries. Liège, especially, tried to hold on to its steel industry, but over the decades, factory after factory closed down. Here it is worth citing at length a 2011 article that appeared in the Dutch newspaper *NRC Handelsblad*, titled "Last Gasp of the Illustrious Steel Industry around Liège." In this article Petra de Koning writes about the protests stirred by the decision of ArcelorMittal to close down the last two remaining blast furnaces once constructed by Cockerill:

> The metal workers in Liège have a British hero cast in bronze and an invisible enemy from India [i.e., Lakshmi Mittal, the owner of ArcelorMittal]. In the nineteenth century, John Cockerill from Lancashire made Wallonia into one of the richest areas in the world by constructing blast furnaces and steel factories. That prosperity has long gone, though the people of Liège themselves still like to call steel the *backbone* of their region.
>
> . . .
>
> Thousands of steel workers from Wallonia, Flanders, France, and Germany have protested in the past week against the closing. On the Municipal Square of Seraing, a border town of Liège . . . they heard their union leaders say that Lakshmi Mittal has "no heart" and is leading a company that is "the pest and the cholera." John Cockerill's statue on the same square was holding in his hands a flag of the socialist FGTB union. On the other arm there was a balloon of the Christian union, CSC. Banners read: We are all children of Cockerill. And also: Cockerill is ours. Because the people from Liège never talk about ArcelorMittal. For them the company is still called "Cockerill."
>
> . . .
>
> On the side of the square is Yvette Vanoppen (65). Until her retirement she worked for the province of Liège in the "employment" department. "The steel industry," she says, "touches on the roots of almost each family in this region. Everyone in their family has somebody who is financially dependent on steel. There is also an entire layer of the population who are difficult to retrain or to get employed if that industry goes down."[47]

Also in Wallonia, though, new sectors have emerged, including agroalimentary, chemical, and pharmaceutical industries. In recent decades, the region has actively sought to transform itself into a knowledge-based economy, through research and development parks, collaborations between the academic and commercial sectors, and so-called spin-offs, companies that exploit scientific research commercially. Most of these activities have developed along the axis Louvain-la-Neuve-Namur-Luxembourg, which has replaced the coal axis as Wallonia's economic backbone. More recently, the former industrial area near Mons saw the emergence of a "Digital Innovation Valley" that comprises over a hundred firms operating in new digital technologies, including Microsoft, IBM, and HP.[48] One of the motors behind the development of this mini Silicon Valley has been Google, which in 2010 began operation of its data center in St. Ghislain, near Mons, which was the company's first outside the United States. Google's move to the Borinage fits into the company's wider strategy to store its data in postindustrial space where land is relatively inexpensive and energy and water are readily available. Google states that the St. Ghislain location presented the "right combination of energy infrastructure and developable land," while its authorities displayed a "strong vision for how the Internet can bring economic benefits and jobs to the area."[49]

Another main reason the Nord appeals to multinational investors is its unaltered strategic location in northwest Europe. This geographical capital has not always been self-evident. "Why construct a highway between Paris and Lille when there are only fields?" French opponents of the A1 national highway wondered out loud. The road took fifteen years to build and was only finished in 1969. Similarly, the Belgian newspaper *La Libre Belgique* feared that one could "play marbles" on the East-West *route de Wallonie*, the construction of which was started in 1962. As European integration has continued to progress, though, and especially since the 1985 inauguration of the Schengen Area (which facilitated free movement of persons between France, West Germany, and the then already "borderless" Benelux countries), Wallonia and Nord-Pas-de-Calais have literally positioned themselves at the crossroads of northwest Europe. Over the last decades, Lille and Liège have developed into major high-speed train hubs connecting Paris, Cologne, Frankfurt, Brussels, Randstad Holland, and, since the opening of the Channel tunnel in 1994, also London. A year earlier, Lille began operation of a new international railway station that carries the ambitious name "Lille Europe," a station that is seen both from the exterior and the interior in *L'humanité* (figs. 2.14 and 2.15). When traveling east from Lille Europe, across the border and with a transfer in Brussels, one arrives at the newly renovated Liège-Guillemins station, which is characterized by equally European and forward-looking architecture. At the same time, the station's impressive glass and steel vault may be interpreted as a monument to the city's industrial heritage (see figs. 2.16 and 2.17).

Figure 2.14. The Lille-Europe railway station as seen in *L'humanité* (Bruno Dumont, 1999).

Figure 2.15. Pharaon waiting for the Eurostar to London (*L'humanité*).

Figure 2.16. The construction of the Liège-Guillemins railway station as seen in Thierry Michel's documentary *Métamorphoses d'une gare* (2010).

Figure 2.17. *Métamorphoses d'une gare*.

The Nord is not only located at the intersection of the EU's economic and political centers, it is also a product of European integration itself. Or rather, European integration has helped reveal the Nord as the transnational region it always already was. Starting with the creation in 1975 of the European Regional Development Fund (ERDF), Wallonia and Nord-Pas-de-Calais have received structural European monetary aid in order to stimulate their economic transitions. Since the early 1990s, a large part of this aid has been allocated through the various Interreg programs that both regions have participated in (fig. 2.18). Interreg is an EU initiative that promotes the transnational collaboration between regions in the European Union.[50] It ought to be understood as part of the EU's self-image as forming not only a collection of sovereign nation-states but also a patchwork of small, cross-border, and often overlapping Euroregions.[51] The aim of these Euroregions and Interreg initiatives is to confront economic, environmental, and other challenges that exist across international borders. For example, the French-Belgian border region has had to deal with the pollution left behind by the coal mines. This is why the French North and the Walloon province of Hainaut, under the aegis of their shared trajectory "from black to green," have called into existence an Outil de Contrôle for former coal mining sites.[52] Other domains in which Wallonia and the French North—whether or not in combination with other Belgian and northern French regions—have collaborated include health care, university education, culture (including cinema, as we will see in the

Figure 2.18. EU funding in Nord-Pas-de-Calais (author's photo).

following chapter), and the development of the binational metropolitan area around Lille. As far as this cross-border metro area is concerned, one finds an astute illustration in an Interreg information brochure that emphasizes the importance of Euregional collaboration: "An aerial photograph shows the evidence: seen from the sky the agglomerations that constitute the metropolitan area of Lille and the towns of Tournai, Coutrai, and Mouscron form, or almost form, only one agglomeration. One is in France, the other in Belgium, in two different provinces. The problems posing itself to this so important collective are of its size" (fig. 2.19).[53]

We find even clearer visual evidence of the Nord in the rare maps that combine the aerial picture's blindness for borders with socioeconomic statistics at the regional level. The reason such maps are relatively rare is that most regional data is gathered and published by either national or intranational regional institutions. In the 2000s, though, the French Institut National de la Statistique et des Etudes Economiques (INSEE) created an *Atlas transfontalier franco-belge*, a nine-volume "transborder" atlas of Belgium, northern France, and also parts of Germany and the Netherlands. The atlas was made with the goal to "better understand the evolution of territories, and the physical, human, and economic geography of this collective of 14 million inhabitants."[54] Browsing through this atlas, which is also available online, we observe for example that at the turn of the twenty-first century, the GDP per inhabitant in the French North and the Belgian South was significantly lower than in surrounding areas (fig. 2.20). This difference is partly explained by these regions' relatively low employment rates,[55] which were in turn largely caused by the mismatch between availability of and demand for employment. Figures 2.21 and 2.22 illustrate unemployment and youth unemployment rates in different regions in northern France and Belgium. One doesn't have to squint one's eyes to recognize in these maps the trajectory of the former northern French Walloon coal mining axis. At the same time, these maps reveal some differences between Wallonia and Nord-Pas-de-Calais. While both regions have been "affected by unemployment and precarity,"[56] as the INSEE observes, the Walloon situation remains more "delicate" than that of Nord-Pas-de-Calais, where the unemployment rate showed a slightly more optimistic trend in the beginning of the twenty-first century.[57]

Despite this difference in pace in which Nord-Pas-de-Calais and Wallonia have managed to catch up with their domestic and foreign neighbors, the shared socioeconomic history that has connected these regions since the 1713 fixation of the French-Belgian border continues to prevail. Having sketched this history in word and image, it is now time to analyze how it has found its way to the screen on each side of the border. I began my exploration of the Cinéma du Nord already in the first chapter with the comparative analysis of *Rosetta*, *L'humanité*, *Mouchette*,

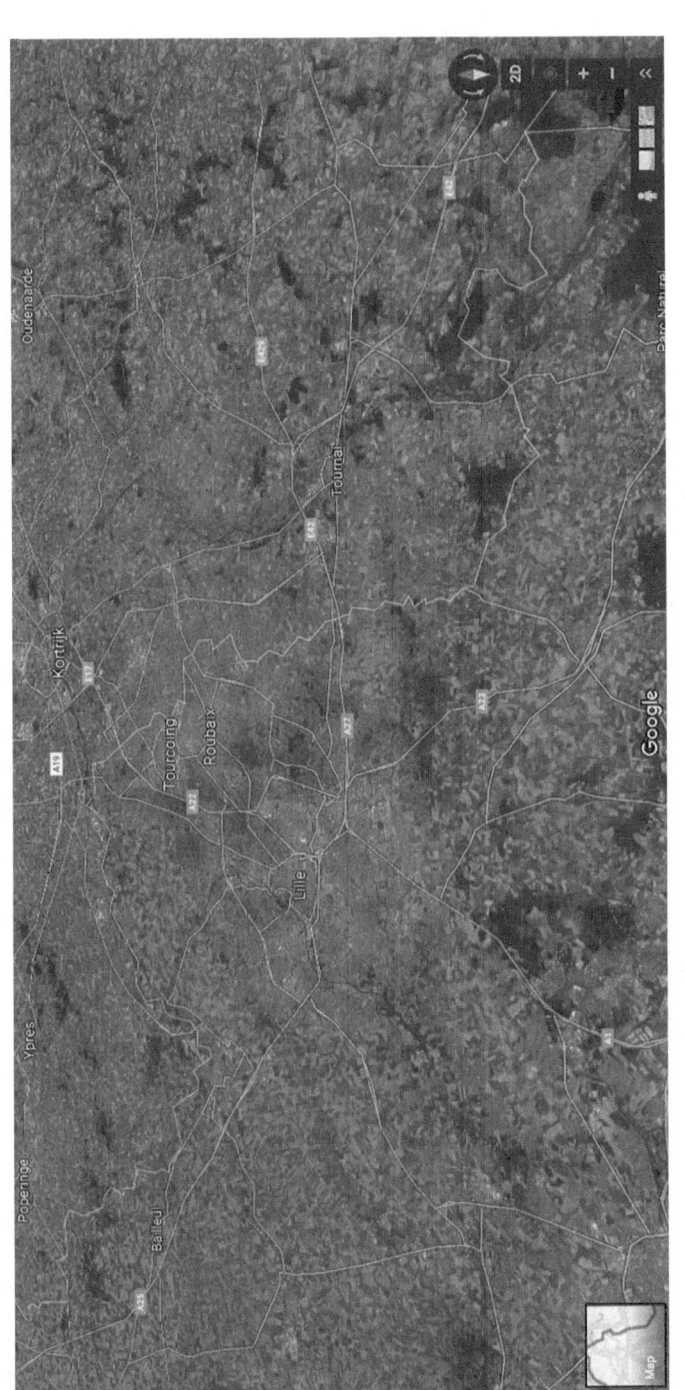

Figure 2.19. The border-crossing metropolitan area around Lille as seen on Google Maps (https://www.google.com/maps/@50.3760898,3.1256745,161591m/data=!3m1!1e3).

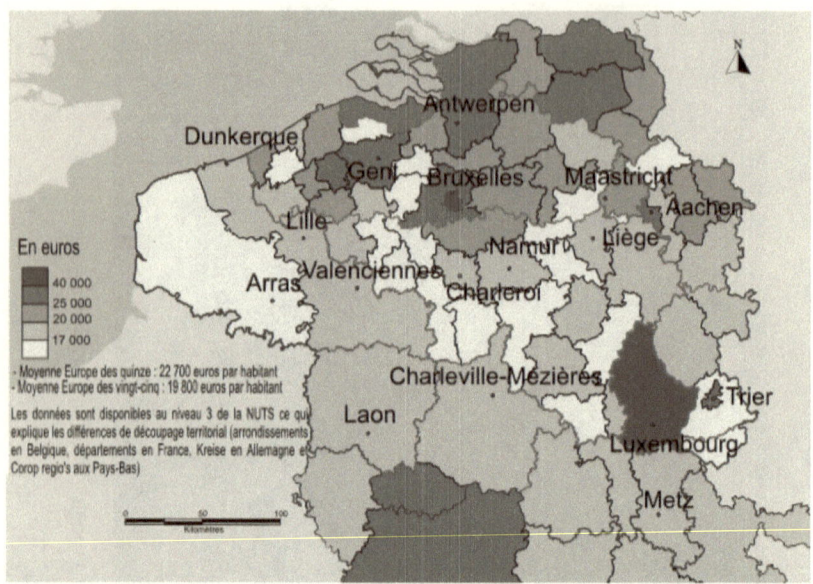

Figure 2.20. GDP per capita in 2000 in northern France, Belgium, Luxembourg, the southern Netherlands, and southwest Germany. *Source:* Pouille et al., *Atlas transfontalier: Tome 3*, 7.

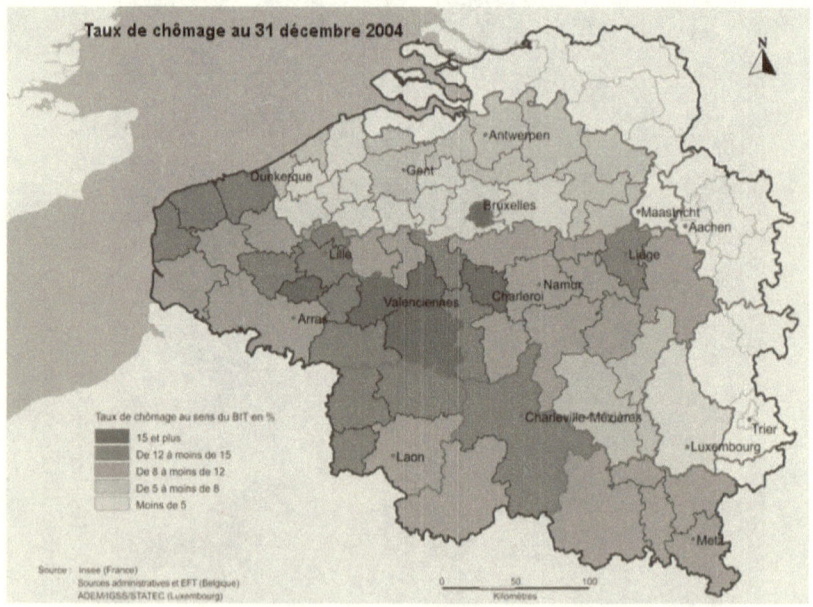

Figure 2.21. Unemployment rates at the end of 2004 in northern France, Belgium, and Luxembourg. *Source:* Pouille et al., *Atlas transfontalier: Tome 4*, 3.

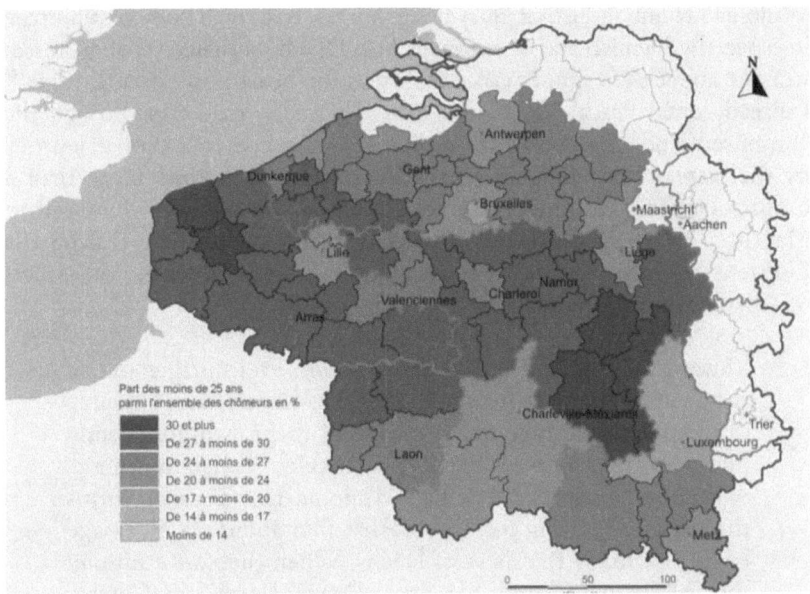

Figure 2.22. Unemployment among people under twenty-five at the end of 2004 in northern France, Belgium, and Luxembourg. *Source:* Pouille et al., *Atlas transfontalier: Tome 4*, 5.

Journal d'un curé de campagne, and *Sous le soleil de Satan*. In this second chapter I have continued this exploration so far through *Bienvenue chez les Ch'tis* and *Borinage* (and, in passing, the documentaries on Cockerill and Liège-Guillemins). The following two sections focus on the Walloon and northern French sides of the Cinéma du Nord, respectively, while they also integrate a comparative analysis between the ways films from either side of the border have given expression to the Nord.

Between Utopia and Dystopia: Wallonia in the Cinema

> Au début, chacun, seul, pensait que bientôt, ou un jour, il y aurait un second grève général, peut-être même une révolution, bien que chacun savait aussi qu'en Belgique le mot "révolution" est toujours un abus de langage. (In the beginning, everyone thought that soon, or one day, there would be a second general strike, perhaps even a revolution, even though everyone also knew that in Belgium the word "revolution" is always an abuse of language.)
>
> —*Pour que la guerre s'achève les murs devaient s'écrouler*
> (Jean-Pierre Dardenne and Luc Dardenne, 1980)

Wallonia's fading industrial glory has given rise to a small body of reportage in especially Flemish and occasionally also Dutch journalism that expresses wonder about the region's crisis reality at the heart of western Europe.[58] I already cited Pascal Verbeken's *Arm Wallonië*, a road trip through the "promised land," framed by its author as a response to a similar journey by the francophone-Belgian journalist Auguste de Winne more than a century earlier.[59] Another example is *Afscheid van Magritte* (Farewell to Magritte, 2004) by the Flemish journalist Guido Fonteyn. Tracing the footsteps of Wallonia's most famous painter, Fonteyn describes the streets of Châtelet, near Charleroi:

> Toward the end of the *Rue des Gravelles*, even further out of the center, beyond the three Magritte-houses, are a couple of dilapidated storage units. In one of them men are silently piling up crates of fruit. Black poverty rules the neighborhood. A shabby bar-hotel-B&B, half Walloon, half Turkish, forms the dreamed setting for a neorealist film about the Borinage or *Le Centre*, or the Aalst of Daens. When they were filming the well-known Flemish film about Daens [*Daens*, Stijn Coninx, 1992; about a Catholic priest in 1890s Flanders, who strives to improve the working conditions in local factories], and the entire cast went to Poland, with the excuse of lacking gray areas closer to home, the location casters had overlooked this part of Châtelet. This is not Poland or East Germany, but Châtelet.[60]

Wallonia's poverty-struck areas evoke, at least to this reporter, the urban wastelands of Italian neorealism. Would this also mean that socially critical and stylistically minimalist form of filmmaking prevail in cinematic accounts of Wallonia and its century of crisis? Browsing through studies of Walloon cinema, the answer is a resounding "yes." Roger Mounèje argues that the Walloon films "that have resisted time most come forth out of the lived social experience of the Walloon population."[61] Frédéric Sojcher calls the "cinema of the real" a certain tendency of Belgian and of Walloon filmmaking in particular.[62] Léon Michaux states that "in Wallonia, documentary nourishes fiction, while fiction films are transparent to the concern with the real, the concern with documentary."[63] Jacques Polet observes in Walloon cinema "a close link to the real" and "the articulation of a social culture that is profoundly nourished by the history of Wallonia, in particular its economic history and industrial mutations."[64] And in the 2011 collection of essays *Cinéma et crise(s) économique(s): esquisses d'une cinématographie wallonne* (Cinema and economic crisis: sketches of Walloon cinematography), Anne Roekens and Axel Tixhon examine "the identity of . . . Walloon, Belgian, and francophone cinema, while they explain its anchorage in a landscape of crisis and economic difficulty."[65] In this same study, Bénedicte Rochet writes, moreover, that "Wallonia's filmmakers have in common that they advocate a cinema of the 'real' in which genres bump into each other, often on the tightrope between reality and fiction."[66]

Walloon cinema is a subset of francophone-Belgian cinema, which further includes francophone films from and/or about the Brussels area (e.g., Chantal Akerman's 1975 *Jeanne Dielman: 23 Quai du Commerce, 1080 Bruxelles* and the 2015 film *Black* by Adil El Arbi and Bilall Fallah, about gang rivalries in the city's Molenbeek and Matonge neighborhoods). Other than *Rosetta* and the earlier-discussed *Misère au Borinage* (whose codirector Henri Storck appears as Jeanne's "first caller" in Akerman's film), the third uncontestable landmark of Walloon cinema is the 1960 fiction film *Déjà s'envole la fleur maigre* (The scrawny flower has already flown) by Paul Meyer. Until the late 1950s, with the theaters dominated by Hollywood and French productions, most Belgian feature-length films were folkloristic or vaudeville comedies with little to no artistic pretensions. The reason for this longtime nonexistence of a Belgian "quality" or "auteur" cinema was above all the unavailability of funds. As Théodore Louis writes, "every filmmaker who toward the end of the 1950s dreamed about shooting, in our country, with Belgian money, outside of the accepted 'norms,' a fiction feature could expect to be treated as either utopian or crazy."[67] Meyer was a utopian. His film began as a project commissioned by the Belgian Ministry of Public Education and was supposed to sing the praises of smooth integration of immigrants in the Borinage. However, after Meyer visited the area and witnessed its misery and strikes with his own eyes and in *Misère au Borinage*, he radically deviated from the State propaganda he had committed himself to and instead made a film much more in line with his earlier Bresson-inspired short *Klinkaart* (The bricklayer, 1955). The production costs of *Déjà s'envole la fleur maigre* soon exceeded the government budget, necessitating Meyer to secure additional loans. He gathered a large cast of nonprofessional actors, including many children, whom he asked to perform their own lives. Upon the final edits, he took the film to a studio in Paris to postsynchronize the dialogues dubbed by French voice actors speaking Italian, Polish, French, and Dutch. The film premiered at the festival of Porretta Terme in Italy, where a jury including Michelangelo Antonioni, Roberto Rossellini, and Luchino Visconti awarded the film the Critics Prize. These neorealist godfathers were joined in their praise by Vittorio de Sica, Giuseppe de Santis, and *Cahiers du cinéma*. In Meyer's home country, the film won the Grand prix d'excellence at the Antwerp National Film Festival, and in 1963 the Cannes Film Festival selected *Déjà s'envole* for its Semaine Internationale de la Critique. The Belgian government was less thrilled, however, and accused Meyer of having abused public funds. The payback of these and other funds nipped Meyer's career as a fiction feature auteur in the bud.[68]

Déjà s'envole la fleur maigre (which only appeared on DVD in 2016) does not only offer the clearest-cut *néorealisme à la wallonne*, it also must be the most *Italian* neorealist film ever made outside of Italy. The film takes its title from a poem by Salvatore Quasimodo, "Già vola il foiore magro." At the start of the film, we hear a female voice singing this poem to the beat of industrial clinking sounds, while a French translation rolls through the frame: "Je ne saurai rien de ma vie, sang obscure et monotone / Je ne saurai qui j'aimais, qui j'aime" (I will know nothing of my life, obscure and monotonous blood / I will only know whom I loved, whom I love). The film tells the story of the large immigrant and in particular Italian immigrant population of the Borinage. The narrative spans a single day and is structured around two opposed trajectories, that of Domenico, who after seventeen years of labor in Marseille, Paris, and the Borinage feels the need to return to his childhood country ("Il faut que je rentre e[t] ritorno a casa"), and that of the young Luigi, who together with his mother and his siblings has just arrived by train in the *pays noir* in order to join his father. Staring out of the bedroom window in his new home away from home, Luigi overhears his parents quarreling. "Why did you ask us to come over?" his mother reproaches his father, "Why do you let him [Luigi's older brother] learn the job of a *chômeur* [an unemployed person]?" The film's third protagonist is the black country itself, which captured by the dreamy gaze of Meyer's lens unmistakably calls to mind the volcanic earth of *Journey to Italy* (Rossellini), much like the family's arrival by train reminds the viewer of *Rocco and His Brothers* (Visconti).

The film's poetic climax is the encounter between Domenico and Luigi on the *terril*, or slag heap, a man-made mountain dug up from the earth. "Tout ce que tu vois d'ici du haut du terril, c'est le Borinage" (All you see from here from the *terril* is the Borinage), Domenico explains the industrial landscape to Luigi in a shot that merges the points of view of the old man and the young boy (fig. 2.23). "La miniera, charbonnage." Cut to a shot of kids playing, sliding down the dusty hill on steel disks (fig. 2.24). "Disoccupazione, chômage." Cut back to the children, whose laughter and speed is cross-cut with the indiscernible movement of a couple of snails caught in close-up, and as a pun on the Flemish word for *terril*, *slakkenberg*, which literally translates as "snail mountain." The kids' joyous descent contrasts with the priest's uphill struggle in an earlier scene. Like all priests in the Nord—from Van Gogh to Bresson's *curé*—he is tormented by existential doubts. On his way to the crucifix on top of the *terril*, he loses his hat. A young boy fetches the hat and also gives

Figures 2.23–2.25. *Déjà s'envole la fleur maigre* (Paul Meyer, 1959).

the priest one of the herrings (fig. 2.25) he has just stolen from a street vendor (who is heard promoting his merchandise in Dutch: "Verse haring!"). The priest hands the boy half of the flowers he has just picked, asking the boy whether he ever goes praying at the cross. "No," the boy answers and throws the flowers onto the ground. The boy, like Luigi and like all the other children, whether Belgian, Italian, or Polish, know the truth about their world. They gather it from their parents' quarrels, they hear it from wise men like Domenico, and they feel it in their stomachs. *Borinage, charbonnage, chômage*: Borinage, coal mining, unemployment. Rather than sugarcoating this truth with the scrawny flowers of religion, the children fight it with their own fables. They slide down the hill, they dance, they play in the ruins—with reference to Rossellini's *Germany Year Zero*—and they eat, with dirty faces, Domenico's imaginary bonbons. "Nous sommes tous des comédiens," the old man preaches to his young audience, "le terril ne sert plus à rien" (We are all comedians, the slag heap no longer serves any good).

The *terril* is *the* icon of Walloon cinema, which is a cinema largely shot in the industrial centers of the Borinage and the Liège basin. In some films the *terril* serves as the narrative setting itself, whether for struggle, wandering, or play. Other than *Borinage* and *Déjà s'envole la fleur maigre*, this is the case in *Pays noir, pays rouge* (Thierry Michel, 1975), *Les Convoyeurs attendent* (Benoît Mariage, 1999), and *Ultranova* (Bouli Lanners, 2005). Or it appears in the background, as a black giant looming over the brick houses, as it does in *Jeudi on chantera comme dimanche* (Luc de Heusch, 1967), or as a green hill that over time has seamlessly integrated itself into the horizon, as in *Hiver 60* (Thierry Michel, 1983), *Marchienne de vie* (Richard Olivier, 1993), *La Raison du plus faible* (Lucas Belvaux, 2006), and the Dardennes' *La Promesse* (1996).

The *terril* being the iconic image of Walloon cinema, its iconic event is the "strike of the century," which in the winter of 1960–1961 paralyzed Belgium, and in particular Wallonia, for almost five weeks.[69] The Belgian Communist Party organized this general strike in response to the austerity policies proposed by the center-right-wing Eyskens government. In Wallonia, the protestors also demanded structural economic reforms as well as the federalization of Belgium. The government ultimately crushed the protests, during which four people were killed by police violence. The strike left deep traces in Belgian politics and turned out be the last big show of force of the Walloon labor movement. From that winter on, large-scale street confrontations have made way for the so-called Rhineland model, a controlled market economy structure in which trade unions, employers, and the government negotiate in order to seek a consensus.[70]

Among the cinematic offshoots of this general strike are *Vechten voor Onze Rechten* (Fighting for our rights, 1962) by the Flemish Frans Buyens, a found-footage agitprop film that speaks the language of the class struggle. The film is a montage of moving and still images, from found footage of street protests to TV images of corrupt politicians, and from neon ads to Congo (which in June that year had gained independence from Belgium). A second example is *Pays noir, pays rouge* (Black country, red country, 1975) by Thierry Michel, a poetic documentary that combines images of life and crisis in 1970s Charleroi with testimonies of workers who participated in the big strike. Both films pay homage to *Misère à Borinage*. Moreover, *Pays noir, pays rouge* quotes *Déjà s'envole fleur maigre*, as it intercuts shots of people dancing at a street fair with shots of laughing children sliding down a *terril*. In 1982, Michel returned to the big strike with *Hiver 60* (The winter of 1960), a reenacted docudrama about the protests in the Belgian South that also includes footage from *Vechten voor Onze Rechten*.[71]

Also for the Dardennes the collective spirit of the strike of the century has been foundational. At the turn of the 1980s, the brothers made two militant videos through their first production company, Dérives. The first is *Lorsque le bateau de Léon M. descendit la Meuse pour la première fois* (When the bark of Léon M. went down the Meuse for the first time, 1979), the other *Pour que la guerre s'achève les murs devaient s'écrouter* (For the war to succeed the walls had to crumble, 1980).[72] Both films integrate archival footage of Wallonia's socialist heydays with testimonies by Cockerill employees who at the time were involved in the strikes. *Pour que la guerre* follows Edmond, the former editor of a clandestine newspaper. Retracing his movements and reenacting his habits, Edmond recalls the optimism of the strike's early days, when he and his comrades peacefully breached a police line, while singing the International, and while being cheered by people leaning out of their windows also singing the International. Similarly, in *Lorsque le bateau* Léon recalls the "unequaled sense of fraternity" that the strike stirred in "people who were not used to taking responsibility." The film follows, in black and white, the maiden voyage of the boat Léon has built, "the boat of the last survivors of a revolutionary language condemned to death by history." And both films connect the memory of 1960 to the present, an "end of the century deprived of history" in a desperate need of "the myth of revolution."

In their early careers, the Dardennes thus showed themselves quite nostalgic for this revolutionary spirit that once materialized in the streets of Liège and Charleroi. At the end of *Lorsque le bateau*, the narrator wonders out loud:

> Quel est le langage révolutionaire non condamné à mort par l'histoire? . . . Quel est à faire le bateau lorsqu'au appel de sa sirène ne répondaient que les appels d'autres sirènes? . . . Allait-il pour suivre son voyage parce que les ailes de la mouette continuent de desiner dans le ciel les rivages de l'Utopie? (What is the revolutionary language that has not been condemned by history? . . . What would the boat do if other sirens were the only to answer to its sirens? . . . Would it continue its journey because the wings of the seagull keep on drawing the banks of utopia in the sky?)

It's in the light of this quest for a utopian vocabulary that one needs to understand the *appel au réalisme* the Dardennes made with their early documentary work, films also through which they inscribed themselves in Wallonia's rich social documentary tradition, from Storck to Michel. At the same time, their documentaries from this period show an experimental touch clearly inspired by the videos Jean-Luc Godard had made earlier that decade together with Jean-Pierre Gorin and with the Dziga Vertov Group.[73] *Pour que la guerre* opens with three ways "to begin the film," and *Lorsque le bateau* shows sharp close-ups of the gestures connecting Léon's thirty-three years at Cockerill to the construction of his boat. Both films, moreover, pair found footage with reflections about the use value of such footage, and more in general on cinema's ability to do justice to history and potentially rekindle glimpses of utopia in the present.

Walloon cinema thus moves between the dystopia of crisis and the utopia of a people, a pendulum swing that, other than by mining and the labor movement, frequently engages the themes of immigration and racism. A key work in this light is the 1994 TV documentary *Marchienne de Vie*, directed by Richard Olivier. *Marchienne de Vie* grasps the social discontent that exists among parts of the white population in the multiethnic Marchienne-au-Pont, one of the poorest neighborhoods in Charleroi.[74] The documentary was broadcast by the RTBF and stirred quite some controversy, as it gave voice to populist and xenophobic sentiments that, as Verbeken writes in his aforementioned travelogue, didn't stroke with "the most intimate self-image of Wallonia: that of a straightforward, warm, cosmopolitan immigration region where all of Europe came together."[75] It is instructive to compare *Marchienne de vie* to *Déjà s'envole la fleur maigre*, which forty years earlier had also courageously attacked the postcard image of Wallonia as a melting pot of cultures. The films' strategies are very different, though. Whereas Meyer's film dreams up an ephemeral magic mountain that unites children from all cultural backgrounds in their misery, *Marchienne de vie* is much more gritty in its questioning of the Walloon dream. One of Olivier's interviewees tells about the gradual degradation of the "big family" he felt part of in the early seventies after having just migrated from Algeria to Charleroi: "There was tons of work . . . and money, too much money. In those days there was no racism. But since the closure of the mines we have started to feel that people became aggressive . . . because of the lack of work."

The third example of a film that engages the region's immigration history that I'd like to highlight is the 2017 documentary *Enfants du hasard / Children of Chance* by Thierry Michel and Pascal Colson. For this film Michel and Colson "infiltrated" for a year a class of children around the age of twelve, taught by Madame Brigitte, who is about to retire. All but one of the children in this class is of Walloon-Turkish heritage. When asked who among them has a grandfather who worked in the mines, they all raise their hand. One girl knows to tell that "life was hard and [that] it wasn't very pleasant underground." At the same time the film shows that as the region's mining sites are being demolished, also the people's collective memory of them fades. Then, in March that year, the class, like the rest of Belgium, is shaken up by the bombings in the Brussels subway and airport. The film shows the class discussing what could have possibly motivated these events. When their teacher observes that the majority of the students is Muslim like the attackers, a girl corrects her: "But not in the same way, Madame" (figs 2.26–2.28).

In an RTBF reportage around the release of *Enfants du hasard*, one of the pupils who was followed for this documentary observes that "it's just a film, but it's not just a film, it tells our lives, it tells the lives of our grandparents."[76] The girl's remark not only sums up *Enfants du hasard*, it captures Walloon cinema in general, its cinema of life and lived existence. As we have seen, the Walloon cinema of the real originated around 1930 with the first Walloon social documentaries. Since then also many of its fiction films integrate elements of documentary, staying true to Storck's adage that "a good fiction is first of all a good documentary."[77] Above all, Walloon cinema is a strongly *rooted* cinema. Its films are almost always shot on location, its narratives mostly take place in the historical present, and many of its actors, whether professionals or amateurs, are originally from the region.[78] In some cases these actors play "themselves," like in *Déjà s'envole la fleur maigre*. In other cases their Walloon identities serve as the "raw" materials for their fictional appearances, as in *Rosetta*. At the same time, and while regionally rooted, Walloon cinema, and especially Walloon *fiction* cinema, tends to touch upon notions and tap into sentiments that transcend their immediate settings. In a neorealist vein that integrates socialism with an often secular-Catholic humanism, Walloon

Figures 2.26–2.28. *Enfants du hasard* (Thierry Michel and Patrick Colson, 2017).

cinema employs the particularity of its region's landscapes, towns, and people in order to construct images and narratives that lay claim to a more universal human condition. As Jacques Polet writes, this "rootedness pregnant of universality" (*enracinement porteur d'universalité*) is the dialectical fundament of the Walloon cinema of the real:

> [The Walloon cinema is] a particular cinema that is nonetheless capable of universalization: a regional cinema that wholeheartedly assumes its object, yet not so much a regionalist cinema that succumbs to the temptation of the painterliness of the local. Ultimately it is a cinema that, in its expression of Wallonia, bears witness to the fact that the true universal is always concrete.[79]

A recurring theme in Walloon cinema is that of the small person's struggle for the good or at least a *better* life in the face of economic hardship, often in narratives that are partly goal-driven, partly wandering, and that combine melodrama and documentary with the "love and rejection of the real" that André Bazin so much revered in Italian neorealist cinema.[80] Most Walloon films express, moreover, a belief in an idea of "humanity" according to which people have the power to act ethically and to retain their dignity even when confronted with dehumanizing conditions. Finally, most Walloon fiction films have a poetic, lighthearted, tragicomic, or otherwise redemptive touch, and often they end on a somewhat hopeful note. This intertwined engagement with a particular regional experience, on the one hand, and a more universally "human" condition, on the other, is fundamental to Walloon realism. Walloon cinema produces films that, while depicting, employing, or even exploiting the particularity of *these* people and *their* realities, make intelligible and felt the more general question, "What is left of humanity in a time and space of crisis?"

I already discussed the examples of *Déjà s'envole la fleur maigre*, which alchemically transforms the harsh reality of *Borinage, charbonnage, chômage* into the fragile flower of Quasimodo's poem. And there is of course *Rosetta*, in which the Dardennes' earlier longing for a collective utopia gives way to a young woman's fight for a normal, working-class life. There are numerous other examples, all worth listing, because Walloon cinema is quirky, subtle, funny, harsh, moving, and miraculous, all at once, so I'll list a few: *Jeudi on chantera comme dimanche / Thursday We Will Sing Like Sunday* (Luc de Heusch, 1967), yet another story of the big strike, which ends happily on a commercially sponsored marriage;[81] *Du beurre dans les tartines / Bread and Butter* (Manu Bonmariage, 1980), a TV documentary about a small company in crisis; *Le Grand paysage d'Alexis Droeven / The Wide Landscape of Alexis Droeven* (Jean-Jacques Andrien, 1981), the story of a young farmer who sees his livelihood threatened by EU policies; *Australia* (1989), also by Andrien, which narrates the decline of the Verviers glass industry; *Et la vie* (Denis Gheerbrant, 1991), a French film whose travels take us to *terrils* both in Wallonia and in Nord-Pas-de-Calais; *Les Convoyeurs attendent / The Carriers Are Waiting* (Benoît Mariage, 1999), a black-and-white tragicomedy about a Charleroi-based family that makes it to the new millennium (fig. 2.29); *Les Enfants du Borinage: lettre à Henri Storck* (Patric Jean, 1999), a video-letter to the father of Walloon cinema; *La Raison du plus faible / The Right of the Weakest* (Lucas Belvaux, 2006), a socialist heist thriller set in Liège in which a group of men take what they deserve; *Eldorado* (Bouli Lanners, 2008), a road movie through the promised land; and *Illégal / Illegal* (Olivier Masset-Depasse, 2010), a *j'accuse* of Belgian and European immigration policies. Some of these films aestheticize the bleakness of their industrial settings in high contrast, black-and-white photography (*Jeudi on chantera*, *Les Convoyeurs attendent*),[82] while another transforms the Walloon landscapes into a Wild West setting (*Eldorado*). Finally, some films explore, directly or indirectly, the region's integration into the EU, into this union as a migration fortress (e.g., *Illégal*, the Dardennes' *La Silence de Lorna*), or as a common market (*Le Grand paysage*). These films' critique of "Europe" could not contrast more starkly with the ideal of a united Europe that Storck envisioned in his only (and commercially unsuccessful) fiction feature: *Le Banquet des fraudeurs* (*The smugglers' banquet*, 1952), a Belgian-German production partially financed with Marshall Plan funds

Figure 2.29. *Les Convoyeurs attendent* (Benoît Mariage, 1999).

and a plea for a utopian, borderless Europe narrated in a fictive town at the Belgian-German-Dutch border.[83]

And what about that other border, the one between France and Belgium that defines the Cinéma du Nord? While there are quite a few films that depict the regional and linguistic border between Wallonia and Flanders (e.g., *Le Grand paysage d'Alexis Droeven*, Alain Berliner's 1998 telefilm *Le Mur*), the French-Belgian border is rarely felt in Walloon cinema,[84] which is a first difference between the Walloon and northern French sides of the Cinéma du Nord.

Not Paris: Nord-Pas-de-Calais in the Cinema

> Une route qui va de Paris qui va jusqu'au Calais, après c'est la mer et puis l'Angleterre. (A route that goes from Paris that goes until Calais, after that it's the sea and then England.)
>
> —From the 1994 film *Rosine*, directed by Christine Carrière

Unlike as in Walloon cinema, there are many films set in the French North that depict French-Belgian relations. There is a number of films about smuggling communities, like *La Maison dans la dune / The House on the Dune* (Georges Lampin, 1951), an adaptation of a 1932 novel by Van der Meersch.[85] The border plays a role in Jean Renoir's *Le Crime de Monsieur Lange / The Crime of Monsieur Lange* (1936), a film that breathes the spirit of the Front Populaire government. There are several adaptations of *Germinal* (1913, 1963, 1993), in which the northern French mines import Belgian workers in order to break up a strike. Finally, *Rien à declarer / Nothing to Declare* (2010) by Dany Boon, in the vein of his earlier *Bienvenue chez les Ch'tis*, uses the 1993 abolishment of customs control at the French-Belgian border to depict the mutual prejudices of the French of the North and the Belgians of the South.

This list of examples may make it seem that the French North has always been a significant presence in French cinema, but this is not the case. As François Baudinet writes in *Le Nord et le cinéma* (1998): "The history of the [French] North in the cinema is first of all an interrogation of the question of the unseen, of the 'disappearance' of the North on the screen, of the 'unfilmable.'"[86] Similarly, Alexandrine Dhainaut observes:

> The camera of filmmakers has often preferred the light of the South to the capricious sky of the North. The films that have been shot in the region (those in which the North is clearly identifiable) can be counted on the fingers of one hand. As far as the directors who have chosen the region are concerned, they have essentially come there to film *malheur*, moroseness, or social decay.[87]

The claim that the French North has hardly seen any film crews at all throughout its history is a little exaggerated. In his *Les Tournages des films dans le Nord et le Pas-de-Calais* (2008) Daniel Granval lists over two hundred films shot or partly shot in the region, including the films listed at the start of this section (with the exception of the 1963 *Germinal*, directed by Yves Allégret, which was shot in Hungary).[88] But Dhainaut does raise two crucial facts about the relation between cinema and the French North. The first is that, until very recently, the region has remained relatively underrepresented in French national cinema. The second is that films that *do* depict the region often caricaturize it as an *enfer du Nord*, a northern Hell.

There are four reasons for the relatively low number of cinematic productions in the French North up until the mid-1980s.[89] The first is the long-term existence of negative stereotypes about the French North elsewhere in France, mostly related to its coal mining history and its climate. That climate, though definitely not *as* arctic as it has sometimes been depicted, is the second reason why many filmmakers used to avoid the French North. With its high precipitation rates and capricious skies, Nord and Pas-de-Calais form challenging and potentially expensive shooting locations for directors and producers who wish their films to reflect a consistent light and landscape appearance. Therefore for many decades production teams working on historical dramas with narratives set in the French North dislocated their outdoor shooting mostly to eastern Europe. Directly related, and the third reason for the relative invisibility of the North in French cinema, is the ironic fact that many of the region's old quarters and historic sites were destroyed during the very same sieges and battles depicted in those historical dramas (e.g., the siege of Arras in *Cyrano de Bergerac* [Jean-Paul Rappeneau, 1990], which was also shot in Hungary). Fourth, until the French New Wave, most French films were shot and edited in the studios of Nice, Marseille, and Paris. This situation only gradually and partially changed with the increasing popularity of location shooting and the emergence of regional production companies and TV channels. Even with these changes, though, the proximity of Nord-Pas-de-Calais to Paris and its vast cinematic infrastructure for a long time continued to slow down the development of a truly regionally rooted northern French cinema: a cinema that takes to heart the region's specificity *and* that is its product.

Such a northern French regional cinema only really took off in the 1990s. Since the start of that decade, and for many of the same reasons that prevented earlier generations of filmmakers to work in the region (its coal history, its capricious skies), the North has become one of the most significant filmmaking sites in France, after Paris and Ile-de-France.

As René Prédal writes with reference to Dumont, Xavier Beauvois (two of the most acclaimed directors from the region), and Maurice Pialat (who shot three films there):

> These filmmakers have found [in the North] places, people, a temporality, and a light that paradoxically gives their stories a universal impact: they show *this* region while addressing all spectators. This anchoring situates things in working-class and farmers' milieus, whereas in Paris the cinema tends to only speak of the bourgeoisie. The province imposes new behaviors and in particular a bigger role for the body instead of tightening up everything with the word, an "evil" endemic to the Parisian film. . . . The North, in particular, offers characters who resist much more to intellectual analysis and, because of that, touch the audience differently. In sum, their silences, an empty everydayness, permit the arrest of the essence of even the human being who has been completely obscured by the perpetual movement of Paris [*l'essence même de l'homme complètement occultée par le mouvement perpétuel de Paris*].[90]

Prédal's analysis resonates with my earlier characterization of Walloon cinema as a regionally rooted cinema that taps into more universally "human" sentiments. Much like their Walloon colleagues, French filmmakers, including those *not* from Nord-Pas-de-Calais, have embraced the places and people of the North in a way that is at once place-specific and that transcends its particular subjects and settings. But does northern French cinema's anchorage in the "real" indeed emanate directly from the region's socioeconomic and geographic reality, as Prédal suggests? Does the French North "impose" a certain aesthetic in which affective encounters with bodies and landscapes "naturally" prevail over the long, philosophical digressions of a cinema "tightened up with the word"? And is the rootedness of northern French cinema truly regional, or it is also somewhat of an imported product? These are difficult questions to answer. While it is tempting to understand the northern French appeal to a regional essence—in itself, of course, a contestable notion—as the inevitable expression of such an essence, one needs to keep in mind that the marriage between the French North and a regionally anchored realism is still fairly young. In order to retrace the origins of that marriage, it is necessary to situate the North in the history of French national cinema.

Up until the New Wave, French cinema was dominated by psychological, studio-shot realism, as François Truffaut lamented in his 1954 pamphlet "Une certaine tendance du cinéma français" (A certain tendency in French cinema).⁹¹ For a great part, this tendency resulted from the fact that many films were adaptations from literary classics set in a remote past. Truffaut writes that what "annoys" him about the "tradition de la qualité" is its distinction between "filmable" and "unfilmable" scenes. Truffaut continues that whereas in cinema's first decades those unfilmable scenes used to be simply omitted, around 1940 screenwriters started to invent "*equivalent* scenes, that is to say, scenes as the novel's author would have written them for the cinema." In Truffaut's view, there is no such thing as an "unfilmable scene"; unfilmable scenes only exist for "metteurs-en-scènes," upon which he joins André Bazin in his praise of the "auteur" Bresson for his adaptation of *Journal d'un curé de campagne*.

Truffaut would have likely been less positive about most other adaptations of novels set in the French North. Examples include the many adaptations of Hugo's *Les Misérables* (1862)⁹² and of Alexandre Dumas's *Les Trois mousquetaires* (1844),⁹³ or the 1938 film *Mollenard* by Robert Siodmak, an adaptation of a novel by the Walloon author Oscar-Paul Gilbert. Like Renoir's aforementioned *Le Crime de Monsieur Lange*, *Mollenard* captures the spirit of the Front Populaire, though primarily in terms of story and not so much in that of style. Similarly, the various adaptations of Van der Meersch's *La Maison dans la dune* and *Germinal* (for which Zola paid many observational visits to mining towns and for which he descended into the operational coal pit of Denain)⁹⁴ are only selectively faithful to the naturalism of their novels. As Paul Renard argues, in the spirit of Truffaut:

> While these films reactualize and reinvigorate the stereotypical images of the North, they almost always water down the realism of the novelists by which they are inspired, whether it is the epic realism of Zola, the satirical realism of Gilbert, or the melodramatic realism of Van der Meersch. They attenuate, for example, the Zolanian violence. Capellani and Allégret suppress the episodes in which the grocer is castrated by the starving women . . .⁹⁵

I agree with this modernist, New Wave–inspired critique, which equally applies to the 1993 *Germinal* adaptation of Claude Berri (who at the time of his film's release was attacked by left-wing critics for deliberately omitting the Marxist and anarchist discourses present in Zola's narrative).⁹⁶ At the same time, these films need to be seen as part of the lineage of a socially critical realism, or neorealism, in northern French cinema, if only because they draw attention to a region for a long time ignored in French cinema. As far as Capellani's *Germinal* is concerned, the film was one of the first features almost entirely shot on location. Only some of the interior scenes, including those that take place down in the pits, were shot in a studio. All the other scenes Capellani shot in the streets or at the mining site of Auchel, near Lille, where a crowd of local extras complemented a professional cast of actors from the Comédie Française. As Daniel Granval writes, this "collaboration with the inhabitants of Auchel was very precious to the film crew, and in the evenings the actors joined the real miners in their card games."[97]

Two other landmarks in the northern French cinema of the real—and that like *Germinal* document the life and hardship in and around the mines—are the 1931 French-German talkie *Kameradschaft / La Tragédie de la mine* (The mine tragedy / comradeship), directed by Georg Wilhelm Pabst, and *Le Point du jour* (1949) by Louis Daquin. Pabst based his film on the dust explosion that took place in 1906 in a pit in Courrières, near Lens, which killed 1,099 miners, including many children, which made it the worst mine disaster in European history ever. Though the narrative is set around and also "underneath" the French-German border, parts of the film were filmed in Noeux-les-Mines, in Pas-de-Calais. Originally Pabst wanted to end the film on a pessimistic note, with the separation of German and French mining communities by nationalist sentiments. Censors, however, imposed a more optimistic ending. The style of the film is quasi-documentary and expresses, in the words of Tangui Perron, a "humanist and internationalist philosophy,"[98] an aesthetic that mostly resulted from Pabst's decision to supplement his professional cast with nonprofessional actors recruited from the local population. As a French journalist reported from the set:

> [T]he extras play a[n] . . . active part. With a charming patience. Pabst explains what they need to do as occasional actors. . . . I expected hesitations, laughter, discomfort. I was surprised by the sincerity, the truth with which a young man and an old woman in the foreground played their roles. The woman did not feel like laughing: she is a widow and her husband died in the mine. The young man goes down into the pits every day. They were told: "Act like there is a fire in the pit." They understood.[99]

Like *La Tragédie de la mine*, Daquin's *Le Point du jour* was filmed with a mixed cast of professionals and amateurs. The film shows the everyday lives of miners and their families in Liévin, near Lens, where the film was also shot. *Le Point du jour* engages, moreover, the region's political present. Daquin was a member of both the French Communist Party and the Confédération Générale du Travail, the first major confederation of trade unions in France. During the shooting of his film he was closely monitored by the mine management, who forbade him to make any reference to class struggle, silicosis (which at that time had just been recognized as a miner's disease), or the tragedy of Courrières. This is why the film refers to this disaster as "Ostrevent," while sizing down the body count to "more than 300." The film's tone is critical nonetheless. As Perron writes, "a film without strike or dust explosion, and devoid of all miserableness," *Le Point du jour* was a commercial failure, but the film meant "the departure point for France of a social, or socialist, neorealism."[100]

Although that tradition of northern French neorealism goes back to the early days of cinema, the presence of the North in French national cinema only blossomed into a truly regionally rooted northern French cinema in the 1980s, when France began to turn toward the regions, both politically and cinematically. Other than the 1913 *Germinal*, *La Tragédie de la mine* (1931), *Le Point du jour* (1949), and *Journal d'un curé de campagne* (1951), the clearest foreshadowings of this regionally rooted cinema are the three films Pialat made in the region: his feature-length debut *L'Enfance nue / Naked Childhood* from 1968, *Passe ton bac d'abord / Graduate First* from 1978, and *Sous le soleil de Satan* from 1987. A director, screenwriter, and actor who originally wanted to become a painter, Pialat came to filmmaking late. He was the contemporary of New Wave filmmakers such as Godard, Truffaut, and Chabrol, but he only made his first feature-length film when the New Wave proper was already over. *L'Enfance nue* is a critique of the French New Wave, of its modernism, its obsession with Paris, and above all of the distorted image of French childhood this movement had created in Pialat's eyes. This did not prevent Pialat from working with Truffaut, who coproduced *L'Enfance nue*. What makes this collaboration all the more interesting is that *L'Enfance nue* forms a critical response to Truffaut's *Les 400 coups / 400 Blows* from 1959. Both films tell the story of a boy adrift, and both do so in a stripped-down cinematic language. Here the parallels end. Pialat's portrait of French youth is simultaneously much more negative and much more positive than Truffaut's. Whereas Antoine in *Les 400 coups* wages his struggle against the old France in the epicenter of the Nouvelle Vague, the childhood of the ten-year-old François (Michel Terrazon) in *L'Enfance nue* unfolds in a forgotten France that is truly naked and devoid of play. First François is sent by his mother to a home for wayward children. From there he goes to a foster home, until the family gives up on the unruly child, in revenge for which he drowns their cat. Whereas the initial lightheartedness of *Les 400 coups* ultimately runs aground in the dead end of its final freeze frame, the overall bleakness of *L'Enfance nue* ends on a sincere spark of faith in the protagonist's future (figs. 2.30–2.33). These differences also play out stylistically. Truffaut's sparkling handheld black-and-white images are as playful and restless as Antoine, but ultimately remain at a deliberate distance from their protagonist, who as a result remains somewhat of a mystery to the viewer. In *L'Enfance nue*, in contrast, the long takes are gray despite their colors and the long shots intimate in their Bresson-inspired stasis. There is not much mystery to François: he just wants to be loved.

L'Enfance nue, *Sous le soleil de Satan*, and *Passe ton bac d'abord* (which tells the story of a group of adolescents in Lens who're asked to invest in their future in a milieu of unemployment and disillusion), are the most poignant forerunners of a regionally anchored northern French cinema. Like Walloon cinema, northern French cinema displays a tendency for the real. Many of its films engage the region's economic crisis, like *Faut-il aimer Mathilde?* (Edwin Baily, 1993; whose heroine tries to figure out her life in an industrial town near Lille), *Chacun pour soi* (Bruno Bontzolakis, 1998; about two childhood friends from the Côte d'Opale who decide to join the army when they find no work), *Rien à faire* (Marion Vernoux, 1999; in which an unemployed man and woman run into each other in a supermarket), and *Ça commence aujourd'hui* (Bertrand Tavernier, 1999; about a school director in the unemployment-struck Anzin who gradually becomes the voice of the poor). Northern French cinema shares with its Walloon neighbor, moreover, a secular-religious humanism, as found for example in *Pierre et Djemila* (Gérard Blain, 1987), *Rosine* (Christine Carrière, 1994), *La Vie rêvée des anges* (Erick Zonca, 1998), and *Sauve-moi* (Christian Vincent, 2000). And like in Walloon cinema, many northern French films engage the topic of migration and cultural tensions between ethnic groups, including *Pierre et Djemila*, *Sauve-moi*, *Karnaval* (Thomas Vincent, 1999), *Welcome* (Phillipe Lioret, 2009), *Happy End* (Michael Haneke, 2017), *Vent du Nord* (Walid Mattar, 2017; a coproduction with Tunisia and Belgium), and the films that Bruno Dumont set and shot in his home region (*La Vie de Jésus*, *L'humanité*, *Flandres*, *Hadewijch*, *Hors Satan*, *Ma Loute*, as well as the TV miniseries *P'tit Quinquin* and *Coincoin et les z'inhumains*).

As far as this theme of migration is concerned, both *Pierre et Djemila* and *Sauve-moi* are set in Roubaix, which has the largest French Arab population in Nord-Pas-de-Calais, and both films use love stories to challenge racial stereotypes. The former is a modern, bicultural *Romeo and Juliet*, the latter revolves around the encounter between the French Arab Mehdi and the Romanian Agatha in the city's *parts moches*, its seedy parts. While both these films are structured around conventional

Figure 2.30. *L'Enfance nue* (Maurice Pialat, 1968).

Figure 2.31. *Les 400 coups* (François Truffaut, 1959).

heterosexual romances, other films take a more unconventional approach, like Carrière's *Rosine*, which revolves around the friendship between the fourteen-year-old title character and the French Maghreb Yasmina. The film ends on a slightly absurdist tracking shot of a marching band parading through the outskirts of a small industrial town alongside "a road that goes from Paris that goes to Calais," as the protagonist, in voice-over, situates the narrative in the film's opening sequence. And then there are, as stated, Dumont's northern French films, almost all of which involve

Figure 2.32. *L'Enfance nue*.

Figure 2.33. *Les 400 coups*.

self-consciously caricatural confrontations between "French-Catholic" and "French Arab Muslim" culture. These confrontations appear as side plots in *L'humanité* or in *P'tit Quinquin*, or center stage in *Hadewijch* (2009), in which the aspirant nun Céline *vel* Hadewijch (as Julie Sokolowski's character is named in the credits) joins a French Arab cell after she has been sent on leave from the monastery of Mont-des-Cats in French Flanders. Following her suicide attack in the Paris subway, she is miraculously saved by a simple yet sensitive northern French christ in a closing sequence that calls to mind the end of *L'humanité*, in which Pharaon also looks offscreen to the Lord present in his absence (fig. 2.34, cf. fig. 1.21).

As argued in relation to *L'humanité*'s treatment of its minor character of the French Algerian arrestee, I am somewhat critical of Dumont's engagement of the region's migrant population. While I see that the characters of Yassine and Nadir Chikh (Karl Sarafidis and Yassine Salime) in *Hadewijch* and that of Mohamed Bhiri (Baptiste Anquez) in *P'tit Quinquin* are, like the French Maghreb "dealer" in *L'humanité*, tongue-in-cheek and perhaps even mildly provocative caricatures, their plot lines are definitely less fleshed out than those of their ethnically northern French colleagues, as a result of which social caricature slips into cliché. This is different, for example, in Thomas Vincent's *Karnaval*, one of the highlights of northern French cinema and like *Rosetta* and *L'humanité* a film from 1999. *Karnaval* tells the story of the coincidental romance between Larbi (Amar Ben Abdallah) and Béa (Sylvie Testud) during the Carnival of Dunkirk. He is a French Arab youth who is tired of being exploited by his father; she works in a supermarket and is married. When they first meet, they kiss, but when he goes looking for her the next day, she says that "hier c'était Carnaval, c'était un baiser du Carnaval" (yesterday it was Carnival, it was a Carnival's kiss). *Karnaval* delights in the Carnival spectacle—in its songs, costumed participants, and papier-mâché street giants. At the same time, the film captures the exclusionary or even downright xenophobic sentiments that may accompany such strong regional community sense.

Figure 2.34. *Hadewijch* (Bruno Dumont, 2009).

While these tensions between ethnic-cultural groups are not significantly different from those found elsewhere in western Europe, in recent years the French North has also been the stage for a migration crisis that exceeds regional proportions, namely, the encampment near Calais of migrants from the Middle East and Africa who hope to cross the Channel (Pas-de-Calais). This encampment, informally named "The Jungle," originated in its first form in 1999 and by 2005 it housed over six thousand people living in shantytown conditions. The camp was raided by the police in October 2016, when some of the migrants were evacuated to other parts of France. The Calais encampment has been the subject of several films, both fiction and documentary, both online and offline. A first example is *Welcome* (2009) directed by Philippe Lioret, about a swimming coach who tries to help a young Iraqi-Kurd immigrant. The film is a critique of French immigration laws, including a law that makes it illegal to help illegal immigrants (*sans-papiers*). The Calais encampment also formed the inspiration for Michael Haneke's *Happy End* from 2017. The film takes place in Pas-de-Calais, but instead of portraying the encampment directly, it vivisects, in Haneke's trademark fashion, bourgeois indifference toward what is happening in their backyard at the crossroads of Europe. Finally, and as far as online films about the encampment are concerned, I consider *With Love from Calais* (2016) by the British Manjinder Virk the most interesting.[101] This short film integrates documentary with fiction and alternates interviews with the scripted story of a young British aid worker who doesn't want to return to the UK, both for humanitarian reasons and marriage problems back home. As she walks through the camp's burning remains, the camera, accompanied by strings that are a tad overdramatic, keeps an eye for poetry: a girl with a red balloon, a makeshift home with written on it the words "lieu de vie," and a giant tag "LONDON CALLING" (with someone, an actor or a "real" person, in lieu of the "I") (figs 2.35–2.38).

The Calais encampment, in combination with structural economic crisis and a decreased belief in the corruption-plagued Parti Socialiste, has provided fertile ground for the rise of xenophobic sentiments, that is to the extent that the electoral successes of Marine Le Pen's right-wing populist party National Front (FN) may be taken as an indicator of such sentiments. In 2015, the FN almost obtained control of Nord-Pas-de-Calais-Picardie, for decades a socialist stronghold. In 2017, during the first round of the French presidential elections Le Pen came out on top in the region, by then called Hauts-de-France, while in the second round she obtained almost one in two votes there, with Pas-de-Calais and Aisne (previously in Picardy) as the only two departments in France

Figures 2.35–2.38. *With Love from Calais* (Manjinder Virk, 2016).

where she beat Emmanuel Macron. During the campaign leading up to these presidential elections, there was the release of *Chez Nous / This Is Our Land*, a 2017 French-Belgian coproduction directed by the Walloon Lucas Belvaux and starring Émilie Dequenne (who gained fame as Rosetta), making the film a prime example of the Cinéma du Nord. In *Chez Nous*, Dequenne is Pauline Duhez, who works as a nurse in the imaginary town of Hénart in Pas-de-Calais. During house visits, she is confronted day in day out with social misery and with people's stories about the disappearance of social services, like the bus service to Lens that was discontinued a while ago. Then one day Pauline is approached by the local doctor, who is involved in the Rassemblement National Populaire, a right-wing populist party that promises a free and independent France "by and for the people." Would she be willing to represent the party in the upcoming municipal elections? Pauline hesitates. She thinks of her father, a former steel industry worker and above all a lifelong socialist. She also thinks of her patients, many of whom have a migration background. But ultimately she lets herself be convinced by party leader Agnès Dorgelle (Catherine Jacob), who is clearly modeled after Le Pen. The National Front was, as expected, not thrilled with *Chez Nous* and considered it, in the words of vice president Florian Philippot, "downright scandalous to, in the middle of the presidential elections, two months before the vote, release in French theaters a film that is clearly anti-FN."[102] In response, Belvaux stated that "this is not a militant film, but a committed film, a *film citoyen* made to provoke discussion," and that he wanted to denounce the manipulative strategy of the FN, a "discourse that does not correspond to what the party profoundly proposes."[103]

In its northern French campaigns, the FN has indeed toned down its xenophobia and instead placed emphasis on socioeconomic issues. The reason is that the French North, like Wallonia, is a region in which migrants have integrated into socioeconomic and cultural life for decades, and in which "traditional" northern French culture—itself a product of sedimented migrations—has opened up to migrant labor and culture for decades. In order to illustrate this shift in discourse by the FN, I cite a report by BBC journalist Henri Astier from the town of Hénin-Beaumont, Pas-de-Calais, which also formed the main inspiration for *Chez nous*. The town was captured by the FN earlier that year in the first round of the communal elections. Astier reports:

> To carry a left-wing mining town in a region ravaged by pit and factory closures, [elected mayor] Mr. Briois had to do more than beat the FN's traditional drum. He has soft-pedaled on ideology to emphasize practical support. . . . Making the FN brand appealing to Hénin-Beaumont voters has meant muting

the party's traditional anti-immigration message. Xenophobia, notes Octave Nitkowski, a prominent local blogger and author, does not sell well in a town built on wave after wave of foreign workers: "First there were Belgians, then Italians, Poles, and North Africans. There are no separate communities. Everyone has mixed blood," says Mr. Nitkowski—who himself has Polish, French and Arab ancestors. "That's why the front had to base its campaign on social issues."

Two months into the FN's rule, the town hardly feels hostile to migrants. In the central square, two halal butchers facing each other are doing brisk business. A headscarf-covered doll stares out of the window of an Islamic bookshop. Several residents of foreign origin appear to be well disposed toward Mr. Briois. "Whenever I've seen him he has treated me with respect and courtesy," an Algerian-born man says. "I won't turn my back on him now that he is mayor."

This does not mean that there is no racism in Hénin-Beaumont:

> For some the new, inclusive image presented by the FN is only a facade. Marie-Françoise Gonzalez, who runs a sandwich shop on the square, believes that although local FN have sanitized their language, they remain "fascist" at heart and their victory has encouraged prejudice among residents. "Racism is on the rise," she says, "I see it in my own shop. I hear things I haven't heard in 15 years! I am appalled."
>
> The problem for the local left is that it is bleeding voters and many are going over to the FN—not just in Hénin-Beaumont but across the region. A retired dentist from neighboring Billy-Montigny who describes himself as a lifelong socialist says he voted for FN for the first time. He is not alone. The National Front leader there—who, tellingly, is a former communist—doubled his score in six years.[104]

In Wallonia, in the meanwhile, the cultural and political climate has remained comparatively stable. The Parti Socialiste has remained relatively strong, even though as in France it has been plagued by scandals, which is part of the reason why in 2017, the party for the first time in thirty years remained excluded from the Walloon government coalition. In the meanwhile, and unlike the situation in northern France, right-wing populist parties (Démocratie Nationale, Wallonie d'Abord) have remained relatively marginal, despite Liège and Charleroi (alongside certain neighborhoods in Brussels) having been labeled as breeding grounds for Islamic extremism, a topic the Dardennes have brought center stage in *Le Jeune Ahmed* (whose protagonist calls to mind Rosetta). This difference between Wallonia and the French North in terms of their political tendencies is largely explained by the long-standing tension between Flanders and Wallonia, a tension that has come to dominate Belgian politics, and in which Walloons for long have been at the receiving end of xenophobic discourses promoted by the Flemish movement as they are currently channeled by the Vlaams Belang and the Nieuwe Vlaamse Alliantie (New Flemish Alliance).

This fact that Wallonia and the French North, despite their shared socioeconomic trajectory, are part of very different national contexts, also has manifested itself in the Cinéma du Nord. In many respects Walloon cinema and northern French cinema are two halves of a whole in terms of their engagement of crisis in the Nord. But they are also very different halves. Whereas Walloon cinema's regional rootedness is "pregnant of universality" and does not "succumb to the temptation of the painterliness of the local" (Polet), northern French cinema is much more regional*ist*, for two reasons. The first reason is that whereas a Walloon fiction feature cinema emerged organically out of its documentary roots, a tradition with which it has always retained strong ties, northern French fiction cinema has emerged relatively independently from the region's documentary traditions and—as I will argue in more detail in the next chapter—needs to be understood in the context of the partial decentralization of France and of French national cinema from the 1980s onward.[105] In other words, and to stay on the metaphor of rootedness, whereas Walloon cinema is a small old forest that has germinated over decades out of its seeds of misery, northern French cinema is of a more recently planted, state-coordinated nature, even though there are some really old trees in the northern French cinema, like Capellani's *Germinal*.

The other reason that explains the difference in text and texture between Walloon and northern French cinema is that whereas Wallonia is the southern, francophone half of an internally divided, predominantly bilingual Belgium, the French North, and in particular the former region of Nord-Pas-de-Calais, is only a small part in the very northwestern tip of a traditionally centralized French nation-state. As a result, Wallonia and the French North occupy very different places in their respective national discourses, a difference that is also felt on-screen. Many recent films set or partly set in Nord-Pas-de-Calais depict the region as one that is different from more southern parts of France, in terms of geography, climate, and culture. Dumont's films, for example, present the North as a space remote from Paris, from its authorities and its culture, while both *En avoir (ou pas)* (Laetitia Masson, 1995) and *Karnaval* stage oppositions between Nord-Pas-de-Calais and more southern parts of France. The former juxtaposes a cold and windy Boulogne-sur-Mer to a warmer and jazzier Lyon; the latter contrasts the rain of Dunkirk to the sun of Marseille. While some of these oppositions contain an essence of truth—it *is* colder in the French North than at the Côte d'Azur—they generally also hold a stereotypical, essentialist dimension. It is not even so much that these films depict the French North in an overly negative or positive fashion, as is the case in *Bienvenue chez les Ch'tis*; it is more that they present the region's landscapes, towns, and people in ways that make it seem those very landscapes, towns, and people give rise to narratives and situations, whether tragic or comic, that might as well as have been set elsewhere in France. In this respect, the rootedness of the northern French film is of a less dialectical and more caricatural nature than that of its Walloon counterpart. Like Walloon cinema, northern French cinema turns its region into a space of fairy tales and modern myths, but northern French cinema does not testify "to the fact that the true universal is always concrete," as Polet writes about Walloon cinema. Instead, northern French cinema tends to essentialize the particularity of its region. Especially Dumont proves that this essentialism does not have to be uninteresting or problematic per se. On the one hand, his films strongly rely on the particularity of the French North and its local actors. On the other hand, they ultimately dehistoricize the region by transforming it into a stage of struggle between a primordial, mute nature and an omni-signifying, secular-religious notion of humanity. Similarly, *Nord* (1991) by Xavier Beauvois uses the French North as the narrative site for a universal tragedy. The film tells the story of Bernard, acted by Beauvois himself, and the disintegration of his family. Had the film been titled differently, we could have interpreted this retelling of the Oedipus legend as one that merely *happens* to be set in the French North, but as a result of the film's title, Bernard's path to darkness is presented as one always already predestined by his northern French identity.

With this in mind we reach a provisional:

Conclusion

In sum, the Cinéma du Nord is a transnational, interregional cinema primarily defined by economic crisis. It's a storytelling cinema, and the story it tells is that of the Nord, including the fact that the Nord is cut through by the French-Belgian border. Sometimes this border appears explicitly, as in the *Germinal* adaptations and *Rien à déclarer*, or it manifests itself more implicitly, through the differences in how the shared reality of Wallonia and Nord-Pas-de-Calais has found expression in each of their regional cinemas. Both Walloon and northern French cinema display strong tendencies for socially critical and stylistically austere forms of realism, for a cinematic ethics and aesthetics that, while regionally rooted, also expresses an idea of human life that transcends its particular settings. This dialectic is felt at both sides of the border, with the note that the northern French cinema of the real, much more than its Walloon counterpart, is also a regional*ist* cinema that essentializes the French North's particularity, including its geographic location within the hexagon. This difference is explained by the conditions under which these regional cinemas developed over the course of the twentieth century. Whereas a distinctly Walloon cinema already began to emerge in the 1930s with *Borinage*, a truly regionally rooted northern French cinema did not take off until the late 1980s, even though the lineage of films that engage northern French socioeconomic reality goes back to the early decades of cinema. And whereas Walloon fiction cinema has always retained strong ties with its documentary origins, from its emergence in the 1960s with *Déjà s'envole la fleur maigre* and *Jeudi on chantera comme dimanche* to the present, in the French North the traffic between the region's fiction-feature auteur cinema and its documentary traditions has remained comparatively small.

Of Giants, Angels, and Humans

The Cinéma du Nord is a critical fairy tale, a fairy tale rooted in crisis, and as is the case in fairy tales the Cinéma du Nord contains creatures that tickle the imagination, like giants, both metaphorical ones, like the *terrils* emerging from the horizon, and real ones, as in *Karnaval* and *Quand la mer monte* (Yolande Moreau and Gilles Porte, 2004). The last film is named after a song by Raoul de Godewaersvelde, a popular singer from Lille, who five years after his suicide in 1977 was resurrected as a processional giant in his native streets. The phenomenon of the processional giant merits closer attention, because it is also found in Belgium, both in Wallonia and in Flanders, as well as in Belgian cinema, as for example in Storck's *Les Fêtes de Belgique* (1972), a documentary series about Carnival and folklore in Belgium. Made of wicker frames covered with papier-mâché and textiles, the giants can be up to nine meters (twenty-nine feet) in height and weigh up to 350 kilograms (770 pounds). They represent biblical figures, local heroes, or traditional professions such as "fisher," "miner," or "lace maker," and often they are related to each other through family ties. The giants are carried through the streets of places like Douai, Cassel, Mons, and Brussels at the occasion of local and regional holidays, including Carnival and street fairs. The ritual originated on the Iberian Peninsula and dates back to the late Middle Ages, when the humanlike and grotesque giant joined and at once represented the taming of the figure of the dragon, which first appeared in pagan rites in late twelfth- to early thirteenth-century Portugal. Whereas the dragon symbolized the negative pole of Manichaean thought, the human giant personified the strength of the city. As the French historian Henry de Lumley writes:

> Once conquered, [the dragon] . . . becomes a benevolent animal. Associated with the power of water, with sources, marshes, and rivers, the dragon is submitted to a patron saint or a local hero, who is often assimilated to Saint George, the dragon tamer par excellence. . . . Unlike the dragon, the human giant appears at the end of the fourteenth century to personify the survival of the city in the face of exterior and interior disorders. Symbolically, the citizens, aided by noble or ennobled giants, gained their independence through conquering sinister creatures emerging out of the sea, forests, or deserted land that threatened civilized life.[106]

Over the course of the sixteenth century and with the peak of the Spanish Empire, the ritual traveled to other parts of Europe, including the southern Catholic-minded provinces of the Low Countries (including Flanders, which at the time also incorporated the "burgraviates" of Lille and Douai, both in France now, as well as Tournai, now in Wallonia). In 2005, the UNESCO recognized the "Processional Giants and Dragons in Belgium and France" as one of the world's "masterpieces of the oral and intangible heritage of humanity."[107] The persistence of these and related traditions, like Carnival itself, is yet another aspect that the French North and the Belgian South have in common, and thus a further "proof" of the existence of the Nord as a border-crossing reality.

A concept of a region, the Nord is immanent to the practices, discourses, and conditions of existence shared by the people of the Belgian South and the French North. One encounters these shared realities in films made on both sides of the border, but whereas socioeconomic crisis is the theme that dominates most Walloon films, many films set and shot in the French North tend to portray the region primarily along cultural and geographical lines. To a large extent this difference can be attributed to the fact that, more than Walloon cinema, northern French cinema—from its social realism to its blockbusters—has a tendency toward genre films, especially toward lighter genres such as melodrama and tragicomedy. This difference is in turn largely explained by the fact that whereas Walloon cinema is part of a francophone regional cinema that operates as a small national cinema, northern French cinema is part of the colossus that is French national cinema. Elements of a regionalist, northern French essentialism are not restricted to the family film; we also encounter them in more heavy-handed productions such as *Nord* and *L'humanité*. The latter, as I have argued, turns the region's landscapes and towns into a stage for the struggle between the primordial forces of *la bête humaine* and a "humanity" seeking to contain and redeem those forces, like the giant taming the dragon. *L'humanité*, like *Rosetta*, thus employs a secular-Christian vocabulary in order to express a world in which life-shaping institutions, including the Church, have waned in power.

Rosetta and *L'humanité* are not alone in this secular-Christian strategy. Two other films that explicitly engage Christian heritage in northern French culture are *Rosine* (Christine Carrière, 1994) and *La Vie rêvée des anges / The Dreamlife of Angels* (1998), directed by Erick Zonca. Among the angels of Zonca's film is Isa (Élodie Bouchez), but is she *really* an angel? Isa is a twenty-something drifter washed ashore in Lille. She gets by working factory jobs and selling handmade postcards (figs. 2.39 and 2.40). She fails to save one life (that of her friend Marie), but she saves another (Sandrine). Is that enough in order for her to be considered an angel? More than human and less than divine, angels herald the event. They announce life, they guard life. Sometimes they fight, and sometimes, perhaps, they fail. But do they dream? If there were a God, Isa would have been an angel. However, as Rosine writes to the "country priest" in her resignation letter from the church choir: "je crois toujours pas en votre Dieu, parce qu'il n'est pas disponible. Il s'occupe pas de filles comme moi. . . . En attendant je fais chanteuse" (I still don't believe in your God, because he's not available. He doesn't look after girls like me. . . . In the meanwhile I become a singer). Rosine's dream is Isa's dream is Rosetta's dream. It's the dream of a "normal" life, not the good life, but a *better* life. It's a dream also shared by the female factory employees in the concluding tracking shot of *La Vie rêvée des anges*. The camera frames the women one by one, in close-up (fig. 2.41), pausing briefly on each of their faces, upon which it moves on again. The shot is telltale of the Cinéma du Nord. Like the close-up endings of *Rosetta* and *L'humanité*, or the shots of children in *Déjà s'envole la fleur maigre* and *Enfants du hasard*, it makes felt the presence of *these* people and *their* lives, while it expresses a belief in cinema's potential to give voice to "humanity" by investing the single shot with a simultaneously affective and conceptual power. It is a belief that ruptures, perhaps somewhat naively, with critiques of representation and realism as they have been

Figures 2.39–2.41. *La Vie rêvée des anges* (Erick Zonca, 1998).

raised since the 1960s onward, in cinema and in philosophy. As such, the Cinéma du Nord partakes in a broader wave of new realism in world cinema from the last quarter century. This new realism in the wake of modern critiques of representation and realism is the topic of chapter 4. Before that, I continue my analysis of the Cinéma du Nord, which is not only a cinema that engages crisis on-screen, but also an industry emerging from that same crisis.

3

Cinéma du Nord, a Euregional Cinema

Le cinéma belge, c'est bon pour l'économie! (Belgian cinema is good for the economy!)

—Alain Jennotte in the Walloon newspaper *Le Soir*

Tout en restant exigeants sur la qualité artistique des films, nous augmentons encore notre impact économique: les tournages soutenus par le CRRAV ont généré plus de 11 millions d'euros de dépenses en région. (While we remain demanding when it comes to the artistic quality of films, we are still increasing our economic impact: the shootings supported by the CRRAV have generated over 11 million euros of expenses in the region.)

—2010 report of the Centre Régional de Ressources Audiovisuelles of Nord-Pas-de-Calais

∽

IN ORDER TO FURTHER UNDERSTAND the coincidence of *Rosetta* and *L'humanité* at Cannes 1999, we need to stay seated for their final credits. From *Rosetta*'s closing titles (fig. 3.1) one learns that the film is a Belgian-French coproduction with as main partners Les Films du Fleuve (the production company Jean-Pierre Dardenne and Luc

Dardenne founded in 1996 in Liège, on the banks of the Meuse), the Radio Télévision Belge Francophone (RTBF, the public broadcasting organization of the French Community of Belgium), and ARP Sélection (a French production and distribution company). In addition, the film received financial support from the Centre du Cinéma et de l'Audiovisuel de la Communauté Française de Belgique (CCA, a public agency that promotes the production of films and other audiovisual media in the French Community of Belgium), the Télédistributeurs Wallons (a public organization that unites television distributors in Wallonia), the Walloon regional government (Sodedi[1]), the Belgian National Lottery, the French pay television channel Canal Plus, and the French Centre National de la Cinématographie (CNC, since 2009 the acronym of Centre National du Cinéma et de l'Image Animée).

I'm most interested here in the contribution *Rosetta* received from the Walloon regional government. In fact, the region committed itself to the film only *after* the Dardennes' triumph at Cannes. As Philippe Reynaert, one of the main promoters of Walloon cinema in the last two decades, explains:

> From the moment the Dardenne brothers obtained this Palme d'Or at Cannes, the majority of Walloon representatives wanted to jump onto the bandwagon. And the Dardennes had the courage to say: you didn't help us, you don't jump onto anything. And we arrived at the very surrealist situation, which is also a Belgian invention, that the Walloon region coproduced the film *Rosetta* after its Palme d'Or. It's one of the least risky investments we've ever made, because the film was finished. The only thing that remained to be done was to change the credits in order to list the Walloon region among the coproducers. At that moment we had a core to mobilize ourselves around, and to tell ourselves: let's strike while the iron is hot; this event will help us to gear up.[2]

Reynaert spoke these words during a conference that was held in 2001 in the northern French city of Valenciennes on the topic of regional cinematic infrastructures in France and francophone Belgium. At that conference Reynaert represented Wallimage, of which he has since been the president. Wallimage is an investment fund for the audiovisual industry created by the Walloon government earlier that year, less than two years after *Rosetta*. Wallimage finances individual film, television, and media productions, as well as audiovisual service companies in the region.[3] Wallimage is an economic rather than a cultural fund: The organization bases its investment decisions not, or at least not primarily, on the artistic merits of a film, but on its expected benefits for the region's economic development. Reynaert again:

> We try to create a fertile ground for producers in the region, by investing money in their films, or in the films of foreign producers. . . . And we ask these films' coproducers to spend one and a half times as much [in the region] than we invest ourselves. The regional expenses aren't a pure and strict matter of territorialization. We absolutely don't insist that the film is shot in Wallonia, where we do not have the variety of landscapes you are lucky to have in the French regions. We simply say: when we invest €200,000 in a film, we want €300,000 spent in the region, on the hiring of technicians and actors, on artistic rights, on a scenario, etc. Expenses we consider equally eligible include hotel and restaurant costs. . . . We have an entire range of eligible expenses.[4]

Reynaert contrasts the funding policy of Wallimage to that of its northern French equivalent, then called the Centre Régional de Ressources Audiovisuelles (CRRAV, since 2013 Pictanovo, also after Nord-Pas-de-

Figure 3.1. *Rosetta*.

Calais merged with Picardy).⁵ More than in Wallonia, the northern French funding policy is geared toward audiovisual projects that increase the region's transnational visibility, and that give a boost to its cultural and tourism sectors. Specifically, the CRRAV's 2001 funding guidelines stipulated that, to qualify for financial support, a film needs to be either produced by a company established or shot for at least "an important part" (50 percent) in the region.⁶

The CRRAV was one of the coorganizers of the roundtable conference in Valenciennes, which was the third in a series of four conferences on film production in the francophone-European world. (The other organizer was the Commission Nationale du Film France, a state funding portal agency for film producers interested in shooting in France.)⁷ In Valenciennes, the CRRAV was represented by its president Christian Vanneste and vice president Jean Cortois.⁸ As can be read in the conference's proceedings, the two men explained that Nord-Pas-de-Calais, like Wallonia, approaches its promotion of the audiovisual sector as part of a broader, mainly economic vision, with the goal to achieve a synthesis between culture and economy. The region's first objective is, so they stated, to stimulate the industrial infrastructure for film and television productions, while its second objective is to facilitate organizations that work on new audiovisual recording and distribution technologies. Here Vanneste and Cortois mention the region's creation of an *arc numérique*, or digital portal, for the stimulation of new forms of employment "in a region that has severely suffered from an industrialization based on a few heavy industries,"⁹ while they also refer to examples of individual films supported by the CRRAV, including *L'humanité*. Looking at the closing titles of Dumont's film, other than the CRRAV, *L'humanité* credits the coproducing partners 3B Productions (a small French production company), Arte France Cinéma (the production division of the French-German television network Arte), and, as participating partners, the CNC, the French Ministry of Culture, and Canal Plus (fig. 3.2).¹⁰

This cross-section of funding and production structures in Wallonia and Nord-Pas-de-Calais serves as an introduction to this chapter's perspective on the Cinéma du Nord. The chapter's guiding question is: "What explains the remarkable stream of cinematic productions that have emerged from Wallonia and the French North, especially since the early 1990s?" Whereas in chapter 2 I analyzed the Cinéma du Nord as a cultural movement, in this third chapter I discuss it as an infrastructure of film production. And whereas in the previous chapter I mainly discussed films as audiovisual texts, in the following pages films figure above all as the products of an inherently transnational industry.

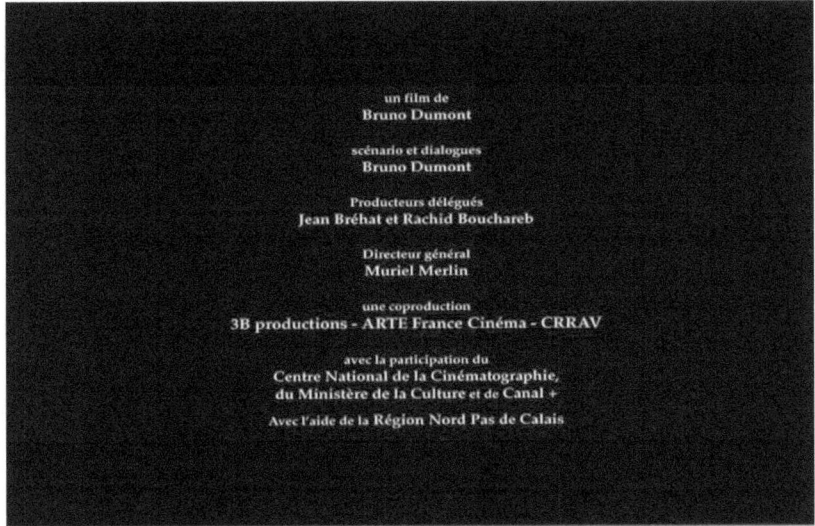

Figure 3.2. *L'humanité*.

Transnational Coproduction (the Example of *Route 181*)

In order to understand the Cinéma du Nord as an open network cinema at the crossroads of northwestern Europe, it is important to first consider the question, "What actually determines a film's nationality?" Generally speaking, film programs and databases list the country from which the majority of a film's funding originated first, the second country second, and so forth. However, as is explained on the website of the Lumière Database (a collaboration between the European Audiovisual Observatory and the European Union's MEDIA program) there actually exist "no widely accepted international or even European definitions of the criteria to be used to determine the country of origin of a film."[11] As a result, it sometimes happens that a film listing reports an international coproduction's countries of origins differently than the film's own credit sequence. For example, the Internet Movie Database (IMDb) lists *Rosetta* (according to its own credits a "Belgian-French coproduction") as a primarily French production,[12] while the Lumière Database lists *L'humanité* (a wholly French production according to its credits) as a French-Belgian coproduction.[13] It seems safe to state, though, that "BE/FR" and "FR" are *Rosetta*'s and *L'humanité*'s most accurate country-of-origin designations. That said, my discussion of these films as "Walloon" and "northern French," respectively, would not have been that much different had their production nationalities been slightly different. The reason is that production nationality is of course only one of the factors that determine the identity under which a film circulates in programming, journalistic, academic, and cinephilic discourses. Other determining factors are the nationality or nationalities of a film's director(s), screenwriter(s), and its cast, a film's narrative setting(s) and shooting location(s), and its language(s), including its visual language, because images are also culturally coded.

For example, film scholars have generally discussed *Route 181: Fragments of a Journey in Palestine-Israel* (2003) by Michel Khleifi and Eyal Sivan as a Palestinian film, because of Khleifi (a Palestinian who in 1970 moved from Israel to Belgium), and because of the film's subject matter. The film travels along the 1947 UN border between Palestine and Israel, documenting a series of encounters Khleifi and Sivan (who is from Israel) had with Palestinians and Israelis whose lives are marked by this border. While *Route 181* is undeniably Palestinian in its thematics and politics, the film is a Belgian-French-British-German coproduction. Surprisingly, however, in their contributions to *Dreams of a Nation: On Palestinian Cinema* (ed. Hamid Dabashi, 2006) neither Joseph Massad nor Bashir Abu-Manneh mention this fact, nor does the selected filmography of Palestinian cinema at the end of the edited collection.[14] This is not to say that *Dreams of a Nation* fully ignores Khleifi's Belgian connection. Khleifi himself briefly discusses the work he did for francophone-Belgian television in the late 1970s; in another essay, Omar Al-Qattan recalls his first encounters with Khleifi in the mid-1980s at the Institut National Supérieur des Arts du Spectacle (INSAS), the film and theater school in Brussels where Khleifi studied and subsequently taught; and both Al-Qattan and Hamid Naficy discuss the funding history of Khleifi's 1987 *Urs al-jalil / Noce en Galilée* (Wedding in Galilee, 1987), an Israeli-French-Belgian-Palestinian coproduction, and the first Palestinian feature that received major international acclaim (the film won the International Critics' Prize at the 1987 Cannes Film Festival).[15]

Khleifi's work is part of Palestinian cinema, but it is equally part of Belgian, and more specifically francophone-Belgian, cinema. Khleifi obtained Belgian nationality in 1980 and he has described himself as "a Palestinian Arab who was born in a Christian family, who grew up in Israel, and who lives in Belgium."[16] Khleifi's most Belgian film is his 1993 *L'Ordre du jour* (Order of the day, 1993, FR/BE/LU), an adaptation of the novel by the Belgian author Jean-Luc Outer and a parable of Belgian bureaucracy. It is therefore no surprise that Khleifi's name appears in almost all studies of Belgian cinema. For example, in *Ça tourne depuis cent ans: une histoire du cinéma francophone de Belgique* (1995), Emmanuel d'Autreppe describes *Noce en Galilée* as a film that "incarnates a big success of an ecumenical and cosmopolitan cinema;"[17] in 1993, a special magazine issued on the occasion of the twenty-fifth anniversary of the CCA film selection committee lists Khleifi as one of the filmmakers who have put Belgian-francophone cinema on the map, along with Chantal Akerman, Jean-Jacques Andrien, the Dardennes, and André Delvaux;[18] and in *La Kermesse héroïque du cinéma belge* (1999), Frédéric Sojcher observes in relation to Khleifi's first feature-length film *La Mémoire fertile / Fertile Memory* (1980, BE/NL/PS/DE) that the Palestinian-Belgian filmmaker "has an approach of reality that paradoxically brings him close to a Belgian documentary gaze, the 'documented point of view' he has learned at the INSAS and that derives in a straight line from Henri Storck."[19]

Both cinemas Khleifi belongs to are those of communities whose rights have been and continue to be contested, albeit of course with very different means and stakes. While Palestinian cinema is an exilic cinema of a nation without a nation-state, francophone-Belgian cinema is the cinema of the French Community of Belgium, which in 2011 changed its name to "the Wallonia-Brussels Federation" (a name change that, as stated in the previous chapter, has remained unacknowledged by both Flanders and the Belgian federal constitution). And what about the Cinéma du Nord? The Cinéma du Nord at once is and isn't a stateless cinema. The space and community it is rooted in and that it expresses—Wallonia "plus" Nord-Pas-de-Calais—does not really add up to a nation and therefore also not to a nation lacking and dreaming of a state. Instead, the Cinéma du Nord is immanent to a simultaneously material and imagined reality shared by two region states that exist across and despite the French-Belgian border that cuts through it.

Argument

This chapter is organized as follows: first I will examine the emergence of the regional cinemas of Nord-Pas-de-Calais and Wallonia within the contexts of French and francophone Belgian cinema, respectively. Next I will analyze the occasional collaborations between these two regional cinemas. Whereas northern French cinema has been a forerunner region in a traditionally very centralized national cinema, Walloon cinema is a substantial subset of a regional cinema that functions largely as a small national and inherently transnational cinema within an internally split Belgian cinema. This difference in structure between Walloon and northern French cinema creates an imbalance within the Cinéma du Nord, especially insofar as the production of fiction features is concerned. Whereas almost all Walloon fiction features, and francophone-Belgian features in general, are coproductions with France, most films set and shot in the French North are 100 percent French productions, this despite the fact that in recent decades Belgium has become France's main coproducing partner. The reason for this imbalance internal to the Cinéma du Nord is that "Paris" is not just the economic heart of French national cinema but of francophone cinema at large, including francophone-*Belgian* cinema, which over the decades has become partly assimilated by its big southern neighbor. In the context of this Parisian-centered force field, during the 1990s and into the new millennium Wallonia and the French North (and specifically Nord-Pas-de-Calais, before its merger with Picardy into Hauts-de-France) have developed into small yet significant centers of film production. This development has been spurred by the active and sporadically collaborative efforts of the Walloon and northern French governments to promote audiovisual production within their borders. Those efforts, in turn, have been part of these regions' broader, "European" endeavors to reinvent themselves economically and culturally after decades of recession. In sum, this chapter traces the emergence of the Cinéma du Nord as a cinema that at once expresses and is driven by the Nord's uneven socioeconomic transition. In doing so, the chapter continues the investigation started in chapter 2 of the Cinéma du Nord as a transnational regional cinema that short-circuits economy and culture, fiction and reality, history and dreams.

Terre d'Images:
Northern French Cinema within French National Cinema

Films have been made in and about the French North since the early twentieth century, but it is only relatively recently that one can speak of a northern French cinema that is also regionally produced. The main reason for this longtime nonexistence of a northern French film production industry is the proximity of Paris. As a case in point, when in the early 1930s the first northern French production company set up shop, it did so not in the North itself but in the French capital, from where it coordinated a handful of films (including two films about the Roubaix textile industry).[20] Two decades later, in 1950, RTF-Télé-Lille established the first professional TV studios in the region, which also gave a small boost to film production.[21] It would, however, not be until the second half of the 1980s, with the launch of the CRRAV and its regional fund for film and media productions, that northern French cinema began to emerge as a forerunner region within France's traditionally very centralized national cinema.

In order to understand the emergence of northern French cinema, it is necessary to look at some key chapters in the history of post–World War II French national cinema and, in particular, at the role of film funding in that history. In 1946, the French national government created the Centre National de la Cinématographie (CNC), an overseeing body for the French film industry that largely replaced the Vichyite Comité d'Organisation de l'Industrie Cinématographique (COIC). Initially attached to the Ministry of Information, the CNC was transferred in 1947 to the Ministry of Industry and Commerce, from where it was transferred on, in 1959, to the Ministry of Culture, which is its current home. In 1948, the CNC laid the basis for its Fonds de soutien, since 1959 named the Compte du soutien, by creating a system of *soutien automatique*. This "automatic support" was meant to create a counterweight to the tide of American imports and consisted of a subsidy that benefited the vast majority of French productions and coproductions. The system was financed through a levy on box office receipts of both French and non-French productions. The amount of support a film was to receive was prorated according to the box office sales of a producer's previous production. During the 1950s, when the subsidy ranged from 15 to 25 percent of a film's production costs, this redistribution measure was relatively effective in its goal to stimulate French film. But the system of automatic support had two main limitations. The first was that the pressure that higher ticket prices put on box office sales partly offset the subsidy. Second, the subsidy tended to favor established, risk-averse producers over younger, more experimental producers, while it excluded first-time producers altogether.[22]

In other words, this system of market regulation favored, above all, the Tradition de la Qualité and not so much the auteur film, to paraphrase François Truffaut's 1954 "A Certain Tendency of French Cinema," a diatribe against the established cinematic order. Together with fellow *Cahiers du cinéma* critics, including Eric Rohmer, Jacques Rivette, Jean-Luc Godard, and Claude Chabrol, Truffaut proclaimed a *politique des auteurs* according to which cinema is an art rather than a mere form of entertainment and directors artists rather than executive technicians. Supported by a general climate of burgeoning cinephilia, the *Cahiers* critics revolutionized the discourse around cinema. In 1957, the French parliament passed a law that recognized the moral copyright of authors to their creations. Two years later Truffaut's *Les 400 coups* was selected as France's submission to the Cannes film festival, only a year after he had been refused a press pass to that same festival. "We have won," as Godard triumphed in response, "by having created the acceptance for the principle that a film by Hitchcock, for example, is as important as a novel by Aragon. Thanks to us, film auteurs have once and for all entered the history of art."²³ In the same years that the *jeunes turcs*—as Bazin referred to his rookie colleagues—laid the basis for the Nouvelle Vague, the French national government developed its system of *aide sélective* (selective aid), a type of financing that is allocated on the basis of a project's artistic qualities. In 1953, the CNC started to experiment with a *prime à la qualité* (reward for quality) for short films. In 1955, due to pressure by the so-called Group des 30 (among whom were Alain Resnais and Alexandre Astruc) and the increasing success of French cinema at international festivals, the CNC also extended the *prime* to feature-length productions. As Resnais observed in the late 1950s, "thanks to the *prime à la qualité*" young talent started to make films.²⁴ But also already established filmmakers benefited from the system, like Robert Bresson, who received F50 million for *Un condamné à mort s'est échappé / A Man Escaped* (1956, FR).²⁵ In 1959, Minister of Culture André Malraux replaced the *prime* by the *avance sur recettes* (advance on receipts), a financing regulation for feature-length productions that exists until this day. This advance is an interest-free loan that is awarded to a filmmaker or producer for an artistically promising project. The loan must only be repaid insofar as a film's box office revenues permit. The *avance* regulation came at a strategic moment, because with the releases of *Hiroshima mon amour* (Resnais, FR/JP), *Les Cousins* (Claude Chabrol, FR), and *Les 400 coups* (for which Truffaut was chosen best director at Cannes), 1959 was also the year that the New Wave rose to full force. In subsequent years, the advance on receipts certainly helped to intensify the wave's momentum, though there are also many films associated with this movement and its immediate aftermath that were produced entirely on private funds. As Truffaut reassured Rohmer after he had been denied funding for *Ma nuit chez Maud* (1969, FR) (a moral tale in which Pascal's wager meets sexual temptation): "You can make it without the *avance sur recettes*. I'll take care of it. I ask some friends to put money into it."²⁶

The advance on receipts system needs to be understood in the context of France's politics of cultural exceptionalism. Charles de Gaulle inaugurated this doctrine in February 1959, four months after the foundation of the Fifth Republic, through the creation of a Ministry of Culture. At the head of this ministry was André Malraux. The men's vision on the role of culture in French society was patriotic and centralist inasmuch as it was modern and emancipatory, at least in its intentions. Distancing themselves from the elitist Beaux-Arts politics of the Fourth Republic, De Gaulle and Malraux favored a democratization of the access to *la culture française*, with an emphasis on the definite article. This French culture was above all a Parisian culture, and in order to disseminate that cultural word all over the hexagon, Malraux initiated a network of *maisons de la culture*, or culture houses. In his address of the National Assembly at the occasion of the inauguration of this initiative, Malraux clearly had no intention to hide his Parisian-centered vision. "There is only one democratic culture that counts, which means something very simple," he stated, "it means that it is necessary that through these *maisons de la culture* the things we are trying to make in Paris will spread to each French department, and that every sixteen-year-old, however poor, can have true contact with his or her national patrimony and with the glory of the spirit of humanity."[27] Cinema played a pivotal role in this mix of cultural patriotism and paternalism, for reasons of the medium's mass potential, and also because Malraux and De Gaulle, in their ambition to strengthen France's international prestige vis-à-vis the United States, found legitimatization in the New Wave discourse around auteurism. In turn, some filmmakers saw allies in the General and the author of *La Condition humaine* (1933). As Frédéric Depétris writes in his study *L'Etat et le cinéma en France* (2008):

> The universalist pretensions of the "auteur-filmmakers" of the New Wave [perceived] an echo, or a political "translation," in the positions and interventions of De Gaulle and Malraux. [The] wish to inscribe French cinema—which at that moment was seen as a minor mode of expression—into the history of art [occurred] through universalist self-positionings.[28]

According to Chabrol, for example, De Gaulle equated revival: "The General arrives, the Republic changes, France is reborn,"[29] and in a similar patriotic vein, Rohmer was of the opinion that "the most beautiful American films" awoke in him "the regret that France . . . [had] extinguished the torch of a certain idea of man in order for it to be lit again across the ocean, in short that France [had] to admit its defeat on a terrain of which it is the legitimate owner."[30]

Meanwhile, French cinema was sailing into turbulent waters. Following the postwar "golden age," between 1957 and 1969 annual box office entries plummeted from over 400 million tickets sold to less than 200 million, a decline that can be partly attributed to the rise of television.[31] In this same period, the production of feature-length films "*à l'initiative française*" (a category that includes both wholly French productions and international coproductions with a French majority share) dropped, from 142 in 1957 to eighty-six in 1967. This development yielded a discourse of crisis in which producers, distributors, and theater owners urged protective measures in order to safeguard a national cinema culture. In response, in 1967, the French government sharpened the eligibility criteria for the *soutien automatique* and from then on strictly earmarked its funds for films *à l'initiative française*.³² This protective measure was unable, however, to resuscitate investments in the French auteur film. Whereas in the early 1960s the advance on receipts made up almost half of the funds distributed by the CNC (both automatic and selective aid), in the 1970s this percentage dropped to less than 25 percent, an indication of the fact that France was leaving the production of films more and more up to the market.

In the 1980s and the early 1990s, culture again became the affair of the state it had been under Malraux and De Gaulle, as the conviction that "cinema and television [*l'audiovisuel*] are not commodities like others" firmly took root.³³ With that phrase France managed to rally other European countries for its position that, in order to prevent a further *cocacolonisation* of national cultures, film and television productions should remain excluded from the General Agreement on Tariffs and Trade (GATT). In 1993, this "culture war" even spilled over to the box office, when French politicians pitched Berri's *Germinal*—France's largest production to date—against *Jurassic Park*.³⁴ Though France lost this symbolic battle, it largely succeeded in the international political arena. In 1992, the Treaty of Maastricht confirmed the notion of cultural exception, while the GATT agreed to postpone the issue, which effectively meant that individual nation-states could continue to protect their cultural industries.³⁵

The main advocate of France's renewed politics of cultural exceptionalism was Jack Lang, minister of culture between 1981 and 1993 (with an interruption in the period 1986–1988) and a member of the Socialist Party like then president François Mitterrand.³⁶ During his two terms Lang implemented an interventionist politics that in some people's eyes came close to a nationalization of culture, starting with his 1981 initiative to raise the culture budget to 1 percent of the total national budget.³⁷ Lang's measures especially affected the film and television industries. He put in place an antitrust policy in order to dissolve the large Pathé-Gaumont group, granting more space to independent distributors and exhibitors. He stimulated the decentralization of distribution and exhibition structures, by creating a special aid fund, as well as the Agence pour le Développement Régional du Cinéma (ADRC). And, along the same decentralizing lines, Lang transformed the *maisons de la culture* from the "modern cathedrals" that Malraux had envisioned them as into culturally diverse and popular *centres culturels* and *centres de recherche et d'action culturelle* (centers for cultural research and activity).³⁸ Lang's reforms equally transformed film funding. As Susan Hayward writes, "Lang had 'a certain idea' of French cinema; . . . he believed fervently that it was the State's responsibility to facilitate the filmmakers' task."[39] Above all, Lang's goal was to increase the audience numbers for French film. He doubled the *avance* budget and, to stimulate new talent, he split the CNC's selection committee into one division for projects by established filmmakers and another division for first and second films.[40] He also created a tax shelter in order to encourage private investments[41] as well as a financing mechanism directed at big-budget productions, this as a counterweight to US blockbusters.[42] And he installed an export aid for French films that had proven themselves either at national box offices or at the main international festivals.

Lang initiated, moreover, several measures that intervened in the relation between the television and film industries. Starting in the early 1980s, France began to deregulate its television market. In 1984, the subscription channel Canal Plus started its operations, followed shortly by the free private channels La Cinq and TV6. In 1987, the French government privatized TF1, leaving Antenne 2 and France Régions 3 as the only public channels. At the same time, the state kept exerting its influence on French television, and in fact, as Depétris writes, was "never as interventionist as during [this] period of privatization."[43] As far as television's interface with cinema was concerned, new laws bound all channels to quota for French film and television productions, and in 1986, after he had already made television funding a CNC responsibility, Lang created a *taxe audiovisuelle*, which obligated TV channels to contribute around 5.5 percent of their annual revenues to the CNC's *compte de soutien*. As a result, television's contribution to this account increased from 8 percent in 1985 to 53 percent in 1989.[44] Finally, in 1991 the Assemblée Nationale voted in favor of a law that mandates TV channels to invest at least 3 percent of their annual revenues in film productions.[45]

Initially, Lang's measures seemed to turn the tide. Audience figures stabilized and French cinema saw the birth of a new movement of spectacular, high-production-value films that became known as the *cinéma du look*, examples of which are *Diva* (FR/US) from 1981 by Jean-Jacques Beineix and Luc Besson's 1985 *Subway* (FR). Following this brief upheaval, however, French cinema returned to its state of crisis. Despite the new abundance of funds, the number of French films produced and coproduced dropped to 1960s levels—from 208 in 1981 to eighty-nine in 1994—a paradox that is largely explained by the tendency of private investors and television channels to concentrate on a small number of high-profile productions. In this same period, audience numbers resumed their free fall as well, especially audience numbers for domestic productions: from ninety-five million in 1981 to thirty-five million in 1994 (including audience numbers for international coproductions in which France had a majority share). In 1991, French productions only had a 28 percent domestic market share (compared to 50 percent in 1981), while the market share of American productions had risen to 61 percent (compared to 35 percent in 1981).[46]

At this moment that the culture war seemed lost, France's strategy of controlled deregulation of its cinema and other audiovisual industries started to bear fruit, at least in quantitative terms. Even though the presence of American films on French screens has remained strong, more than half of the increase in audience numbers between 1994 (124 million) and the mid-2010s (around 200–210 million) can be attributed to French productions and coproductions. During this same period, the annual production of films *à l'initiative française* more than doubled, from eighty-nine to over two hundred. Especially remarkable in this context is the large share of films by first-time filmmakers. As chart 3.1 illustrates, from the early 1990s onward, first films have made up well over a third of the annual output of feature-length productions. But as the same figure also demonstrates, life is precarious in French cinema, because about half of the filmmakers who secure the funds for a first feature-length film never make a second one. In the words of Michel Marie, there exists "a

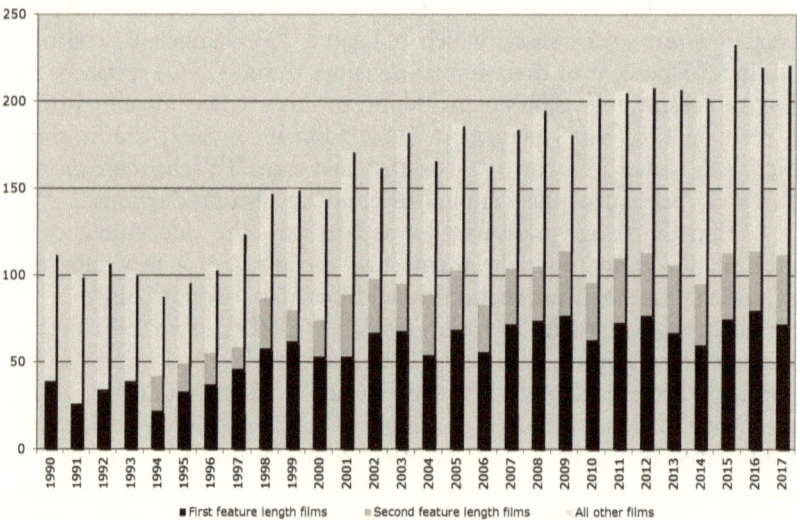

Chart 3.1. Annual production of the first and second feature-length French initiative films (1990–2017; no data available for second films between 1990 and 1993). *Source:* Annual CNC reports 2012 and 2018.

privilege to youth and to the 'first time' [in French cinema], and it is certainly not easy to become old in [it]."⁴⁷ The reasons for this state of affairs have been addressed convincingly by the Club des 13, initiated by Pascale Ferran. In their 2008 manifesto, titled *Le Milieu n'est plus un pont mais une faille* (The center is no longer a bridge but a fault), this collective signals an overproduction in French national cinema, while, in their view, the average quality of French productions has declined. The group shows itself particularly concerned about the "bipolarization" of French cinema: the increasing split of the country's cinematic output into big-budget productions (over €10 million) and small-budget productions (€800,000 to €3 million), while "films dits 'du milieu'" (mid-range films), "nonetheless the life of cinema and its renovation," are under threat.⁴⁸

This renewed discourse of crisis contrasts sharply with the jubilant embrace that many French critics had given the flood of first films in the early 1990s. *Cahiers du cinéma* exclaimed in 1993 that "the new cinema has arrived," baptizing this "new New Wave" as the "jeune cinéma." The *Cahiers* critics emphasized, though, that "not every first or second film is *jeune cinéma*," but that the latter directly emanates from a "country that is spontaneously inhabited" by filmmakers whose work displays the "sort of immediate affinity between the decisive moment that one throws oneself into the water in order for the film to exist and the prolonged adolescence of a group or an individual in the state of apprenticeship."⁴⁹ The essay mentions the examples of Arnaud Desplechin, Laurence Ferreira Barbosa, Cedric Kahn, and Patricia Mazuy. In subsequent years, some other filmmakers who have been associated with the revival of the French auteur film include Olivier Assayas, Jacques Audiard (also part of the Group des 13), Xavier Beauvois, Christine Carrière, Pascale Ferran, Jean Pierre Jeunet, Matthieu Kassovitz, Gaspard Noé, François Ozon, Sandrine Veysset, Christian Vincent, and Bruno Dumont.⁵⁰ Most of these filmmakers were born around the beginning of the New Wave, and all of them have worked and continue to work in that movement's auteurist legacy. Beyond those facts, though, it is difficult to pin down what exactly unites these filmmakers. For some this has been reason to question the label *jeune cinéma* altogether. For example, in her essay "Was There a Young French Cinema?" (2015), Jacqueline Nacache writes that "all attempts to define the young French cinema run up against [the] impossibility" of mapping contemporary French cinema,⁵¹ while Will Higbee even calls it a "catch-all term" that displays "a fetishistic approach to 'youth' . . . and an excessive reverence for the myths and the legacies of the nouvelle vague."⁵² I partly agree, though I would also argue that, starting in the early 1990s, there have been several tendencies in French cinema that exceed a nostalgia for a New Wave that will never be again. At the beginning of the next chapter I will return extensively to these tendencies; here I will highlight two of them: the influence of television on French cinema and the increased integration of the regions in French cinema.

To start with the former: as Higbee observes, the *jeune cinéma* is also a *jeune ciné-télé*.[53] From the late 1980s onward, French cinema has become increasingly dependent on funds from terrestrial television stations. In the second half of the 1980s, as the result of the audiovisual tax pushed for by Lang, the financial share of television companies in the *Compte de Soutien* rose from 8 to over 50 percent. By the early 2000s, the vast majority of French films was cofunded by television, even though in nominal terms the funding stream from television to cinema remained minimal[54] (a paradox that is explained by the regulation that when a French TV channel coproduces a film, it gains the right to broadcast that film two instead of the regular three years following its theatrical release[55]). Inevitably, this presence of television in French cinema has affected the types of films produced. As Hayward argues, "many films . . . are overdetermined in favor of televisual rather than cinematographic practices. Thus considerations of pacing, soundtrack and narrative are patterned around the exigencies of broadcasting rather than screening. . . . Obviously, this progressive normalization of the product for the small screen leads to a hegemonic style that has little to do with cinematic writing."[56]

But television has also given creative impulses to French cinema. Think here especially of the French-German network ARTE (Association Relative à la Télévision Européenne). Whereas Canal Plus's commitment to a diverse French cinema is primarily driven by the legal stipulations regulating its commercial imperative, for ARTE this support is integral to its more general mission of diffusing culture and the arts. Founded in 1992, this network has made a crucial contribution to the emergence of the young French cinema, both through its production arm La Sept Cinéma and its programming policy. In 1994, ARTE produced and broadcast nine TV films of about an hour each as part of the series *Tous les garçons et les filles de leur âge / All the Boys and Girls of Their Age*, a landmark event in the rejuvenation of French auteur cinema in the 1990s. *Tous les garçons et les filles* presents a youthful perspective on contemporary France. ARTE commissioned the series of films from a combination of established and new auteurs, including Claire Denis, Olivier Assayas, Patricia Mazuy, André Téchiné, Cédric Kahn, and Chantal Akerman. Most of these films also had a longer feature-length theatrical version. For example, Assayas's *La Page blanche* formed the basis for his *L'Eau froide* (1994, FR). Following the series, ARTE has coproduced films such as *Beau travail* (Claire Denis,

1999, FR) and *Ressources humaines* (Laurent Cantet, 1999, FR/UK), both of which premiered on TV. In 2000, ARTE made a new series of six TV films under the title *Gauche/droite* (*Left/Right*), which includes Zonca's *Le Petit voleur* (The little thief, FR) and Cabrera's *Nadia et les hippopotames* (FR). Both films only had a very limited theatrical run, but especially the latter is a much-cited example of the return of politics in French auteur cinema.

The second tendency characteristic of the *jeune cinéma* I want to emphasize here is the increased role and visibility of the French regions. This development started in the late 1990s, when several "regional" directors broke through in Cannes. As Thomas Bauder writes in *Le Jeune cinéma français* (ed. Michel Marie, 1998):

> Without debate, 1997 was the year that witnessed . . . the emergence of a cinema deliberately anchored in the regions: Robert Guédiguian finally acclaimed in Marseille and in Cannes thanks to his social story from the town of Estaque [a fishing village near Marseille]; Manuel Poirier hailed on the Croisette with his tribulations of a Spaniard and an Italian Russian in the Bigouden region [in Bretagne]; and finally, Bruno Dumont, giant of the North, newly arrived at the Riviera, descending straight from the hills of Flanders with his *Vie de Jésus*. That is how it goes with the topography of French cinema, expanding to the South, to the West, to the North.[57]

This partial decentralization of French national cinema has to be understood in the context of the partial decentralization of the country's administrative structures. Since 1982, the French regions have held a significant degree of autonomy on the terrains of infrastructure, education, and culture. This has also allowed the regions to develop their own cinema and television politics. Even though the vast share of public and private funds available for films *à l'initiative française* has continued to be administrated by institutions located in Paris and the Ile-de-France region, by the late 2000s all of France's twenty-two metropolitan regions (and three of its five overseas regions) dedicated a part of their budget to cinema and television. Moreover, all regions but two (Champagne and Picardy, which until the creation of Hauts-de-France incidentally were the regions bordering Nord-Pas-de-Calais) coproduced or sponsored at least one feature-length production. The highest-spending regions have been, unsurprisingly, Ile-de-France and Rhône-Alpes (the capital of which is Lyon, France's second-largest metropolitan area). Perhaps more surprisingly, the region that throughout most of the 1990s and 2000s ranked third in terms of its financial support for cinema and television was Nord-Pas-de-Calais.[58]

Nord-Pas-de-Calais was among the first French regions that introduced an audiovisual funding policy. In the first years of Lang's period as minister of culture, the region became part of a pilot project in which the ministry, via the CNC, financially supported the emergence of production companies in the French regions. In 1985, this resulted in the creation of the Centre Régional de Production Cinématographique et Audiovisuel (CRPCA), which became known as Cercle Bleu, in Villeneuve d'Asq near Lille (where the founding president Michel Vermoesen ran a *salle art et essai*). In its first five years, Cercle Bleu had the legal entity of an *association* (nonprofit organization) and received subsidies from both the CNC and the Conseil Régional du Nord-Pas-de-Calais. In 1990, the association was dissolved and replaced by a private structure, after which, between 1993 and 2003, the company's ownership was largely transferred to *La Voix du Nord*, the regional newspaper of Nord-Pas-de-Calais.[59] In that same year, in 1985, also the CRRAV commenced operations. In 1990, the CRRAV launched a regional aid fund for film and television productions. Among the first productions supported by this fund was Berri's 1993 *Germinal*. Instead of shooting his film in a cheaper, eastern European location, Berri wanted to make it in the French North itself. The Conseil Régional recognized the economic opportunities for its unemployment-stricken region, and then president of the council, Marie Christine Blandin, pushed for an extraordinary F10 million (US$1.8 million) in *avance sur recettes* for Berri's film.[60] The investment turned profitable. Not only did the film's box office success allow for the restitution of the loan, *Germinal* also generated around F40 million of expenses in the region and many temporary jobs (though it should be noted that the extras were paid only F200—about US$35—per day).[61]

Following *Germinal*, the CRRAV developed into a significant nonexecutive, minority coproducer that became a model for other regional funding structures. In 2011, the CRRAV operated on a budget of about €5 million, almost €3 million of which went to seventy-eight individual productions, including fiction features, shorts, animated films, documentaries, TV dramas, and art videos.[62] Other than *Germinal*, *Bienvenu chez les Ch'tis*, *La Vie rêvée des anges*, *Quand la mer monte*, and almost all Dumont's films, some examples of films coproduced by the CRRAV (which since 2013 is called Pictanovo) that have drawn national and international attention are: *Ça commence aujourd'hui* (Bertrand Tavernier, 1999, FR), *Joyeux Noël* (Christian Carion, 2005, FR/BE et al.), *Le Scaphandre et le papillon / The*

Diving Bell and the Butterfly (Julian Schnabel, 2007, FR/US), *Un conte de Noël / A Christmas Tale* (Arnaud Desplechin, 2008, FR), *Welcome* (Philippe Lioret, 2009, FR), *La Vie d'Adèle / Blue Is the Warmest Color* (Adbellatif Kechiche, FR/BE/SP, 2013), *La Tête haute / Standing Tall* (Emmanuelle Bercot, 2015, FR), and *Happy End* (Michael Haneke, 2017, FR/AT/DE). Many of these films are by filmmakers from, or who identify as from, the region, including Dumont, Desplechin, Baily, and Carrière. Others are by filmmakers from elsewhere in France (Berri, Zonca), or from other countries (Schnabel, Haneke), in particular Belgium (Masset-Depasse, Moreau). The cinema of Nord-Pas-de-Calais is thus not only a regionally rooted cinema, it is also a *cinéma d'accueil*, an open crossroads cinema fertilized by the funds and facilities available in the region, which is a characterization that holds true for the Cinéma du Nord in general. Had it not been for the CRRAV, films such as *Entre ses mains* (Anne Fontaine, 2005, FR/BE) and *La Vie rêvée des anges* (Zonca, 1999, FR) would have likely been shot and set elsewhere in France. As Granval points out in relation to these two films, which both have narratives that now seem anchored in the region: while Fontaine, before she got involved with the CRRAV, just had the idea to situate her film's narrative "in the provinces," Zonca "didn't know Lille before filming there." "For [Zonca] the subject of his film [was] universal. He could have shot it anywhere."[63]

The CRRAV coproduction that has probably attracted the most international attention, both acclaim and controversy, is *La Vie d'Adèle* directed by Kechiche, which is the second Palme d'Or winner shot in the region, after Pialat's *Sous le soleil de Satan*. Shot in Lille, Roubaix, and also Brussels, *La Vie d'Adèle* is an adaptation of Julie Maroh's graphic novel *Le Bleu est une couleur chaude* (2010), a story of lesbian love that also takes places in the French North. I would argue, however, that the film fails to do justice to the original, in the first place because Kechiche was accused of "moral harassment" by the lead actresses (Léa Seydoux and Adèle Exarchopoulos) and other crew members,[64] and second because of the film's male gaze that imposes itself onto the queer romance. On a side note, this gaze could not be more different from the queered voyeuristic gaze found in the gay cruising thriller *L'Inconnu du lac* (Alain Guiraudic, FR), which that same year in Cannes won the Queer Palm.

In conclusion to this section: to a large extent northern French cinema results from the region's desire to manifest itself as a *terre d'images*, a country of images, as was the CRRAV's slogan until its 2013 merger with the *Pôle Image* into Pictanovo, which also calls itself "the Lille Region Image Community."[65] Not all of these images cast the region in a favorable light. As former CRRAV president Christian Lamarche stated in 1999 about the region's 112,000 euro support[66] for *L'humanité*: "We don't focus so much on anti-miserabilist shorts nor on tourism leaflets, but on art works.... Together we debated whether we should endorse *L'humanité*.... The region decided that it was a great film."[67]

Yes We Cannes: Francophone-Belgian Cinema in Its Walloon Manifestation

It was a great film. Such was, as we have seen, also the Walloon government's response to *Rosetta*, though only retroactively. *Rosetta* is a Walloon film and the Dardennes are among the flag-bearers of a regionally rooted Walloon cinema, there is no doubt about that. Interestingly, though, the brothers also appear in several recent studies of *French* national cinema.[68] The borders between French and francophone-Belgian cinema are indeed porous, and many of the Dardennes' films are coproductions with France, which somewhat justifies this French appropriation of the two-time Palme d'Or winners. Most of these studies, however, pay little to no attention to the specificities of film production in Belgium. Moreover, the reverse situation (i.e., a book on Belgian cinema that discusses a French-Belgian coproduction *à la majorité française* by a French director and with a strictly French cast) would simply be odd. The reason for this imbalance is, of course, that Belgian cinema is French cinema's small neighbor. What is Belgian cinema? Does it exist in the first place? Many studies of Belgian cinema open with such questions, as for example *Ça tourne depuis cent ans: une histoire du cinéma francophone de Belgique* (1995), edited by Philippe Dubois and Edouard Arnoldy. Dubois and Arnoldy start their introduction with the anecdote of a 1990 exhibition about Belgian art in the Musée d'Art Moderne de la Ville de Paris. This exhibition also included a section on cinema, curated by Dominique Païni, then president of the Cinémathèque Française, who concluded his opening speech with the words: "Le cinéma belge, ça existe; je l'ai rencontré" (Belgian cinema exists: I have encountered it). Dubois and Arnoldy take Païni's statement as symptomatic for what they call the "mirror stage" in which Belgian cinema still found itself in the early 1990s, as at that time Belgian cinema was, so they argue, still in need of affirmation, in particular by its French mother. They write:

> Not only does [Païni's statement] express the functioning of an external gaze (French, moreover, but that's alright) on our cinema (really? it exists? surprising!), but fundamentally it also testifies to certain realities of the gaze Belgian cinema casts upon its own cinematographic identity: its timidity ..., its embarrassment ..., its discomfort, ..., its insecurities ...,

its flotations. . . . Are we sure of this existence? Why do we doubt it? Is it the "cinema" or the "Belgian" that poses the problem?[69]

With this last sentence Dubois and Arnoldy hint of course at the long-standing tensions between francophone Belgium, in particular Wallonia, on the one hand, and Flanders and the Flemish community, on the other.[70] Inevitably, the Flemish-francophone divide has left its traces in Belgian cinema, which over the decades has largely been split into a Flemish and a francophone cinema, while within francophone-Belgian cinema one can further identify a distinctly Walloon cinema, or in the words of Jacques Polet, a "Belgian francophone cinema in its Walloon manifestation."[71] More than a quarter century after the exhibition in Paris, and at a moment in which Belgium is one of the best-represented countries in the international film festival circuit, this internal split remains the reason that some critics continue to call into question the existence of Belgian cinema. In a special dossier from 2009 on the "new Belgian cinema" that was published in the French film magazine *Positif*, Yolande Moreau (*Quand la mer monte*) observes, for example, that "Belgian cinema" only exists insofar as "there is a Flemish cinema and a Walloon cinema."[72] Amd about a decade later, almost all theatrical screenings of Belgian films are preceded by a leader that brands the film either as *made in* Flanders or the self-declared Wallonie Brussels Federation (fig. 3.3), thus affirming Belgian cinema's divided nature film after film.

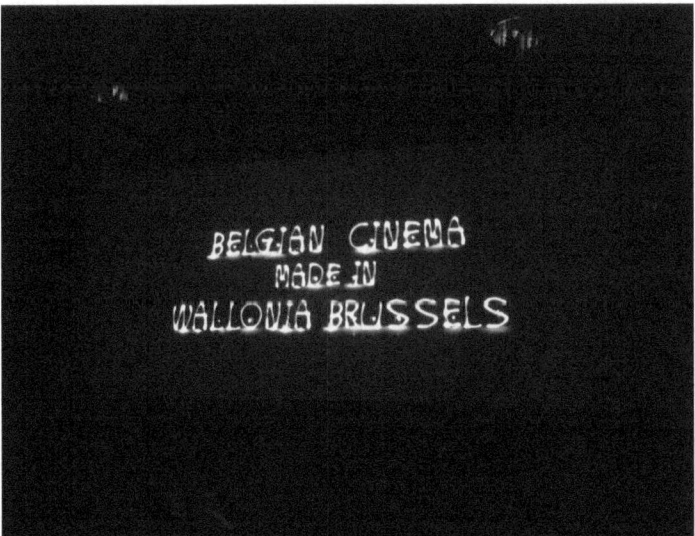

Figure 3.3. Leader preceding francophone-Belgian films (author's photo).

A good place to start examining this national Belgian cinema that often does not appear as a single cinema is the 1952 royal decree that inaugurated the first Belgian program of government funding for cinematic productions. As Frédéric Sojcher writes in his three-tome *La Kermesse héroïque du cinéma belge* (1999), this "first and last effort of the [Belgian] state to create and develop a *national* cinema" came at a moment when "Belgium's unitary flame still sparkled with all its force."[73] This program, administered by the Ministry of Economic Affairs, was inspired by the French system of automatic aid and consisted of a bonus scheme for Belgian producers of features, shorts, and newsreels. Five years later, the Belgian government created a selection committee in charge of subsidies to productions based on subjective quality criteria. This selection process remained very rudimentary, however, and in reality the majority of Belgian productions continued to be eligible for government support. Specifically, the 1952 decree stated that a Belgian feature was good for a subvention of 13 percent of its gross box office sales following the first five years after its release, "as long as [the government's] budgetary limits permitted." For shorts and newsreels the percentages were 5 percent (for three years) and 3 percent, respectively. A 1957 law slightly altered the decree in order to prevent hastily produced shorts attached to successful, foreign features from guzzling the budget. From then on the subvention accorded to a short could not exceed its production costs.[74]

In order to understand why this subvention program failed in its mission to create a unified Belgian cinema, it is necessary to give a brief overview of Belgian cinema in the half century that preceded the royal decree. In the first decades of the twentieth century Belgium hardly saw any structural investments, whether public or private, in a national film industry.[75] As Dubois writes, in these decades "the steel industry and the colonial expansion [had] all priority and no-one [wanted] to really invest in cinema."[76] As a result, in the silent era, and continuing in the first decades of the talkie, foreign and in particular American and French productions dominated the Belgian market, while those Belgians interested in a film career left for Paris. Among the most celebrated members of this Belgian connection in Paris were the screenwriters Albert Valentin and Charles Spaak, who cowrote Jean Renoir's *La Grande illusion / The Great Illusion* (1937, FR), and the director Jacques Feyder, who gained fame with *La Kermesse héroïque / Carnival in Flanders* (1935, FR/DE). Based on a screenplay by Spaak and full of references to Flemish painting, *Kermesse héroïque* tells the story of a small town in Flanders under Spanish occupation. Despite the film being a French-German coproduction entirely shot in French studios, Feyder's meticulously crafted period piece is his most Belgian film and the first Belgian auteur feature avant la lettre (the film also had a German version, *Die Klugen Frau*, which was much to the liking of Joseph Goebbels).[77] In the early 1930s, Belgian cinema entered its so-called "heroic period," an era that lasted for roughly thirty years and that was characterized by three main tendencies. The first was that of a popular cinema without much artistic pretensions (e.g., the comedies of Gaston Schoukens, which made fun of the Brussels accent). Second, Belgian cinema saw the emergence of a small *cinéma d'essai* (e.g., Edmond Bernhard's 1957 *Waterloo*, Paul Haesaerts's visual essays on Picasso). Third and above all, these years were marked by the burgeoning of Belgium's acclaimed documentary tradition, which, other than Storck, had a main pioneer in Charles Dekeukeleire, who especially for his early films (*Impatience* [1928], *Visions de Lourdes* [1932]) found inspiration in French avant-garde filmmaking.[78] Storck and Dekeukeleire made many of their films on public funds. Even though the Belgian government did not actively promote a national film industry in this era, it did support pedagogical and tourist films through its Commisariat au Tourisme, which started to commission films in the mid-1930s, mainly from already established filmmakers. As Sojcher writes, "the goal was always to distribute a 'postal card' image of folklore and national landscapes. It was up to the filmmaker to find a way to transform the commissioned project into a cinematographic mise-en-scène worthy of its name."[79]

In addition, the Belgian government commissioned films through its Fonds Colonial de Propagande Economique et Social, which was the driving force behind Belgian colonial cinema (e.g., André Cauvin's *Bongolo* from 1952, as well as several productions Dekeukeleire and Storck participated in). Finally, in the middle of these thirty "heroic" years, there was the Film Guild, which controlled the production, distribution, and exhibition of films during World War II, this in collaboration with the German occupying authorities. Among the most prominent members of this guild was Storck, who became president of the production section in September 1943. A year earlier, Storck had started working on his five-part *Boerensymphonie / Farmer's Symphony* (1942–1944), a eulogy on rural Belgium cofinanced by the National Corporation of Agriculture and Alimentation, an institute created in 1940 by Flemish nationalists. While it would maybe go too far to call Storck a collaborator, I agree with Sojcher that it is difficult to unite the image of Storck as the father of Walloon cinema and the Marxist militant of *Misère au Borinage* with that of the opportunist who showed himself willing to make films at all costs.[80]

In 1947, spurred by the continued lack of interest on the part of the Belgian state to foster a national film industry, the Belgian filmmaking community united itself into the Comité National des Travailleurs du Film (National Committee for Film Workers). Vice president of this committee was, again, Henri Storck. In a publication titled *Cinéma belge, où en es-tu?* (Belgian cinema, where are you at?) Storck wrote the following about the virtual absence of a Belgian cinema: "Our country is the victim of the exiguity of its domestic market. . . . Only the State is able to oppose the protective measures that foreign producers benefit from in their home countries with similar measures to the benefit of Belgians."[81]

Under the pressure of this committee the Belgian government launched, in 1952, its bonus scheme. While this regulation meant a paradigm shift in the history of Belgian cinema, it failed, however, in its objective to create a national Belgian film industry. The allocated budget proved much too small, and, more fundamentally, in a small country automatic aid is much less effective than in countries with large domestic markets such as France and Italy. As the Belgian producer and cinema economist Jean-Claude Batz analyzes: "In the case of a small country, too small even to effectively set up a quota protection system, the automaticity of aid, through lack of the necessary support (the market), constitutes the most illusory, the most deceiving of solutions."[82] Batz spoke these words in 1963 at the Free University of Brussels, during a colloquium he had organized on the problems of film production in Belgium. This colloquium came at a strategic moment, for a number of reasons. First, a year earlier, the INSAS film school had opened its doors in Brussels;[83] second, following their creation in 1953 the public broadcasting organizations Radio Télévision Belgique (RTB) and Belgische Radio- en Televisieomroep (BRT) had proven themselves as important platforms for Belgian filmmakers; and third, in the early 1960s, Belgian cinema had garnered some international acclaim for the features *Déjà s'envole la fleur maigre* and *Meeuwen Sterven in de Haven / Seagulls Die in the Harbor* (Rik Kuypers, Ivo Michiels, and Roland Verhavert, 1955), the first Belgian film officially selected for the Cannes Film Festival.[84] In the report that came out of the Brussels colloquium Batz writes: "the point is not to 'help' cinematographic production [in Belgium]—which is practically nonexistent—but to create it."[85]

The Belgian government did indeed honor this call for state intervention in Belgian cinema, though in a very different way than Batz had envisioned. Even though Batz's report breathed a Belgian unitary spirit, it implicitly favored international, and in particular Belgian-French, coproductions, which was a concern for the Flemish minister of culture, Renaat van Elslande. Here it is important to know that since 1961 Belgium has had separate Flemish and francophone ministers of culture. Initially both ministers operated from within a single Ministry of National Education,[86] but in 1964 Van Elslande successfully pushed for the creation of a Selection Committee that administered a system of selective aid for Flemish-language films.[87] Following the 1968 split of the Ministry of National Education into two separate ministries, the French Community of Belgium created its own system of selective aid modeled on the French *avance sur recettes* regulation, which put a definitive end to the dream of a unitary Belgian cinema.

The period 1964–1968 is generally considered to mark a watershed in the history of Belgian cinema, because of this simultaneous creation and communitarization of government support for the Belgian auteur film, and also because of André Delvaux's pivotal film *De Man die Zijn Haar Kort Liet Knippen / The Man Who Had His Hair Cut Short* (1965, BE), which was cofinanced by the BRT and the Ministry of National Education.[88] However, in the *Encyclopédie des cinéma de Belgique* that accompanied the 1990 *L'Art en Belgique* exhibition in Paris that I opened this section with, Patrick Leboutte proposes an alternative periodization of Belgian cinema. Leboutte distinguishes between three periods: the pre-1958 period, or what he calls the "gestation years"; the period 1958–1974, or the "Knokke years" (after the EXPRMNTL film festival in Knokke-le-Zoute);[89] and the post-1974 period, or what he labels the "commission years." Leboutte further characterizes the second of these periods as a "cinema of examples [*cinéma fait d'exemples*],"[90] an expression he borrows from Païni, who in the same *Encyclopédie* observes a certain "dilettantism" stirred by the longtime absence of a developed cinematic infrastructure. It is, Païni writes, "as if the Belgian filmmakers had adapted themselves to this situation made of administrative difficulties and indifference, by adopting an excessively proud viewpoint: 'We could do it if we wanted. The proof? We do it once but only once.' There is a tendency to the *unique* in Belgian cinema."[91] Sojcher wholeheartedly disagrees with this alternative periodization proposed by Païni and Leboutte and instead he defends the conventional periodization while he also extends it. The three periods Sojcher distinguishes between, and that organize the respective volumes of his *Kermesse héroique*, are: 1896–1965 ("documentaries and farces"), 1965–1988 ("the deforming mirror of cultural identities"), and 1988–1996 ("the European carousel"). Sojcher takes serious issue with the notion of "a cinema of examples." In his view, Païni and Leboutte fetishize the longtime improvised state of film production in Belgium and in doing so ignore Batz's economic lessons. "Leboutte and Païni," Sojcher writes, "want to 'rehabilitate' an exceptional cinema, made with little means, in commercially unexploitable formats or lengths. Is there not a dangerous snobbism here, one that would like to make us believe that one acquires cinematographic successes independently of all financial constraints?"[92]

Underlying these quarrels about the periodization of Belgian cinema is the question whether a Belgian cinema exists in the first place. To take 1964–1968 as a watershed is to acknowledge the divide internal to Belgian cinema and perhaps even of Belgian culture at large. As Sojcher argues, "following the installation of the Selection Committee for Flemish film, one can no longer really speak of a 'national production.'"[93] Païni and Leboutte's *Encyclopédie*, in contrast, frames itself as an endeavor to unthink the divide internal to Belgian cinema. Rather than referring to that divide, the plural "cinémas" in its subtitle refers to the different stages of development of one and the same national cinema.[94] Belgian cinema exists, as Sojcher also affirms through the subtitle of his study. It exists as a split cinema, but it also exists beyond that split. It does so in several ways. First of all, both before and after the communitarization of Belgian culture, there have been Belgian filmmakers who work both in French and Flemish and on both Flemish and francophone Belgian funds. Examples include Storck (whose 1972 *Les Fêtes de Belgique / Feesten in België* is a true Flemish-francophone Belgian coproduction),[95] Delvaux (author of the francophone *Belle* [1973, BE/FR] and the dutchophone *Vrouw tussen Hond en Wolf / Woman between Wolf and Dog* [1972, BE/FR], and Marion Hänsel (author of *Sur la terre comme au ciel / Between Heaven and Earth* [1992, BE/FR/SP/NL] and *Between the Devil and the Deep Blue Sea* [1995, BE/FR/UK]).[96] Second, since 2006 the francophone and Flemish regions have committed themselves to collaborate on a limited number of annual "intranational" coproductions (e.g., *Black* from 2015), this in a modest attempt to spur an all-Belgian film culture.[97] Third, I do agree with the unitarist camp (Païni, Leboutte) that there is a certain Belgian cinematic affect, a *belgitude*, that, however hard to pin down, can be felt in both Flemish and francophone-Belgian productions. That said, ultimately I follow Sojcher in his observation that an adequate funding structure is a prerequisite for a sustainable auteur cinema. This especially holds true for nations with small domestic markets. One can therefore conclude with Sojcher that the communitarization of film funding in the mid-1960s also implied the communitarization of Belgian cinema.

Toward the end of the era that traditional European film countries saw their cinemas rejuvenate into new waves, francophone Belgium thus saw the birth of a new cinema. For a large part, this cinema owes its identity to precisely the fact that it was born in the modern auteur era. Whereas in France critics and filmmakers proclaimed auteurism as part of their oedipal struggle against cinematic tradition, francophone Belgian cinema, by lack of such a *cinéma du papa*, has been much less iconoclastic in its modernity. As Philippe Dubois writes, "if modernity feeds itself on rupture and rejection . . . Belgium clearly lacked nourishment. Whence, perhaps, a less 'reactive' but also a more positive modernity. Nothing to destroy, everything to build."[98] Globally speaking, francophone-Belgian cinema is characterized by a certain lightness, a lack of pretension, and, in the words of Maryline Laurin, a sense of "mischievous or biting humor that foregrounds a self-mockery, a strong ability to make fun of oneself without self-denigration."[99] One encounters this *belgitude* in such international successes as *C'est arrivé près de chez vous / Man Bites Dog* (Rémy Belvaux, André Bonzel, Benoît Poelvoorde, 1992, BE), *Ma vie en rose* (Alain Berliner, 1997, BE/FR/UK), *Une liaison pornographique / A Pornographic Affair*, Frédéric Fonteyne, 1999, BE/FR/CH/LX), and *Nue propriété / Private property* (Joachim Lafosse, 2006, LX/BE/FR). One equally finds it in the Walloon cinema of the real, from *Déjà s'envole la fleur maigre* to *Jeudi on chantera comme dimanche*, and from *La Raison du plus faible* to *Les Convoyeurs attendent*. Moreover, in response to Luc Dardenne's worry following *Rosetta* that "people may even start to accuse us that we have no sense of humor,"[100] I would argue that even this film has its sparse moments of lightness (think of Riquet's poor gymnastic skills, which for a split second make Rosetta forget her misery).

This preceding characterization of the Belgian cinematic spirit as a certain lightness also applies to what we could call its *cinéma de l'imaginaire*, the other dominant tendency in francophone-Belgian cinema alongside its cinema of the real. This cinema of imagination and the imaginary spans from the magic realism and surrealism of André Delvaux to films such as *Quand la mer monte*, *Toto le héros* (Jaco van Dormael, 1991, BE/FR/DE), *Between the Devil and the Deep Blue Sea* (Hänsel), *Home* (Ursula Meier, 2008, CH/FR/BE), the very low-budget productions of the "cineaste de l'absurde" Jean-Jacques Rousseau, and the films by Bouli Lanners, including *Eldorado*, *Les Géants / The Giants* (2011, FR/BE/LX) and *Les Premiers, les derniers* (2016, FR/BE). As becomes clear from the fact that some of the films I list here as examples of the *cinéma de l'imaginaire* I discussed earlier as examples of the Walloon *cinéma du réel*, these two tendencies are closely intertwined. As Vincent Thabourey argues: "This [Belgian] cinema defines itself by a surprising pendular movement between the social observation and a pure fantasy that inscribes itself in a historicity that is perfectly taken on. It finds its singularity in a permanent provocation, a facetious rebellion that never forgets to accord a tender and consoling benevolence to the human being."[101] Crucial to this unity in diversity is the smallness of francophone-Belgian cinema. Many of its filmmakers attended the same film schools, and also on screen one often encounters the same faces. For example, Fabrizio Rongione (Riquet in *Rosetta*) and Jérémie Renier (Bruno in the Dardennes' *L'Enfant*) also appear in Lafosse's *Ça rend heureux* and *Nue propriété*, while Olivier Gourmet, a Dardennes regular, also has roles in Meier's *Home* and *Quand la mer monte*. This last film's cast, in turn, includes Bouli Lanners, who equally appears in *Toto le héros*, *Les Convoyeurs attendent*, and his own *Eldorado*, and so on. The other reason for the frequent encounter between reality and imagination in francophone-Belgian film is that it often steeps the struggle for the good-or-at-least-a-better life in dreams and fantasy. In the spirit of De Sica's *Miracle in Milan*, francophone-Belgian, and in particular Walloon, realism redeems raw reality with everyday magic. Think of *Déjà s'envole la fleur maigre* and *Les Convoyeurs attendent*, or of *Le Gamin au vélo*, the Dardennes' sunny take on *Bicycle Thieves*. Moreover, many Walloon films that don't explicitly engage crisis still make felt the region's reality. Bouli Lanners, for example, transforms the region's fields, forests, and industrial landscape into widescreen North American–like settings for an absurdist road movie (*Eldorado*) and a summer vacation fairy tale (*Les Géants*) (figs 3.4 and 3.5). At the same time his films' big plains and arcadian hills remain unmistakably Walloon, with the "once upon a time" of their narratives grounded in the historical present. In his more recent *Les Premiers, les derniers*, Lanners crosses over into France, in order to transform the northern French fields of La Beauce, near Chartres, into a fucked-up yet super-sweet biblical Wild West in which, as per the gospel according to Matthew, "the last will be first and the first will be last" (fig. 3.6).

As a final point in this characterization of francophone-Belgian auteur cinema: it is a cinema integrated in European funding structures, as is argued by the subtitle of Sojcher's third volume of his *Kermesse héroïque*: the "European carousel." Sojcher locates the start of this period in 1989, which was the year the Council of Europe created its Eurimages fund. Two years later the EU launched the first of its MEDIA programs, which are aimed at the strengthening of the audiovisual industries in Europe. A film that would have probably not seen the light had it not been for these European programs is *Toto le héros*, winner of the Caméra d'or at Cannes 1991 and Belgium's "film event of the decade."[102] For some commentators this acclaim has been reason to embrace Van Dormael's film as the dawn of a European cinema. Sojcher writes that "soon the Toto-mania exceeded the simple Belgian framework, and the European programs, Eurimages and especially MEDIA I, always presented it as the living proof of their actions."[103] Leaving aside the question of whether Eurimages and MEDIA have indeed contributed to a European cinematographic identity (and here it is good to keep in mind that the costs of an average Hollywood production amount to about twice the annual budget of Eurimage) in the wake of *Toto le héros*, Belgium, and particularly francophone Belgium, has become a true "laboratory of European cinema."[104]

Also several of the examples of Walloon cinema that I discussed in the previous chapter received financing from either or both of these funds, including *Les Convoyeurs attendent*, *La Raison du plus faible*, *Eldo-*

Figure 3.4. *Eldorado* (Bouli Lanners, 2008).

Figure 3.5. *Les Géants* (Bouli Lanners, 2011).

Figure 3.6. *Les Premiers, les derniers* (Bouli Lanners, 2016).

rado, *Illégal*, and many of the Dardennes' films (though not *Rosetta*).[105] I write "Walloon cinema," but does such a distinctly Walloon regional cinema actually exist? "All depends on the definition one wants to give it," Sojcher states in response to this question. "Are we speaking about a cinema *of* and *from* Wallonia [*de Wallonie*], or about a specifically Walloon identity translated into cinema?"[106] Based on the second definition, two of the earliest Walloon feature-length films are *Déjà s'envole la fleur maigre* (1959) and *Jeudi on chantera comme dimanche* (1967). The former, however, left its director financially ruined, while the latter was directed by Luc de Heusch from Brussels and is based on a screenplay by the Flemish Hugo Claus (author of the 1983 novel *Het Verdriet van België / The Sorrow of Belgium*). *Jeudi on chantera*, moreover, was one of the first features cofinanced by the Ministry of French Belgian Culture, making it a francophone-Belgian film set in Wallonia rather than a Walloon film. It was only around the turn of the 1980s that a Walloon fiction cinema made by Walloons and "purposely expressive of [Wallonia's] own history and culture"[107] began to take shape. Among its early highlights are Andrien's *Le Grand paysage d'Alexis Droeven* (1981)—according to *Le Monde* "the first grand film of a Walloon cinema"[108]—and Michel's *Hiver 60* (1982) (mostly for its subject matter, because the film was almost entirely shot in Brussels).[109] In the following decade, in the 1990s, two production companies were founded in Liège, namely, the Dardennes' Les Films du Fleuve (1994) and Versus (1999). In 2001, as discussed at the beginning of this chapter, the Walloon region launched Wallimage. Technically, the mission of Wallimage is economic and not cultural. However, in its public presentation Wallimage clearly *does* affirm a Walloon cultural identity, as evidenced by the red T-shirts with the slogan, "Wallonia, yes we Cannes!" that the organization distributed at the 2001 Cannes festival. Wallimage's implicit embrace of a Walloon cinematic identity has to be understood within the broader context of the relatively late emergence of a cultural self-awareness in a region that constitutionally is not a cultural region. As the Walloon historian Jean Pirotte writes:

> Initially looked down upon with some sulkiness by Walloons nostalgic of a unitary Belgium, Wallonia exists more and more in the facts. For this region, recently called into existence and constrained in its emergence by a difficult economic context, the identity question raises itself with acuity: it is a matter of mobilizing all actors—not only the political ones, but also the social, cultural, and economic ones—around a Walloon project. In order to do so, the Walloon region certainly has weapons, but it is also seriously lacking some: the cultural domain does not belong to the regions but to the communities.[110]

Because of this divide in competencies between the Walloon region and the French Community of Belgium, it is impossible to identify a fully distinct Walloon cinema within francophone Belgian cinema at large. This is illustrated for example by the promotional document *10/10* (*Dix sur dix*), which was published in 2010 by the Ministry of the French Community of Belgium in collaboration with Wallonie-Bruxelles International (a suborganization of the Centre du Cinéma that manages the international relations of Wallonia and the French Community of Belgium) and Wallonie-Bruxelles Image (which promotes francophone-Belgian films internationally). This originally English document targeted at Anglo-Saxon and northwestern European distributors lists the "Walloon" Bouli Lanners, Joachim Lafosse, and Fabrice du Welz, among seven other emerging francophone-Belgian filmmakers (fig. 3.7).[111]

In the 2000s, francophone-Belgian cinema, and Belgian cinema in general, experienced a surge of funds. In 2003, the Belgian federal government launched its Tax Shelter (Incitant Fiscal), a "Loch Ness monster of Belgian cinema"[112] that through a system of fiscal exemption incites private parties not operative in the audiovisual industry to invest in Belgian audiovisual productions and production companies. Though EU competition laws stipulate that this system has a cultural and not an economic objective, also here the industry and art of cinema blend into one another. Some feared that the Tax Shelter would only stimulate "commercial" films and harm "auteur" productions. This fear has been somewhat justified by the

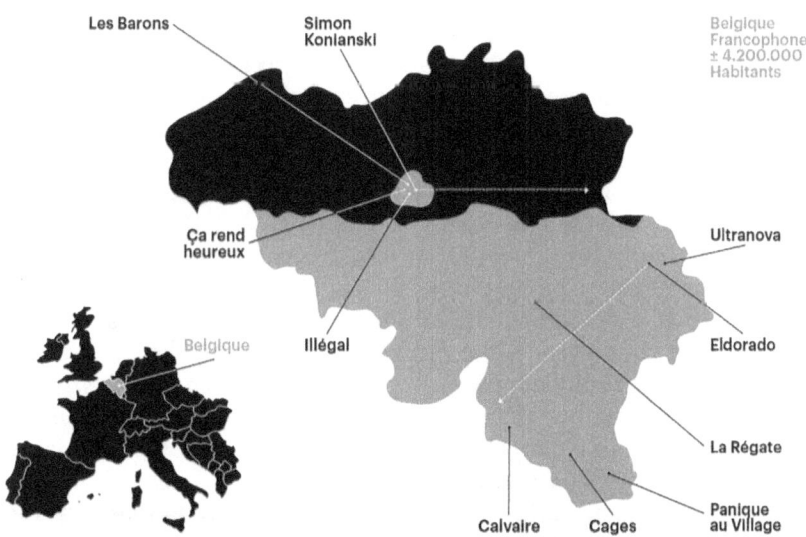

Figure 3.7. Young filmmakers in francophone Belgium. *Source: 10/10.*

tendency among intermediary investment companies to circumvent production companies altogether. In reaction to this tendency, in 2005 Versus and Les Films du Fleuve, together with two other production companies, created their own intermediary organization, Inver Invest, which seeks to convince investors to also support films that are less likely to become box office hits. At the same time, others are of the opinion that the Tax Shelter has actually benefited the Belgian auteur film. According to Henry Ingberg, then general secretary of the French Community of Belgium, "the real capital of the cinematic industry is originality and creation. Our best commercial successes are also our auteur films! In our country it is the auteurs who carry cinema."[113] The second reason why economy and culture are per definition entangled in the Tax Shelter's structure is that it strictly applies to investments in Belgium, much like Wallimage promotes investments in the Walloon region. This Tax Shelter thus links the protection of a Belgian cultural identity, a *belgitude*, to economic protection. The Tax Shelter is also much more generous, and therefore more protective, than similar regulations in neighboring countries. Not all have been happy with this situation, especially not in France, where some have lamented the delocalization of French films to Belgium. In 2010, the northern French CRRAV even called the Belgian Tax Shelter a form of "slightly unloyal competition in the production of feature-length films."[114]

Belgium's favoring of a homemade Belgian cinema has not prevented that francophone-Belgian and by extension Walloon cinema continue to have stronger ties to French than to Flemish cinema. The reasons are many: Belgium's internal linguistic and cultural border; the communitarization of Belgium's advance on receipts regulation and of its public television; the 2004 coproduction agreement between France and the French Community of Belgium;[115] the rising costs of cinematic productions (which are harder for small countries to cope with); EU regulations that stipulate that a cinematic production can be financed by public funds for only a maximum of 50 percent of its total costs;[116] French institutions such as Canal Plus, ARTE, and the CNC, which all have a strong investment in French national cinema; the French distribution market; the relatively low appeal of francophone films in Flanders (even a box office hit like *Bienvenu chez les Ch'tis* had late and only very limited success in the region[117]); the Cannes Film Festival and its traditional sympathy toward homegrown directors; and finally the fact that Belgian's most important film schools are primarily francophone. All of these factors contribute to the situation that, seventy years after the emergence of a Belgian connection in Paris, the cinematic border between francophone Belgium and France is still more porous than the one internal to Belgian cinema.

At the Crossroads of Europe

This porosity of the French-Belgian cinematic border becomes especially evident when one considers the role that French-Belgian coproductions have played in both francophone-Belgian and French cinema. France has always been the primary coproducing partner of the French Community of Belgium, and since the early twenty-first century French-Belgian coproductions have made up even more than two-thirds of all feature-length productions endorsed by the French Community of Belgium (chart 3.2). Vice versa, and perhaps more surprising, over the course of the 2000s and 2010s Belgium has also become the most important coproducing partner of France, before Italy and Germany. As chart 3.3 shows, between 2002 and 2015 there were 445 international French-Belgian coproductions in which either French or Belgian parties held a majority share, which make up 40 percent of all coproductions France was involved in over this period. Of these productions, 313 were à l'initiative française, the other 132 were primarily Belgian.[118] Since 2005, these French-Belgian projects fall under the new coproduction agreement France and the French Community of Belgium signed in 2004 in Cannes. This *Accord cinématographique* differs in two respects from the 1962 agreement between France and Belgium that it replaces (though the original agreement still regulates French-Flemish coproductions). First, whereas the original agreement stipulated that the proportion of the financial input of each of the country's coproducer(s) amounts to at least 20 percent, under the new agreement this percentage is only 10 percent. This is especially important for Belgian producers, for whom up until 2004 it was nearly impossible to garner the funds necessary for a minority share in coproductions of over €10 million. The reduction of this lower limit has led to an increase of high-budget French-Belgian coproductions with a financing structure "très majoritairement française" (with a very large French majority share),[119] in which the Belgian portion is almost always financed through the Tax Shelter. The second major difference between the 1962 and 2004 agreements is that the new agreement also stipulates an artistic collaboration. The minor coproducing country has to minimally provide 1) an author (director, scriptwriter, et al.) or an executive technician; and 2) an actor in a primary role, *or* two actors in secondary roles, *or* a second author or second executive technician.[120]

The artistic component of the French-Belgian coproduction agreement is much more specific than comparable paragraphs in other coproduction agreements both France and Belgium have signed with other countries, and as such it is indicative of the blurred border between French and francophone-Belgian cinema. This partial integration of Europe's

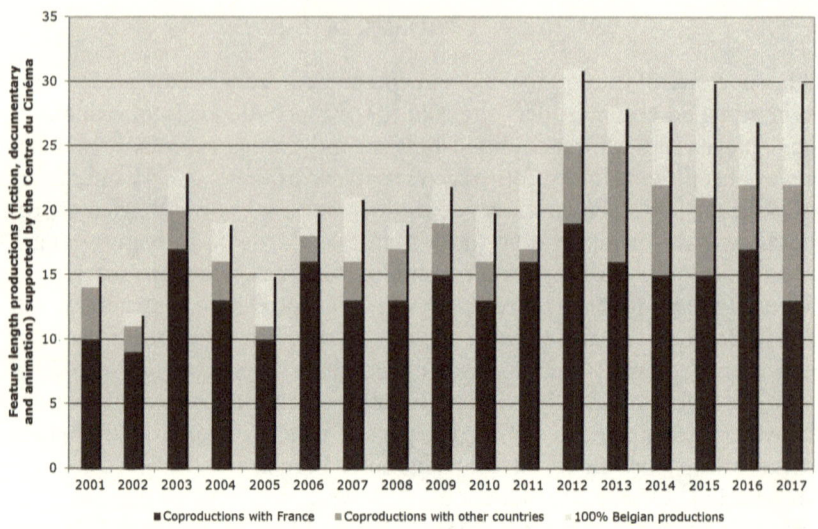

Chart 3.2. Coproductions with France in francophone-Belgian cinema, 2001–2017. *Source:* CCA.

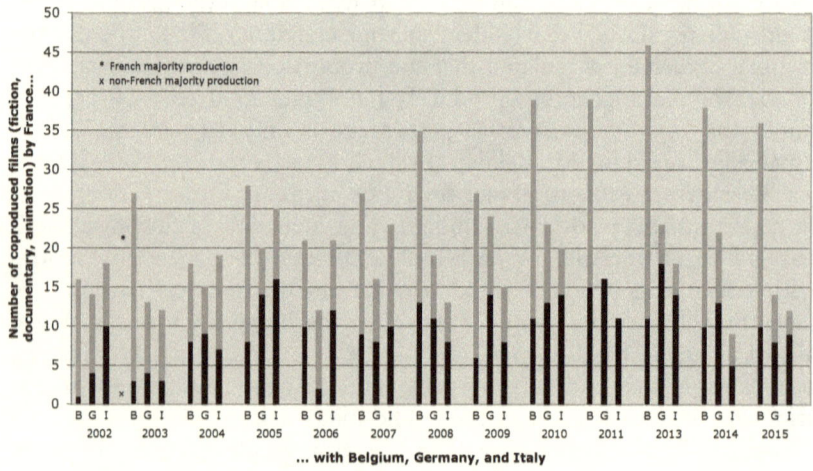

Chart 3.3. France's main coproducing partners, 2002–2015. *Source:* CNC.

largest national cinema, on the one hand, and one of the world's most visible small cinemas, on the other hand, has also manifested itself in the Cinéma du Nord, in particular on the Walloon side. Almost all of the films I discussed as "Walloon" in the previous chapters are coproductions with French parties, in particular the CNC, Canal Plus, and ARTE. In contrast, the northern French component of the Cinéma du Nord largely consists of all-French productions and contains very few coproductions with Belgium. The first reason for this imbalance internal to the Cinéma du Nord is, of course, that in France it has always been much easier than in Belgium to find the financial resources for an entirely domestic production. The second reason is that the main Belgian funding sources (Wallimage and the French Community of Belgium) only invest in films that have an economic or cultural link to Belgium, while similarly the CRRAV, and since 2013 Pictanovo, have also required a production connection to their region. As a result and somewhat ironically, for a long time cross-border coproductions that involve financing parties from both Wallonia and the French North were almost impossible by stipulation. Such coproductions only started to take off in the early 2000s. In 2003, the CRRAV and Hainaut Cinéma (which promotes the film and audiovisual industry in the Walloon province of Hainaut) initiated the three-year project "Audiovisuel Wallonie-Nord-Pas-de-Calais," this under the aegis of the EU's Interreg III structural aid program. Financed 40 percent with EU funds, the project sought to stimulate the emergence of a cinematic and audiovisual "Euroregion" across the French-Belgian border. As then CRRAV president Christian Lamarche stated, the goal of this collaboration was to "arouse synergies in [the] two regions by permitting for example a producer from Nord-Pas-de-Calais who wants to make films on both sides of the border to work with a Belgian director."[121] In order to achieve this interregional collaboration, the parties involved created a transnational fund for shorts that cofinanced several films, including *Dans l'ombre / In the Dark* (2004, BE/FR/CH) by the Belgian Olivier Masset-Depasse.

It was also a film by Masset-Depasse, his feature *Cages* (BE/FR) from 2006, that was the first fruit of the collaboration agreement that the CRRAV and Wallimage signed in 2004.[122] As Vincent Leclerq from the CRRAV stated about the negotiation process: "We discussed some interesting projects and decided to do something together. At first it seemed impossible—the criteria of both funds were that more than half of the shooting had to take place in the region—which makes it an equation impossible to solve. . . . But if there is one thing that is necessary in international coproductions it is flexibility." In its original script, *Cages* was set in Wallonia, but because of the lack of postproduction facilities in Nord-Pas-de-Calais, the partners agreed to change both story and shooting location to the Belgian-Flemish North Sea coast. That way half of the shooting could be done in Nord-Pas-de-Calais and half in

Belgium. In order to fully solve the equation, Wallimage and the CRRAV agreed that the Walloon investment would be higher than that of the French North (€250,000 and €150,000, respectively, on a total budget of almost €2 million).[123] Following *Cages*, Wallimage and the CRRAV have collaborated on one more feature-length film, namely, Anne Fontaine's *Entre ses mains* (2005), which takes place in Lille. In addition, there have been several features for which the CRRAV participated together with one of the other main institutional actors in francophone-Belgian cinema, including the RTBF and the Bureau d'Accueil des Tournages Cinéma de la Province de Hainaut-Belgique (BATCH). With this last organization the CRRAV collaborated for example on Dumont's *Hadewijch*, which travels between Paris, Nord-Pas-de-Calais, and an unspecified location in the Middle East, but which was also partly shot in the Hôpital Notre-Dame à la Rose in the Walloon town of Lessines, just north of Mons. Between 2009 and 2012, furthermore, the CRRAV, Wallimage, and also the Flemish VAF (Vlaams Audiovisueel Fonds) collaborated on the CASPER initiative (Creative Animated Series in the Euro Region), which stimulated the production of animated projects, "while approaching them, from the beginning, from a Euroregional vision."[124]

While the ongoing partnerships between Wallonia and the French North continue to produce cross-border coproductions, it is important to emphasize that I define the Cinéma du Nord more broadly than such direct collaborations. Rather, I see these collaborations as further evidence for the Nord's existence as a cross-border region. The Nord exists in relation to the border it traverses and at times renders invisible. The existence of the Nord is real, but the Nord is also internally split. It is therefore only logical that, however porous the cinematic border between Belgium and France may have become, the Cinéma du Nord remains an internally split cinema, in terms of industrial infrastructure, and, as argued in the previous chapter, in terms of the types of cinematic expressions it has given rise to. Formulated differently, the Cinéma du Nord exists despite its internal split. It expresses and, at the same time, is the product of the realities shared by the French North and Wallonia, and the realities shared by northern French and Walloon cinema. Like these regional cinemas individually, the Cinéma du Nord is both a rooted cinema and an open *cinéma d'accueil*, whose emergence has largely resulted from the structural efforts by Wallonia and the French North to attract investors to generate new discourses around their regions. These efforts have a clear economic component, in that both Wallonia and the French North only fund films that are largely produced in the region. As the francophone-Belgian newspaper *Le Soir* headlined in 2010, at the occasion of the cooperation agreement between Wallimage and Bxlimage, "Belgian cinema is good for the economy," adding that "in 2009 the 'historical' investment line of Wallimage, which exists since 2001, registered a record fallout" and that on average "each of the 3.6 million euro invested generated expenses of 3.69 euro for the totality of the concerned productions, amounting to fifteen films."[125] Similarly, in 2010 the CRRAV stated in its annual report that "while we remain demanding when it comes to the artistic quality of films, we are still increasing our economic impact. . . . On average each euro invested in a film yields four euro, of which three in audiovisual expenses, essentially in salaries for technicians and actors."[126] This analysis does not include the indirect economic benefits that film production may have had for Wallonia and the French North, nor does it include the qualitative effects on these regions' self-image and their national and international visibility. It is beyond doubt, though, that cinema has played and continues to play a crucial role in the Walloon and northern French efforts to restructure and reprofile themselves as vibrant Euroregions.

This claim finds further support in the fact that in the late 2000s Wallonia and Nord-Pas-de-Calais, both individually and together, have expanded their cinema and television strategies to newer forms of audiovisual media. In 2006, Wallonia saw the birth of the Pôle Image de Liège, which "firmly planted in the heart of Wallonia, Belgium, and Europe" unites audiovisual service companies in the Liège region (such as EVS Broadcast Equipment, the world's leading producer of digital broadcast video production systems).[127] Since 2010, this Pôle Image has been affiliated with Wallimage. In turn, both Wallimage and the Pôle Image fall under the umbrella of the Technologies Wallonnes de l'Image, du Son et du Texte (TWIST) cluster, which, financed by the Walloon Region, stimulates synergies between companies that operate in the audiovisual sector. Similarly, in 2009 Nord-Pas-de-Calais, in collaboration with Wallimage and the Vlaams Audiovisueel Fonds, founded its own Pôle Images. Established in three locations in the French North, this structure united cinema, digital video, gaming, and virtual worlds, and represented around two hundred companies, schools, research teams, and professional organizations in the region.[128] In 2013, the CRRAV and Pôle Image merged to form Pictanovo. "We need more force to exist beyond the regional borders," Pictanovo's first president, Michel-François Delannoy, rationalized the merger, "we need to give perspectives of international development to regional actors."[129] For example, among the films Pictanovo supported in recent years is *Vent du Nord*, a French-Tunisian-Belgian coproduction that also received funds through the Belgian Tax Shelter regulation. The film tells two crossing stories: that of Hervé, who becomes a fisher when his factory in the north of France is delocalized to Tunis, and that of Foued, who lives in Tunis and who hopes to build a new life when he gets a job at the new factory, upon which their plots intersect.

Finally, in this overview of cinematic collaboration across the French-Belgian border, I need to mention the Expériences Interactives TransRégionales, a €300,000 funding line for "transmedia" projects launched in 2014 by Nord-Pas-de-Calais and Wallonia (fig. 3.8). In line with the funding strategies of Wallimage and Pictanovo, the goal of this border-crossing initiative was to attract investments to the region and to rebrand its image from a place of misery and unemployment to that of a creative, forward-looking, and Euregional hub. As Cineuropa reports, "the objective of the partnership between Pictanovo and Wallimage is

Figure 3.8. "It's in the Nord we make TransMedia foam." *Source:* Cineuropa.

the collaboration of artists, entrepreneurs . . . and researchers in two regions, while supporting significant projects made in partnership with other regions. Only projects involving business and/or research centers of the two regions are eligible."[130] Among the projects funded are: *What the Fake: Selfies?!* (a participatory online documentary on new communication practices among adolescents), *Monsieur et Madame Flash* (a transmedia web series that investigates what it means to succeed today), and the "serious game" *L'Homme au harpon*, which puts the player in the shoes of a prisoner on their uneven path of reintegration.[131] In this last project, online gaming meets the Cinéma du Nord, as *L'Homme au harpon / The Man with the Harpoon* (2015) is also a TV series and a feature-length documentary directed by Isabelle Christiaens and broadcast by the RTBF and ARTE. In both the series and the documentary, the camera follows the forty-five-year old Alain, who after having served a third of his fourteen-year sentence for attempted murder in the Walloon prison of Nivelles now starts his long struggle back into society. In the game, hosted on the RTBF website (http://www.rtbf.be/harpon/), the player is asked to choose their own avatar. They can become, for example, a single young mother who has been sentenced to seven years for having sold cocaine to another young woman (who subsequently overdosed on the drugs). In the beginning of the story our protagonist—let's call her "Rosetta"—receives a moral blow right away. First, she is turned down by her parents ("How do you dare to still ask us something?"), then by the employment office: "Work, you're dreaming, honey. If you believe there is a place for everyone in the world, you're fooling yourself [*tu te fous le doigt dans l'oeuil*]. . . . You'll have to get by with €45 in welfare." From here on, it is up to the players' choices whether Rosetta will be granted a second chance at a "normal" life.

Google, Van Gogh, the Louvre-Lens, and a *Terril* of Coats

In conclusion to this chapter, I would like to relate the Cinéma du Nord to the story of two cultural-economic giants who in recent years have set foot in the Nord: Google and the Musée du Louvre. As I already wrote in chapter 2, in 2010 Google opened a data center in Saint-Ghislain, near Mons in the Borinage, the company's first outside of the US. Since that year, the company has manifested itself as an advocate of culture in the region. In 2012, Google teamed up with the Mundaneum museum in Mons. This museum commemorates the work of Belgian information pioneers Paul Otlet and Henri Lafontaine, who in the late nineteenth century developed the Decimal Classification System, "a search engine on paper" and "a way to classify the world."¹³² Subsequently, Google supported Mons as Europe's 2015 Cultural Capital, "where culture meets technology."¹³³ Part of this event was the restoration of the former house of Vincent van Gogh in the nearby town of Wasmes (fig. 3.9; see also fig. ix in the photo series following this chapter), where that year Google's logo appeared on a banner, alongside the corporate footprints of ING, BMW, and the EU. According to the company's "Head of Free Expression & Community," Google's presence has created an opportunity for the Borinage "to go from the nineteenth to the twenty-first century, from the old industry to the new."¹³⁴ Something that the head of free expression does not mention, though, is that part of Google's choice for the still-unemployment-stricken Borinage is the strategic location close to Brussels and that city's EU offices. As the *Financial Times* astutely observes, Google's effort "to portray itself as a friend of European culture" comes at a moment "pressure increases from regulators and traditional content industries in Europe over copyright issues and the company's privacy policies."¹³⁵

South of the French-Belgian border in the meanwhile, the Parisian Louvre has started a satellite museum on a former mining site in Lens. The construction of the museum was largely financed by the Nord-Pas-de-Calais region. At the eve of the museum's opening in 2012 the region's president, Daniel Percheron, stated that "what we want is a Bilbao effect," this in reference to the Basque town in northern Spain, where a similar Guggenheim satellite has helped to rejuvenate the

Figure 3.9. The Van Gogh house in the Walloon town of Wasmes (auhor's photo).

region's image.[136] The Louvre-Lens stretches out over a park of twenty hectares (fifty acres) that still reveal the railroad tracks that connected the pits. The museum itself is a low and light Japanese design that blends nicely into the landscape, with *terrils* rising at the horizon. Inside there are two main spaces. One is the Galérie du temps (fig. 3.10) with a permanent and free exhibition of objects mostly brought over from the Paris depots. The other is a space for temporary and ticketed exhibitions such as *Des animaux et des pharaons* and *Les Désastres de la guerre* (from the Napoleonic Wars to drones). In many respects the Louvre-Lens has lived up to its expectations. A year after its opening, the museum had employed two hundred and indirectly created four hundred other jobs, and in its first two years the museum attracted over 1.5 million visitors, from the region, from the rest of France, and from abroad (especially Belgium), making it the best-visited regional museum in France.[137] But the museum has also been a subject of critique. *La Tribune de l'art*, for example, observes the "intellectual emptiness" of the *Galérie du temps*, while Didier Rykner writes that "it is a little bit like zapping through art history, or art history in 30 minutes for beginners. The visitor passes, through 205 works, from 3300 before to 1850 after Christ, and it challenges those who never set foot in a museum—the main audience explicitly targeted by the project—to understand something."[138] While this exhibition setup is still a matter of preference, what struck me most about the museum was the sheer absence of northern French accents or engagement with the region's history. Apart from the North Sea fish

Figure 3.10. The Galérie du temps in the Louvre-Lens (author's photo).

served in its restaurant and a display in the museum shop with Ch'ti beer, regional tourist guides, and Marguerite Yourcenar's *Archives du Nord*, the region is missing from the Louvre-Lens. On top of that, in an informational video in the space downstairs a man who introduces himself as "the voice of Louvre-Lens" explains the museum's two missions. The first is to "go to all audiences, including audiences far from culture [*éloignés de la culture*—see fig. 3.11]," the second to "demythify the museum without ever sacralizing it." In that second mission the Louvre-Lens mostly succeeds, as the museum visualizes the Louvre depot. In its first mission, however, one hears the uncomfortable echo of De Gaulle and Malraux, disseminating La Culture from Paris to the far corners of the hexagon (and beyond, because the Louvre also has a satellite in Abu Dhabi). As Magali Lesauvage writes:

> All these intentions, however beautiful, are the proof of an unconscious condescendence and paternalism. Universalist and imperialist, the Louvre here gives itself as mission a sort of evangelization through culture that seems to forget the contemporary culture (except for the [nonpermanent] presence of Carnival giants in the exhibition).
>
> "All to Lens," the museum PR says. But rather than bringing the Louvre to Lens, couldn't one bring the people of Lens to the Louvre . . . ?[139]

Figure 3.11. The Louvre-Lens addressing "those at a remove from culture" (author's photo).

In its defense, the museum has been somewhat responsive to these critiques. In 2015, for example, it asked supporters of the Lens soccer team (whose stadium is right next to the museum) to contribute their "fetish objects" to an exhibition around Euro 2016.[140] Then again, and to add to the critique of the museum, in that same year the inhabitants of the former *corons* (miners' houses) across the street of the museum were asked to move, as the city needed the space for a luxury hotel.[141]

Back across the border, in the Borinage at the site of the Musée des Arts Contemporains de la Fédération Wallonie-Bruxelles (MAC's), which is located in the early nineteenth-century Grand-Hornu mining complex, the *corons* are still inhabited. In the spring of 2015, MAC's had a breathtaking exhibition by the French artist Christian Boltanski, titled *La Salle des pendus* (Room of the hanged). In one of the rooms, visitors had to find their way through a soft maze of semi-translucent curtains. In another room, twenty-nine matrix displays counted, in real time as it were, the seconds lived by twenty-nine persons, punctuated by the sound of a throbbing heartbeat. And in yet another room, a large hall, there was a wall-filling memorial of rusted biscuit boxes, on each of them the name, and in some cases also a photograph, of a former miner from the region (figs. 3.12–3.14). The exhibition's highlight was another maze, this one of miners' jackets, hanging like they used to hang from the ceilings in the *salles des pendus*, as the miners referred to their locker rooms. This maze led to a room with a *terril* of coats with, suspended above it, hanging from the ceiling, a single lamp whose light was absorbed by the textile giant, this in memory of the Walloon coal dust that once absorbed the sun (fig. 3.15).

La Salle des pendus breathes the equally site-specific spirit of the Cinéma du Nord. As I have argued in the first two chapters, the Cinéma du Nord roots its inquiry into "humanity" in the particular cultures and communities of the French-Belgian border region. As I have demonstrated in this third chapter, the Cinéma du Nord is also an industry rooted in the economies of Wallonia and Nord-Pas-de-Calais. The Cinéma du Nord is a cinema *made in the Nord*, "made" both in the sense of "created" and "produced." Conversely, cinema has helped the Nord to reimagine and rebrand itself: away from its dark and grim past, toward a green, bright, and also silicon future. "Cinema is good for the economy!" In the Nord it certainly has been, not only because the interplay between artistic imagination and state support has generated welcome exposure for the region, attracting people and business, but also because the Cinéma du Nord has helped pave the way for the development of Wallonia and the French North into the Euregional transmedia hubs they are today.

Figures 3.12–3.14. Memorial of biscuit boxes. From Christian Boltanski's *La Salle des pendus* in the Musée des Arts Contemporains de la Fédération Wallonie-Bruxelles (author's photos).

Figure 3.15. *Terril* of Coats. From Christian Boltanski's *La Salle des pendus* in the Musée des Arts Contemporains de la Fédération Wallonie-Bruxelles (author's photo).

i–ii. The Liège-Guillemins train station.

Excursion

From the Nord, with Love

Most research for this project was done in Paris and online, but I have traveled quite a bit in Wallonia and Northern France, and whenever I now visit the "Nord" (which is around the corner from Dutch Limburg, where I grew up) inevitably my gaze is colored by cinema. What follows is a series of photographs that capture the Cinéma du Nord insofar as its notion has latched itself onto my outlook on the region, on its land- and cityscapes. The journey starts at the Liège-Guillemins train station—at once nearby and very far from Rosetta's home—from where we travel to the Borinage, up and down the *terril d'Hornu à Wasmes*, via the memory of Van Gogh, to *temps jadis*. We then take the train to Lens and travel, via the majestic *chevalement de la Fosse no. 1* in Liévin—cinematically located at the Rue des Frères Lumières!—and onward to the Côte d'Opale, where Bruno Dumont shot some of his films, including *Jeannette, l'enfance de Jeanne d'Arc* (2017) and *Jeanne* (2019). Finally, we take Charleroi's phantom subway (which was never taken into operation) into a miraculous Nord, where borders blur, cherry trees are struck by lightning, and one-way roads are tagged with love.

iii–iv. *Terril* in Wasmes, Wallonia.

v–viii. *fleurs du terril.*

ix. Maison Van Gogh de Colfontaine in Wasmes.

x. Brasserie Van Gogh in Boussu.

xi. Maison Van Gogh in Mons.

xii. Charbonnage de Frameries.

xiii. Charleroi.

xiv. Mons.

xv. Charleroi.

xvi. Marcinelle.

xvii–xviii. Lens.

xix. Liévin.

xx–xxii. Liévin.

xxiii–xxiv. Dunes de la Slack (the shooting location of Bruno Dumont's *Ma Loute*).

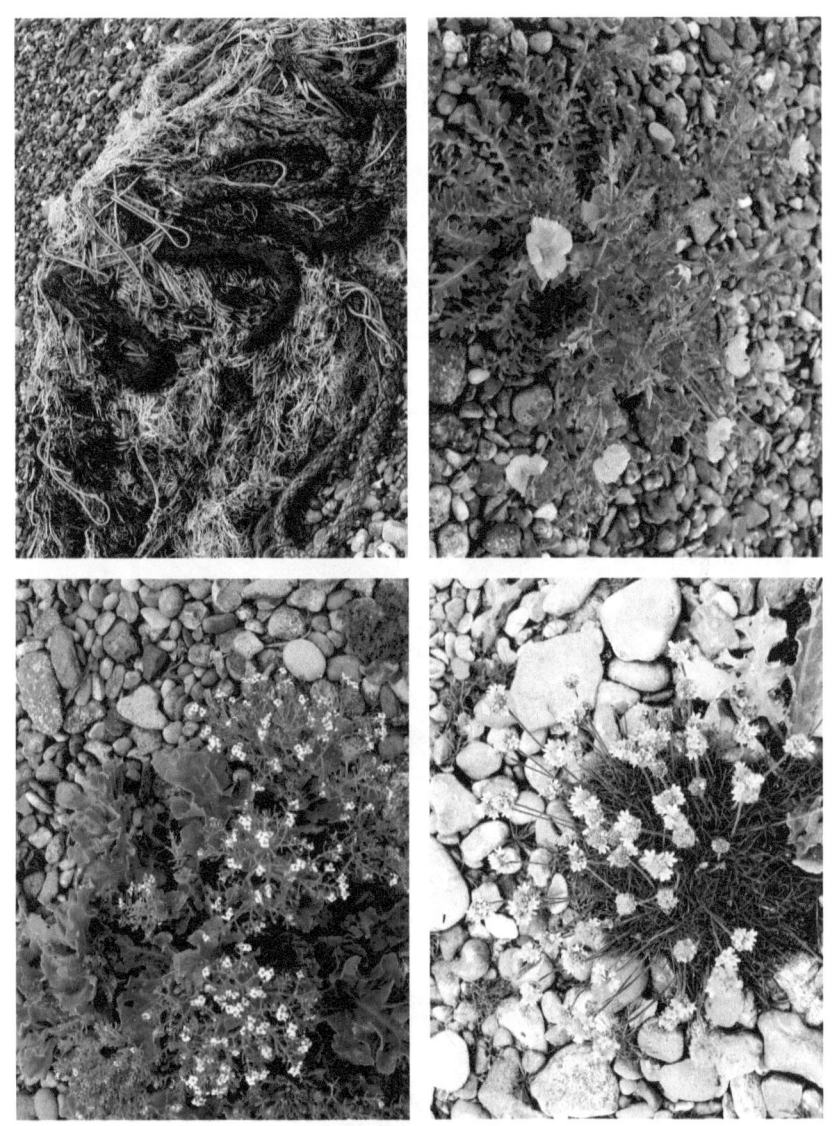
xxv–xxviii. *fleurs de la pierre.*

xxix–xxx. Charleroi's phantom subway.

xxxi. Charleroi.

xxxii. Liège.

xxxiii. Borinage.

xxxiv. Valenciennes.

4

New Realism after the Modern Cinema

THE CINÉMA DU NORD IS not only an expression and product of the French-Belgian border region, its turn-of-the-millennium realism also needs to be understood within francophone-European and, more broadly, world cinema from the last three decades. As discussed in the previous chapter, over the course of the 1990s and the 2000s France saw a surge in films by young filmmakers, a *jeune cinéma français* that was received by many critics as a revival of the New Wave auteur tradition. This "new New Wave" became associated, moreover, with a return of political engagement, for two main reasons. The first is the open letter *Le Monde* published on February 12, 1997. With this *appel à la désobéissance* (appeal to civil disobedience) fifty-nine French and also a few Belgian filmmakers distanced themselves from a law proposed by the French government that would obligate citizens to denounce *sans papiers*, undocumented immigrants. "We, French filmmakers," the letter reads, "we are all guilty, every one of us, of having recently sheltered clandestine foreigners. We have not denounced our foreign friends."[1] Among the filmmakers who signed the letter were Pascale Ferran, Olivier Assayas, Philippe Lioret (who made *Welcome* about the Calais refugee crisis), the northern French Arnaud Desplechin, and also the Walloon Lucas Belvaux (director and writer of the 2017 film *Chez nous*, a critique of the Front National). The letter inspired similar public statements by other groups, including writers, and created the momentum for a large-scale street protest in Paris later that month. Under this pressure the government withdrew the law proposal, reason for *Libération* to triumph that the film world had proven that the Left was still alive in France.²

The other reason the young French cinema has been linked to a return of politics is that a lot of its films share a new realism that ruptures with the spectacular *cinéma du look* of the 1980s.³ This new realism, as Martine Beugnet writes:

> . . . is characterized by its provincial locations, its use of non-professional actors, and its documentary feel. Some writers have called it a *cinéma des petites gens*, literally, "the cinema of the small people"—the homeless, the unemployed, the manual workers and small shopkeepers, the inhabitants of the suburbs, of provincial towns and villages, groups of individuals neither particularly beautiful nor glamorous, who are rarely seen in major roles on-screen.⁴

These "small people" range from the farming communities of Dumont's *Flandres* and Sandrine Veysset's *Y'Aura-t'il de la neige à Noël? / Will It Snow for Christmas?* (1997) (fig. 4.1) to the migrants of Lioret's *Welcome* (fig. 4.2) and the Dardennes' *La Promesse*; from the banlieues inhabitants of *La Haine* (Mathieu Kassovitz, 1995) and Céline Sciamma's 2014 *Bande de filles* (whose protagonists, like Rosetta, above all wish "to be normal") to the school classes of *Être et avoir* (Nicolas Philibert, 2002) and *Ça commence aujourd'hui* (a 1999 film by Bertrand Tavernier set in the French North after the shutting down of the mines); and from the women of *La Vie rêvée des anges* (Zonca) and *Ressources humaines* (Cantet) to the social outcasts of Agnès Varda's *Sans toit ni loi / Vagabond* (1985) and *La Raison du plus faible* (Belvaux). By bringing these characters to the screen, young French realism has expanded the scope of French cinema, not only in terms of its subjects and stories but also geographically, as it has decentralized French cinema—away from Paris toward the regions and the banlieues.

But the *jeune cinéma* has also drawn some severe criticism. One of the most provocative attacks, and at the same time one of the most astute analyses of the young French cinema, is a 1998 essay by Mathias Lavin and Stéphane Delorme, titled "Petits arrangements avec le jeune cinéma français" (a play on Ferran's 1994 film *Petits arrangements avec les morts*), which was published in the short-lived journal *Balthazar* (named after Bresson's film). "The common denominator, the big affair of the young French cinema," the two write in this whirlwind of a critique, "is not cinema but *life*. Cinema is absolutely not interrogated in its form. It is envisioned as a mould that has already acquired its perfect and definitive

Figure 4.1. *Y'Aura-t'il de la neige à Noël?* (Sandrine Veysset, 1997).

Figure 4.2. *Welcome* (Philippe Lioret, 2009).

form, the most *minimalist* form, in order to receive 'life,' the only object worthy of its name."[5] Even though Lavin and Delorme admit that films such as *La Vie rêvée des anges* (Erick Zonca, 1998) and *Mange ta soupe* (Mathieu Amalric, 1997) provide "agreeable entertainment," and while they praise Dumont for his treatment of bodies in *La Vie de Jésus*, they argue that too many of the recent auteur films subordinate cinema to the "real," or lose themselves in "intimist" anecdotes centered around "me, me, me, the little me."[6] They reproach the young French filmmakers for their *mimetism*, a tendency to render every screen event and image transparent. From Assayas to Xavier Beauvois, and from Cédric Kahn to Laurent Cantet: in their eyes all these filmmakers are too concerned with capturing preexisting ideas of contemporary reality rather than creating new cinematic worlds. "Cinema," they write, "is no longer thought" but is instead "conceived of as an illustration of a psychological history, of a discourse that would do very well without images." All in all, Lavin and Delorme lament what they see as a revival of the realist aesthetic favored by *Cahiers du cinéma*, "from Bazin to Daney," while they mourn the disappearance of the "great filmmakers" of the 1960s and 1970s who "launched themselves on the route traced out by Bresson."[7] The young filmmakers, they note as they ratchet up their critique, above all lack an aesthetic project. "Certainly," they admit:

> ... there are differences between Desplechin, Beauvois, or [Noémie] Lvovsky [author of the much-acclaimed *La Vie ne me fait pas peur / Life Doesn't Scare Me* from 1999]. But are they of the sort of the ones between Godard, Rohmer, Resnais, and Demey at the start of the sixties? One can very well imagine a character of Ferran enter a film by Lvovsky, but how could one imagine a character of Rohmer in *L'Année dernière à Marienbad* [Resnais, 1961] or *Les Carabiniers* [Godard, 1963]? The example is grotesque.[8]

Lavin and Delorme therefore show themselves unconvinced by young French cinema's alleged return of the political. "Unfortunately, the generosity of the gesture," they write about the *appel à la désobéissance*, "does not take away the perfect nullity of this act."[9]

In a 2001 follow-up essay also published in *Balthazar*, Lavin and Delorme extend their critique to young French cinema's on-screen political agenda. In their view, films such as *Ressources humaines* (Cantet) and *Nadia et les hippopotames* (Dominique Cabrera) (like *Rosetta* and *L'humanité* both from 1999), lack a radical aesthetics and instead get bogged down in class caricature. As far as aesthetics is concerned, Lavin and Delorme specifically target the frequent use of the handheld camera, whose "coming and going ... is accompanied by a ... minimal montage that contents itself with linking up shots."[10] They give the examples of Desplechin's *Ester Kahn* ("Even in the only scene worthy of interest ... the camera is trembling and films the actors half crouched over, as if the operator was shivering with cold") and Assayas's 1998 *Fin août, début septembre* ("the camera seems to play hide-and-seek with the bodies, struggling to find the most ugly framing possible: a piece of shoulder here, the back of a head there").[11] The "most funny example," though, they consider to be *Rosetta*: "When the warrior has (finally) calmed down (it's mealtime), the camera continues to hop on its place, and in order to provide a little bit of action hides itself behind the gate, allowing the corner of the wall to navigate into the frame. One is inevitably reminded of bad fantastic films, when the monster hides itself behind its victim."[12]

Lavin and Delorme get carried away a little, but they do have a point. Many turn-of-the-millennium French films *do* create very similar universes, grasp back to rather conventional modes of storytelling, and overall lack the aesthetic boldness of the French New Wave and its immediate aftermath. However, in their sweeping dismissal of a Bazinian cinema that puts its faith in reality and their simultaneous nostalgia for Bresson, the critics lose sight of the influence Bresson's work has had on some of the authors they reference, including the Dardennes and Dumont. Lavin and Delorme base themselves, moreover, on a rather reductive understanding of cinematic realism. First of all, they ignore the dialectical nature of Bazin's film philosophy, according to which realism in art goes beyond mimesis and "can only come forth out of artifice." This is why Bazin saw his cinematic ideal realized in *Ladri di biciclette / Bicycle Thieves* (De Sica, 1948) as much as in *Journal d'un curé de campagne* (Bresson, 1951). While the former in Bazin's words achieves a "perfect aesthetic illusion of reality" resulting from the disappearance of actors, story, and sets, the latter constitutes a "triumph of cinematographic realism" that hands back "the screen, free of images . . . to literature." The result is the same in both cases: "no more cinema," that is to say, the meticulously crafted illusion thereof.[13]

My second objection against Delorme and Lavin is that their juxtaposition of realism and its revival in young French, and more broadly francophone-European, cinema, on the one hand, and a radical modernism that links Bresson to New Wave and post–New Wave directors including Godard and Eustache, on the other, oversimplifies the triangular relationship between Italian neorealism, the French New Wave, and the long tradition of "Bazinian" realism: from Vigo and Renoir, via Bresson and Pialat, to Dumont and the Dardennes. That triangle is the focus of this chapter, which explores the revival of a socially critical and often humanist realism in the wake of modern critiques of realism and representation in francophone-European film and philosophy. Building on Beugnet's definition cited earlier, I understand new realism as an ethics and aesthetics of filmmaking that 1) reinvents earlier practices, and in particular the Italian neorealist practice, of depicting the everyday lives of ordinary people for the globalized age, and 2) revives a belief in cinema's promise to capture reality, however defined, while showing the influence of television and mobilizing the haptic potentials of new digital image and sound technology. New realism is a cinema of life, so I agree with Lavin and Delorme, "life" understood as both the biological body-mind and its sociocultural trajectory from cradle to grave. In its most compelling forms new realism integrates both notions of life. It does so when it renders intelligible and sensible the question: "How does the transition from a strong industrial to a more precarious and diversified, postindustrial economy affect the social fabric, down to the structures of people's quotidian existence?"

First and foremost, new realism addresses this question by telling stories. It's a storytelling cinema, and as such it moves away from what Gilles Deleuze has theorized as the "modern cinema" and its deconstruction of stories. In Deleuze's terminology, one could consider new realism as a renewed cinema of the "action image," by which Deleuze in his *Cinema* books refers to the type of plot-driven image that became dominant under cinema's classical paradigm (e.g., Classical Hollywood, the French *cinéma du papa*). At the same time, new realism, in its most interesting forms, also transforms the "action image" into what I call the *acting/acted image* that turns the tension between its acting subjects in front of the camera and its acted on-screen characters into the simultaneous subject and object of art. Yet before diving deeper into a Deleuzian and post-Deleuzian classification of cinematic signs, it is necessary to address the age-old question:

What Is Realism?

In order to understand new realism we first need to explore the tension between cinematic realism and realist cinema, that is to say, between a realism that supposedly belongs to the medium of cinema and a realism achieved by cinematic means. An organic point of departure to start examining this tension is the film philosophy of André Bazin. In his essay "Rethinking Bazin: Ontology and Realist Aesthetics" (2006) Daniel Morgan critiques the "generally accepted standard reading" of Bazin that cinema is realist "insofar as it comes closest to or bears fidelity to our perceptual experience of reality."[14] According to Morgan, that reading rests on two propositions. The first is that Bazin would pose a determinate relation between cinematic realism and the ontology of the photographic image. Second, Bazin would posit that the photographic image is a trace of a past, profilmic reality. Morgan refers to this second proposition as the "index argument," as it is in line with the parallel, first drawn by Peter Wollen, between Bazin's ontology of the photographic image and the concept of indexicality as theorized by the American semiotician Charles Sanders Peirce. Here indexicality is understood as a sign's direct physical connection to its referent, say that of a footprint to a foot, that of a barometer to the air pressure, or that of a photograph to the reality that was once in front of the camera.[15] Morgan rejects both propositions. In his view, Bazin's claim that the photograph is "the object itself, freed from the conditions of time that govern it"[16] is much stronger than the index argument allows for. In addition, Morgan disagrees with the notion that Bazin would have favored directors such as Orson Welles, Jean Renoir, and the Italian neorealists because of their films' mimetic qualities. Instead, Morgan proposes an understanding of Bazinian realism that goes beyond mere verisimilitude. Bazin, he argues, "not only rejects verisimilitude as an essential component of *realism*, at various points coming close to directly opposing it to realism. He is also explicit that perceptual or psychological realism is an inadequate criterion for realism."[17] Morgan proposes to think of Bazinian realism as an open set of styles that, though not necessarily driven by verisimilitude, share an *acknowledgment* of the photograph's privileged relation to reality. This way, Morgan reasons, one can account, for example, for Bazin's acclaim of *Journal d'un curé de campagne*, which through its final shot of a crucifix ultimately takes flight from verisimilitude: "Bazin will argue that the spiritual existence Bresson is interested in cannot be shown. . . . What Bresson does, as Bazin sees it, is give us this spiritual state, and at the same time acknowledge the ontology of the medium, by *negating* the visual dimension of the image."[18]

Morgan's synthesis of Bazin is convincing on the whole. The only aspect I don't agree with is his presentation of the "index argument," the argument that Bazin is a realist because he would see a determinate relation between the ontology of the photographic image and a realist aesthetics. As discussed, Morgan rejects this argument, because according to his reading of Bazin objects exist in the present, with a positive value.[19] The photographic image, so Morgan reasons, is not just a sign that *refers* to its object; it is an object in and of itself that *partakes* in the reality of the object that it *re*-presents. The photograph *is* its object, *minus* the latter's temporal contingency, and for that reason the photograph is more than a mere index. After all, Morgan writes, "no one argues that a footprint *is* a foot or that the barometer *is* the air pressure, despite the fact that there is a direct, non-subjective causal relation between them."[20] True, for Bazin the photographic image is not a trace of a past reality, but a reality in and of itself. However, Morgan passes over the fact that for Peirce the index is a more general category than one of signs that are, or have been, in direct physical contact with the objects they refer to. Morgan mentions the footprint, as per Lev Manovich's claim that "cinema is the art of the index; it is an attempt to make art out of a footprint,"[21] but Peirce's own privileged example of indexicality was the pointing finger, a sign that affirms the existence of its referent without its necessarily touching or having touched that referent, like the exclamation "There!"[22]

Does the "index argument" hold true when one takes the index in this broader connotation? It's a difficult question to answer. Peirce was a monist and as such he was a fervent critic of a Cartesian mind-body dualism. In an early essay, "Questions Concerning Certain Faculties Claimed for Man" (1868), Peirce rules out the epistemological ground of a first intuitive thought. Instead he argues that all cognition is mediated by previous knowledge and that the only cognizable thoughts are thoughts in signs, thoughts being signs themselves, thought-signs. "To say," Peirce writes, "that thought cannot happen in an instant, but requires a time, is but another way of saying that every thought must be interpreted in another, or that all thought is in signs."[23] In other words, signs operate in, through, and around us, and in a later essay, Peirce even goes as far as speculating as to whether the entire universe is composed "exclusively of signs," a position that brings him close to Spinoza's equation of God and Nature.[24]

As far as the photographic image is concerned, Peirce writes, in a much-cited passage:

> Photographs, especially instantaneous photographs, are very instructive, because we know that they are in certain respects exactly like the objects they represent. But this resemblance is due to the photographs having been produced under such circumstances that they were physically forced to correspond point by point to nature. In that aspect, then, they belong to the second class of signs, those by physical connection.[25]

A photograph is an index, but "in certain respects" it is also an icon (the type of sign that relates to its referent through resemblance, like a drawing). A photograph is both an image and an object. It's an image with a certain thickness that forms a "footprint" of the object it represents (or more precisely of the light reflected by that object when photographed). But to complicate matters, does the photograph not also "point to nature" precisely because of its unrivaled iconic qualities, which would contradict the definition of the index as a sign that yields no insight into its object? And does the fact that one's recognition of a photograph's indexicality depends on the prior knowledge of the "circumstances" under which that image-object was produced not contradict Peirce's earlier claim that the index-object dyad exists independently of the sign's interpretant? Peirce never really resolved this paradoxical nature of the photograph, which, I would argue, has to do with the potential contradiction between his premise that every sign is a sign *to an interpretant*, and his simultaneous claim that the index-object bond is independent of an interpretant. The only way to resolve this contradiction is by positing that an object's indexicality is always already mediated by the iconic or symbolic aspects also part of that object. This is because an immediate index can only be understood as an emptied-out symbol, a signifier without signified, whose object is the interpretant's very inclusion in the chain of signification. Such a "pure" index would be a sign that interrupts processes of signification and as such is akin to the Lacanian gaze of the real, which equally arrests the decentered subject in their inclinations to make sense.[26]

Even more than in Peirce's discussion of photography, in Bazin's ontology of the medium the index-icon distinction collapses:

> This automatic genesis [of photographic images] has overturned the psychology of the image. The objective nature of photography confers on it a power of credibility absent from all other pictorial work. Whatever the objections of our critical spirit may be, we are forced to believe in the existence of the object represented, actually *re*-presented, rendered present, that is to say, in time and space. Photography benefits from a certain transference of reality from the thing to its reproduction.[27]

This passage starts off as a historical-phenomenological argument about the way photographs appear to and have changed human perception, but it subsequently slides into the ontology promised by the title of Bazin's essay. The photographic image, by its very nature, instills in its beholder the belief that its representation partakes in the reality of its object. Bazin thus goes one step further than Peirce, and in fact goes where Peirce could not have gone without contradicting his monism. Like Peirce, though, Bazin was a monist, despite the fact that his humanist ontology often flirts with the blissful revelation of the things in themselves so much longed for by Bresson's *curé*. In Peirce's terminology, for Bazin the photograph is an index precisely because it is an icon. It's a sign that stands in a direct physical relation to the object it resembles, thereby offering the viewer a glimpse of a fragment of objective reality presented "in all its virginal purity to my attention and consequently to my love."[28]

Now, how does Bazin move from this aesthetics of reality captured by "the impassivity of the lens" to his aesthetics of cinematic realism, considering the fact that for him cinema is not only photographic objectivity in time but "also a language"?²⁹ As we have seen, Morgan argues that for Bazin realism is a heterogeneous set of styles that, without it necessarily mimicking reality, acknowledges the photograph's ontology. I agree, but I would also add that even more than an aesthetic category, realism for Bazin is an ethics according to which cinema, in its "purest" manifestations, redeems human perception in a way that surpasses the photograph's mummification of facts. Realism in cinema, Bazin emphasizes over and again, is only achieved through artifice. As Cesare Casarino puts it, realism for Bazin is a practice that returns to reality what it has borrowed from it, while also adding interest to that return payment.³⁰ This "added measure of reality" takes different forms and may even exceed the domain of representation, as it does in *Journal d'un curé de campagne*, where the black cross, "the only visible trace left by the assumption of the image," bears witness to "that whose reality was only a sign."³¹ The passage is instructive, because like Bresson's film itself it employs a Catholic vocabulary, while at the same time it grounds itself in a materialist-existentialist worldview according to which there is nothing beyond the mundane existence of things. Cinema's promise for Bazin is to melt these seemingly opposite positions (the one spiritual, the other material) and to orient our gaze downward to people and things, rather than at a phantasmagoric sky, while keeping up the viewer's hope for salvation. The medium and art of cinema fulfills this Bazinian promise when it makes us see that, in the words of the *curé*, *all is grace*.

Neorealism

Other than in Bresson, Bazin recognized his ideal of pure cinema in Italian neorealism. Indissolubly associated with the shoestring, newsreel-like aesthetic that characterized its emergence in 1940s Italy, neorealism, so Bazin would have agreed with Rossellini, "is above all, a moral position from which to look at the world. It then became an aesthetic position, but at the beginning it was moral."³² Bazin further defines this moral stance as a "fundamental humanism" that expresses a simultaneous "love and rejection of reality" and that as such cannot be reduced to an a priori political or religious agenda. "The recent Italian films," he writes, "are at least prerevolutionary. They all reject, implicitly or explicitly, through humor, satire or poetry, the social reality they are using, but they know, even when taking a clear stand, to never treat this reality as a means to an end. . . . They do not forget that before being something to be condemned, the world *is*, quite simply."³³ Bazin praises the neorealists for not subjugating their events to preexisting dramatic structures, and to instead allow those events to manifest themselves as samples of the everyday. In doing so, these films achieve in his vision a synthesis between the laws of the theater and cinema's antitheatrical, "novel-like potential" to give primacy "to events over actions, to succession over causality."[34] The result is a cinema that renders its narrative momentum immanent to the plot-space, or plane of narration, allowing that plane to emerge directly from the historical reality it engages.[35] Bazin writes about *Bicycle Thieves*: "It is a spectacle, and what spectacle! However, in nothing does [De Sica's film] depend on the mathematical principles of drama, the action does not preexist as an essence, it ensues from the preliminary existence of the narrative, it is the 'integral' of reality."[36]

In *Cinema 1: The Movement-Image* (1983), Deleuze makes a very similar argument about *Bicycle Thieves*. "There is no longer a vector or line of the universe which extends and links up the events, the rain can always interrupt or deflect the search fortuitously; the voyage of the man and of the child."[37] Inspired by Bazin, Deleuze locates Italian neorealism at the junction of the transition structuring his *Cinema* books: from a classical cinema of movement (*Cinema 1*) to a modern cinema of time (*Cinema 2*). Deleuze theorizes this transition as cinema's self-liberation of "the sensory-motor link" that connects character perception to action, and that, more in general, ties all plot elements into a cohesive forward-driven momentum. This link is strongest in what Deleuze calls the cinema of the "action image," the type of narrative cinema that became dominant before World War II, in particular in Classical Hollywood, in which narrative situations prompt character actions that in turn prompt new situations, and so on, until closure is reached. Neorealism loosens the sensory-motor link without fully breaking it. Neorealism still respects the rules of continuity editing and, more generally, stays part of a classical paradigm that sees the screen as a window on a self-contained Cartesian space-time. At the same time, neorealism produces what Deleuze refers to as "any-spaces-whatever" (*espaces-quelconque*), screenscapes that, unlike the plot-spaces of the "old realism," do "not yet appear as a real setting."[38] These any-spaces-whatever are undetermined planes that stand in a relation of mutual determination with the indeterminacy of the characters who populate and traverse them, because in neorealism character action, to paraphrase Bazin, no longer preexists the plot-space but instead is rendered immanent to that space.

Bazin forms a crucial influence on Deleuze's account of neorealism, but does Deleuze also share Bazin's fundamental, Catholic-inspired humanism? When concentrating on the narrative hinge between *Cinema 1* and 2, the answer seems to be negative. Deleuze begins the first chapter of *Cinema 2* by stating that "against those who defined Italian Neorealism by its social content, Bazin put forward the fundamental requirement of formal aesthetic criteria."[39] I agree with the last part of this observation, but I would also argue that what makes the vague yet persistent longing for redemption in Bazin's notion of pure cinema so compelling is precisely its integration of an aesthetics of reality with an ethics of representation that *also* depends on neorealism's social content. "Neorealism" for Deleuze is not exactly what it is for Bazin. Whereas the any-space-whatever forms an ontological category, a glimpse of the "plane of immanence" that can really be invoked by *any* space, Bazin's spectacle of reality—a concept he borrows from Cesare Zavattini—is simultaneously an epistemological and a sociohistorical category. On the one hand, the spectacle of reality is defined by the contingency of the present moment. On the other hand, it refers to a historical reality, in particular the everyday experience of the street and the workplace, of the insignificant, of people who in themselves are not very "cinegenic," but who in the films of Rossellini, De Sica, Visconti, and Fellini become the subjects of art.

Of course, "ordinary" people have populated the film screen since the Lumières, and they appear prominently in the classical genres of the western and the melodrama. But especially in pre–World War II narrative cinema, or what Deleuze calls the cinema of the action image, people were rarely portrayed in their everyday lives, in their routines and their struggle for a better life. In its choice of stories, settings, shooting locations, and actors, Italian neorealism was the first large-scale cinematic movement that ruptured with this representational paradigm. In the words of Zavattini, the neorealists "were bored to death with heroes more or less imaginary" and instead sought to establish an encounter with "the real protagonist of everyday life."[40] The neorealist spectacle of reality thus constituted a doubly mimetic revolution: It constituted an aesthetic rupture with pre–World War II psychological realism, and at the same time, at the level of subject matter, it meant a democratization of the worlds cinema creates.

It is instructive to analyze this democratization of cinematic representation alongside the representational revolution in literature about a century and a half earlier. Italian neorealist cinema reiterated the transformation of what Jacques Rancière has called the distribution of the sensible previously performed by the early nineteenth-century novel. By "distribution of the sensible" (*partage du sensible*) Rancière refers to the way particular genres or styles became associated with the representation of certain social groups. Before the literary novel, under what Rancière calls the representative regime, the genre of tragedy was reserved for noble subjects, while the lighter genre of comedy dealt with the profane and the ordinary (though not necessarily with the everyday). The aesthetic regime ruptures with these representational hierarchies and instead turns all and everything into the potential subjects of art. According to Rancière, the emergence of the aesthetic regime coincided with that of literature as such. Literature created "a new sensorium," Rancière writes, a more democratic way of "linking a power of sensory affection and a power of signification."[41] Rancière disagrees with interpretations of the crisis of representation in art as a transition from realism to nonfigurative modes of artistic expression. In his view, it was the realist novel that emancipated resemblance from representation, an argument Rancière sees corroborated by nineteenth-century critics who accused Flaubert of making everything "equal, equally representable."[42]

For Rancière, the politics of the realist novel is precisely this inclusion of objects, persons, and situations previously not deemed worthy of artistic rendering in the first place. Besides Flaubert, the novelist Rancière considers emblematic of the new aesthetic sensorium is Honoré de Balzac. "Perhaps Balzac's and Flaubert's sentences were mute stones, but those who uttered this judgment also knew that, in the age of archeology, of paleontology, and of philology, stones speak too."[43] Rancière continues that the realist novel is determined to give voice to "the mute witnesses of communal history."[44] This is why in Balzac's stores all things—art and kitsch, prose and poetry, old and new stuff, useful and useless objects, "an Indian pipe, a pneumatic machine"—get mixed up into "a poem without ending."[45] Balzac, the self-declared "secretary" of modern reality,[46] thus asks the reader to become a window-shopper who witnesses the sellout of the hierarchies that defined the ancien régime. "One does not consume in Balzac's stores, one reads in them the symptoms of the new times, one recognizes in them the debris of a collapsed world, one encounters in them the equivalent of defunct mythological divinities."[47]

Rancière's claim that Balzac was one of the first to breach representational hierarchies is not entirely new. In *Mimesis* (1946), Erich Auerbach already presented Balzac, along with Stendhal, as the "creator of modern realism," precisely because of his detailed descriptions of the contemporary, everyday world.[48] Auerbach points out that Balzac's mimetic descriptions are not mere potpourris of persons and objects liberated from their anonymity, but renderings of the organic and often demonic unity of the milieu of which they are a part.[49] Every milieu in Balzac, Auerbach argues, "becomes a moral and physical atmosphere which impregnates the landscape, the dwelling, the furniture, implements, clothing, physique, character, surroundings, ideas, activities, and fates of men, and at the same time the general historical situation reappears as a total atmosphere which envelops all its several milieus."[50] Auerbach emphasizes that Balzac's "atmospheric realism" focuses primarily on the middle and lower bourgeoisie, whether Parisian or provincial, whereas it pays relatively little attention to the lower strata of society.[51] Nevertheless, and despite their social-conservative undertone, Balzac's novels contain the seed of a critique of capitalism. As Rancière writes, "when Marx invites the reader to descend [*s'enfoncer*] with him into the hells of capitalist production . . . his textual reference is borrowed from Dante's *Divine Comedy*. But the hermeneutic gesture he accomplishes, that, is borrowed from the poetics of the Balzacian *Human Comedy*."[52]

In *Le Père Goriot* (1835) Balzac himself, by voice of his narrator, states the following about this hermeneutic gesture: "Paris is a true ocean. Throw in your plumb, you will never know its depth. Traverse it, describe it!"[53] Following its protagonist's furious quest to *parvenir*, the novel maps the city's socioeconomic structures. In the words of Georg Lukács, by providing us with such an "infinitesimal fraction . . . of the incommensurable reality of its time,"[54] Balzac's oeuvre captures the totality of a capitalist system whose economic and ideological structures are ever closer integrated. Balzac, and "great realism" in general, manages to do so in Lukács's view when literature does justice to the "dialectical unity of appearance and essence," penetrating the "surface of capitalism [that] appears to 'disintegrate' into a series of elements driven toward independence."[55] This position was met by severe criticism from Theodor Adorno, who accused Lukács of reducing political literature to social realism. According to Adorno, Lukács remained "indifferent to the philosophical question of whether the concrete meaning of a work of art is in fact identical with the mere 'reflection of objective reality.' "[56] For these same reasons Adorno did not share Lukács's love for Balzac. The "entire *Comédie humaine*," Adorno writes, "stands revealed as an imaginative reconstruction of the alienated world, i.e. of a reality no longer experienced by the individual subject."[57]

Regardless of who was right in this quarrel, I would argue that every practice called realist in the critical sense of the term predicates itself on a notion of totality and, concomitantly, the ambition to, in an at least somewhat objective manner, provide insight into the socioeconomic relations that structure the desires and experiences of the modern subject. This also holds true for Italian neorealism. Like the realist novel, most neorealist films integrate their documents of everyday life into allegories of power relations. Take again the example of *Bicycle Thieves*. While I agree with Bazin and Deleuze that the search for the stolen bicycle appears as a series of chance events, the protagonists' increasingly aimless wanderings also have a clear mapping function. From the nuclear family to the trade union, from the pawn shop to the *Porta Portese*, and from the church to the fortune teller: *Bicycle Thieves* traverses and describes—to paraphrase

Balzac—the Italian capital in order to render visible the structures that determine the indeterminacy of so many of its inhabitants. In addition, while mapping postwar, everyday life, many neorealist films also express a hope for change. Far from Balzac's ironic, at times Godlike outlook on his scale model of contemporary France, the neorealists sought to imagine a new and more ethical Italy, an outlook that, as we have seen, Bazin described as a humanist love and rejection of reality.

Bazin wrote these words in 1948, so still before De Sica made *Umberto D* and *Miracle in Milan*. They are two of the films in which neorealism reached its humanist heights. Ironically they are also two films that at the time were received as the end of neorealism proper for their taking flight from reality, both in terms of subject matter and aesthetically. While the partially studio-shot *Umberto D* strays far from aesthetic austerity or the illusion thereof, *Miracle in Milan* ends on the ascension, on stolen broomsticks, of Toto and his fellow poor to a place where "good morning really means good morning" (fig. 4.3). Of course, neorealism did not end with these films, but it certainly underwent a transformation in the 1950s, if only because "the economic miracle" that was Italy did. While in its early years Italian neorealism took its characters from the poor and the proletariat, placing them in narratives that usually end on a redemptive note, over the course of the 1950s (e.g., Rossellini's *Europa '51* [1952] and *Viaggio in Italia / Journey in Italy* [1954] and into the 1960s, the neorealists expanded their scope to Italy's new bourgeoisie, while their outlook on the nation became increasingly bleak. Other than Rossellini, two "second-generation" neorealist directors who had a large share in this ongoing revolution of Italian cinema in the face of Italy's launch into modern capitalism were Michelangelo Antonioni and Pier Paolo Pasolini.[58] The former's *Cronaca di un amore / Story of a Love Affair* (1950) and *L'Eclisse / Eclipse* (1962) are critiques of bourgeois alienation as vitriolic as those found in Flaubert. The latter's *Accattone* (1961) and *Mamma Roma* (1962)—which star the neorealist icons Anna Magnani (Pina in *Rome Open City*) and Lamberto Maggiorani (Antonio in *Bicycle Thieves*), respectively—carry the dream of a new Italy to its symbolic grave, in passion stories far removed from Toto's minimally Christian miracles in Milan.

As far as *Miracle in Milan* is concerned: had De Sica had the disposal of twenty-first-century technologies, he would have likely used CGI for the special effects (which were now done by the American Ned Mann). Special effects—and more generally images or image elements that disrupt the ordinary—are rare in neorealism, which is the first parallel between neorealism and the realism that revived in turn-of-the-twenty-first-century cinema. Some notable exceptions are found in the films of

Dumont (e.g., Pharaon's levitation) and, outside francophone Europe, the work of the Chinese filmmaker Jia Zhangke (whose first feature *Xiao Wu* from 1997 is, like the Dardennes' *L'Enfant*, a variation on Bresson's *Pickpocket*). I am thinking of the instances of realism turning miraculous in *Still Life* (2006), or the animated sequences in *The World* (2004) (figs. 4.4 and 4.5). They are moments of what Bazin would have called "pure cinema" that, much like the final scenes of *Miracle in Milan* and *Diary of a Country Priest*, disrupt mimesis in order to reveal reality's ambiguity more clearly. As Dudley Andrew writes in *What Cinema Is!* (2010): the animated sequences in *The World* "celebrate and contribute to the intoxicating freedom of the digital, and yet . . . they are circumscribed by the human and social drama which they interrupt like holes in cheese. Jia Zhangke is, it turns out, a modernist, devoted to the kind of discovery that the neorealists made their mission."[59] Or as Jia himself states in a *Cahiers du cinéma* dossier titled "Bazin in Asia," the spaceship in *Still Life* isn't a departure from realism but "corresponds to the reality of the Three Gorges Dam. I'm a realist filmmaker. But I should answer to this question: What is realism today?"[60]

From Neo to New: Miraculous Realism

The beginning of an answer to Jia's question is given by Anthony Scott, who in 2013 identified a global wave of new realism, "less a style than an impulse," that "surfaces, with local variations" all over the world.[61] Other than francophone-European *jeune cinéma* and sixth-generation Chinese filmmaking (e.g., the films by Jia or Wang Xiaoshuai's *Beijing Bicycle* [2001], yet another variation on *Bicycle Thieves*), new realist epicenters have been Romanian postrevolutionary cinema (e.g., Cristi Puiu's *The Death of Mr. Lazarescu* [2005] and Christian Mungiu's *4 Months, 3 Weeks, 2 Days* [2007]), the Iranian New Wave (e.g., Jafar Panahi's *The Circle* [2000], Abbas Kiarostami's *Ten* [2002]), New Austrian cinema (e.g., Jessica Hausner's *Lovely Rita* [2001] and Ulrich Seidl's *Import/Export* [2007]), Italian neo-neorealism (e.g., Gianni Amelio's *Il Ladro di bambini* [1992] and Matteo Garrone's *Gomorrah* [2008]) and American independent filmmaking (e.g., Kelly Reichardt's *Rosetta*-inspired *Wendy and Lucy* [2008] and Sean Baker's *The Florida Project* [2017], with its miraculous iphone ending).[62] The realism of these films is in many respects the neorealism of the immediate postwar period. It's a realism made on relatively modest budgets and shot on location that combines dramatic narratives with a documentary feel and a "natural" style of acting. And like neorealism, new realism is a cinema that depicts the world from the perspective of the "small people." There are also differences between new realism and neorealism, both in terms of aesthetics and of content. In terms of aesthetics, first of all new

Figure 4.3. *Miracolo a Milano* (Vittorio de Sica, 1951).

Figure 4.4. *Still Life* (*Sanxia haoren*; Jia Zhangke, 2006).

Figure 4.5. *The World* (*Shijie*; Jia Zhangke, 2004).

realism, even more than neorealism, is a storytelling cinema in which plot development is motivated by character psychology. In Deleuze's terminology, new realism creates a less loosened-up, more conventional form of the action image than neorealism did. Instead its images are often highly emotionally invested in its protagonists' lives. But new realism, in its most interesting forms, also challenges the sensory-motor link in other ways, by overstretching it until it bursts or almost bursts, for example, by repeatedly skipping establishing shots, as is the case in *Rosetta*, a film that like its protagonist has no time to wander in the neorealist fashion. Second and related, even more than is the case with neorealism, the new realist image is defined by an intimist and affective texture that goes hand in hand with, as Lavin and Delorme observe in their critique of the *jeune cinéma*, a concern for human life and a desire to bear witness to life. Third, whereas in most Italian neorealist films sound was almost always postsynchronized, resulting in a degree of distance between image and sound, in new realism the convention is direct sound, as a result of which the viewer is even more inserted into the situations created.

To this one can add that in recent years new realism has also evolved as a digital aesthetic, for example, because digital shooting allows for an added degree of flexibility, especially when improvising with amateur actors. To cite Jia again, this time about his short *In Public* (2001), which is the first film he shot in digital video: "It was as if multiple persons were walking in procession along a river. The digital camera allows you to discretely insert yourself into the procession, while at the same time maintaining a certain distance with respect to it, to follow its rhythm, its pulse, without stopping to look at it, to continue that way, and to enter a mental study."[63] Similarly, Laurent Cantet has embraced the simultaneous physical proximity and observational distance toward the world that DV allows. Cantet states about the shooting of *Entre les murs / The Class* (2008), a film that at once inserts itself into and keeps an observational distance from this school class, whose interactions feel at once scripted and "real":

> I wanted the recording to follow the improvisation work done in studios [*ateliers*], with the same liberty. For that reason HD video was indispensable. I had noticed it when making *Ressources humaines*, the cost and the heaviness of 35mm leave little room for improvisation. Moreover, things got a little fossilized at the moment of shooting. For *Entre les murs*, in contrast, I wanted to shoot continuously for twenty minutes [with three cameras] without interruption, even if nothing happened, because I knew that one remark could be enough to trigger things. . . .

> I was quickly persuaded that the shooting plan required three cameras: a first one always directed at the teacher; a second one on the student standing central in the scene that we were turning; and a third in order to allow digressions: a chair balancing on one leg, a girl cutting her friend's hair, a student who is daydreaming and then all of a sudden starts paying attention—the everyday details of a classroom that we would have never been able to construct.[64]

And of course, also shooting with analog means a certain intimate distance between camera and the acting/acted subject is possible, as is proven by *Rosetta* and *L'humanité* (though since his TV series *P'tit Quinquin* Dumont has shot digitally). What speaks, though, from these quotations of Jia and Cantet, and what speaks from new realism's images, is a desire to observe its protagonists from up close both in terms of shot length and affective investment, this even more than was the case in neorealism, which also often captured its characters from a distance as it shows them wandering in plot-space.

As far as differences in content between new realism and neorealism are concerned: While at the beginning of this section I listed the new realist examples by national cinemas (sixth-generation Chinese filmmaking, postrevolutionary Romanian cinema, etc.), an important cause for the global nature of new realism is of course the increasing transnationalization of national cinemas.[65] Vice versa, new realism expresses human life in the era that local, regional, and national communities are increasingly integrated into global networks. As Fredric Jameson writes, in his concluding remarks to *Aesthetics and Politics* (the 2007 edited collection that includes the essays by Lukács and Adorno cited earlier):

> Under these circumstances, the function of a new realism would be clear; to resist the power of reification in consumer society and to reinvent that category of totality which, systematically undermined by existential fragmentation on all levels of life and social organization today, can alone project structural relations between classes as well as class struggles in other countries, in what has increasingly become a world system.[66]

Jameson makes this call for a new realism with respect to the literary novel, but elsewhere, in *The Geopolitical Aesthetic* (1995), he formulates a similar argument about realism in cinema.[67] There Jameson raises, moreover, the question, "Under what circumstances can a necessarily individual story with individual characters function to represent collective processes?" His answer: "Allegory thereby fatally stages its historic reappearance in the postmodern era . . . and seems to offer the most satisfactory (if varied and heterogeneous) solutions to these form-problems."[68]

While I agree with Jameson that new realism maps a globalized totality, I would argue that allegory also has its limitations. This becomes clear for example from a comparative analysis of the following three films that all employ a mosaic narrative structure that cuts back and forth between different story lines: *Code inconnu* (2000) directed by Michael Haneke, *Babel* (2006) by Alejandro González Iñárritu, and Jia's *The World*. Of these three attempts to allegorize the global system, I consider only *The World* a success. The reason is precisely that Jia's film is allegorical to just a limited extent, and may in fact be read as a commentary on the insufficiency of allegory in our age. Whereas *Code inconnu* and *Babel*, in their almost Balzacian endeavor to piece together story fragments from all over the world, ultimately subject those fragments to the grand statements about the disconnection between people suggested by their titles, *The World* limits its scope to the small world of its protagonists (who all work in a theme park near Beijing called "The World," which features scaled replicas of global landmarks like the Eiffel Tower and the Taj Mahal). In doing so, *The World* manages to capture the *immanence* of global networks: from tourism to women trafficking, from the clothing industry to labor migration.

Jia's films are among the most powerful examples of a transnational new realism that reinvents the neorealist love and rejection of reality for the globalized digital era. It's a new realism that, in the words of Martin O'Shaughnessy, bears witness to "the fragments left behind once globalization has passed through the social terrain."[69] Similarly, as Lauren Berlant observes in *Cruel Optimism* (2011) in relation to Cantet's *Ressources humaines* and *L'Emploi du temps / Time Out* (2001):

> Even the most local perspective in these films is an outcome of globalization and neoliberal restructuring: none of these dramas would occur without shifts in state tax, labor, and welfare policy that promote the disempowerment of unions, a corporate culture that suppresses wages, benefits, and workers' rights, and the concomitant expansion of production systems scattered across spaces in Europe, Korea, and elsewhere.[70]

Berlant defines global new realism as a "cinema of precarity," a witnessing mode of the contemporary capitalist "fraying" of socioeconomic structures all over the globe and across classes. By "precarity" Berlant understands the "politico-affective" condition to which human existence is reduced once the good life fantasy is no longer available. Scraping by, the precarious subject lacks, above all, a narrative, and constantly has to adapt herself to the challenges posed by the present. The films of Cantet or the Dardennes, Berlant argues, engage this solitary struggle, while they explore new forms of community: "The cinema of Precarity attends to the proprioceptive—to bodies moving in space performing affectively laden gestures—to investigate new potential conditions of solidarity emerging from subjects not with similar historical identities or social locations but with similar adjustment styles to the pressures of the emergent new ordinariness."[71]

This "Precariat" that Berlant sees the seeds of in new realist cinema is conceptually close to what autonomous Marxism has called "multitude." Like "Precariat," the notion of multitude originates from the desire to imagine forms of collective resistance beyond "proletariat" and "the people." Whereas "proletariat" presupposes a traditionally Marxist vision on society, "multitude" cuts through traditional class categories, and in doing so disconnects resistance from the labor process. And whereas "people" refers to a homogeneous group that can be represented and controlled by institutions (e.g., political parties, the Church, trade unions), "multitude" seeks to express, rather than represent, a heterogeneous, self-expressive swarm of singularities who are involved in the same, nonteleological movement. "Multitude" is thus a simultaneously historical and ontological category that expresses a mode of communal existence particular to our globalized, post-Fordist age, while it at the same time confronts the precarity fundamental to the human animal. As Paolo Virno writes in *A Grammar of the Multitude* (*Grammatica della moltitudine*, 2003):

> That which has always been true, is only now unveiled. The multitude is this: a fundamental biological configuration which becomes a historically determined way of being, ontology revealing itself phenomenologically. One could even say that the post-Fordist multitude manifests *anthropogenesis* as such on a historical-empirical level; that is to say, the genesis itself of the human animal, its distinguishing characteristics.[72]

A class beyond class, and a community beyond the people, the multitude is a form of collective human life beyond humanity. Whenever the multitude actualizes itself, however ephemerally and locally, and whenever it manifests itself as *a* multitude, one can speak of a miracle, an *immanent* miracle. I take this concept of "immanent miracle" from Alessia Ricciardi, who introduces it in a comparative analysis of *Miracle in Milan* and Michael Hardt and Antonio Negri's 2000 book *Empire*, which cites *Miracle in Milan* as one of its inspirations. *Miracle in Milan*, Ricciardi writes, "may be said to allegorically depict, in the final flight of the poor, the paradoxical capacity of neorealist film to convert pessimism into an act of immanent faith, as a miracle can only emerge from a contingent and immanent perspective."[73] This same nontheological, immanent faith in a new world for which we do not yet have a grammar Ricciardi equally identifies in *Empire* and its attempt to conceive of new forms of collectivity, to think a multitude. But Ricciardi also critiques *Empire* for its somewhat Christian ending that disrupts "the book's otherwise ecumenical spirit."[74]

The final pages of *Empire* do indeed catch the reader off guard by a deus ex machina in the form of Saint Francis who, so Hardt and Negri write, during his lifetime "posed a joyous life, including all of being and nature, the animals, sister moon, brother sun, the birds of the field, the poor and exploited humans, together against the will of power and corruption."[75] To a certain extent, and in defense of *Empire*, the book's finale may be understood in the light of the "humanism after the death of Man" that the authors identify in the late Foucault (especially in his work on sexuality). "How is it possible," they ask, "that the author who worked so hard to convince us of the death of Man, the thinker who carried the banner of antihumanism throughout his career, would in the end champion these central tenets of the humanist tradition?" Hardt and Negri resolve this paradox by arguing that Foucault's posthuman humanism in fact forms a logical continuation of his Nietzschean project: "Once we recognize our posthuman bodies and minds, once we see ourselves for the simians and cyborgs we are, we then need to explore the *vis viva*, the creative powers that animate us as they do all of nature and actualize our potentialities."[76] This may all be true, and yet these reflections, so I agree with Ricciardi, do not fully account for the book's miraculous conclusion on Saint Francis, who is also known as the "alter Christus" (as he received the same stigmata as the original Christ). In his visitation the reader recognizes an old-fashioned humanism from before the death of man that models its ideal of "human" on a white, male, Western subject. It is the secular-Catholic humanism, moreover, that also inspired many first-generation Italian neorealists films, including Rossellini's *Francesco, giullare di Dio* (*The Flowers of St. Francis*, 1950) and *Miracle in Milan*, in which Toto, like Saint Francis, is an alternative Christ for the poor.

Also the new realism of the Cinéma du Nord is, as we have seen, frequented by alternative christs, in particular in the films of the Dardennes (*Rosetta*, *L'Enfant*), Dumont (*La Vie de Jésus*, *L'humanité*, *Hadewijch*, *Hors Satan*), and before them Pialat (*Sous le soleil de Satan*), who are all filmmakers who, to paraphrase Lavin and Delorme, launched themselves on the route traced out by Bresson (though not necessarily in the way these critics had in mind). South of the Nord, the francophone-European new realism is not as explicitly Christian in its inspirations, but in its overall concern with the "small people," young French cinema's new realism has definitely displayed a certain humanism and, directly related, a belief in the cinematic image to bear witness to human life, often in rather conventional, classical-realist modes of storytelling. This renewed belief in representation, and this reinvigorated belief in cinema's ability to offer a window onto an increasingly globalized world, is a turn away from critiques of representation and humanism as found in modern French film and philosophy, including the film philosophies of Godard and Deleuze. At the same time, like new realism both Deleuze and Godard, and the French New Wave filmmakers in general, have shown themselves inspired by not only Bresson (in the modern way Lavin and Delorme refer to), but also by Italian neorealism and by Bazin's writings on neorealism and Bresson. In order to understand young new realism's relation to the modern cinema of the New Wave, it is therefore necessary to understand modern cinema's own inspiration by neorealism.

The Modern Cinema

Bazin died a day after Truffaut started shooting *Les 400 coups*, and we can therefore only speculate as to whether Bazin would have been prepared to modernize his cinematic ideals in response to the much more self-conscious, fragmented, and also playful aesthetics of the French New Wave. What is certain is that Bazin's writings inspired the *Cahiers* filmmakers, even though the *exact* way is difficult to determine, as Dudley Andrew argues in *Opening Bazin* (2011):

> The phrase "Nouvelle Vague" should be read as a play on words, a historical inversion that transforms the first term into a noun and the second into an adjective. Thus "New Wave" becomes "vague news," or uncertain gospel." Indeed what the New Wave directors received in the transmission from Bazin can only be called vague. Truffaut, Godard, Rohmer, Chabrol—all of them disagreed with the Bazinian criteria for cinematic value: don't they champion "small subjects," set against the "important topics" their master had always believed went hand in hand with great cinema? Still, they absorbed his lessons about Renoir and Rossellini (the play of amateurism, the mixture of actors and ordinary people), and they generally agreed with the key principles of his ontological realism.

But how can one stick to so-called Bazinian ideas and yet oppose their historical, sociological, and political consequences? Failing to apply the general idea of cinematic realism in their treatment of individual films, one after the next, the New Wave critics had to remain "vague" if they were to remain Bazinian in any sense at all. This was especially true as their own films moved further from rendering a conception of the world, becoming increasingly focused on a conception of cinema (although Bazin preached that one should not divorce these). Still a larger transmission occurred, larger because much more vague: the transmission of a philosophical idea, which does not personally belong to Bazin, though he knew how to phrase it properly: the idea of mimesis.[77]

To further specify the last part of Andrew's argument: the idea of mimesis the New Wave generation took from Bazin was a deliberately *vague* idea. Like the neorealists, the New Wave directors sought to capture the indeterminate, fleeting nature of the present moment. Unlike the neorealists, and in particular the first-generation neorealists, the New Wave was not so much concerned with staying faithful to everyday reality. In difference with Bazin's doubly mimetic ideal of a cinema that puts its impressions of profilmic life in the service of a simultaneously aesthetic and historical idea of reality, the New Wave integrated a sense of the street into its *l'art-pour-l'art* approach to filmmaking above all concerned with "cinema." At its most modernist and philosophical, the New Wave discards the Bazinian emphasis on reality as a stable external referent for cinematic value, and instead foregrounds its own artificiality.

In the *Cinema* books, Deleuze welcomes this rupture as one that affirms life, "life" understood in the Nietzschean sense as an all-expressive, preindividual will-to-power. "The neorealist resolution," Deleuze writes, "still retained a reference to a form of the true, although it profoundly renewed it, and certain authors were freed from it in their development. But the New Wave deliberately broke with the form of the true to replace it by the powers of life, cinematographic powers considered to be more profound."[78] According to Deleuze, the New Wave thus completed the crisis of action set in motion by neorealism, and in doing so liberated cinema from the already loosened-up sensory-motor link that governs classical narrative realism, in particular that of Classical Hollywood. Deleuze sees "the sign of a new realism" in films such as *Tirez sur le pianiste* (Truffaut, 1960), *Paris nous appartient* (Rivette, 1961), and *Les Carabiniers* (Godard, 1962). Unlike the old realism of the action image, this new realism is not concerned with "making-true" but with "making-false" (*faire-faux*): "clumsy fights, badly aimed punches or shots, a whole out-of-phase of action and speech replace the too perfect duels of American Realism."[79] The new realism Deleuze embraces here is in almost all respects the opposite of the new realism of young French cinema. It's the *expressive* realism of a cinema of time that subsumes and shatters the *representational* realism of a cinema of movement.

Let's have a closer look at the philosophical underpinnings of the transition from movement to time that connects the *Cinema* books. David Rodowick draws a convincing parallel between this transition and the emergence of poststructuralist theory in France. "Only in France," he writes, "was this experimentation philosophically possible. From *The Order of Things* to *Cinema 2: The Time-Image*, there runs a Nietzschean thread that passes between philosophy, film theory, and film practice as an extraordinary examination of time and history both in philosophy and in cinema."[80] That Nietzschean thread is the expression, both in concept and image, of the modern crisis of representation. As Foucault argues in *The Order of Things* (*Les Mots et les choses*, 1966, four years after Deleuze's book on Nietzsche), whereas in the classical world there is a distance between discourse and things, a distance that allows people to classify their reality into representations from which they themselves remain absent, in the modern world—or what Foucault calls the modern episteme—the fundamental difference between discourse and things disappears. Everything has become a sign, to paraphrase Peirce, including the human subject who, so Foucault writes, is revealed in their finitude, "a fundamental finitude which rests on nothing but the [limitation of man's] own existence as fact."[81] In the final pages of *The Order of Things*, Foucault unveils the drive behind his "archaeology of the Same," namely, to reach beyond this all-too-human finitude and confront the unthought that is man's "double." It's a dangerous expedition, for as we know from *doppelgänger* legends, to literally encounter oneself is to encounter Death.[82] This death of the human form is precisely what Foucault heralds. "Human," after all, is only a recent invention, and with the modern episteme nearing its ineluctable end, the human face, "drawn in sand at the edge of the sea," will soon be engulfed by the waves of the "new pure present" that also finds expression in Deleuze's time image.[83] As Deleuze emphasizes at the end of his book on Foucault (1986, a year after *Cinema 2*), this death of the human form and the concomitant arrival of the "superman" is a conceptual revolution rather than the actual disappearance of living human beings. "It is the advent of a new form that is neither God nor [hu]man and which, it is hoped, will not prove worse than its two previous forms."[84]

To return to cinema: historically speaking, the medium was born under the modern episteme, but what Deleuze calls the cinema of movement still corresponds to the classical episteme. Cinema only became truly modern with its transition to time, liberating camera and spectator from their "invisible" confinement. Among the most poignant expressions of this cinematic reiteration of the crisis of representation are Godard's *Les Carabiniers / The Carabineers* and *Le Mépris / Contempt*, both from 1963, and both films inspired by Rossellini. *Les Carabiniers* was based on a screenplay by the Italian filmmaker (who on his turn took the story from a 1945 play by Beniamino Joppolo), while *Le Mépris* is a variation on *Viaggio in Italia*, including its tourist gaze, but minus its miraculous conclusion. To start with *Les Carabiniers*: A gritty black-and-white, newsreel-style neorealist film sliced up with Rembrandt reproductions, fashion ads, and World War II footage, *Les Carabiniers* is a film about war, representation, and the representation of war in film. In the beginning, Ulysses (Marino Masé) and Michel-Ange (Patrice Moullet) enlist to fight in name of the king, and it's the king's name that guarantees that they will be duly compensated for their heroic deeds once the king has won the war. Until then, however, they will have to content themselves with images, literally. Ulysses and Michel-Ange bring home piles of postcards that correspond to categories and subcategories of things: means of transport > rail transport: diesel engine, BB-9003. Or: monuments > antiquity > the pyramids, the Parthenon, and so on for seven more minutes. Representations: that is what Ulysses and Michel-Ange have fought for, *plus* the firm belief that those representations have a direct referent in reality and perhaps even partake in that reality itself (as do photographs according to Bazin's ontology).

As their names emphasize, the epistemological enclave Ulysses and Michel-Ange inhabit is a combination of the Foucauldian classical and preclassical epistemes. In the preclassical episteme there was no fundamental difference between words and things. Culture and nature still formed an organic whole, while discourse had no need for representations, as it already spoke the univocal language of things. It's the world of the *Odyssey*, for example. As Fritz Lang explains in *Le Mépris*: "The world of Homer is a real world. The poet belonged to a civilization that developed in harmony with and not in opposition to nature. The beauty of the *Odyssey* lies precisely in this belief in reality as it is." Lang speaks these words to Paul (Michel Piccoli), who in the eyes of the German director makes the mistake of projecting his own modern, neurotic odyssey (his relationship trouble with Camille, performed by Brigitte Bardot) onto the one he is adapting for the screen. Shot in Technicolor and Cinemascope, *Le Mépris* opens with a long take filmed on location at the Cinecittà studios. The shot shows a film crew working on a tracking shot. While the on-screen camera slowly rolls toward the viewer, a male voice-over recites the credits, concluding on the statement that "according to Bazin, cinema substitutes for our gazes a world that accords itself to our desires" and that "*Le Mépris* is the story of that world" (Le cinéma, disait André Bazin, substitue à nos regards un monde qui s'accorde à nos désirs. Le Mépris est l'histoire de ce monde). The quotation the film attributes to Bazin is in fact a misquotation of a different *Cahiers* critic, but, nonetheless, captures Bazin's cinematic ideal fairly well.[85] For Bazin, cinema, at those moments it creates the illusion of its own disappearance, holds the redemptive power to set reality free of its contingencies. Godard does not seem to share this idealism. In line with Michel's claim in *Le Petit soldat* (Godard's third film that was released in France in 1963, after it had been banned for three years) that "cinema is truth twenty-four times a second," Godard over and again affirms a modern paradigm in which signs and images have lost their intrinsic value, and in which the classical distance between observer and representation is shattered.[86] As the on-screen camera reminds us at the end of the opening sequence of *Le Mépris*: *We* viewers are the subjects of the film's vivisection of modern love.

Speaking about love: What happened to the neorealist "love" necessary for "the birth of the new image"? Deleuze raises this question at the end of *Cinema 1*, where he expresses the worry that in a modern, falsifying cinema all images start to resemble the clichés they seek to expose, with the result that images do not really express anything anymore except for their belonging to a world of images. Deleuze recognizes the same concern in Godard: "We will find in Godard formulas which express the problem: if images have become clichés, internally as well as externally, how can an Image be extracted from all these clichés, 'just an image,' an autonomous mental image?"[87] Deleuze invests his hope in the time image and its liberation of cinematic expression, thereby offering a glimpse of the death of the human form. As he writes about the crystal image, the type of time image that expresses time most directly, "it is time that we *see in the crystal* . . . ," "the perpetual foundation of time, Cronos and not Chronos. This is the powerful, non-organic Life which grips the world."[88]

The *Cinema* books cannot be seen separate from Deleuze's more general, lifelong ontology of difference, his endeavor to think life, understood as a pre-individual, posthuman intensity. The passage from the movement-image to the time-image that structures Deleuze's cinema philosophy—from a classical cinema that depends on a "form of the true" to a modern cinema that creates its own truths—corresponds to a transition that "happened a very long time ago in philosophy."[89] It is the passage from Descartes-Kant-Hegel to Spinoza-Nietzsche-Foucault, from dialectics to immanent causality, from representation to expression, from the human to the posthuman, from forms of discourse that clearly delineate narrative points-of-view to a free indirect discourse in which "we no longer know what is imaginary or real, physical or mental,"[90] and from the diachronic to the synchronic, that is to say, the eternal return of the new pure present. When thus seen from the perspective of this thread that runs through and that connects *Cinema 1* and *Cinema 2*, the return of more conventional and overtly humanist forms of realism can only be taken as a regression, leading cinema back to a more naive, less critical and self-reflexive state. To a certain extent this is indeed the case, because as I agree with Lavin and Delorme's criticism of the young French cinema of life, new realism has not revolutionized cinema in the way neorealism and the New Wave did. Yet in its most interesting manifestations, the young new realist cinema of life does create a kind of cinema that appears missing from Deleuze's taxonomy of images. To identify such a cinema is to identify a potential blind spot in Deleuze's immanentism at large.

Deleuze's work has been an important influence on this project. Other than the *Cinema* books, my transregional outlook on the Cinéma du Nord is inspired by his writings on space, concepts, and immanence. In *What Is Philosophy* (*Qu'est-ce que la philosophie?*, 1991) he and Félix Guattari write: "The plane [of immanence] is like a desert that concepts populate without dividing up. The only regions of the plane are concepts themselves, but the plane is all that holds them together. The plane has no other regions than the tribes populating and moving around on it."[91] Concepts and planes are inseparable. Philosophy extracts them from language, and all philosophy begins with rolling out a plane that is always already populated by concepts. The plane itself is not conceptual but forms the pre-philosophical condition of possibility or "image" of thought. It's a risky place also: "We head for the horizon, on the plane of immanence, and we return with bloodshot eyes, yet they are the eyes of the mind."[92] What has the philosopher seen on their journey? What causes the afterglow in their eyes? Was it a *monstrum* perhaps, an inassimilable, purely indexical, gazing sign, a signifier without signified that leaves the subject speechless and without direction in their effort *à faire sens*, confronting thought with the unthought living at its decentered heart? And what if this monster has a human face?

The Acting/Acted Image
(the Example of *A Nos amours*)

New realism offers that human face. It is a cinema of life, in a humanist sense. New realism distances itself from the modernist, bourgeois, literary-minded, and Parisian-centered New Wave, from which it at the same time reclaims the neorealist heritage of an "idea of mimesis" in order to render visible the margins and the marginalized at the turn of the twenty-first century. New realism restores, moreover, the neorealist belief in the truth of the image, a faith crushed under cinema's modern episteme. But new realism's opposition to and critique of the New Wave is complex. New realism also inherits from the New Wave. First of all, young French cinema returns to the auteur model, to its production process and its shooting on modest budgets. Second, new realism's focus on economically and geographically marginalized subjects has proto-new-realist precedents in the New Wave, like Claude Chabrol's chronicles of provincial life and the wanderings of a young woman, played by Sandrine Bonnaire, through the any-spaces-whatever of Agnes Varda's *Sans toit ni loi* (1985). Above all, new realism continues the long French tradition of socially critical humanist realism, whose flame during the New Wave era was kept alive above all in the films of Bresson and Pialat. The former's *Pickpocket* was released in 1959, the year of *Les 400 coups*, while the latter belonged to the same historical generation as the New Wave auteurs but only made his first film when the New Wave proper had already passed. Bresson is a recurring figure in Deleuze's *Cinema* books. Pialat, however, who by the publication of *Cinema 2* (1985) had made seven feature-length films, shines in his absence from the two volumes. Does this absence testify to a blind spot in Deleuze's cinema narrative, and in his posthuman philosophy of expression at large?

As Deleuze explains from the outset of *Cinema 1*, his project "is not a history of the cinema" but "an attempt at the classification of images and signs."[93] It is a classification of cinematic forms of life. The narrative that runs through *Cinema 1* and *2* is at once linear and non-linear. At some points, Deleuze presents the transition from movement to time as a loose diachronic trajectory: "around 1948, Italy; about 1958 France; about 1968 Germany."[94] Elsewhere, he presents it as a synchronic process, emphasizing that the "direct time image" is not a post–World War II invention but "a phantom which has always haunted the cinema [that] it took modern cinema to give a body to."[95] The reverse situation holds equally true: also once the promise of the modern time image had become flesh, as for example in the French New Wave, the classical cinema of action continued to be around. "The greatest commercial successes always take that route," Deleuze writes about the persistence of the action image, "but the soul of the cinema no longer does," because it "demands increasing thought."[96]

As far as Pialat is concerned: would his absence from the *Cinema* books mean that Deleuze did not consider films such as *L'Enfance nue*,

La Gueule ouverte / The Mouth Agape (1974), and *A nos amours / To Our Loves* (1983) part of cinema's soul as it had actualized itself in post–New Wave France? For Deleuze, the post–New Wave French cinema that *mattered*, that materialized cinema's soul, was a cinema of bodies: "Since the New Wave, every time there was a fine and powerful film, there was a new exploration of the body in it."[97] As examples, Deleuze lists films by Chantal Akerman, Jean Eustache, Jacques Doillon, and Philippe Garrel. In his view, these auteurs enriched the modern cinema that was being constructed on the "ruins . . . of the action-image" with a voyeurism of "postures" and "attitudes," like Jeanne Dielman's real-time potato peeling, or the infinite *pas-de-trois* of Eustache's *La Maman et la putain* (1973). Under the influence of this voyeurism, so Deleuze argues, postures and attitudes undergo an "imperceptible passage" to "gesture." Deleuze takes the concept of "gesture" or "gest" from Bertolt Brecht, while he also generalizes its definition as a "link or knot of attitudes" that does not depend on a preexisting narrative structure but that "carries out a direct theatricalization of bodies, often very discreet, because it takes place independently of any role."[98] Other than the examples already mentioned, Deleuze considers John Cassavetes emblematic for cinema's passage to gesture. Deleuze writes:

> The greatness of Cassavetes' work is to have undone the story, plot, or action, but also space, in order to get to attitudes as to categories which put time into the body, as well as thought into life. When Cassavetes says that characters must not come from a story or plot, but that the story should be secreted by the characters, he sums up the requirement of the cinema of bodies: the character is reduced to his own bodily attitudes, and what ought to result is the gest, that is, a "spectacle," a theatricalization or dramatization which is valid for all plots.[99]

Pialat's cinema of bodies has often been compared to that of Cassavetes, but the difference between the two is even more revealing, because it explains why Deleuze passes over Pialat in his discussion of the French post–New Wave era. Philippe Lubac formulates the difference between Pialat and Cassavetes as follows: "John Cassavetes' actors *perform* unpredictability, whereas, in Pialat, actors such as Monsieur and Madame Thierry [*L'Enfance nue*] *are* unpredictable."[100] Similarly, Kent Jones writes:

> Where the breaks in a Cassavetes film are strictly behavior-oriented, getting at the essential unpredictability of people, Pialat's often feel like frayed-edge manifestations of Tarkovsky's

"pressure of time." The exquisite agony of the moment, which must always come to an end, the transience of experience, eternally invigorating and just as frustrating—few filmmakers have ever come as close to capturing it on film.[101]

Pialat brought to great heights the dialectic between the acting body in front of his camera and the performed body presented on-screen. His films establish a short circuit between the acting and the acted, by which I do not mean the mere coincidence of actor and character, whether that coincidence results from the becoming-character of an actress whose performance is so virtuous that it becomes eerie (e.g., Juliette Binoche / Anne in *Code inconnu*), or takes the form of an amateur acting himself as good or bad as he is able to (e.g., Lamberto Maggiorani / Antonio in *Bicycle Thieves*). In both examples, the character appearance is highly affective but also somewhat one-dimensional and, in the case of *Code inconnu*, even a little cold and clinical (precisely the affects Haneke is after in his ruthless critique of the Western bourgeois subject). No, by the acting/acted short circuit I mean that *je ne sais quoi* that happens when the tension between the acting and the acted reaches such a height that acting almost but not quite breaks down and gives way to acts acting through the body trying to hide itself in the act. At such instances, the acting and the acted body appear at one and the same time, separate yet held together by the real, sparkling nonacted joy of acting that has taken possession of the person who's acting that she's not acting, and that somehow, in all its colors, is transferring itself to the other side, the screen, the site of the acted. What one sees in this flash that is the acting/acted body is not merely the becoming-human of the on-screen character, but above all the becoming-actor of the person in front of the camera.

Pialat knew what he wanted, sort of, intuitively, but that is the point, and his challenge was to bring that intuition alive. Kent Jones recalls an anecdote he was told by Elsa Zylberstein, who played a sex worker in *Van Gogh* (1991): "Working with Pialat was like trying to walk a straight line in a funhouse after downing a quart of vodka. Lightning in a bottle—a motto, a working principle, an instinct, a way of life. 'Stop—what you're doing now, that's exactly what I want,' he would tell Elsa. 'What?' she would ask. 'You just lost it!' 'What did I just lose?!?' "[102] Or take *A nos amours*: The film captures the coming-of-age of the fifteen-year-old Suzanne as much as it captures the becoming-actress of Sandrine Bonnaire, who Pialat had "discovered" through a call for extras. As is often the case with Pialat, *A nos amours* is an explicitly imperfect film with ellipses that do not get accounted for and loose ends that are never tied up. The film was based on a script by Arlette Langmann, but during the shooting Pialat frequently deviated from the script, and he had his actors improvise many of the scenes. This method of working made Pialat the true inheritor of Jean Renoir. As Alain Bergala writes in *Cahiers du cinéma*: "Like Renoir, Pialat must be convinced that the search for perfection has never made the force of an artwork and that cinema's worst enemy is a *plan* ["plan" and "shot"] to be carried out, the architect's blueprint that Renoir has always hated. Like Renoir he prefers to paint the bouquet from the side that he has not prepared it."[103]

In *A nos amours*, Pialat's strategy of the making-impromptu of staged situations reaches its apogee in the family dinner near the end of the film, a scene through which Pialat shows his allegiance to the French realism of the 1930s, to Renoir but also to Marcel Pagnol. Pialat had not written out this fifteen-minute scene, nor had he prepared his actors for the return of the never-named father, played by Pialat himself.[104] This dinner scene starts with a diatribe between the father/Pialat and his brother-in-law Jacques (played by Jacques Fieschi) about the position of auteur cinema in France. The dialogue picks up on an actual polemic Pialat had at the time with the film journal *Cinématographe*, for which Fieschi worked.[105] Then the father and the camera turn their gazes toward Suzanne (Bonnaire), the only person in this crazy family who still loves him. "N'est-ce pas mademoiselle Suzanne?" (Right, Miss Suzanne?), he asks his daughter. Suzanne remains silent for a second, pensive, biting her nails, on her guard. "T'es comme eux?" (Are you like them?), her father continues. "Non mais," Bonnaire improvises. "Mais en ce moment," Pialat steps up the pressure, while the camera still frames Suzanne/Bonnaire seated between her possessive brother and her rather dull fiancé, "qui a raison, eux ou moi? Où tu es?" (But who is right now, they or I? Where do you stand?) "Elle a pas à choisir?" (She doesn't have to choose), Jacques, offscreen, jumps in. "Ah, pourquoi?" (Why?), Pialat ignores Jacques, upon which his gaze and the camera pan back to Suzanne, "Où tu es-toi?" (Where do you stand?). "Moi je suis là" (I'm here), Suzanne responds, while her pensiveness gives way to a disarming smile, acted or not (figs. 4.6–4.8).

This scene could not contrast more with the alienating obsession with bodies Deleuze saw, and that he wanted to see, in post–New Wave cinema. Contrary to the voyeuristic, thought-provoking, and distancing outlook on postures and attitudes that in their passage to gesture express the preindividual, prehuman power of the false, the obsession with bodies found in Pialat's films, but also in those of the Dardennes and Dumont, produces an intimate, affective cinema that affirms but also examines a notion of "humanity." Like the time image, this acting/acted image is not a recent invention. One encounters elements of it everywhere cinema

Figures 4.6–4.8. *A Nos amours* (Maurice Pialat, 1983).

creates the affective illusion of integrating flashes of human life into its staged realities, whether fictional or documentary. The acting/acted image is the fundamental humanism of cinema's ontology, a humanism somewhat repressed, perhaps, in the *Cinema* books. It is a kind of cinema that goes as far back as that staged documentary in which we see workers acting that they are not acting that they are leaving the Lumière factory. But one equally encounters this acted/acting image in the French New Wave. Think for example of the largely improvised interview with François / Jean-Pierre Léaud at the end of *Les 400 Coups*, a scene Pialat quotes in his *L'Enfance nue*.

The acting/acted image is Deleuze's blind spot for post–World War II forms of cinema, and especially of the forms of French cinema around him, that appeal to affect rather than to thought, and that affirm a rather classical idea of human life. This blind spot manifests itself most clearly in the elements of a progress narrative that Deleuze, especially in his discussion of neorealism, weaves through his rendering of cinema's transition from movement to time. In this narrative, Deleuze mainly concentrates on neorealism's protomodernist aspects, while he underscores what Bazin called neorealism's "fundamental humanism," that is to say, its weak spot for precarious subjects combined with its Christian longing for grace, secular or not. In addition, in his discussion of the New Wave and post–New Wave Deleuze mainly concentrates on those films and those aspects of films that corroborate his posthumanism inspired by Spinoza, Nietzsche, and Foucault. There indeed exists such a philosophical parallel between Deleuze and the New Wave directors, in particular Godard, but to draw that parallel too tightly leads one to ignore the intimist, nonfalsifying, and at times plainly humanist side of the New Wave and post–New Wave soul of French cinema.

The life image is thus not only a reaction to the New Wave modern cinema, in some cases it is also integrated into it. One of the best examples is *Cléo de 5 à 7* (1962) by Agnès Varda. The film follows Cléo almost real-time on her wanderings through Paris, while capturing her frantic state of mind. Cléo is anxious about the test results of her tumor that she will receive later that day. Will the ominous tarot reading that the film opens on be validated by reality? Do the cards, shot in color, predict the otherwise black-and-white plot? In terms of cinematography and editing the film is akin to *A bout de souffle* (Jean-Luc Godard, 1960), but whereas Michel dies, *Cléo de 5 à 7* ends on a redemptive, perhaps even humanist, note—a belief in love and a true connection between two souls, however uncertain their future (Cléo still does need to undergo chemo therapy, while her love is a soldier on leave about to return to the French-Algerian War).

In the last two decades Varda made a series of intimate essay documentaries that integrate social commentary, a reflection on cinema, as well as portraiture, including self-portraiture: *Le Glâneur et la glâneuse / The Gleaners and I* (2000, an ode to small digital cameras), *Les Plages d'Agnès / The Beaches of Agnès* (2008, in which she celebrates her eightieth birthday and an ode to her deceased husband Jacques Demy), and *Visages Villages / Faces Places* (2017). In this last film Varda teams up with JR, a *photograffeur* and street artist who flyposts giant black-and-white photographs in public locations, and who in his refusal to take off his sunglasses reminds Varda of Godard. The film documents the road trip through France that Varda and JR make in the latter's photobooth mini-van. The trip begins in Bruay-la-Buissière in the French North, where the two create a series of portraits of miners, which they then stick onto the *corons*, the old miners' houses, which are about to be demolished. The series includes the portrait of Jeanne, in her own words "la dernière des survivantes," as she refuses to leave her house. Jeanne recalls how as a child she and her friends used to feast on the "pain d'alouette," the leftover baguette that the workers brought back up from the mine. From the North, Varda and JR continue to move down south, while they stage themselves into the image in Varda's trademark lighthearted, minimally fictive style: to Normandie, to the Vaucluse, to the Alpes-de-Haute-Provence, to Sainte-Marguerite-sur-Mer, and finally to Rolle in Switzerland, Godard's hometown. Varda and Godard have a rendezvous, but the latter doesn't show. There's no acting in Varda's disappointment in her long-term friend, but she is consoled by her new friend JR, who *finally* takes off his sunglasses and shows his eyes to her, though not to the viewer, as the blurry image renders the point-of-view of Varda's declining eyesight. As Varda reminisces earlier in the film: once Godard, when both she and he were still young, and when Godard in fact was the same age (thirty-three) as JR now, once in that distant past, Godard also took off his sunglasses for her and allowed himself to be photographed as a person, letting go for a moment of the carefully crafted artist-persona who always wants to be in control of the image, including his self-image. Godard's no-show in *Visages villages* (which doesn't appear to be staged) frankly is a missed opportunity. Looking at Godard's latest films, though, his refusal to become part of a montage he has no control over can be understood. Whereas Varda over the course of her career became increasingly playful, in the late Godard there is little room for play. The late Godard is dead serious and concerned above all with Love with a capital *L*, understood as the montage of two souls, not in the fragile and intimate way in which Varda and JR convince the viewer of their true human connection, but in a very abstract way in which montage is supposed to produce a spark of Grace of the kind we also sense a longing for in the Dardennes, Dumont, and before them Bresson.

The Question of Grace in Francophone European Film Philosophy

This is a good moment to bring Alain Badiou into this conversation. In his 1997 book on and somewhat controversial posthumous critique of Deleuze, Badiou juxtaposes Deleuze's monism to his own philosophy of the event. Badiou writes, with reference to Pascal's wager and *Journal d'un curé de campagne*:

> It can be said that [for Deleuze] there is nothing new under the sun because everything that happens is only an inflection of the One, the eternal return of the same. It can equally be said that everything is constantly new because it is only through the perpetual creation of its own folds that the One, in its absolute contingency, can indefinitely return. These two judgments are ultimately indiscernible. We must then wager, in the same sense as does the country priest at the end of Bernanos's book [and of Bresson's film], but without needing for this any other God than the God of Spinoza (Nature): "What does it matter? All is grace." Which has to be punctuated as follows: "All" *is* grace. For what is, is nothing other than the grace of the All.[106]

Grace for Deleuze is the immanent miracle of what Spinoza calls beatitude, "the love by which God loves himself."[107] For Badiou this way of thinking about grace is a contradiction in terms. Badiou rules out that Being can be thought as All. This is not to say that he rules out grace. For Badiou, grace, rather than that it emerges from within Being (as it does according to Deleuze), is the event, which disrupts Being from the outside. The event is constitutive, moreover, of the subject. To act ethically, and to be a subject of truth as Badiou calls it, is to remain "lastingly faithful" to the event, to that hitherto unimaginable, life-changing encounter, like Paul to Christ. "This is precisely what Paul calls grace," Badiou argues in *Saint Paul: The Foundation of Universalism* (*Saint Paul: La Fondation de l'universalisme*, 1997), "that which occurs without being couched in any predicate, that which is translegal, that which happens to everyone without an assignable reason. Grace is the opposite of law insofar as it is what comes *without being due*."[108]

In *Neither God nor Master: Robert Bresson and Radical Politics* (2011), Brian Price argues that Badiou's materialist theory of grace as event helps us to see the consonance between Bresson's early, expressly religious films and his increasing concern with youth culture in his later-life career. But Price also sees something more radical at work in Bresson. Price finds in Bresson a critique of Christianity that goes further than Badiou's secularization of Paul. Already in his early work, he argues, Bresson overlays the notion of divine grace with a more secular conception of chance. "My intention is to think," Price writes, "of grace not as analogous to chance but as a correction to the notion of grace and election itself."[109] To stay with this difference between grace and chance: whereas grace is a narrative, chance is the radical absence thereof. From the perspective of the nonbeliever, of the nonbeliever in the Catholic sense, "grace" makes sense of chance as it imposes onto it God's unfathomable logic. To be the subject of grace is to be chosen. To be the subject of chance is to be lucky, or not, in one's endeavors. Moreover and crucially, whereas grace implies a rupture in time—a before and after the miracle—chance is always part of a continuous series. There is no single, isolated throw of the dice. Now, Badiou's notion of the event, though secular in its self-presentation, shares the temporality of grace. The subject only becomes the subject of truth by recognizing the event as event, first of all when the event miraculously disrupts the status quo, and subsequently in the event's wake, when the subject stays committed to its truth. For Badiou, truth thus precedes practice. For Deleuze, in contrast, practice and truth are in a relation of mutual determination to the point that they become indistinguishable from one another. Deleuze, so I agree with Badiou, fully immanentizes grace and at his most posthuman perhaps does away with grace altogether.

My problem with Badiou's theory of the event is that is presupposes a relatively stable notion of subjectivity, a subject that lives in the wake of and to some degree holds on to something that is now past. But while there are indeed life-changing events, events that change the lives of individuals (e.g., falling in love), communities (e.g., a declaration of independence), and perhaps even the world (e.g., 9/11), an event is always part of a series of larger and smaller events, which are in turn embedded into a continuum. I thus agree with a Spinozist-Deleuzian ethics of subjectivity that sees the subject as an ever-unfolding decentered organic process that moves through the perpetual present, where past and future short-circuit.

There is also a parallel between Badiou and Deleuze. Despite their diametrical differences, Badiou and Deleuze share a longing for grace that, however immanent or secular, resonates with the Catholicism of the French intellectual tradition from which they emerged. The same can be said about Godard, their contemporary, or more precisely *late* Godard, because, as already observed in chapter 1, the young Godard still had some trouble grappling with Bresson's Catholic vocabulary for a disenchanted world. In the interview from 1966 that Godard and Michel Delahaye had with Bresson, Godard identifies two tendencies in Bresson's work. "You are," Godard says, "on the one hand, a humanist, on the other hand, an inquisitor. Is that reconcilable, or . . . ?" "Inquisitor?" Bresson asks, "In what sense? Not in the sense. . . ." The conversation continues:

> GODARD: Oh, not in the sense of the Gestapo, of course. But in a sense, let us say . . .
>
> BRESSON: Not in the sense of the Inquisition? Saint Dominic? . . .
>
> GODARD: Oh, yes, all the same . . .
>
> BRESSON: Oh! . . . No. No . . .
>
> GODARD: Or then, let us say particularly: Jansenist.
>
> BRESSON: Jansenist, then, in the sense of austerity . . .
>
> GODARD: Yes, but all the same, there is something else, and the word Inquisitor . . .
>
> BRESSON: Really, Inquisitor! You do not mean that I assert my way of seeing things. For yes, I assert—I cannot do otherwise—my way of seeing, of thinking, my personal view, but as everyone who writes does . . . In the end, if Inquisitor there is, I would say then that I go seeking in people what I find that is most subtle and most personal.
>
> GODARD: Yes, but there is at the same time a frightening aspect . . .
>
> BRESSON: The Question, then.
>
> GODARD: Yes, The Question.
>
> BRESSON: As you say: of course, I put the Question.
>
> GODARD: There![110]

Finally, the two film philosophers are on the same wavelength. Bresson continues to explain his methodology as "a questionnaire in the unknown," upon which Godard observes that this would bring him close to Pascal, a humanist and an Inquisitor too. Toward the end of the interview, Bresson explains his cinematography as one that is open to an unknown "that happens to us, all the time." But the questionnaire is not a quest. The unknown emerges "not because one intended to find this unknown, which cannot be found, because the unknown is discovered and not found." And here Bresson cites Picasso: "one finds at first, and then one seeks."[111] *Je ne cherche pas, je trouve.*

At certain moments in this meandering conversation, titled "The Question," Godard has a hard time understanding Bresson, despite or maybe precisely because of his outspoken veneration for the filmmaker. "I have the impression," Godard states, "compared with you, of not making cinema."[112] What is this idea of cinema, this pure cinema, that Godard, along with Bazin, finds in Bresson and that he feels he's lacking himself? One finds seeds of an answer in the quotation in *Le Mépris* that Godard falsely attributes to Bazin: "Cinema substitutes for our gazes a world that accords itself to our desires." Or in the quotation in *Histoire(s) du cinéma* that he falsely attributes to Saint Paul: "The image will come at the time of the resurrection." The creation of that Image, of such a true, premodern, and prelinguistic image that says "adieu au langage," and that, as Daniel Morgan writes in *Late Godard* (2013), returns its disparate elements to "something like a unified whole,"[113] requires a miracle. Such a miracle happens, perhaps, in *Nouvelle vague* (1990), when the levitating camera captures Richard's and Elena's reconciliation, while an intertitle confirms that "Amor Omnia Vincit" ("Love conquers all," fig. 4.9).[114] A miracle definitely happens in *Je vous salue, Marie / Hail Mary* (1985). We witness the birth of a child (who may or may not be Christ), we see a donkey who reminds us of Bresson's Balthazar (who also may or may not be Christ), and we hear Joseph paraphrase to Marie the ending of Bresson's *Pickpocket*: "O Marie, quel drôle de chemin j'ai dû faire pour arriver jusqu'à toi" (Oh Marie, what a long strange road I had to take to reach you). As Morgan argues: "The miracle at issue would be less about the intrusion of the supernatural into the natural than about the possibility of two people coming together."[115] Indeed, if there is one theme that defines late Godard, and that the late Godard inherited from the young one, it is the Question of Love, which is the Question of the Image. As Godard states in *King Lear*, while wearing a "Picasso" t-shirt: "Image is a pure creation of the soul. It cannot be born of a comparison, but of a reconciliation of two realities that are more or less far apart." We here have Godard in a nutshell. Love for Godard is the montage of two souls, of the transmission of an image that overcomes, and that in doing so, says "adieu" to language. Such an image, such a true image, is not merely the coming together of two abandoned souls; it is the event of love, the creation of a new, collective inner world.

The obvious film through which to further explore Godard's notion of love is *Éloge de l'amour / In Praise of Love* (2001). A eulogy to love, the film is also a eulogy to Bresson. In its first black-and-white half we see the film poster of *Pickpocket* juxtaposed to a young couple, and waiting in line for the movie theater, the man of an elderly heterosexual couple recalls again the last line of Bresson's 1959 film: "*O Jeanne* . . ." In the film's color-saturated second half, an unnamed young woman reads out loud from *Notes sur le cinématographe*: "It's not a question of directing someone but of directing oneself," and "Let feelings bring out events, not the other way around."[116] *Notes sur le cinematograph*, which is Bresson's declaration of cinematic faith, appeared in 1975, so almost a decade after Godard's interview with him. That interview, by the way, was clearly on Godard's mind while making *Éloge de l'amour*. "Je ne cherche pas, je trouve," Mr. Rosenthal (Claude Baignières) cheers up Edgar. "Picasso," the latter identifies the citation (fig. 4.10).

What does Godard find in *Éloge de l'amour*, and what do we find out about love? In the film's first half we follow Edgar, who is working on a project for which he still needs to find a vessel. Is it a play, a novel, a film? The project expresses the four stages of love: the encounter, physical passion, the separation, and the reconciliation. These stages are told through the stories of three couples of different generations. Let's say that the young couple is called Perceval and Eglantine, Edgar instructs one of his actresses, while he explains to her that she will have to not merely interpret the particular story of Perceval and Eglantine "but a moment in history, the big History that moves through [them], the moment of youth." The mythological figure of Perceval we know from his quest for the Holy Grail, but when he is over for dinner at the Fisher King's castle he fails to inquire about the object when it is passed in front of him. He fails to ask The Question. Perceval searched, but he did not find. Eglantine is a character in *The Canterbury Tales*. Pious as she is, she is fascinated with courtly love. The credo engraved in her brooch is the same as that of Godard's *Nouvelle vague*: "Amor vincit Omnia."

In order to tell the story of love in *Éloge de l'amour*, Godard tells another story. In the second part of the film, the viewer again encounters Edgar, who is now working on a study on the role of Catholicism in the French Resistance. This connection between love, Resistance, and Christianity Godard has inherited from Bresson. Godard once provocatively called Bresson's *Les Dames du Bois de Boulogne* (1945) "the one true film of the French Resistance," and in *Histoire(s) du cinema* (section

3A, 1998) he juxtaposes the last words Agnès speaks to her lover to the words Charles de Gaulle spoke to the Free French: "Il faut lutter."[117] Once again, love conquers everything. This connection between love and Resistance resonates with Badiou's writings on love. Also for Badiou love is militant. Love is a truth procedure, a radical commitment to the event of the romantic encounter, to the experience of difference. The event is like a miracle. You cannot search for it, it finds you, though you need to be open to it. In his own essay interview *Éloge de l'amour* (2009, together with Nicolas Truong, and which may or may not be a reference to Godard's film) Badiou states: "What is universal is that all love proposes a new experience of truth on what it is to be two and not one. That the world may be encountered and experienced in a different manner than by a solitary conscience," upon which he cites Saint Augustine: "That's why we love to love."[118] Also Godard cites Augustine in his *Éloge de l'amour*: "The measure of love is love without measure."

Godard's film essays take a very different approach to questions of truth and love than Badiou's ontology of the event. While I agree with Morgan that Godard's films "make arguments,"[119] they do not present theses. Godard's films wander like the essays of Montaigne.[120] Godard, like Picasso, does not search; he finds. There nevertheless seems to be an intellectual romance between Badiou and Godard. The philosopher makes a brief appearance on the cruise ship in *Film socialisme* (201), where he gives a lecture on Husserl in front of an empty auditorium, subtitled in broken English as: "geometry as origin / return to geometry / ourselves partof [sic] geometry."[121] And Badiou's ideas seem to be present in Godard's intimate 3-D philosophical drama *Adieu au langage* (2014), for example, when Gédéon (Kamel Abdeli) states that the two greatest inventions are infinity and zero, which are also important concepts for Badiou.

To leave Badiou for now, and to return, once again, to Bresson: besides a notion of love, the other Bressonian transmission in Godard's late work is his employment of actors. Godard's characters are always acting, and their acting is always revealed, through montage, through the frequent dissociation of sound and image, and—especially in his later-life films—through the citations and declamations he has his actors speak. If there is one thing that defines late Godard, it is a profound melancholia, a longing for History that manifests itself for an important part in the acting, whether by professionals (e.g., Bruno Putzulu who plays Edgar) or amateurs (e.g., Marine Battaggia, who plays Florine in *Film socialisme*, a young woman who works at a gas station, and who will "kill you if you make fun of Balzac" [fig. 4.11]). (The reason, by the way, there are so many gas stations in Godard's films is not just that his characters like cars, and especially *American* cars, but also that the French word for gas is *essence*, a double entendre most explicit in *Je vous salue, Marie*: "Ton père va bien? . . . Toujours dans l'essence?" Marie's answer: "Non il veut le quitter.") There is something Bressonian about the acting in late Godard, in which the performativity of Belmondo and Léaud has given way to the pensiveness of characters locked up in themselves, characters who are alone even when they are together, and who speak in monologues even when they are in conversation. Their mouths produce language, but it is not these actors-characters themselves who speak, but History that speaks through them, as in Edgar's project. Like Bresson, Godard turns his actors into vessels for a more universal vision on Humanity, and like Bresson's, Godard's universe is in need of redemption, of a militant love bound up with History, and of a cinema of the Image more primary than the word that runs off with Roxy the dog, acted by Godard's own dog, in *Adieu au langage*.

But not *all* is grace in late Godard. If there is grace at all in his films, it is always already caught up in a horizontal and vertical montage in which sparks of harmony are immediately countered by stabs of dissonance that remind one of the constellation under which his filmmaking was born: the crisis of representation. Think of the snippets of Bach crosscut with a roaring train in *Je vous salue, Marie*, or the apocalyptic sequence of moving and still images in the third movement of *Film socialisme*, whose ominous sounds carry over into *Adieu au langage* and *Le Livre d'image* (2018). In contrast, in the miraculous realism of the Dardennes and Dumont, grace is very normal. Like late Godard, the Dardennes and Dumont inherit from Bresson. This is clearest in *Rosetta* and *L'humanité*, variations on *Mouchette* and *Journal d'un curé de campagne*, respectively, and both films rooted in crisis. In *Rosetta*, this crisis manifests itself in the title character's christlike struggle for "a normal life," starting with a job, while *L'humanité* turns crisis reality into a backdrop for its carnal-spiritual quest for "humanity." Over the course of these quests, the Dardennes and Dumont take recourse to Bresson's secular-yet-humanist Catholicism, according to which God may or may not exist—"What does it all matter"—with as the main difference that the Dardennes and Dumont let their protagonists live where Bresson did not.

As far as the Dardennes are concerned, the recurring Question in their "challenge to the being of cinema" is, so I agree with Sarah Cooper, "to kill or not to kill?"[122] It is a question that the Dardennes have faced repeatedly. Do we want Rosetta to follow in Mouchette's footsteps? Will Olivier strangle Francis in *Le Fils* (a variation on the story of Abraham and Isaac)? And what about Lorna, what price does she have to pay for her silence? Or is this not the kind of cinema that demands an eye for an eye? In the case of Bruno in *L'Enfant* (a variation on Bresson's *Pickpocket*

Figure 4.9. "Amor Omnia Vincit" (*Nouvelle vague*, Jean-Luc Godard, 1990).

Figure 4.10. "Je ne cherche pas, je trouve" (*Éloge de l'amour*, Godard, 2001).

Figure 4.11. "Si vous vous moquez de Balzac, je vous tue" (*Film socialisme*, Godard, 2010).

and Pasolini's *Accattone*, in turn a variation on the passion story), the Dardennes did actually consider the possibility of death. Luc Dardenne writes in his journal: "Accattone dies but there is the music of Johann Sebastian Bach. Mouchette dies but there is the music of Monteverdi. What if Bruno dies and there is no music?"[123] Bruno lives though, like Rosetta, Francis, and Lorna. Yet with Lorna it's different. If there is any hope for salvation in her case, that salvation needs to come from beyond the image. Whereas the Dardennes' four preceding fiction films end in the middle of a face-to-face encounter, Lorna's flight forward leads her to an isolated cabin in the middle of the woods. While collecting firewood she raises her gaze, hoping for it to be returned, but except for a bird nothing is there (fig. 4.12). "I won't let you die, ever," she speaks to the imaginary child in her womb, the conception of which she attributes to Claudy, the addict-christ in whose murder she had a part, "I let your father die. You'll live." In the following shot Lorna is back in the cabin. She ignites the stove and closes the shutters, almost fading out the image. "We'll sleep now, we'll leave tomorrow morning." And then, for the first time in the Dardennes' cinema, there is nondiegetic music. No Bach or Monteverdi as would have been the case in neorealism, but a handful of chords from a Beethoven piano sonata that leave space for a secular interpretation of all of this (much like Van Morrison's "Gloria" in their later film *Deux jours, une nuit* is at once Christian and secular). Lorna lies down, the music stops. "Sleep tight," she speaks, caressing her belly, in a double reminiscence of Rosetta (both of Rosetta's secular bedtime prayer—"Your name is Rosetta"—and of her giving birth to the unpainted Easter egg). And with the frame going fully black now, the music resumes,

Figure 4.12. *Le Silence de Lorna* (Jean-Pierre Dardenne and Luc Dardenne, 2008).

a tiny bit louder this time, as if seeking to compensate for what the image cannot give the viewer, but without fully silencing Lorna's breathing, thus staying true also, in a new realist fashion, to direct sound.

Are we at ease with this secular-Christian humanism for a world without God, a humanism that refuses to dwell in crisis (as a critique of capitalism would) and instead ideologically subsumes crisis with its redemptive closure effects? Are we at ease with these films' miraculous twists, wrapping up the contingency of reality? To be a humanist nowadays without burning oneself too badly requires miracles. We already knew this from *Miracle in Milan*, and we are reminded about it by Dumont. Dumont's new realism, insofar as the term applies at all to his work, forms a special case. Whereas the Dardennes only give us strictly immanent, human miracles—Riquet's forgiving of Rosetta (who's not an angel), Olivier's forgiving of Francis (who's not Isaac), the friendship between Igor and Assita in *La Promesse*, Bruno's tears, the sunny sky in *Le Gamin au vélo* (a variation on *Bicycle Thieves*)—Dumont's quests for redemption almost always cross from the real to the surreal, from the possible to the magical and possibly also the transcendent. The clear exception is *Twentynine Palms* (2003), a modern retelling of "Adam and Eve" set in the unredemptive Californian desert. The film ends on the observation, spoken by a police officer who's framed in an extremely long shot, that the male protagonist "looks like he has been through a meat grinder." Based on the preceding scene, and with the merciless desert wind torturing the speakers, the viewer can do nothing but confirm the officer's report. Dumont's only unequivocal new realist film is his first feature, *La Vie de Jésus*, that is to say up until this film's final shot, where we all of a sudden see Freddy, who also is a secular Christ, stretched out in the field, where the viewer expects him to be in jail. Where *La Vie de Jésus* ends, *L'humanité* begins: explicitly negativizing the realism that the Nord calls for, an approach equally found in the other stories Dumont set and shot in the Nord (*Flandres, Hors Satan, Hadewijch, P'tit Quinquin, Ma Loute,* and *Coincoin*). They all draw the viewer into new realist worlds populated by new realist characters, but they do so only to emphasize a deviation from the real. In terms of form they disrupt the realist illusion through their self-referential and, especially in the case of *L'humanité*, overtly aestheticized style. In terms of narrative: whereas new realism, like neorealism before it, largely develops its characters along socioeconomic lines, Dumont's protagonists are motivated by more primary, natural forces. They are *bêtes humaines* at once biological and spiritual, immanent and transcendent. It's therefore no surprise that such a large part of the Cannes audience showed itself upset by *L'humanité* back in 1999. Dumont's films *are* hard to stomach, as they uproot layers of our humanist soil that one would perhaps rather leave unthought.

In conclusion to my analysis of the Cinéma du Nord: despite these differences both the Dardennes and Dumont have in common that they make a cinema of life. It's a cinema that at the end of the day affirms an at once particular and universal notion of humanity. And it is a cinema that affirms the lives of their actors mixed up in their fictional characters. Bresson was able to sacrifice Mouchette and the *curé* because by treating his actors as models, he could separate the acting, profilmic person from the acted, on-screen persona. At least such was his wager. For the Dardennes and Dumont, in contrast, the acting and the acted are highly integrated. The particular "love and rejection of reality," to paraphrase Bazin, that drives their films turns the actors, whether amateurs or professionals, not into models, but affirms them—self-reflexively, but also somewhat problematically—as acting/acted *humans*, while their humanist Catholicism is of a more secular, milder, and optimistic nature than Bresson's. Both the Dardennes and Dumont resuscitate a belief in the Image, a belief that goes hand in hand with their positive and redefinition of "humanity," their longing for redemption that obscures a true critique of the social conflict they engage (obliquely in Dumont, center-stage in the Dardennes, sliced-up in Godard). Whereas for Godard, an Image can only be a spark of montage, the Dardennes and Dumont look for that spark in the single shot, in the close-up of a human face: Rosetta's face trembling from fear and exhaustion, or Pharaon, lost in light, while he takes upon his sloping shoulders the guilt of humanity, with a small *h*. Their miracles, so rooted in the lived realities of the Nord, speculate, in a somewhat nostalgically humanist fashion, about a beyond-the-image, a world where Rosetta and Pharaon can, finally, live *happily ever after*.

Epilogue

Posthumanism

> For most people think they sufficiently understand a thing when they have ceased to wonder at it.
>
> —Spinoza, *A Theologico-Political Treatise*

∞

Following the critical fairy tale of the Cinéma du Nord, I would like to engage the main question that its turn-of-the-millennium new realism poses to the critical posthuman viewer: Is it possible to fully do away with a humanism according to which people have an innate drive toward community, with an idea of the human as a social animal that lives in harmony rather than in dissensus, with a sense of control that perpetuates in this era of global capitalism and climate catastrophe? To be human is to tell stories, stories of humanity, of individual and collective existence as it is shaped—from cradle to grave—by parochial power structures, from the nation-state to mass-employment industries, from political parties to trade unions, from schools to hospitals, and from the Church to the nuclear family. The posthuman, in contrast, emerges from the crisis of Humanity and Representation and lacks such a *normal human* overarching story, for better or worse. The posthuman is a *scattered* and *shattered* subject—if "subject" is still the right word—for whom such distinctions as work versus free time and public versus private space increasingly collapse. The posthuman works from home or shops online from work, while maintaining long-distance relationships with friends and family all over the globe, or across the room. The posthuman travels with the economic seasons and may be in between jobs even when at work (say, while driving for Uber). The posthuman is in between things in general and lives in the perpetual present. The posthuman lives in the networked space of ever smarter and greener city regions. The posthuman lives transnationally (like in the Nord). The posthuman shares (car, house, pictures, life stories), though not for free. The posthuman seeks love online. The posthuman has a rich emotional palette that oscillates from anxiety (Will I ever find a job, significant other, stable life?) to euphoria (I found work, love, a sense of belonging!). The posthuman lives in neighborhoods, where pockets of traditional local culture struggle, while glocal "authenticity" thrives. The posthuman recycles, and perhaps even dreams of a nomadic existence on a decentralized grid. The posthuman is from the time that machines are better at telling the difference between humans and machines, and that machines are perhaps even better—and certainly more efficient—at meeting our "human" needs. The posthuman belongs to the cloud rather than to a mass, and as such I take this conceptual figure as synonymous with what Gilles Deleuze called the *dividual*. Already, in 1990, Deleuze writes in "Postscript on Control Societies": "We're no longer dealing with a duality of mass and individual. . . . Individuals become '*dividuals*,' and masses become samples, data, markets, or '*banks*.'"[1] Again, for better or for worse.

For worse, in the posthuman platform society social infrastructures and public spaces are increasingly infiltrated by the norms and values of predominantly American tech corporations, which disrupt not only traditional markets (housing, transport, health care) but also, and above all, any ideal of democratic representation and transparency. It's a world also in which, little by little and driven by an ideology of a rediscovered locally produced heterogeneity that allegedly disrupts traditional economic sectors, all and everything becomes the potential "content" of an ever more homogeneous new American Dream, designed in Silicon Valley, whose truly disruptive effect is precisely that its infrastructures separate form from content. The posthuman world, moreover, is one of increasing segregation within and between societies. It's the world of Rosetta, for example, to whom I will return shortly, or of the precarious labor and ecological threats that facilitate our everyday communications and travels (think of energy-guzzling datacenters, or the blood minerals in our phones). For the better, the posthuman challenges borders. In this respect, I'd like to think of my endeavor in chapters 2 and 3 to identify the Cinéma du Nord as a transregional north wind immanent to crisis as a posthuman, slanted perspective. Moreover, in its most progressive connotation, the posthuman queers life, love, and language, thereby challenging traditional and modern humanisms that model their notion of "human" on a male, heterosexual, white, European subject.

Does this make the posthuman antihumanist? In *The Posthuman* (2013), Rosi Braidotti writes that "the radical thinkers of the post-1968 generation rejected Humanism both in its classical and its socialist versions. The Vitruvian ideal of Man as the standard of both perfection and perfectibility was literally pulled down from his pedestal and deconstructed."[2] Indeed, Foucault heralded the Death of Man; Irigaray has constructed a new vocabulary based on feminine embodiment in critique of the phallocentric logic of Man; and Deleuze's thinking, as Braidotti writes in *Nomadic Subjects* (2011), "bypasses the binary structure of sexual difference altogether and works toward in-depth exploration of the multiple sexualities inherent to a subject in terms redefined as transversal, collective, and dynamic."[3] However, and to stay with Deleuze, what do we make of the vestiges of Humanism in his speculations about cinema's "Catholic quality" to restore the belief in the "link between man and the world, in love or life"? And what to make of the fact that many of the filmmakers whom Deleuze considers exemplary for the transition from a classical cinema of representation to a modern cinema of expression equally employ such a Christian humanist vocabulary, like Rossellini, De Sica, and Godard? Deleuze writes in *Cinema 2* that "the cinema must film not the world, but belief in this world, our only link."[4] He sees protomodernist sparks of such a belief in the late Rossellini, for instance in *Joan of Arc at the Stake* (1954), even though, as he writes, the filmmaker's paradoxical Christianity does not fully abandon the classical "ideal of knowledge." That ideal of knowledge, Deleuze continues, collapses with Godard, in whose films "the 'good' discourse, of the militant, the revolutionary, the feminist, the philosopher, the film-maker, etc., gets no better treatment than the bad." Godard, according to Deleuze, restores belief in the world, in *this* world, "before or beyond words." His films do so by giving discourse to the body "before discourses . . . before things are named," and here Deleuze cites the example of *Je vous salue, Marie* (1985): "What did Joseph and Mary say to each other? What did they say to each other *before*? Give words back to the body, to the flesh."[5]

However, while invoking this minimally Catholic language in neorealism and late Godard, Deleuze shows himself rather blind to issues of gender and sexuality in his *Cinema* books, including the fact that in Godard's films bodies are always coded along strict gender and heteronormative binaries. Can one imagine a homosexual or trans character in Godard's universe? Whereas in early Godard (e.g., *A bout de souffle*, *Masculin Féminin*) this gender stereotyping may still be understood as part of the filmmaker's performative deconstruction of Classical Hollywood, in late Godard the male-female trope has become part of a nostalgic reiteration of the same old Question, "What remains of grace in a world without God?" The problem with Godard and especially with *late* Godard, and the problem with Deleuze's repeated embrace of Godard as an exemplary modern filmmaker, is not that the Godardian universe, however fragmented and self-conscious in its self-presentation, is entirely populated with heterosexual men and women. The problem is that the terms of the question of grace that runs from *Je vous salue, Marie* to *Adieu au langage* are not neutral, but are steeped in an audiovisual vocabulary bound up with the patriarchal Word. Godard thus somehow, and through the back door, over and again affirms a Christian paradigm by explicitly questioning that paradigm in its own language. And here it's good to call to mind the insight of Bresson's *curé* that "the desire to pray already is a prayer, and . . . God would not desire more." As I have argued in chapter 1: to explicitly question "God" is already to implicitly affirm Him, because the Christian God lives precisely in the Question of his existence.

As I have demonstrated in chapter 4, Godard inherits this longing for a secular grace from Bresson, and so do the Dardennes and Dumont, with the difference that whereas in Godard every spark of grace is immediately sliced into a montage, in the miraculous realism of the Dardennes and Dumont grace is very normal. Here it is instructive to compare *Rosetta* and *L'humanité* to *Miracle in Milan*. As I also argued in the final chapter, in *Empire* Michael Hardt and Antonio Negri invoke De Sica's and Zavattini's films as an inspiration for their posthuman humanism. However, Hardt and Negri ignore the Christianity of this cinematic fable, much like they leave untheorized their study's own utopian ending on the miraculous visitation of Saint Francis, the alter-Christ. Like in *Miracle in Milan*, in *Rosetta* and *L'humanité* the rediscovered belief in humanity (with a small *h*) is of a secular nature. Unlike De Sica's fairy tale and the heterogeneous multitude with which it flies off, Rosetta's and Pharaon's lonely struggles express a decreased faith in collective action, in the communist utopia-to-come, and in the social-democratic ideals of solidarity and emancipation. In sum, whereas the neorealist humanism of *Miracle in Milan* reveals a posthuman tendency even though it was born on catholic soil, the humanism of the Dardennes and Dumont is of a more classical and perhaps somewhat reactionary nature. It's a cinema that invests its protagonists' quests for "humanity" with a moral stake that sees the human form as the center of ethics.

To focus for a final time on *Rosetta*: This film, as noted also by Lauren Berlant, is a privileged example of a new-realist "cinema of precarity" that witnesses the global fraying of socioeconomic structures.[6] Berlant writes in *Cruel Optimism* that "the Dardennes represent consciousness under present systemic economic, political, and intimate conditions . . . where if you're lucky you *get* to be exploited."⁷ True, *Rosetta* gives us the title character's precarious struggle for a normal life, but Berlant, like Rancière, misses the affective spiritual mind game *Rosetta* plays with its viewer. More than Rosetta's precarity itself, the film's real subject is the emotional response it teases from its viewer while secretly telling them a passion story in which Rosetta is the holy virgin and christ at once. *Rosetta*, unlike so many new realist films, is not an explicitly humanist film. For that, its flirtations with a Christian audiovisual vocabulary for a world without God are too smart. But the film *does* define "human" implicitly, in that it ultimately integrates its perverted passion story into a classical male quest motif in which, as in *Miracle in Milan* and *L'humanité*, the main male character is the humanizing agent and Rosetta herself the passive recipient of "humanity." Partly as the result of its own game strategy, partly despite its own implicit humanism, *Rosetta* is thus a testing ground. The film compels critical, posthuman viewers to analyze to what extent their worldview holds on to the uncritical desire for a "human" face amid a reality in which it is no longer clear what a life looks like, a world in which people are defined by work despite the fact that many are denied access to it.

One equally senses such unprocessed vestiges of humanism in Deleuze's yearning in *Cinema 2* to believe in love or life, the link between the human (from beyond the Death of Man) and the world, *this* world. Other than in *Cinema 2*, this minimum of humanism shines through in between the lines of Deleuze's 1995 essay "Immanence: A Life." Halfway through that essay, Deleuze gives an example of *a* life, with an emphasis on the indefinite article. The example is from a passage in Charles Dickens's *Our Mutual Friend* (1864–1865), in which a man who is held in contempt by his community is found dying, upon which bystanders "suddenly" try to save him, meeting his slightest vital sign with love, "to the point where, in his deepest coma, this wicked man himself senses something soft and sweet penetrating him."⁸ The love withers again, however, once the man regains his strength and returns to life. According to Deleuze, it is precisely at that infinitely small juncture between these two stages, between life and death, that "*a* life playing with death" becomes visible, as in a flash. Deleuze writes:

> Between his life and his death there is a moment that is only that of a life playing with death. The life of the individual gives way to an impersonal and yet singular life that releases a pure event freed from the accidents of internal and external life, from the subjectivity and objectivity of what happens, a "Homo tantum" with whom everyone empathizes and who

attains a sort of beatitude. It is a haecceity [thisness] no longer of individuation but of singularization: a life of pure immanence, neutral, beyond good and evil, for it was only the subject that incarnated it in the midst of things that made it good or bad. The life of such individuality fades away in favor of the singular life immanent to a man who no longer has a name, though he can be mistaken for no other. A singular essence, a life . . .[9]

Up until this example, Deleuze, as in an act of performative tautology, has circled around the affective concept of "a life," equating it to the "immanence of immanence," "A LIFE," and—with reference to Spinoza—"complete bliss." Yet with the Dickens example something happens. Suddenly "a life" has become "a *human* life," against the grain of Deleuze's own argument that the flash of life recognized by the bystanders is impersonal, nameless, and freed of individual subjectivity. The fact is, though, that Deleuze, in his illustration of *a* life, does not call to mind, say, a bicellular organism, but instead takes recourse to an example of a singular suffering life insofar as it is recognized by a community's empathy and even compassion, that is to say, by a human and humanizing collective that shows itself inexplicably touched by, and that gathers around, a *Homo tantum*, a human without qualities, but minimally "human" nonetheless. This minimum of humanism is not a problem per se, and Deleuze's choice of example perhaps demonstrates that when speaking about a concept that poses itself at the limit of discourse, that in fact poses itself *as* that limit, a minimum of humanism cannot be avoided. Only a being in discourse can be affected by this limit, which is a being usually referred to as "human." According to this reasoning, "a life" is indeed always already anthropomorphized as a human life, even when it is encountered in living beings considered non- or posthuman, like plants, animals, angels, gods, or cyborgs. I am aware that I read a degree of humanism into Deleuze's philosophy of life that that philosophy itself probably does not agree with. It's a risk worth taking, because my point is that Deleuze's philosophy itself insufficiently acknowledges the humanist connotations of the vocabulary and examples in and through which it equates "love" and "life."

This minimally humanist belief in love or life also radiates from the sudden appearance of Saint Francis at the end of *Empire*, who like Toto in *Miracle in Milan* sought to inspire a heterogeneous multitude of the poor, or what Berlant in *Cruel Optimism* refers to as the Precariat. As Hardt observes elsewhere, Berlant's writings on affect show parallels to that of Spinoza and Deleuze. According to Hardt, Berlant meets these thinkers "in a political project for non-sovereign subjects."[10] He argues that Berlant, like Spinoza and Deleuze, critiques an understanding of the subject as a sovereign individual in control of their destiny and instead thinks of the subject as a nonsovereign mode of being immanent to the power relations affecting it. Hardt argues, moreover, that, much like Spinoza's ethics (according to which a subject achieves joy by increasing their power to be affected) Berlant's explorations of the passions show us that "the only path toward achieving the good life must be constructed with and through the affects."[11] This path of self-causality is uneven, because the same attachments that bring the subject joy may also cause them sadness in other ways. In Hardt's view, the strength of Berlant's philosophy is that it navigates "this tangled terrain of complex, contradictory affects," and here Hardt cites Berlant's "eminently Spinozian formulation" that "a relation of cruel optimism exists when something you desire is actually an obstacle to your flourishing."[12]

In response to Hardt, Berlant shows herself skeptical about this attempt to map a Spinozist/Deleuzian "relational realism" onto her more vernacular analysis of the condition of self-deluding optimism that defines the post-Fordist subject. "What is joy?" she rightly asks, upon which she argues that

> one thing that makes Hardt's essay difficult and the thought it remediates troubling . . . is the aspiration toward the end of chance as though that end were possible, if indeed one is truly and constitutively open and committed to attending to being in relation. Maybe this is a simple problem: perhaps the end of chance lurks as a horizon but being in life remains a project of what [Timothy] Brennan calls "discernment," which here would be the capacity to judge what increases one's power to be affected by joy and to act from its teaching about the appetites and ethics. But formally, Hardt still wants it both ways, a little: the essay contains caveats but ends up bringing you the joy of joy.[13]

As Berlant suggests, a Spinozist/Deleuzian nonprescriptive ethics may seem tautological, but I don't think it is. I would argue that rather than that such ethics is oriented at the elimination of chance, it is a lifelong process in and through which the almost-but-not-quite decentered, scattered and shattered posthuman subject renders themselves conscious of, and while doing so challenges, their "human" tendency to construct life stories, while negotiating their equally "human" sense of being exposed to chance. Those stories, which are story fragments, are self-humanizing survival techniques as much as they are, indeed, often cruel in their optimism. To become conscious of one's all-too-human tendency to project oneself into the future may lead oneself to be less affected by the sense of chance, but it doesn't eliminate that sense itself. It is a posthuman ethics of belief and intuition, a belief that it is possible to have a link with the world and to act ethically, and to develop—and here I agree with Hardt—a sense of knowing how to act and to increase one's power to be affected. It's a sense of knowing also that, as per Berlant's reply to Hardt, seeks to let go of judgment and that loosens the attachment to a project, to a life narrative.

I take belief and intuition as synonyms, belief as in Deleuze's belief in love or life and intuition as in what Spinoza calls the third kind of knowledge, the "love by which *Nature* loves itself, not insofar as it is infinite, but insofar as it can be explained through the essence of the human mind, considered under a species of eternity"[14] (and note that I here take the liberty to substitute "God" with the more gender-neutral "Nature," as per Spinoza's own equation of God and Nature right at the start of his *Ethics*). What is intuition? Whereas for Spinoza affect, or the first kind of knowledge, is the inadequate knowledge of particular sensations, and reason, or the second kind of knowledge, is the adequate knowledge of universals, intuition is adequate knowledge of the essence of particular things. In this context "adequacy" is the degree to which an idea expresses its own cause. To adequately know the essence of a singular thing is to know its movement within the flux of Nature, or immanent causality. To know intuitively means to understand Nature through the essence of a singular thing that serves as a lens through which the body-mind "perceives" Nature—not a lens in the sense of a magnifying glass held between one's conscious perception and Nature (the kind of perception that pertains to reason), but in the sense of a crystal ball from within which the eyes of the mind—which "are demonstrations"[15]—surrender themselves to the world's necessity, considered under a species of eternity, or what Deleuze refers to as the eternal pure present of the time-image. Crucially, intuition does not take the form of a series over the course of which the cause of a cause of a cause (ad infinitum) becomes clear. Instead, intuition is an immediate and embodied knowledge by which the "mind senses those things that it conceives in understanding no less than those that it has in the memory."[16] Spinoza thus avoids the Cartesian trap of infinite regression. As Deleuze writes in *Expressionism in Philosophy* (*Spinoza et le problème de l'expression*, 1968):

> It is always [Nature that] determines any cause to produce its effect; so [Nature] is never, properly speaking, a "distant"

or "remote" cause. Thus we do not start from the idea of [Nature], but we reach it very quickly, at the beginning of the regression; for without it we would not even understand the possibility of a series, its efficiency and actuality. *Whence it little matters that we proceed through a fiction.* The introduction of a fiction may indeed help us to reach the idea of [Nature] as quickly as possible without falling into the traps of infinite regression.[17]

This necessary speculative fiction that the subject proceeds through is the condition of possibility of intuition itself. Deleuze points out that whereas the greater part of the *Ethics* (down to section 5, proposition 21) is written in the language of reason, the remainder of its fifth and final section is written in the language of intuition (or at least seeks to explore, in its controlled poetry, what such a language could sound like). With this shift in voice Spinoza implicitly acknowledges the impossibility of proving the possibility of intuition. Intuition is a belief, after all, a secular belief in the immanent miracle of embodied knowledge. Spinoza's entire philosophy is predicated on this belief and it takes out an advance on the truth by ruling out negativity, that is to say, by proclaiming truth as the standard of itself and what it is not.[18] By consequence, the third type of knowledge is not really third, but the condition of possibility of life itself, of the infinitely positive, spiraling dialectics without *Aufhebung* between affect and reason.[19]

Perhaps these reflections on intuition and belief may all seem a march on place, in that they do not give much of an answer to the question of how to act in posthuman times. But that is also somewhat the point: the attempt to think a nonnormative, nonjudgmental, anarchist ethics that lets go of preconceived ideas of how one is supposed to act, or how others are supposed to act. Whereas the modern human individual, through the power and parochial care of subjectifying structures, was compelled to partake in societywide, lifelong, and rather homogeneous stories, the posthuman dividual is "subject" to ever more invisible networks of control that monitor, profile, screen, track, and trace them, but that, at the same time, also provides them with the tools and techniques to experience a sense of control over an ever more individualized everyday life. The posthuman is particularly skilled in dividing their attention, once again for better or worse. The posthuman "mindfully" compartmentalizes, and in difference with the rigid and digital algorithms that define the control society, exerts a *soft control* over their time and space in order to be present with and attend to tasks, things, others, and themselves. The posthuman thus seems more emancipated and experiences more individual freedom, a higher sense of freedom that may also be a source of anxiety, the existential stress of lacking a life narrative along which to propel oneself into the near future. The posthuman is strictly secular (also when the times are postsecular) and renounces all longing for grace, for a narrative that transcends the immanence of things. But the posthuman dividual is not without stories, stories of humanity. The posthuman, like their classical and modern predecessors, is resilient and keeps producing and attaching themselves to individual and collective life narratives, however shattered and scattered, in the negotiation of chance.

Therefore, for the posthuman to act intuitively, to act out of the belief in the possibility of increasing their power to be affected, is to recognize—and in doing so challenge—an attachment to the fictions, and to the humanist and normative vestiges of those fictions, through which one exercises a sense of control over the acting/acted body-mind, the fictions also through which societies weave a sense of social texture. To act intuitively is to acknowledge one's anxieties, which is where change starts. Intuition is not a spark of insight, as in what Badiou calls the Event, but a process of embodied knowledge that unfolds over time. Intuition is a minimum sense of agency immanent to the body-mind, or, in Spinoza's terminology, immanent to *conatus*, the anarchic preindividual and prehuman tendency of desire, the minimum of inclination to go in some direction rather than another. To act intuitively is to choose to choose, to dance, to choose to dance, and to create new anchors, or story shards, in midair. Intuition is to dwell in wonder and to continue to believe, however naively, in the possibility of authenticity, in a strictly *non-nostalgic* fashion, that is in such a way that does not confuse a drive for authenticity with the delusional desire for an unmediated past, say an offline and wireless Paradise Lost. Intuition is organic anarchy, a belief in expression and expressive politics (rather than representational democracy). Intuition is to live more locally, both in physical and discursive terms, and to disintegrate one's everyday practices and discourses as much as possible from global capitalist structures, with the understanding that local communities may be oppressive and normative to the extent one needs to escape them, whether through physical migration or into online communities. To live more locally, that is to say, to consume and produce and more generally to affect and be affected, in smaller yet inclusive communities, is the only way to scale down one's footprint while the planet is burning (in a sense that the distinction between literal and metaphorical speech has vanished), and to express one's belief in the many links through which the local and the everyday are tied up with processes of socioeconomic and cultural segregation between and within communities, the contradictions inherent to capitalism. It's the only way, moreover, to acknowledge that from time to time one may feel a "sudden" spark of empathy, and perhaps even a minimal emotion of interhuman solidarity, when confronted with suffering life, whether its form belongs to a being considered "human," or to another animal. To increase one's power to be affected, and to be truly posthuman in posthuman times, is therefore to pay attention to the vestiges of humanism in one's minimum of belief in the link with a shattered world and, over the course of that process, open up to more inclusive forms of love or life. To be posthuman, in the miraculously realist sense of the word, is to increasingly exist in the present, as it is shaped by past experience and as it stretches out into the near and somewhat foreseeable future over which the scattered subject still experiences a sense of control. To be posthuman is to face one's freedoms and anxieties, to be softer also, softer in one's self-control, in order to melt borders (patriarchal, national, personal), and trust that one way or another the eyes of the mind will discover new patterns in the clouds.

Acknowledgments

If ideas have a definite beginning in the first place, the idea for this book was born in the sky, in a plane from Amsterdam to Toronto, while I was watching *Rosetta* on my laptop. Ideas sometimes come in midair, or arrive in the middle of the night, but they are never fully one's own. They are also shaped by the places and institutions one works and is supported by, the communities one lives in and traverses, and the people one loves and is loved by. First of all, I would like to acknowledge the funding I received from the following institutions while working on this project: the American Council of Learned Societies, the Huygens Scholarship Program of the Dutch government, the Prins Bernard Cultuurfonds (the Netherlands), the Banting Postdoctoral Fellowship (Canadian government), and, at the University of Minnesota: the Center for German and European Studies (and its patron Hella Mears), the Graduate School (and the Harold Leonard Memorial Fellowship in Film Study), as well as the Department of Cultural Studies and Comparative Literature. At the State University of New York Press, I thank James Peltz, Rafael Chaiken, Murray Pomerance, Ryan Morris, and Dana Foote. At *Camera Obscura*, I thank in particular Chip Badley. Part of chapter 1 was previously published in *Camera Obscura* 97 (2018), under the title "Hunting for Easter Eggs in the Dardennes' *Rosetta*," and this material is republished here by permission of Duke University Press. From my time at the University of Minnesota, and Minneapolis more broadly, I thank Cesare Casarino (who has made me see that cinema too is a form of thought). I also thank Timothy Brennan, Robin Brown, Thorn Chen, Andrea Gyenge, Rembert Hueser, Brad Johnson, Brendan McGillicuddy, John Mowitt, Verena Mund, Nichole Neuman, Adair Rounthwaite (for her many comments and insights in earlier stages of this project), Shaden Tageldin, Jonathan Thomas (for introducing me to the films of Bruno Dumont), and François Vozel. A special thank-you to Richard Leppert for his academic guidance during and beyond my PhD trajectory. A special thank-you also to Chelsea Reynolds for her brilliance and openness, which has helped me to shift my thinking in new directions. In Belgium, I thank Jean-François Hogne for a miraculous day in and around the Borinage, documented as part of the excursion that follows chapter 3. In France, I thank Patrick and Jo Vozel for a wonderful stay in the North of France. In Toronto, I thank Brian Price. I also thank Christine Lucy Latimer, for her unbridled enthusiasm and belief, and Kathleen and John Watt, just for being really warm people! In the Netherlands, I thank Tessa de Boer for her suggestions about the map that opens this book. I also thank Markus Haringa, Fabian de Kloe (for our photo expeditions to Liège), as well as the people of Saint Michel in Maastricht and the Frederik Hendrikschool in Amsterdam for hosting me many times, in particular Robert Buzink and Jos Winters. I thank my brother Ivo. Above all, I thank my parents, for their continuous support throughout the years.

Minneapolis-Amsterdam-Maastricht-
Paris-Toronto-Utrecht, 2008–2020

Notes

A North Wind

1. Luc Honorez, "La Bataille de l'humanité est gagnée: la formidable baffe du jury aux professionels de la profession," *Le Soir*, May 25, 1999, 12; "Vent du Nord," La Voix du Nord, May 25, 1999, 1; "A Rosetta, pour l'humanité," *Le Monde*, May 25, 1999, 1. See also "Palmarès festival de Cannes dont Palme d'Or aux frères Dardenne pour Rosetta," video, *Soir 3* (France 3), May 23, 1999, http://www.ina.fr/cannes/1997-2010/video/CAC99022160/palmares-festival-de-cannes-dont-palme-dor-aux-freres-dardenne-pour-rosetta.fr.html (accessed February 23, 2013). Here and in the rest of this book: unless otherwise noted, translations of quotations are mine.

2. Derek Malcolm, "Belgian Film's Surprise Cannes Victory," *Guardian*, May 24, 1999, 2; Jean-Michel Frodon, "Le jury du 52e Festival décroche la palme de l'exigence," *Le Monde*, May 25, 1999.

3. "Ouverture du festival," video (France 2), May 12, 1999, http://www.ina.fr/fresques/festival-de-cannes-fr/fiche-media/Cannes00335/ouverture-du-festival-1999 (accessed February 21, 2013).

4. Serge Toubiana, "Le Cinéma retrouvé," *Cahiers du cinéma* 536 (1999): 22–23.

Introduction

1. Jacques Rancière, "Le Bruit du peuple, l'image de l'art: à propos de *Rosetta* et de *L'Humanité*," *Cahiers du cinéma* 540 (1999): 111, my translation.

2. See Romain Sublon, "[cinéphilies:] Bruno Dumont et Julie Sokolowski," *Cut* (2009): cutlarevue.fr/2009/11/26/cinephilies-bruno-dumont-et-julie-sokolowski/ (accessed March 3, 2013).

3. Benedict de Spinoza. *The Chief Works of Spinoza:* A Theologico-Political Treatise *and* A Political Treatise, trans. R. H. M. Elwes (New York: Dover Publications, 1951), 86.

4. Spinoza, *Chief Works*, 84.

5. Dudley Andrew, "An Atlas of World Cinema," in *Remapping World Cinema: Identity, Culture and Politics in Film*, ed. Stephanie Dennison and Song Hwee Lim (London: Wallflower Press, 2006), 21.

6. Andrew, "An Atlas of World Cinema," 26.

7. Andrew Higson, "The Limiting Imagination of National Cinema," in *Cinema and Nation*, ed. Mette Hjort and Scott MacKenzie (London: Routledge, 2000), 73.

8. Nataša Ďurovičová, "Preface," in *World Cinemas, Transnational Perspectives* (New York: Routledge, 2010), ix.

9. Mette Hjort and Duncan Petrie, "Introduction," in *The Cinema of Small Nations* (Bloomington: Indiana University Press, 2007), 16. See also Mette Hjort, *Small Nation, Global Cinema: The New Danish Cinema* (Minneapolis: University of Minnesota Press, 2005).

10. Janelle Blankenship and Tobias Nagl, "Introduction: Towards a Politics of Scale," in *European Visions: Small Cinemas in Transition*, ed. Janelle Blankenship and Tobias Nagl (Bielefeld: Transcript Verlag, 2015), 25.

11. Thomas Elsaesser, "The Mind-Game Film," in *Puzzle Films: Complex Storytelling in Contemporary Cinema*, ed. Warren Buckland (Chichester: Wiley-Blackwell, 2009), 16.

12. Alain Jennotte, "Le cinéma belge, c'est bon pour l'économie," *Le Soir*, February 3, 2010, 36.

13. A. O. Scott, "In Toronto, Sampling Realism's Resurgence," *New York Times*, September 10, 2008, http://www.nytimes.com/2008/09/11/movies/11fest.html (accessed March 10, 2013).

14. Lauren Berlant, *Cruel Optimism* (Durham: Duke University Press, 2011), 201.

15. Rosi Braidotti, *The Posthuman* (Cambridge: Polity Press, 2013), 23.

16. Gilles Deleuze, *Cinema 2* (London: Continuum, 2005), 165.

17. Michael Hardt and Antonio Negri, *Empire* (Cambridge: Harvard University Press, 2000), 91.

18. Charles Taylor, *A Secular Age* (Cambridge: The Belknap Press of Harvard University Press, 2007), 13–14.

19. Jürgen Habermas, *Europe: The Faltering Project*, trans. Ciaran Cronin (Cambridge: Polity, 2009), 59, 63.

20. John Caruana and Mark Cauchi, "What Is Postsecular Cinema? An Introduction," in *Immanent Frames: Postsecular Cinema between Malick and Von Trier* (Albany: State University of New York Press, 2018), 4.

21. Taylor, *A Secular Age*, 549.

Chapter 1

1. In the screenplay of *Rosetta*, this opening scene reads as follows:

1. Intérieur—Atelier/Fabrique de surgelés—Jour.

La nuque, le dos de Rosetta (dix-sept ans) déboulant un escalier, traversant l'atelier. Elle est revêtue d'une combinaison-plastique verte et coiffée d'un bonnet hygiénique. Elle est suivie par un homme en chemise/cravate qui tente de lui parler. Elle marche, le visage en colère, croisant quelques ouvriers et ouvrières à leur poste sur la chaîne de refroidissement /empaquettage, eux aussi revêtus d'une combinaision-plastique verte et coiffés d'un bonnet hygiénique. L'homme en chemise/cravate veut la retenir par l'épaule, elle le repousse d'un geste violent. Elle s'approche d'un bureau vitré dans lequel est assise une femme (revêtue d'une combinaison-plastique verte) en train de consulter un écran d'ordinateur.

2. Intérieur—Bureau vitré/Fabrique de surgelés—Jour

Rosetta: C'est vrai que t'as dit que j'étais souvent en retard?

Luc Dardenne and Jean-Pierre Dardenne, *Scénarios*: Rosetta, *suivi de* La Promesse (Paris: Cahiers du cinéma, 1999), 11.

2. Luc Dardenne, *Au dos de nos images (1991–2005), suivi de* Le Fils *et* L'Enfant *par Jean-Pierre et Luc Dardenne* (Paris: Éditions du Seuil, 2005), 66.

3. Philip Mosley, *Responsible Realism: The Cinema of the Dardenne Brothers* (New York: Wallflower Press, 2013), 1–2.

4. Thorn Andersen, "Against the Grain: Adding a Touch of Noir, the Dardenne Brothers Rethink Neorealism in *Lorna's Silence*," *Film Society of Lincoln Center* (2009), http://www.filmlinc.com/fcm/ja09/lorna.htm (accessed April 16, 2010).

5. Andersen, "Against the Grain."

6. Michel Foucault, "The Subject and Power," in *Beyond Structuralism and Hermeneutics* (Chicago: University of Chicago Press, 1983), 214.

7. Foucault, "The Subject and Power," 214–215.

8. Judith Butler, "Bodies and Power Revisited," in *Feminism and the Final Foucault*, ed. Dianna Taylor and Karen Vintges (Urbana: University of Illinois Press, 2004), 192.

9. Berlant, *Cruel Optimism*, 163–164.

10. Joseph Mai, *Jean-Pierre and Luc Dardenne* (Urbana: University of Illinois Press, 2010), 53.

11. Mai, *Jean-Pierre and Luc Dardenne*, 57.

12. Cited in Joan Dupont, "Two Belgian Brothers' Working-Class Heroes," in *Committed Cinema: The Films of Jean-Pierre and Luc Dardenne; Essays and Interviews*, ed. Bert Cardullo (Cambridge: Cambridge Scholars, 2009), 87.

13. François Gorin, "Une journée au Nord," *Télérama*, http://www.brunodumont.com/index.php?option=com_k2&view=item&id=12:a-propos-de-lhumanit%C3%A9&Itemid=53&lang=fr (accessed April 10, 2011).

14. In the film's screenplay, the opening sequence reads as follows: "Il marchait dans le Pas de Calais. La terre n'était pas sourde. Lui respirait à peine et son corps s'humidifiait. A plus de vingt mètres au-dessus de son crâne, bien haut, une alouette à tue-tête son air béni. De la pâture, il franchit une clôture barbelée et gagna des labours. Là, une terre grasse et nue le retint. Son ralentissement—des mottes de limon emportées—l'inquiéta. Il frémissait." Bruno

Dumont, *L'Humanité—écrit pour un scénario*, http://www.brunodumont.com/index.php?option=com_k2&view=item&id=20:sc%C3%A9narios&Itemid=54&lang=en (accessed April 10, 2011).

15. Gorin, "Une journée au Nord."

16. Pancrace Royer, "Le Vertigo: rondeau" (1746).

17. James S. Williams, *Space and Being in Contemporary French Cinema* (Manchester: Manchester University Press, 2013), 46.

18. Jean-Luc Godard and Michel Delahaye, "The Question," in *Robert Bresson*, ed. James Quandt (Toronto: Toronto International Film Festival Group, 1998), 465–466.

19. Robert Bresson, *Notes sur le cinématographe* (Paris: Gallimard, 1975), 35.

20. Steven Shaviro, *The Cinematic Body* (Minneapolis: University of Minnesota Press, 1993), 244.

21. In Gorin, "Une journée au Nord," my emphasis.

22. Robert Sklar, "The Terrible Lightness of Social Marginality: An Interview with Jean-Pierre and Luc Dardenne," *Cineaste* 31, no. 2 (2006): 20, my emphasis.

23. Bresson, *Notes sur le cinématographe*, 37, 39.

24. Bernard Benoliel and Serge Toubiana, "'Il faut être dans le cul des choses': entretien avec Luc et Jean-Pierre Dardenne," *Cahiers du cinéma* 539 (1999): 49.

25. Benoliel and Toubiana, "'Il faut être dans le cul des choses,'" 50.

26. In Bert Cardullo, "The Cinema of Resistance: An Interview with Jean-Pierre and Luc Dardenne (June 2009)," in *Committed Cinema: The Films of Jean-Pierre and Luc Dardenne; Essays and Interviews*, ed. Bert Cardullo (Cambridge: Cambridge Scholars, 2009), 190.

27. Dardenne, *Au dos de nos images*, 137.

28. Gilles Deleuze and Félix Guattari, *Anti-Oedipus: Capitalism and Schizophrenia* (Minneapolis: University of Minnesota Press, 1983), 23.

29. Laura Mulvey, "Visual Pleasure and Narrative Cinema," *Screen* 6, no. 18 (1975): 13.

30. Teresa de Lauretis, *Alice Doesn't: Feminism, Semiotics, Cinema* (Bloomington: Indiana University Press), 140.

31. Margaret Pomeranz, "Interview: The Dardenne Brothers' *Child*," in *Committed Cinema: The Films of Jean-Pierre and Luc Dardenne; Essays and Interviews*, ed. Bert Cardullo (Cambridge: Cambridge Scholars, 2009), 172.

32. Rancière, "Le Bruit du peuple," 112.

33. Martine Beugnet, *Cinema and Sensation: French Film and the Art of Transgression* (Edinburgh: Edinburgh University Press, 1997), 104.

34. Tony Rayns, "*L'humanité*," *Sight and Sound* (October 2000), http://www.bfi.org.uk/sightandsound/review/433 (accessed April 9, 2011).

35. Beugnet, *Cinema and Sensation*, 104.

36. In Gorin, "Une journée au Nord."

37. Jean Mottet, "Mardi 28 novembre 2006: Bruno Dumont," in *La Direction d'acteur: carnation, incarnation*, ed. Frédéric Sojcher (Paris: Éditions du Rocher, 2008), 193–195.

38. Mottet, "Bruno Dumont," 200–201.

39. Giorgio Agamben, *Means without End: Notes on Politics*, trans. Vincenzo Binetti and Cesare Casarino (Minneapolis: University of Minnesota Press, 2000), 57.
40. Agamben, *Means without End*, 59–60.
41. Benoliel and Toubiana, "Il faut être dans le cul des choses," 49.
42. Georges Bernanos, *Nouvelle histoire de Mouchette* (Bordeaux: Le Castor Astral, 2009), 17.
43. Bernanos, *Nouvelle histoire de Mouchette*, 21.
44. Blaise Pascal, *Pascal's Pensées with an Introduction by T. S. Eliot*, trans. W. F. Trotter (New York: E. P. Dutton & Co., 1958), 66–67.
45. Deleuze, *Cinema 2*, 171.
46. Pascal, *Pensées*, 67.
47. Paul Renard, "Les Adaptations cinématographiques des romans," in *Le Nord et le cinéma: contributions à l'histoire du cinéma dans le Nord/Pas-de-Calais*, ed. L'Association Jean Mitry (Pantin: Le Temps des Cerises, 1998), 225–226.
48. André Bazin, *Qu'est-ce que le cinéma (Edition définitive)* (Paris: Éditions du Cerf, 1975), 124.
49. Rancière, "Le Bruit du peuple," 111, emphases in original.
50. Rancière, "Le Bruit du peuple," 111, emphasis in original.
51. Rancière, "Le Bruit du peuple," 112.
52. Kent Jones, "*L'humanité*," *Film Comment* 36, no. 3 (2000): 73.
53. Rancière, "Le Bruit du peuple," 112.
54. Bert Cardullo, "Rosetta Stone: A Consideration of the Dardenne Brothers' *Rosetta*," *Journal of Religion and Film* 6, no. 1 (2002), https://www.unomaha.edu/jrf/rosetta.htm.
55. Dardenne, *Au dos de nos images*, 91.
56. Laura Mulvey, *Death 24x a Second: Stillness and the Moving Image* (London: Reaktion Books, 2006), 183.
57. Elsaesser, "The Mind-Game Film," 30.
58. Laura Marks, *The Skin of the Film: Intercultural Cinema, Embodiment, and the Senses* (Durham: Duke University Press, 2000), xi.
59. Rancière, "Le Bruit du peuple," 112.

Chapter 2

1. Cited in Sheila Johnstone, "Filmmakers on Film: The Secret of the Dardenne Brothers' Palme d'Or Success," in *Committed Cinema: The Films of Jean-Pierre and Luc Dardenne: Essays and Interviews*, ed. Bert Cardullo (Cambridge: Cambridge Scholars, 2009), 103.
2. Bruno Demoulin and Jean-Louis Kupper, eds., *Histoire de la Wallonie: de la préhistoire au XXIe siècle* (Toulouse: Éditions Privat, 2004), 343.
3. Pascal Verbeken, *Arm Wallonië: Een Reis door het Beloofde Land* (Antwerp/Amsterdam: Meulenhoff/Manteau, 2007), 257.
4. Verbeken, *Arm Wallonië*, 37.
5. Cited in Daniel Granval, *Les Tournages de films dans le Nord et le Pas-de-Calais* (Bouvignies: Éditions Nord Avril, 2008), 37.

6. In Nord-Pas-de-Calais, Picard is most spoken in French Flanders, Artois (a former French province that is now part of Nord-Pas-de-Calais), as well as the area around Valenciennes, where Picard is referred to as Rouchi.

7. See Granval, *Tournages des films dans le Nord et le Pas-de-Calais*, 36.

8. Firmin Lentacker, *La Frontière franco-belge: étude géographique des effets d'une frontière internationale sur la vie de relations* (Lille: Presses Universitaires du Septentrion, 1974), 9.

9. The name "Fédération Wallonie-Bruxelles" is used in the broadcastings of the francophone RTBF, but not in those of the Flemish VRT. See "'Ne dites pas 'Federatie Wallonië-Brussel' sur la VRT," 7 *sur* 7, September 29, 2011, http://www.7sur7.be/7s7/fr/3007/Bruxelles/article/detail/1326587/2011/09/29/Ne-dites-pas-Federatie-Wallonie-Brussel-sur-la-VRT.dhtml (accessed April 12, 2011).

A brief anecdote: in 2013 the chair of the Flemish parliament, Jan Peumans, who belongs to the Flemish nationalist N-VA, refused to accept a meeting invitation from his francophone-Belgian colleague, as the invitation was typed on the Fédération Wallonie-Bruxelles letterhead. See: http://www.brusselnieuws.be/nl/nieuws/peumans-weigert-uitnodiging-door-federation-wallonie-bruxelles.

10. Maurits Gysseling and Jules Herbillon, "La Genèse de la frontière linguistique dans le Nord de la Gaulle," *Revue du Nord* 44, no. 173 (1962): 31.

11. The only exceptions were the districts of Eupen and Malmedy, which were reannexed by the Reich. This annexation was reversed again after World War II.

12. As Guido Fonteyn explains, it remains unclear whether Grandgagnage knew that Jesuit and later also Capuchin monks already referred to the southern part of their church provinces as "Germania Inferior Provincia Walloniae." See Guido Fonteyn, *Afscheid van Magritte: Over het Oude en Nieuwe Wallonië* (Antwerp: De Bezige Bij, 2011), 19–21.

13. See Hervé Hasquin, "La Wallonie: d'où vient-elle?," in *Wallonie: atouts et références d'une region*, ed. Freddy Joris and Natalie Archambeau (Mons: Gouvernement Wallon, 1995), 17.

14. Hugh Clout, *The Franco-Belgian Border Region* (London: Oxford University Press, 1975), 6.

15. Clout, *The Franco-Belgian Border Region*, 6. Over the course of history, the drainage pattern of Wallonia and the French North has been altered by the construction of canals and the canalization of rivers. This modification of natural water courses, and construction of new water courses, has in fact increased the visibility of the French-Belgian border, since for protectionist reasons many French canals were left shallower than those north of the border, this in order to prevent large barges from transporting goods from Antwerp and Rotterdam to France.

16. Between 1840 and 1880, the economy of the Walloon regions had an average annual growth rate of 4.4 percent (3.7 for Belgium). See Demoulin and Kupper, *Histoire de la Wallonie*, 252.

17. Demoulin and Kupper, *Histoire de la Wallonie*, 246; Hasquin, "La Wallonie," 32. See also Paul Bairoch, "Niveaux de développement économique de 1810 à 1910," *Annales: Economies, sociétés, civilisations* 20, no. 6 (1965): 1091–1117. In this essay Bairoch lists Belgium as the second industrial power in terms of industrial

development between 1810 and 1880 (tied with the US and, in 1840, also with Switzerland). This classification forms the synthesis of some key indicators of industrialization that Bairoch analyzes for several countries. He distinguishes between direct and indirect indicators. The direct indicators are: the consumption of raw cotton per capita (for which Belgium ranks fourth in 1840, 1860, and 1880, after the UK, US, and Switzerland); the production of cast iron per inhabitant (for which Belgium ranks third in 1840, trailing the UK and Sweden, second in 1860 and 1880, behind the UK). The indirect indicators are: the index of the development of railways; the consumption of coal per capita (for which Belgium ranks second, after the UK, in 1840, 1860, and 1880); and nonmobile steam engines. Finally, Bairoch writes about the industrial power of Belgium in the early nineteenth century: "Even though the data and the estimations are not sufficient in number, it is probable that Belgium—which since 1860 occupies the second place together with the US—situated itself in the beginning of the nineteenth century immediately after the UK in terms of its level of industrial development. It seems therefore that in this country the Industrial Revolution must have begun before the start of the nineteenth century and not in the years 1820–1830 as it has been generally supposed" (1111).

18. Clout, *Franco-Belgian Border Region*, 11.

19. Pierre Pierrard, *Histoire du Nord: Flandre, Artois, Hainaut, Picardie* (Paris: Hachette, 1992), 396.

20. E. A. Wrigley, *Industrial Growth and Population Change: A Regional Study of the Coalfield Areas of Northwest Europe in the Later Nineteenth Century* (London: Cambridge University Press, 1961), 12.

21. Wrigley, *Industrial Growth and Population Change*, 42.

22. F. Codaccioni, "Une puissance industrielle arrivée à maturité," in *Histoire du Nord-Pas-de-Calais: de 1900 à nos jours*, ed. Yves-Marie Hilaire (Toulouse: Éditions Privat, 1982), 65.

23. Jean-Pierre Popelier, *Belges et Français du Nord: une histoire partagée* (Lille: La Voix du Nord Éditions, 2009), 22; Fonteyn, *Afscheid van Magritte*, 139. One of the major dutchophone centers of France was Roubaix in French Flanders, a city of which the population rose from 8,000 to 120,000 during the nineteenth century, an increase that can be largely attributed to Belgian immigrants.

24. Fonteyn, *Afscheid van Magritte*, 138–139. Fonteyn also writes that the 1869 introduction of a system of railway cards hardly slowed down the migration from the Belgian North to the Belgian South.

25. See Anne Morelli, "Les Italiens au Borinage: une longue histoire," in *Cinéma Wallonie Bruxelles: du documentaire social au film de fiction*, ed. W'allons-nous (Virton: W'allons nous, 1989), 104.

26. Michel Quévit and Vincent Lepage, "La Wallonie, une région économique en mutation," http://www.wallonie-en-ligne.net/1995_Wallonie_Atouts-References/1995_ch10-1_Quevit-M_Lepage-V.htm.

27. Pierrard, *Histoire du Nord*, 374. In the Nord and Pas-de-Calais departments the average yields per man per shift in 1930 was 1,100 kg (1.2 tons). In the Walloon mines in 1930, this average amounted to 572 kg (0.6 tons). Dumoulin and Kupper, *Histoire de la Wallonie*, 292. By 1938, the average yields per man

per shift in northern France had remained stable at 1,100 kg. By comparison, in Dutch Limburg, the Saar and the Ruhr, these averages amounted to 2,400, 1,600, and 2,000 kg, respectively. Clout, *Franco-Belgian Border Region*, 14.

28. Dumoulin and Kupper, *Histoire de la Wallonie*, 292. The Walloon glass industry showed a similar development, as the competition in Campine and other Flemish regions profited from its geographical advantages: the presence of coal and sand, as well as the proximity of the seaports of Antwerp and Zeebrugge, and the Albert Channel. Meanwhile, the Walloon blast furnaces had become largely dependent on foreign, predominantly French minerals. For example, in 1929, a "good year" for Walloon steel production, nearly 90 percent of the ten million tons of minerals processed had to be imported.

29. J. A. Sporck, "L'Organisation de l'espace dans la métropole liégoise," *Travaux Géographiques de Liège* 159 (1972): 355–383. Cited in Clout, *Franco-Belgian Border Region*, 14.

30. From "Joyeuse vie" (1851). Victor Hugo, *Oeuvres complètes de Victor Hugo. Poésie IV. Les Chatiments* (Paris: J. Hetzel & Cie; A. Quantin & Cie, 1882), 164.

31. Vincent van Gogh, [Letter to Theo van Gogh. Wasmes, Thursday, December 26, 1878.] (Amsterdam: Van Gogh Museum/Huygens Institute-KNAW), http://vangoghletters.org/vg/letters/let149/letter.html (accessed December 12, 2011).

32. Maxence van der Meersch, *Quand les sirènes se taisent* (Douai: L'Imprimerie Nationale, 1960), 5–6. I partially based my translation on *When the Looms Are Silent*, trans. Frederick Blossom (New York: William Morrow and Company, 1934), 6.

33. Van der Meersch, *Quand les sirènes se taisent*, 78–79; *When the Looms Are Silent*, 75–76, translation modified.

34. The film's added commentary was written by the politician and filmmaker Jean Fonteyne and read by André Thirifays, founder of the Club de l'Ecran (which had ordered *Borinage*) and cofounder in 1938 of the Cinémathèque de Belgique, together with Henri Storck and Pierre Vermeylen.

35. Source: http://measuringworth.com.

36. Marc-E. Mélon, "Misère au Borinage [avec Joris Ivens, 1933]," in *Ça tourne depuis cent ans: une histoire de cinéma francophone de Belgique*, ed. Philippe Dubois and Edouard Arnoldy (Brussels: Communauté Française de Belgique/Wallonie-Bruxelles, 1995), 56.

37. Joris Ivens, *The Camera and I* (New York/Berlin: International Publishers/Seven Seas Books, 1969), 83–84.

38. In the third version of "The Work of Art in the Age of Its Technological Reproducibility" (1939) Walter Benjamin writes: "The newsreel offers everyone the chance to rise from passer-by to movie extra. In this way, a person might even see himself becoming part of a work of art: think of Vertov's *Three Songs of Lenin* or Ivens' *Borinage*. Any person today can lay claim to being filmed." *Selected Writings, Volume 4: 1938–1940*, ed. Howard Eiland and Michael Jennings, trans. Edmund Jephcott et al. (Cambridge: The Belknap Press of Harvard University Press, 2006), 262.

39. The Front Populaire consisted of the French Communist Party, the French Section of the Workers' International, and the Radical and Socialist Party. Combined, these parties gained 63 percent of the votes in the 1936 elections (80 percent of the votes in Nord, 67 percent in Pas-de-Calais).

40. Four months after his signing of the Matignon Agreements, Salengro committed suicide, after having been accused by extreme right-wing groups of having deserted the French army during World War I, an accusation for which no evidence was ever found. The other politician from Nord-Pas-de-Calais in the Popular Front government was Jean Lebas, minister of labor and the former mayor of Roubaix.

41. Demoulin and Kupper, *Histoire de la Wallonie*, 314; Eric Bussière, "Une renaissance économique fragile," chapter 23 in *Deux mille ans du "Nord-Pas-de-Calais": Tome II: De la révolution au XXIe siècle*, ed. Alain Lottin and Eric Bussière (Lille: La Voix du Nord, 2002), 194.

42. Cited in Clout, *Franco-Belgian Border Region*, 14.

43. "The Schuman Declaration—9 May 1950," *European Union*. See: http://europa.eu/about-eu/basic-information/symbols/europe-day/schuman-declaration/index_en.htm (accessed May 19, 2015).

44. Clout, *Franco-Belgian Border Region*, 15–16.

45. Jean Vavasseur-Desperriers, "Les Grandes forces politiques au temps de la reconstruction et de l'expansion," chapter 24 in *Deux mille ans du "Nord-Pas-de-Calais,"* ed. ed. Alain Lottin and Eric Bussière (Lille: La Voix du Nord, 2002), 208.

46. Demoulin, *Histoire de la Wallonie*, 328.

47. Petra de Koning, "Laatste Zucht van de Roemruchte Staalindustrie rond Luik," *NRC Handelsblad*, October 28, 2011, 30–31.

48. See for example: http://www.mons.be/economie/poles-dactivites/digital-innovation-valley-1.

49. Http://www.google.nl/about/datacenters/inside/locations/st-ghislain/ (accessed July 7, 2015). Google's construction of its first datacenter outside of the US has employed about 1,500 and represented an estimated benefit of €900 million for the Walloon economy. See: Etienne Froment, "Le Centre de données de Google dans le région de Mons: un apport considérable pour l'économie belge," *Le Soir*, June 24, 2015, http://geeko.lesoir.be/2015/06/24/le-centre-de-donnees-de-google-dans-la-region-de-mons-un-apport-considerable-pour-leconomie-belge/ (accessed July 7, 2015).

50. The first Interreg programming cycle, Interreg I, took off in 1989 and ended in 1993. The subsequent programming cycles have covered the following periods: 1994–1999 (II), 2000–2006 (III), 2007–2013 (IV), and 2014–2020 (V). Interreg is made up of three strands: strand A, cross-border cooperation; strand B, transnational cooperation; and strand C, interregional cooperation.

51. One of these Euroregions is the Cross-Channel Euroregion initiated by Nord-Pas-de-Calais and Kent in 1987, and expanded with Flanders, Wallonia, and Brussels-Capital in 1991. Furthermore, the Belgian provinces of Limburg, Liège, and the German-speaking Community of Belgium are also part of the Meuse-Rhine Euroregion, which further includes parts of the Netherlands and Germany.

52. See Société de l'Industrie Minérale, ed., *Gestion des anciens sites de carbochimie en Europe. Syntèse du programma Interreg II Ocasicha* (Douai: Les Fascicules de l'Industrie Minérale, 2001). The Interreg IV France-Wallonie-Vlaanderen ran between 2008 and 2013 and focused on the border area involving parts of Wallonia, Flanders, and northern France.

53. Equipe technique INTERREG Nord-Pas-de-Calais, *Regards Transfontaliers INTERREG 2, Hainaut, Nord-Pas de Calais, Picardie* (INTERREG Hainaut, Nord-Pas de Calais, Picardie, 1998).

54. André-Jean Pouille et al., *Atlas transfontalier: Tome 4: emploi-formation-taux de chômage* (Paris: INSEE, 2009). See also http://www.insee.fr/fr/regions/nord-pas-de calais/default.asp?page=themes/ouvrages/atlas/ATLF_accueil.htm#Emploi-Formation (accessed September 10, 2011).

55. According to Eurostat, in 2000 the employment rate in the age range of 15–64 was 61.0 and 60.9 percent in France and Belgium, respectively, but only 51.8 percent and 56.7 percent in Nord-Pas-de-Calais and Wallonia, respectively. See André-Jean Pouille, *Atlas transfontalier: Tome 3: activités économiques—PIB par habitant* (Paris: INSEE, 2005). See also http://www.insee.fr/fr/regions/nord-pas-de-calais/default.asp?page=themes/ouvrages/atlas/03_01_pib_habitant.htm (accessed September 10, 2011).

56. Institut National de la Statistique et des Etudes Economiques, "Nord-Pas-de-Calais," (Paris: INSEE, 2010), http://www.insee.fr/fr/regions/nord-pas-de-calais/default.asp?page=faitsetchiffres/presentation/presentation.htm (accessed September 10, 2011).

57. Whereas over the period 2000–2004 in France on the whole unemployment went up by 0.9 percent, in Nord-Pas-de-Calais's former mine regions unemployment went down. In Wallonia, unemployment went up by 1.4 percent during the same period. See Pouille et al., *Atlas transfontalier: Tome 4*, http://www.insee.fr/fr/regions/nord-pas-decalais/default.asp?page=themes/ouvrages./atlas/04_07_part_des_jeunes_dans_le_chomage.htm (accessed September 10, 2011).

This observation that Wallonia's structural crisis has been more severe than that of Nord-Pas-de-Calais is further confirmed by the fact that between 2007 and 2013 the Walloon province of Hainaut was still the only area in northwest continental Europe that received direct ERDF support (EU support not distributed through the Interreg programs). See "Cohesion Policy 2007–2013," *Europa.eu* (European Union, 2007), http://ec.europa.eu/regional_policy/atlas2007/belgium/index_en.htm (accessed September 10, 2011).

58. A noteworthy Dutch example is the television documentary *Jong in . . . België (Wallonië)* (Young in Belgium [Wallonia]), aired in 2008 by the public television organization VPRO (available online at: http://tegenlicht.vpro.nl/afleveringen/2008-2009/jong-in/jong-in-belgie-wallonie.html).

59. Verbeken writes: "In 1903, the francophone journalist Auguste de Winne wrote *Through Poor Flanders* [*A travers les Flandres*], a classical documentation of a journey through 'holes of sorrow,' where poverty, famine, analphabetism, and exploitation were rampant." Verbeken, *Arm Wallonië*, back cover.

60. Fonteyn, *Afscheid van Magritte*, 11.

61. Roger Mounèje, "Note de l'éditeur," in *Cinéma Wallonie Bruxelles: du documentaire social au film de fiction*, ed. W'allons-nous (Virton: W'allons nous, 1989), 5.

62. Frédéric Sojcher, *La Kermesse héroïque du cinéma belge: Tome I: 1896–1965: Des documentaires et des farces* (Paris: L'Harmattan, 1999), 152.

63. Léon Michaux, *Images et cinéma de Wallonie: une société en mutation* (Brussels: La Médiathèque de la Communauté Française de Belgique, 2000).

64. Jacques Polet, "Un enracinement porteur d'universalité," *Louvain* 133 (2002): 23.

65. Anne Roekens and Axel Tixhon, "Avant-propos," in *Cinéma et crise(s) économique(s): esquisses d'une cinématographie wallonne*, ed. Anne Roekens and Axel Tixhon (Crisnée/Namur: Editions Yellow Now/Presses Universitaires Namur, 2011), 7.

66. Bénédicte Rochet, "Esquisse d'une cinématographie wallonne," in *Cinéma et crise(s) économique(s): esquisses d'une cinématographie wallonne*, ed. Anne Roekens and Axel Tixhon (Crisnée/Namur: Editions Yellow Now/Presses universitaires Namur, 2011), 22.

67. Théodore Louis, "Ambiguité de la fiction: les années 1958–1965," in *Cinéma Wallonie Bruxelles: du documentaire social au film de fiction*, ed. W'allons-nous (Virton: W'allons nous, 1989), 63.

68. After *Déjà s'envole la fleur maigre*, Meyer mainly worked for Belgian public television (RTBF), and he only directed one other feature-length film, *L'Herbe sous les pieds* (Grass beneath the feet, 1977).

69. One of the reasons the protests were less vehement in Flanders than in Wallonia was that the Belgian government exerted pressure on the Catholic trade union and the Catholic Church to discourage the Catholic part of the population from participating in the strike.

70. Moreover, following the refusal of the Belgian Socialist Party and the General Federation of Belgian Labor (GFBL, Belgian's socialist national trade union federation) to let go of their unitary principles in favor of federalism, in the spring of 1961 GFBL leader André Renard launched the Mouvement populaire wallonne (Walloon Popular Movement). In 1970, and largely as the result of this movement's efforts, Belgium was reorganized into three regions (which were federalized in 1993).

71. Thierry Michel also made the documentary film *Chronique des saisons d'acier* (Chronicle of the seasons of steel; codirected with Christine Pireaux, 1981), which depicts the impact of the decline of the Seraing steel industry on the lives of four people from four different generations.

72. Dérives was founded in 1975 and has since produced dozens of documentaries as well as some fiction films. The Dardennes' first film was *Le Chant du rossignol* (The chant of the nightingale, 1978), which has been lost.

73. The Dziga Vertov group was formed in 1968 by Godard and Jean-Pierre Gorin, which produced Brechtian agitprop films such as *Le Vent d'Est* (1969) and *Tout va bien* (1972). The group was disbanded in 1973 out of disillusionment with precisely its remainder of belief in a political cinema, a disillusionment Godard,

together with Anne-Marie Miéville, thematized in *Ici et ailleurs / Here and Elsewhere* (1976). *Ici et ailleurs* is a critical reflection on the earlier unfinished Dziga Vertov project *Jusqu'à la Victoire* (Until victory) that Godard and Gorin made in collaboration with a group of militants from the Palestine Liberation Organization. In September 1970, however, most of these militants were murdered by the Jordanian army, after which Godard and Miéville used the existing footage to make another film. "En 1970 ce film s'appelait *Victoire*," Miéville states. "En 1975 il s'appelle Ici et ailleurs. Ici, une famille française qui régarde la télé. Ailleurs, des images de la révolution Palestinienne." *Ici et ailleurs* thus takes the route Godard had gone earlier with *Les Carabiniers* and *Le Mépris*, by expressing the inherently modern gap between representations and the world (see also chapter 4). The film seeks to visualize and make felt the irrational interval that connects and separates "ici" and "ailleurs," as is emphasized by the recurring shots of a carved Styrofoam "ET." As David Rodowick argues, "in their incommensurability the images of *Ici et ailleurs* return in ever more differentiated series that interrogate the mass media's crowding out of both the memory and actuality of revolutionary struggle." David Rodowick, *Reading the Figural, or, Philosophy after the New Media* (Durham: Duke University Press, 2001), 199.

74. *Du beurre dans les tartines* is part of a television series named *Strip-Tease*, which was produced and broadcasted by the RTBF.

75. Verbeken, *Arm Wallonië*, 89. In 1996, the private TV station RTL commissioned Olivier to make another documentary in Charleroi. In *Au fond Dutroux* (1996) he goes in search of the Charleroi of Marc Dutroux, who in 2004 was found guilty of having kidnapped and sexually abused six girls during 1995 and 1996, and of having murdered four of them. As suggested by his film's title—which can also be understood as "at the bottom of the hole [*trou*]—Olivier partly attributes the crimes of Dutroux to a failed society. In 1999, the event of Dutroux's escape in April 1998 and the police's capturing of him a few hours later, inspired Bouli Lanners to make *Travellinckx*, a fictive documentary in which the protagonist reacts as follows when he hears this news on his car radio: "C'est impossible, c'est une blague . . . Qu'est-ce qu'ils foutent les imbéciles là-haut? . . . Le seul mec, le seul mec qui ne pouvait pas échapper . . . Belgique, un pays de cons. J'ai honte d'être belge."

76. "Enfants du hasard" (RTBF, 9 April 2017), https://www.youtube.com/watch?v=gn2XdSYuIbo.

77. Cited in Polet, "Un enracinement porteur d'universalité," 25.

78. Exceptions are for example the performance of Jeremy Irons in *Australia* (Jean-Jacques Andrien, 1989), and that of Isabelle Huppert in *Nue propriété* (Private property; Joachim Lafosse, 2006).

79. Polet, "Un enracinement porteur d'universalité," 25.

80. Bazin, *Qu'est-ce que le cinéma?*, 263.

81. *Jeudi on chantera comme dimanche* was one of the first feature films that received financial aid from the Ministry of Belgian Francophone Culture, a topic to which I will return in the next chapter. The film was based on a script by the Flemish poet and novelist Hugo Claus.

82. Through a number of its shots, *Les Convoyeurs attendent* cites the works of famous photographers. For example, the film cites Henri Cartier-Bresson's 1963 photograph of a young Mexican girl who is carrying with her a framed painting of a woman. *Les Convoyeurs attendent* substitutes the streets of Charleroi for the shantytown of Mexico City, while the painting becomes an Yves Saint Laurent billboard reading, "In love again." See also Jean-Benoît Gabriel, "La Wallonie révélée: esthétique du paysage industriel chez Benoît Mariage et Bouli Lanners," in *Cinéma et crise(s) économique(s): esquisses d'une cinématographie wallonne*, ed. Anne Roekens and Axel Tixhon (Crisnée/Namur: Editions Yellow Now/Presses Universitaires Namur, 2011), 67–88.

83. *Le Banquet des fraudeurs* was based on a scenario by Charles Spaak and inspired by the formation of the Benelux (Belgium-Netherlands-Luxembourg) in 1948. Originally, the film was planned as a documentary. From a Dutch perspective, the actual "three-border-point" of the Netherlands, Belgium, and Germany is in the town of Vaals, in Dutch Limburg.

84. Two examples of Walloon films that depict the French-Belgian border are *Passeurs d'or* (1948) and *Les Filles des fraudeurs* (1962), both directed by E. G. de Meyst.

85. Van der Meersch's *La Maison dans la dune* has been adapted for the screen twice more: by Pierre Billon (1934) and the Flemish Michel Mees (1988, a Belgian production). Another film based on a novel by Van der Meersch, and one that also depicts the northern French smuggling community, is *L'Empreinte du dieu / Two Women* (Léonide Moguy, 1940).

86. François Baudinet, "Chronique du Nord à l'écran: l'histoire du Nord sous le regard de son cinéma des origines à 1958," in *Le Nord et le cinéma: contributions à l'histoire du cinéma dans le Nord-Pas-de-Calais*, ed. L'Association Jean Mitry (Pantin: Le Temps de cerises, 1998), 154.

87. Alexandrine Dhainaut, "Le Nord au cinéma, victime de ses clichés?" *Il était une fois le cinéma* (2008), http://www.iletaitunefoislecinema.com/chronique/1802/le-nord-au-cinema-victime-de-ses-cliches (accessed February 10, 2012).

88. Granval, *Tournages de films dans le Nord et le Pas-de-Calais*, 11.

89. I largely base these four reasons on the ones listed in Baudinet, "Chronique du Nord à l'écran," 154–155.

90. René Prédal, *Le Cinéma français des années 1990: une génération de transition* (Paris: Armand Colin, 2008), 76–77.

91. François Truffaut, "Une certaine tendance du cinéma français," *Cahiers du cinéma* 31 (1954): 15–29.

92. Victor Hugo's 1862 novel *Les Misérables*—which was adapted for the first time in 1912 by, again, Capellani—unfolds for a part against the backdrop of the industrialized town of "M. sur M," in which we recognize Montreuil-sur-Mer. In reality, though, Montreuil-sur-Mer never was an industrial town. We here thus have one more northern French *anatopism*, in that *Misérables* evokes a *particular*, existing northern French place, while sticking onto it a cultural and economic identity inspired by a more *general*, somewhat objectifying image of the North (much like *Bienvenue chez les Ch'tis* does with Bergues, with the difference

that the latter was made by someone *from* the North). Hugo's response to this critique we know: "It is not important that a story is realistic [*véritable*], but that it is true [*vraie*]." See: http://www.victorhugo2002.culture.fr/culture/celebrations/hugo/fr/fil4_2.htm.

93. *Les Trois mousquetaires* (Alexandre Dumas, 1844) has been adapted numerous times for the screen, in both French and non-French productions. The novel is largely set in the region between Paris and Calais, an area that is depicted as one full of dangers. In George Sidney's 1948 *The Three Musketeers* (starring Gene Kelly and Lana Turner) this region becomes a Technicolor Wild West complete with canyons and rivers.

94. See Guy Dubois and Jean-Marie Minot, *Histoire des mines du Nord et du Pas-de-Calais: des origines à 1939–45* (1991), 22.

95. Paul Renard, "Les Adaptations cinématographiques des romans," in *Le Nord et le cinéma: contributions à l'histoire du cinéma dans le Nord-Pas-de-Calais*, ed. L'Association Jean Mitry (Pantin: Le Temps de cerises, 1998), 225.

96. Will Higbee, "Toward a Multiplicity of Voices: French Cinema's Age of the Postmodern: Part II, 1992–2004," chapter 5 in *French National Cinema (second edition)*, ed. Susan Hayward (London: Routledge, 2005), 301.

97. Granval, *Tournages de films dans le Nord et le Pas-de-Calais*, 48.

98. Tangui Perron, "Nitrates et gueules noires ou le filon minier II," in *Le Nord et le cinéma: contributions à l'histoire du cinéma dans le Nord-Pas-de-Calais*, ed. L'Association Jean Mitry (Pantin: Le Temps de cerises, 1998), 181.

99. Cited in Perron, "Nitrates et gueules noires ou le filon minier II," 181 (from an article originally published in *Pour vous* on September 24, 1931).

100. Perron, "Nitrates et gueules noires ou le filon minier II," 184.

101. Https://vimeo.com/193883175.

102. Marc de Boni, "*Chez Nous*: malgré 8 jours de polémiques, personne au FN n'a vu le film," *Le Figaro*, January 8, 2017, http://www.lefigaro.fr/elections/presidentielles/2017/01/08/35003-20170108ARTFIG00151—chez-nous-malgre-8-jours-de-polemiques-personne-au-fn-n-a-vu-le-film.php.

103. Valérie Sasportas, "*Chez Nous*: le réalisateur du film dénonce 'une manipulation' du FN," *Le Figaro*, February 20, 2017, http://www.lefigaro.fr/cinema/2017/02/20/03002-20170220ARTFIG00145—chez-nous-le-realisateur-du-film-denonce-une-manipulation-du-fn.php.

104. Henri Astier, "How France's National Front captured Henin-Beaumont," BBC News, May 14, 2014, http://www.bbc.com/news/world-europe-27387204.

105. Most of the documentary films produced in Nord-Pas-de-Calais are either TV productions or small productions that only had a very limited theatrical distribution, if any at all. First of all, there are numerous documentary films that testify to the coal mining industry in the region. One recent example we have already encountered with Denis Gheerbrant's 1991 *Et la vie*. Another noteworthy example is *Mémoires de la mine* (1979–1981) directed by Jacques Renard and produced and broadcast by TF1. Through testimonies of mineworkers and former mineworkers, this series of four TV documentaries (*La Mine, La Mémoire, Le Coeur, Le Corps*) covers the history of coal mining in Nord-Pas-de-Calais between 1920 and 1980. In 1985 *Mémoire de la mine* got a sequel, *Blanche et*

Marie, a fiction feature set in 1941 that centers on two young female Resistance fighters played by Miou-Miou and Sandrine Bonnaire. Second, there are several militant films depicting the working conditions of women in the textile industry of Roubaix, including *La Fille de la route* (Louis Terme, 1962) and *Mais qu'est-ce qu'elles veulent?* (Coline Serreau, 1977), a film that also depicts the role of women in the labor movement elsewhere in France. Finally, there are various films engaging the lives of immigrants and their children in Nord-Pas-de-Calais. An early example is *L'Affiche rouge* (Frank Cassenti, 1976). More recently, and especially since the early 1990s, the French North has seen the development of a substantial body of small productions made by "second-generation" immigrants, many of whose films border on the divide between documentary and fiction. Examples are *Le Maboul du quartier* (Riquita, 1991), *Au pays des mille et un puits* (Youssef Essiyedali and Louisette Faréniaux, 1991), and the animated *Une vie de chacal* (Djamel Sellani, 1994).

106. Henry de Lumley, "De la fête à l'identité," in *Géants et dragons: mythes et traditions à Bruxelles, en Wallonie, dans le nord de la France et en Europe*, ed. Jean-Pierre Ducastelle (Tournai: Casterman, 1996), 7.

107. See http://www.unesco.org/culture/intangible-heritage/05eur_uk.htm (accessed March 1, 2012). In the rationale for its inclusion of these traditions on its heritage list UNESCO states: "Although these expressions are not threatened with immediate disappearance, they do suffer from a number of pressures such as the major changes to the town centers, the increase in the number of performance attractions that are unrelated to the giants but which do attract tourists to the detriment of the popular, spontaneous nature of the festival. The success of these other attractions and the lack of proper management slow down the processions and disturb the festival's structure, harming its vitality and dynamism."

Chapter 3

1. Sodedi is an acronym for Société de Développement du Secteur de l'Edition et de l'Audiovisuel, a branch of the Société Régionale d'Investissements de Wallonie, which in turn is an investment unit of the Walloon regional government. See http://www.sriw.be (accessed June 25, 2011).

2. Cited in Commission Nationale du Film France, *Les Collectivités territoriales et la production cinématographique & audiovisuelle: compte-rendu, quatre tables rondes en region* (Paris: Commission Nationale du Film France, 2001), 143.

3. In 2012 Wallimage Coproductions operated on a budget of €4.5 million. See Parlement Wallon (session 2011–2012), *Budgets des recettes et des dépenses de la Région wallonne pour l'année budgéttaire 2012: exposé général: deuxième partie* [4-III a/4-III bcd] (November 21, 2011), 99–103.

4. Cited in Commission Nationale du Film France, *Les Collectivités territoriales*, 143–144. See also Wallimage Coproductions, *Regulations* (2010), http://www.wallimage.be/downloads.php?lang=uk (accessed April 3, 2012), 5.

5. Reynaert also states in an interview: "J'ai fait le tour de tous les fonds régionaux européens et, en réalité, il y a une rupture entre le Sud et le Nord de l'Europe. Dans le Sud, les fonds régionaux fonctionnent par subventions et

trouvent leurs crédits budgétaires qui pourraient relever du tourisme. Curieusement, ce mode de fonctionnement est calqué sur les fonds régionaux américains. À Boston, la responsable du tourisme expliquait à l'un de nos administrateurs qu'ils ont arrêté depuis dix ans d'investir de l'argent dans les brochures administratives pour investir dans le cinéma. Parce que chaque fois qu'un film se tourne à Boston, ça génère des visites de la ville. Les gens veulent voir l'endroit qui figure dans le film qu'ils ont vu. Les Italiens et les Français fonctionnent un peu comme ça. Nous, on fonctionne davantage sur le modèle nord-européen qui est brillamment illustré par les Allemands, chez qui ce sont des incitants financiers qui sont mis en place, incitants dont on espère un effet régional—tant mieux si les sites locaux sont mis en valeur—mais dont on recherche surtout un effet structurant sur l'audiovisuel dans la région. C'est une démarche très différente. L'aspect régional, au sens touristique, est quelque chose qu'on ressentira comme un plus, comme un bonus qu'on sera content d'avoir, mais il n'est pas la clé de la démarche." Cited in Jean-Michel Vlaeminckx, "Wallimage," interview with Philippe Reynaert, *Cinérgie.be: Webzine* 48 (2001), http://www.cinergie.be/webzine/wallimage (accessed April 1, 2012).

    6. Atelier de Production Centre Val-de-Loire (APCVL), *Politiques territoriales de soutien à la production cinématographique et audiovisuelle: guide: mode d'emploi* (Château-Renault, 2001), 66.

    7. The conference in Valenciennes took place on November 23, 2001. The three other conferences were held in Hourtin (Aquitaine), Strasbourg (Alsace), and Vendôme (Centre).

    8. In 2002 Vanneste, who belongs to the center-right UMP, was elected as a member of the French Parliament. In 2006 and 2012 he became the subject of critique for having publicly made homophobic statements.

    9. Commission Nationale du Film France, *Les Collectivités territoriales*, 66, 88–89.

    10. Except for *Twentynine Palms* (2003, FR/DE/US), which was shot in California, all of Dumont's film have been coproduced by or with the financial support of the CRRAV. Details about the financial support that the French regions have accorded to cinematic productions since 2003 can be found on the website of CICLIC (L'Agence Régionale du Centre pour le Livre, l'Image et la Culture Numérique, the equivalent of the CRRAV in the Centre region). From this database we learn that Nord-Pas-de-Calais supported *Flandres* (FR) with €180,000, *Hadewijch* (FR) with €200,000 (in addition to the €300,000 accorded by the Ile-de-France region, where the film was largely shot), and *Hors Satan* (FR) (which is still listed under its original title *L'Empire*) with €175,000. See CICLIC, *Production Guide*, http://www.centreimages.fr/production_guide.php (accessed April 3, 2012).

    11. Lumière Database on Admissions of Films Released in Europe, "Identification of Films in the Lumière Database," http://lumiere.obs.coe.int/web/sources/astuces.html (accessed June 17, 2017).

    12. See http://www.imdb.com/title/tt0200071/ (accessed June 17, 2017).

    13. See http://lumiere.obs.coe.int/web/film_info/?id=12382 (accessed June 17, 2017).

14. Here it is important to note that despite the fact that the Occupied Palestinian Territories do not form an internationally recognized nation-state, the International Organization for Standardization (ISO) does list a "country" code for these territories, that is, "PS," which makes it possible to identify Palestinian productions and coproductions in the "regular" way. See International Organization for Standardization, "FAQs—Answers to Questions Relating to Codes and Names of Specific Countries," http://www.iso.org/iso/country_codes/iso_3166-faqs/iso_3166_faqs_specific.htm (accessed April 8, 2012).

15. Joseph Massad, "The Weapon of Culture: Cinema in the Palestinian Liberation Struggle"; Michel Khleifi, "From Reality to Fiction—From Poverty to Expression"; Bashir Abu-Manneh, "Toward Liberation: Michel Khleifi's *Ma'loul* and *Canticle*"; Hamid Naficy, "Palestinian Exilic Cinema and Film Letters"; Omar Al-Qattan, "The Challenges of Palestinian Filmmaking (1990–2003)," chapters 2, 3, 4, 6, and 8, respectively, in *Dreams of a Nation: On Palestinian Cinema*, ed. Hamid Dabashi (London: Verso, 2006).

16. Cited in Emmanuel d'Autreppe, "Noce en Galilée [1987]," in *Ça tourne depuis cent ans: une histoire du cinéma francophone de Belgique*, ed. Philippe Dubois and Edouard Arnoldy (Brussels: Communauté Française de Belgique, 1995), 107.

17. See for example: d'Autreppe, "Noce en Galilée," 107. For other discussions of the position of Khleifi's work in Belgian cinema, see Marianne Thys et al., *Belgian Cinema/Le Cinéma Belge/De Belgische Film* (Brussels/Ghent/Paris: Royal Belgian Film Archive/Ludion/Flammarion, 1999), 641; Frédéric Sojcher, *La Kermesse heroïque du cinéma belge: Tome III: 1988–1996: Le Carrousel européen* (Paris: L'Harmattan, 1999), 84–85; Philip Mosley, *Split Screen: Belgian Cinema and Cultural Identity* (Albany: State University of New York Press, 2001), 143, 185; and Paul Thomas, *Un siècle de cinéma belge* (Ottignies: Éditions Quorum, 1995), 267–268.

18. "La Commission de sélection a 25 ans," *25 Ans de films en Communauté Française de Belgique: 1967–1992*, special issue of *Pour le cinéma belge* (1993).

19. Frédéric Sojcher, *La Kermesse heroïque du cinéma belge: Tome II: 1965–1988: Le miroir déformant des identités culturelles* (Paris: L'Harmattan, 1999), 193.

20. *Vouloir* (André Jaeger-Schmidt, 1931, FR) and *La Chanson du lin* (George Monca, 1931, FR).

21. Later RTF-Télé-Lille became France 3 Nord-Pas-de-Calais-Picardie, which in 2010 was split into the channels France 3 Nord-Pas-de-Calais and France 3 Picardie.

22. Hayward, *French National Cinema*, 38.

23. Jean-Luc Godard, "Exclu l'an dernier du Festival Truffaut représentera la France à Cannes avec *Les 400 coups*," *Arts* 719 (1959): 5.

24. Cited in Frédéric Depétris, *L'Etat et le cinéma en France: le moment de l'exception culturelle* (Paris: L'Harmattan, 2008), 65.

25. Loredana Latil, "Une métaphore du cinéma français: les sélections du festival de Cannes et la prime à la qualité," http://www.cg06.fr/document/?f=decouvrir-les-am/fr/rr168-cinema.pdf (accessed May 20, 2012).

26. Rohmer citing Truffaut. Cited in "Marie-Christine Barrault: Eric Rohmer [film *Ma nuit chez Maud*]," http://comediennes.org/video/marie-christine-barrault-rohmer-maud (accessed May 17, 2012).

27. Cited in Assemblée Nationale, "Le Ministre et le Parlement," http://www.assemblee-nationale.fr/histoire/andre-malraux/ministre_et_parlement.asp (accessed May 21, 2012).

28. Depétris, *L'Etat et le cinéma*, 55.

29. Depétris, *L'Etat et le cinéma*, 66.

30. Depétris, *L'Etat et le cinéma*, 55.

31. Depétris, *L'Etat et le cinéma*, 78–79.

32. Hayward, *French National Cinema*, 49.

33. Depétris, *L'Etat et le cinéma*, 199.

34. To compare, the budget of *Germinal* was F160 million (around $27 million), that of *Titanic* around $200 million.

35. Yann Darré, *Histoire sociale du cinéma français* (Paris: La Decouverte, 2000), 107.

36. Between 1992 and 1993 and between 2000 and 2002 Lang also was the minister of education.

37. This budget was lowered in 1986, when the right-wing François Léotard became minister of culture. In 1988 Lang restored the cultural budget to 1 percent of the total national budget.

38. Susan Hayward, "State, Culture and the Cinema: Jack Lang's Strategies for the French Film Industry 1981–93," *Screen* 34, no. 4 (1993): 382–383.

39. Hayward, "State, Culture and the Cinema," 382.

40. In addition, in 1983 Lang established the Institut pour le Financement du Cinéma et les Industries des Programmes (IFCIC), which facilitates the financing of cinema and audiovisual productions.

41. This tax shelter allows companies to invest in film productions (for a maximum of 25 percent of the production costs and for a minimum period of five years) through intermediation of a so-called Société pour le Financement du Cinéma et de l'Audio-visuel (SOFICA). In return, companies receive a tax break for 50 percent of the invested amount. In more recent years, EU competition laws have obliged France to weaken these benefits.

42. Hayward, "State, Culture and the Cinema," 388.

43. Depétris, *L'Etat et le cinéma*, 100.

44. As a result, the budget of the Fonds de soutien went from F65 million in 1985 to F548 million in 1987.

45. Hayward, "State, Culture and the Cinema," 387–388; Depétris, *L'Etat et le cinéma*, 119.

46. Source: Centre National du cinema et de l'Image Animée (CNC), *La Production cinématographique en 2011: bilan statistique des films agréés en 2011* (Paris: CNC, 2012); CNC, *La Production cinématographique en 2015* (Paris: CNC, 2016); CNC, *La Production cinématographique en 2018* (Paris: CNC, 2019).

47. Michel Marie, "Vous n-avez rien contre la jeunesse?," in *Le Jeune cinéma français*, ed. Michel Marie (Paris: Nathan, 1998), 3.

48. Le Club des 13, *Le Milieu n'est plus un pont mais une faille* (Paris: Éditions Stock, 2008), 12.

49. Thierry Jousse, Nicolas Saada, Frédéric Strauss, Camille Taboulay, and Vincent Vatrican, "Dix places pour le jeune cinéma," *Cahiers du cinéma* 473 (1993): 28.

50. See Claude-Marie Trémois, *Les Enfants de la liberté: le jeune cinéma français des années 90* (Paris: Éditions du Seuil, 1997); Marie, *Le Jeune cinéma français*; René Prédal, *Le Jeune cinéma français* (Paris: Nathan, 2002); Daniel Serceau, *Symptômes du jeune cinéma français* (Paris: Cerf, 2008).

51. Jacqueline Nacache, "Was There a Young French Cinema?," in *A Companion to Contemporary French Cinema*, ed. Alistair Fox, Michel Marie, Raphaëlle Moine, and Hilary Radner (Malden: Wiley-Blackwell, 2005), 185.

52. Higbee, "Toward a Multiplicity of Voices," 314.

53. Higbee, "Toward a Multiplicity of Voices," 315.

54. See: Hayward, *French National Cinema*, 67.

55. The exception is Canal Plus, which only has to wait one year before it is allowed to broadcast a French production. Like non-encoded French channels, Canal Plus is legally obliged to invest at least 3.2 percent of its annual operating budget in cinema productions. In addition, Canal Plus, unlike other channels, has to comply with a diversity clause stipulating that it has to invest 45 percent of its cinema budget in productions with a budget up until about €5 million. *Accord Canal+ 2005*, http://www.larp.fr/dossiers/?p=631 (accessed August 15, 2012). As a result, Canal Plus has become the principal coproducer of French cinema, including the *cinéma d'art et essai* (e.g., *Rosetta* and *L'humanité*). See Hayward, *French National Cinema*, 69.

56. Hayward, *French National Cinema*, 67.

57. Thomas Bauder, "Les Toiles du Nord," in *Le Jeune cinéma français*, ed. Michel Marie (Paris: Nathan, 1998), 80.

58. In more recent years also Centre and Provence-Alpes-Côte d'Azur have developed substantial policies of support for cinema and audiovisual productions. See Centre Images (Agence Régionale du Centre pour le cinéma et l'audiovisuel), *Soutiens à la production cinématographique et audiovisuelle: régions, départements, villes* (Château-Renault: Centre Images, 2011); Agence France Press, "La Région Ile-de-France, 2e financier du cinéma derrière le CNC," *L'Express*, May 4, 2011, http://www.lexpress.fr/actualites/1/culture/la-region-ile-de-france-2e-financier-du-cinema-derriere-le-cnc_989257.html (accessed June 7, 2012).

59. Among the films coproduced by Cercle Bleu are: *Pierre et Djemila* (Gérard Blain, 1987, FR), *Peaux de vache* (Cow skins; Patricia Mazuy, 1989, FR), and *Inséparables* (Inseparables; Michel Couvelard, 1999, FR). See also Granval, *Tournages de films dans le Nord et le Pas-de-Calais*, 99–100.

60. Florent Leclerq, "A quoi rêvent les Lillois," *L'Express*, March 4, 1993, http://www.lexpress.fr/informations/a-quoi-revent-les-lillois_593598.html (accessed June 8, 2012).

61. Granval, *Tournages de films dans le Nord et le Pas-de-Calais*, 49–50.

62. Source: CRRAV, http://www.crrav.com/crrav_qui.php (accessed June 8, 2012).

63. Granval, *Tournages de films dans le Nord et le Pas-de-Calais*, 104.

64. Clarisse Fabre, "Des techniciens racontent le tournage difficile de 'La Vie d'Adèle,'" *Le Monde*, May 24, 2013, http://www.lemonde.fr/festival-de-cannes/article/2013/05/24/des-techniciens-racontent-le-tournage-de-la-vie-d-adele_3417150_766360.html.

65. "Fusion du Pôle Images et du CRRAV, naissance de Pictanovo," *J'innove en Nord-Pas-de-Calais*, April 8, 2013, http://www.jinnove.com/Actualites/Fusion-du-Pole-Images-et-du-Crrav-naissance-de-Pictanovo.

66. Source: CRRAV, http://www.crrav.com/fichefilm.php?id=290&page=1&perpage=10 (accessed June 19, 2012).

67. Sophie Grassin, "Le Nord fait son cinéma," *L'Express* (October 21, 1999), http://www.lexpress.fr/informations/le-nord-fait-son-cinema_635346.html (accessed June 19, 2012).

68. See for example: Freddy Buache, *Vingt-cinq ans de cinéma français: parcours croisés: 1979–2003* (Lausanne: L'Age d'homme, 2005), 416; Martin O'Shaughnessy, *The New Face of Political Cinema: Commitment in French Film since 1995* (New York: Berghahn Books, 2007); Guy Austin, *Contemporary French Cinema: An Introduction (2nd edition)* (Manchester: Manchester University Press, 2008), 229–231.

69. Philippe Dubois and Edouard Arnoldy, "Ici et ailleurs," in *Ça tourne depuis cent ans: une histoire du cinéma francophone de Belgique*, ed. Philippe Dubois and Edouard Arnoldy (Brussels: Communauté Française de Belgique, 1995), 7.

70. This crisis reached a temporary climax in the years following the 2007 Belgian federal elections. In those years two main issues divided Flemish and francophone-Belgian parties. The first was the question of how to reform the country socioeconomically in the face of the late 2000s financial crisis. Whereas most Flemish parties proposed strong cutbacks on government spending, the francophone parties insisted on income redistribution. The second issue was the controversy about the electoral district of Brussels-Halle-Vilvoorde (BHV), a controversy that dated back to the fixation of the internal language border in 1963. In December 2011, Belgian politics finally entered calmer waters, when after a formation period of 541 days (beating a world record formerly held by Iraq) King Albert II could finally swear in the cabinet of Elio di Rupo, a son of Italian immigrants and the political leader of the francophone Parti Socialiste.

71. Polet, "Un enracinement porteur d' universalité," 25.

72. Yann Tobin, "Entretien avec Yolande Moreau: on n'a rien a perde," *Positif* 576 (2009): 109.

73. Sojcher, *Kermesse héroïque I*, 60, emphasis in original.

74. Sojcher, *Kermesse héroïque I*, 60–61.

75. Sojcher, *Kermesse héroïque I*, 59.

76. Philippe Dubois, "Partir, (ne pas) revenir," in *Ça tourne depuis cent ans: une histoire du cinéma francophone de Belgique*, ed. Philippe Dubois and Edouard Arnoldy (Brussels: Communauté Française de Belgique, 1995), 33.

77. See Sojcher, *Kermesse héroïque I*, 114–115.

78. René Michelems, "Les Trois tendances des années héroïques," in *Ça tourne depuis cent ans: une histoire du cinéma francophone de Belgique*, ed. Philippe Dubois and Edouard Arnoldy (Brussels: Communauté Française de Belgique, 1995), 47.

79. Sojcher, *Kermesse héroïque I*, 30.

80. Frédéric Sojcher, *Pratiques du cinéma* (Paris: Klincksieck, 2011), 199. In his discussion of Storck's questionable role during the years of Belgium's occupation, Sojcher further mentions a letter from March 4, 1941, in which Storck offers his services to the Belgian branch of the German distribution company

Tobis Bruxelles, as well as the filmmaker's involvement in the Institut National de Radiotechnique de la Cinématographie, a film school created under German occupation. In June 1947, Storck wrote a *pro justitia* in which he claims to have been nominated for the Film Guild function without having been consulted first. Storck claims, moreover, to have protested against this nomination and "to have officially resigned in March 1944" without ever receiving an official response. Sojcher, *Pratiques du cinéma*, 199, 290. See also Bruno Benvindo, *Henri Storck, le cinéma belge et l'occupation* (Brussels: Éditions de l'Université de Bruxelles, 2010).

81. Henri Storck, "Cinéma belge, où en es-tu," *Vouloir un cinéma belge* (special issue of the *Bulletin du Comité National des Travailleurs du Film*), June 1949. Cited in Sojcher, *Kermesse héroïque I*, 57.

82. Jean-Claude Batz, *Colloque sur "le problème de la production de films en Belgique": rapport sur le sous-développement de la production de films en Belgique et l'assistance financière et administrative de l'Etat* (Brussels: Institut de Sociologie de l'Université Libre de Bruxelles, 1963), 60.

83. The other main Belgian film school, the Institut des Arts de Diffusion (IAD), was founded in 1959 in Louvain-la-Neuve.

84. Two other noteworthy examples are: *Si le vent te fait peur / If the Wind Frightens You* (Emile Degelin, 1960, BE) and *Il y a un train toutes les heures / A Train Leaves in Every Hour* (André Cavens, 1961, BE).

85. Batz, *Colloque sur "le problème*," 67.

86. In 1961, the francophone Victor Larock was appointed as minister of national education and culture, while the Flemish Renaat Elslande was appointed as minister of culture, adjunct in the Ministry of National Education. In 1963, Larock was replaced by Henri Janne.

87. Van Elslande made this decision largely on the basis of a report by the film critic and BRT programmer Joz van Liempt. In turn, Van Liempt had been much inspired by the subvention system that already was in place in the Netherlands, the Productiefonds voor de Nederlandse film. Van Liempt also became the Selection Committee's first president. Sojcher, *Kermesse héroïque II*, 12.

88. Initially Delvaux's film received bad reviews in Belgium. However, in 1966, upon the film's success at various international festivals, the film had a rerelease in Belgium, upon which it was overloaded with compliments from the Belgian press. Sojcher, *Kermesse héroïque II*, 16–17.

89. This festival took place five times between 1949 and 1974. In 1949, the festival was called Festival International du Film Expérimental et Poétique. The 1958 festival took place in Brussels.

90. Patrick Leboutte, "Un cinéma inimaginable," in Guy Jungblut, Patrick Leboutte, Dominique Païni, *Une encyclopédie des cinémas de Belgique* (Paris: Musée d'Art Moderne de la Ville de Paris/Yellow Now, 1990), 13.

91. Dominique Païni, "Le Cinéma belge, ça existe, je l'ai rencontré," in Guy Jungblut, Patrick Leboutte, Dominique Païni, *Une encyclopédie des cinémas de Belgique* (Paris: Musée d'Art Moderne de la Ville de Paris/Yellow Now, 1990), 9, emphasis in original.

92. Sojcher, *Kermesse héroïque II*, 18–19.

93. Sojcher, *Kermesse héroïque I*, 88.

94. A similar unitarist position on Belgian cinema speaks from another, trilingual encyclopedia of Belgian cinema, *Belgian Cinema/Le Cinéma Belge/De Belgische Film*, edited by Marianne Thys and published by The Royal Belgian Film Archive (which in 2009 was renamed Cinematek, a Dutch-French neologism). This book, as Delvaux writes in the preface, "focuses on films with a significant proportion of home-grown investment, preserving the author's autonomy and a specific Belgian character," and simply divides its object into "the silent era" and "the sound era." Thys, *Belgian Cinema*, 9. To have been truly unitarist though, the authors should have perhaps picked German instead of English as the third language.

95. The main producer of this film was Storck's own fund. Among the other donors were both the Flemish and the Belgian-francophone ministries of education, as well as the RTB.

96. Sojcher, *Pratiques du cinéma*, 221.

97. Since 2009 the VAF and the CCA have each reserved an annual €450,000 in their budgets in order to function as a minor partner in the coproduction of a feature-length film (fiction and animation) primarily financed by the other community. See Vlaams Audiovisueel Fonds, *Jaarverslag 2011* (Brussels: Vlaams Audiovisueel Fonds, 2012), 47.

98. Philippe Dubois, "De la modernité et de ses nuances belges," in *Ça tourne depuis cent ans: une histoire du cinéma francophone de Belgique*, ed. Philippe Dubois and Edouard Arnoldy (Brussels: Communauté Française de Belgique, 1995), 83.

99. Maryline Laurin, "Il était une fois le cinéma belge (4/4): le verdict!," *Cinevox*, March 11, 2012, http://www.cinevox.be/il-etait-une-fois-le-cinema-belge-44-sans-pretention (accessed March 24, 2013).

100. Cited in Vincent Thabourey, "Les Nouvelles saisons du cinéma belge," *Positif* 576 (2009): 92.

101. Thabourey, "Les Nouvelles saisons du cinéma belge," 93

102. Thys, *Belgian Cinema*, 808.

103. Sojcher, *Kermesse héroïque III*, 189.

104. Between 1989 and 1995 Belgian parties participated in eighty-four of the 443 features supported by Eurimages. Of these eighty-four films, twenty-one had majority Belgian financing. Mosley, *Split Screen*, 200.

105. The Walloon films I discussed that received European funding are: *Les Convoyeurs attendent* (Benoît Mariage, 1999, FR/BE/CH), *La Raison du plus faible* (Lucas Belvaux, 2006, BE/FR), *Eldorado* (Bouli Lanners, 2008, BE/FR), and *Illégal* (Olivier Masset-Depasse, 2010, BE/FR/LX).

106. Sojcher, *Kermesse héroïque III*, 198.

107. Mosley, *Split Screen*, 105.

108. Cited in Michaux, *Images et cinéma de Wallonie*.

109. Bénédicte Rochet, "Esquisse d'une cinématographie wallonne," in *Cinéma et crise(s): esquisses d'une cinématographie wallonne*, ed. Anne Roekens and Axel Tixhon (Crisnée/Namur: Editions Yellow Now/Presses Universitaires Namur, 2011), 20.

110. Jean Pirotte, "Une image floue," *Louvain* 133 (2002): 28.

111. The two other copublishers are Wallonie-Bruxelles Images and Wallonie-Bruxelles International, which are both associated with the Ministry of the Francophone Belgian Community. The other filmmakers presented in this document are: Sam Gabarski, Dominique Abel and Fiona Gordon, Micha Wald, Olivier Masset-Depasse, Stéphane Aubier and Vincent Pater, Ursula Meier, and Nabil Ben Yadir. See Boyd van Hoeij, ed., *10/10* (Brussels: Ministère de la Communauté Française de Belgique/Wallonie-Bruxelles International/Wallonie-Bruxelles Images, 2010).

112. Dimitra Bouras and Jean-Michel Vlaeminckx, "Tax Shelter, quatre ans d'existence: le point avec Patrick Quinet et Luc Jabon," *Cinérgie.be: Webzine* 118 (2007), http://www.cinergie.be/webzine/tax_shelter_quatre_ans_d_existence_le_point_avec_patrick_quinet_et_luc_jabon (accessed May 9, 2012).

113. Bouras and Vlaeminckx, "Tax Shelter."

114. CRRAV, *Rapport d'activités 2010*, 5.

115. In 2012, the French Community of Belgium (or Wallonia-Brussels-Federation) had signed coproduction agreements with Portugal, Tunisia, Morocco, Italy, France, Chile, Switzerland, and China, as well as a cooperation agreement with the SODEC in Quebec.

116. Sojcher, *Pratiques du cinéma*, 45.

117. Ivo de Kock, "Bienvenu Chez les Français: Franse Films op Zoek naar een Vlaams Publiek," *Filmmagie* 590 (2008): 46.

118. Centre National du cinéma et de l'Image Animée, *La Production cinématographique en 2011: bilan statistique des films agréés en 2011* (Paris: CNC, 2012), 22; Centre National du cinéma et de l'Image Animée, *La Production cinématographique en 2015* (Paris: CNC, 2016), 26.

119. Centre du Cinéma et de l'Audiovisuel de la Fédération Wallonie-Bruxelles, *Production, promotion et diffusion cinématographiques et audiovisuelles: le bilan 2011* (Brussels: Centre du Cinéma, 2012), p. 9.

120. Centre National du cinéma et de l'Image Animée, *Bulletin officiel du Centre National du Cinéma et de l'Image Animée: accords de coproductions* (Paris: CNC, 2011), 50–51.

121. Cited in Valéry Saintghislain, "Un partenariat Hainaut-Nord-Pas de Calais construire [sic] une 'eurorégion' du cinéma et de l'audiovisuel," *Le Soir*, April 11, 2003, 22. The partners in "Audiovisuel Wallonie-Nord-Pas-de-Calais" were the CRRAV, which contributed €1.79 million (of which 40 percent was financed by the EU), and the Bureau d'Accueil d Tournage Cinéma Hainaut, or BATCH, which contributed €615,000 (also 40 percent of which was subsidized by EU funds).

122. Before the introduction of this official collaboration agreement, both organizations had already jointly invested in the 2002 feature *Va Petite!* (Alain Guesnier, BE/FR/MA).

123. Cine-regio, "'Cages' by Olivier Masset-Depasse," http://www.cine-regio.org/co-production/case-studies/cages/ (accessed June 16, 2012).

124. Wallimage, "Casper, the Friendly Animated Project," October 16, 2009, http://www.wallimage.be/newsfile.php?lang=uk&id=173 (accessed June 20, 2012).

125. Jennotte, "Le cinéma belge, c'est bon pour l'économie," 36.

126. CRRAV, *Rapport d'activités 2010*, 5.

127. Wallimage, "The Pôle Image de Liège Grows with Wallimage Entreprises," December 20, 2010, http://www.wallimage.be/newsfile.php?lang=uk&id=382 (accessed June 20, 2012).

128. Technologies Wallonnes de l'Image, du Son et du Texte, "Launch of the Nord-Pas de Calais Image Pole," http://www.twist-cluster.com/cms/en/news/market-news/248-la . . . (accessed June 20, 2012).

129. Cited in Anne Courtel, "Le CRRAV et le Pôle Images se marient . . . pour le meilleur de l'image," *La Voix du Nord*, January 18, 2012, http://www.lavoixdunord.fr/region/le-crrav-et-le-pole-images-se-marient-pour-le-meilleur-de-l-image-ia26b0n241279 (accessed June 19, 2012).

130. Domenico La Porta, "Pictanovo et Wallimage lancent le fond *Expériences interactives Transrégionales*," Cineuropa, April 4, 2014, http://cineuropa.org/nw.aspx?t=newsdetail&l=fr&did=254550 (accessed July 7, 2015).

131. See: http://transmedia-transregion.com/projets/.

132. See *Google in Mons: European Capital of Culture*, 2015, https://vimeo.com/63885227 and https://www.google.com/culturalinstitute/collection/mundaneum.

133. "Dossier Hainaut: Mons Mons, cité hi-tech," *Le Soir*, January 21, 2012, http://archives.lesoir.be/-titre-dossier-hainaut-mons-mons-cite-hi-tech-titre-_t-20120117-01RLPK.html (accessed July 7, 2015).

134. *Mons 2015 Google soutient la Capitale Européenne de la Culture* (Xavier Flament, 2014), https://www.youtube.com/watch?v=7aAl-fiuUNA.

135. Simon Mee, "Culture: Mons Puts Itself on the Map with Google Deal," *Financial Times*, November 12, 2012, http://www.ft.com/intl/cms/s/0/ce54ad56-1c47-11e2-a63b-00144feabdc0.html (accessed July 7, 2015).

136. Magali Lesauvage, "Louvre-Lens: l'effet Bilbao aura-t-il lieu?," *Exponaute*, December 4, 2012, http://www.exponaute.com/magazine/2012/12/04/louvre-lens-leffet-bilbao-aura-t-il-lieu/ (accessed July 8, 2015).

137. Emmanuel Pall, "Louvre-Lens: quelles retombées économiques?" (France 3 Nord-Pas-de-Calais), December 4, 2013, http://france3-regions.francetvinfo.fr/nord-pas-de-calais/2013/12/03/louvre-lens-quelles-retombees-economiques-370395.html (accessed July 8, 2015); "Le Directeur du Louvre salue le 'miracle' de l'implantation à Lens" (France 3 Nord-Pas-de-Calais), December 12, 2014, http://france3-regions.francetvinfo.fr/nord-pas-de-calais/2014/12/04/le-directeur-du-louvre-salue-le-miracle-de-l-implantation-lens-606546.html (accessed July 8, 2015).

138. Didier Rykner, "L'ouverture du Louvre-Lens," *La Tribune de l'art*, December 4, 2012, http://www.latribunedelart.com/l-ouverture-du-louvre-lens (accessed July 8, 2015).

139. Lesauvage, "Louvre-Lens."

140. Rémi Declerck, "Supporters du RC Lens: donnex vos objects fétiches au Louvre-Lens," *La Voix du Nord*, June 16, 2015, http://www.lavoixdunord.fr/region/supporters-du-rc-lens-donnez-vos-objets-fetiches-au-louvre-lens-ia0b0n2893101 (accessed July 8, 2015).

141. Claire Courbet, "Face au Louvre-Lens, un hôtel 4 étoiles dans des corons," *Le Figaro*, March 5, 2015, http://www.lefigaro.fr/culture/2015/01/23/03004-20150123ARTFIG00394-face-au-louvre-lens-un-hotel-4-etoiles-dans-des-corons.php (accessed July 8, 2015).

Chapter 4

1. The entire statement reads as follows:

Voici le texte de l'appel lancé par cinquante-neuf réalisateurs de cinéma. La liste des signataires, arrêtée au 11 février, devrait s'allonger dans les jours à venir:

Nous, réalisateurs français, déclarons:

Nous sommes coupables, chacun d'entre nous, d'avoir hébergé récemment des étrangers en situation irrégulière. Nous n'avons pas dénoncé nos amis étrangers. Et nous continuerons à héberger, à ne pas dénoncer, à sympathiser et à travailler sans vérifier les papiers de nos collègues et amis.

Suite au jugement rendu de Mme Jacqueline Deltombe, 'coupable' d'avoir hébergé un ami zaîrois en situation irrégulière, et partant du principe que la loi est la même pour tous, nous demandons à être mis en examen et jugés nous aussi. Enfin, nous appelons nos concitoyens à désobéir pour ne pas se soumettre à des lois inhumaines.

Nous refusons que nos libertés se voient ainsi restreintes.

"59 réalisateurs appellent à 'désobeir,'" *Le Monde*, February 12, 1997, 9.

2. See Austin, *Contemporary French Cinema*, 223–224.

3. See, for example: Phil Powrie, "Heritage, History and 'New Realism,'" chapter 1 in *French Cinema in the 1990s: Continuity and Difference*, ed. Phil Powrie (Oxford: Oxford University Press, 1999).

4. Martine Beugnet, "Y'aura-t'il de la neige à Noël? Will It Snow for Christmas; Sandrine Veysset, France, 1997," in *The Cinema of France*, ed. Phil Powrie (London: Wallflower Press, 2006), 247–248.

5. Mathias Lavin and Stéphane Delorme, "Petits arrangements avec le jeune cinéma français," *Balthazar* 3 (1998): 24–25, emphasis in original.

6. Lavin and Delorme, "Petits arrangements avec le jeune cinéma français," 28.

7. Lavin and Delorme, "Petits arrangements avec le jeune cinéma français," 25–26.

8. Lavin and Delorme, "Petits arrangements avec le jeune cinéma français," 32.

9. Lavin and Delorme, "Petits arrangements avec le jeune cinéma français," 27.

10. Stéphane Delorme and Mathias Lavin, "Nouveaux arrangements avec le jeune cinéma français," *Balthazar* 4 (2001): 7.

11. Delorme and Lavin, "Nouveaux arrangements avec le jeune cinéma français," 8.

12. Delorme and Lavin, "Nouveaux arrangements avec le jeune cinéma français," 8.

13. Bazin, *Qu'est-ce que le cinéma?*, 124, 309.

14. Here Morgan refers to the work of Dudley Andrew, Christopher Williams, and Peter Wollen: "Dudley Andrew speaks of Bazin's aesthetic as oriented around a 'deep feeling for the integral unity of a universe in flux' [from *André Bazin*] and elsewhere of realistic styles as 'approximations of visible [or perceptual] reality.' [from *The Major Film Theories: An Introduction*] Christopher Williams argues that, for Bazin, film has 'the primary function of showing the spectator the real world,' which he, like Andrew, glosses as the aesthetic equivalent of human perception.' [from *Realism and the Cinema: A Reader*] Peter Wollen goes so far as to assert that this realism constitutes an anti-aesthetic, the very negation of cinematic style and artifice: 'the film could obtain radical purity only through its own annihilation' [from: *Signs and Meaning in the Cinema*]." Daniel Morgan, "Rethinking Bazin: Ontology and Realist Aesthetics," *Critical Inquiry* 32, no. 3 (2006): 444–445.

15. In opposition to Christian Metz's attempt to construct a theory of cinematic language on the basis of Ferdinand de Saussure's semiology, in *Signs and Meaning in the Cinema* (1969) Wollen grounds his understanding of cinematic signification in the semiotics of Charles Sanders Peirce. Wollen argues that over the course of cinema's history, different directors and theorists have emphasized different semiotic dimensions of the cinematic image. Whereas formalists such as Eisenstein privileged the iconic qualities of the cinematic image, in the realist tradition the indexical aspect of the cinematic image gained dominance. Wollen sees Bazin as the theorist most emblematic of the realist tradition, for the reason that Bazin "repeatedly stresses the existential bond between sign and object." Peter Wollen, *Signs and Meaning in the Cinema* (Bloomington: Indiana University Press, 1972), 125.

16. Bazin, *Qu'est-ce que le cinéma?*, 14.

17. Morgan, "Rethinking Bazin," 458.

18. Morgan, "Rethinking Bazin," 473, emphasis in original.

19. Morgan, "Rethinking Bazin," 448–449.

20. Morgan, "Rethinking Bazin," 450.

21. Lev Manovich, "What Is Digital Cinema?" in *The Digital Dialectic: New Essays on New Media*, ed. Peter Lunenfeld (Cambridge: MIT Press, 2000), 174.

22. Morgan is not alone in this regard. In recent debates about the implications of the digital turn several theorists have referred to the index in order to posit an ontological distinction between moving images recorded on celluloid film and moving images that are stored digitally. Whereas the former would have a physical, indexical bond to the objects they are representations of, the latter would not and therefore lead a virtual existence (see, for example: D.

N. Rodowick, *The Virtual Life of Film* [Cambridge: Harvard University Press, 2007]). This reductive use of the concept of indexicality has been critiqued by Mary Ann Doane, who proposes to distinguish between the index-as-trace (e.g., a footprint) and the index-as-deixis (e.g., a pointing finger), and Tom Gunning, in whose opinion the claim that digital images are nonindexical is "nonsense." Mary Ann Doane, "The Indexical and the Concept of Medium Specificity," *differences: a journal of feminist cultural studies* 18, no. 1 (2007); Tom Gunning, "Moving Away from the Index," *differences* 18, no. 1 (2007): 31.

23. C. S. Peirce, "Questions Concerning Certain Faculties Claimed for Man," in *The Essential Peirce: Selected Philosophical Writings Volume 1 (1867–1893)*, ed. Nathan Houser and Christian Kloesel (Bloomington: Indiana University Press, 1992), 24.

24. "The Basis of Pragmatism," in *Peirce on Signs: Writings on Semiotic*, ed. James Hoopes (Chapel Hill: University of North Carolina Press, 1991), 258.

25. C. S. Peirce, *The Essential Peirce: Selected Philosophical Writings Vol. 2 (1893–1913)*, ed. Peirce Edition Project (Bloomington: Indiana University Press, 1998), 5–6.

26. See also: Niels Niessen, "Lives of Cinema: Against Its 'Death,'" *Screen* 52, no. 3 (2011): 307–323.

27. Bazin, *Qu'est-ce que le cinéma?*, 13–14, emphasis in original.

28. Bazin, *Qu'est-ce que le cinéma?*, 16.

29. Bazin, *Qu'est-ce que le cinéma?*, 14, 17.

30. Casarino proposed this reading of Bazin during the "Cinematic Image" graduate seminar that he taught in the fall of 2008 at the University of Minnesota.

31. Bazin, *Qu'est-ce que le cinéma*, 124.

32. Cited in David Overbey, "Introduction," in *Springtime in Italy: A Reader on Neo-Realism*, ed. David Overbey (Hamden: Archon Books, 1978), 1.

33. Bazin, *Qu'est-ce que le cinéma?*, 263–264.

34. Bazin, *Qu'est-ce que le cinéma?*, 308–309.

35. In *Theory of Film* Siegfried Kracauer develops a very similar argument about neorealism. Kracauer discusses neorealism in terms of the episode, a story "whose common property it is to emerge from, and again disappear in, the flow of life, as suggested by the camera." What sets the episode apart from other categories of fiction film is that it does not present itself as a self-contained story but instead remains "full of gaps" and thereby permeable to the "flow of life out of which it rises." Often the episode film is set in the street, "that province of reality where transient life manifests itself most conspicuously." "From *Open City* to *Cabiria*, *The Bicycle Thief* to *La Strada*," Kracauer writes, "they are literally soaked in the street world; they not only begin and end in it but are transparent to it throughout." Siegfried Kracauer, *Theory of Film: The Redemption of Physical Reality* (London: Oxford University Press, 1960), 251–256.)

36. Bazin, *Qu'est-ce que le cinéma?*, 309.

37. Gilles Deleuze, *Cinema 1: The Movement-Image*, trans. Hugh Tomlinson and Barbara Habberjam (London: Continuum, 2005), 216.

38. Deleuze, *Cinema 1*, 216; Deleuze, *Cinema 2*, 31. Elsewhere, in relation to Bresson's *Pickpocket*, Deleuze defines the any-space-whatever as "a perfectly singular space, which has merely lost its homogeneity, that is, the principle of

its metric relations or the connection of its own parts, so that the linkages can be made in an infinite number of ways" (213).

39. Deleuze, *Cinema 2*, 1.
40. Zavattini, "Some Ideas on the Cinema," 225.
41. Jacques Rancière, "Politique de la littérature," in *Politique de la littérature* (Paris: Galilée, 2007), 23.
42. Jacques Rancière, *Future of the Image* (London: Verso, 2009), 120.
43. Rancière, "Politique de la littérature," 23.
44. Rancière, "Politique de la littérature," 24.
45. Rancière, "Politique de la littérature," 24.
46. Honoré de Balzac, "Society as Historical Organism," in *The Modern Tradition: Backgrounds of Modern Literature*, ed. Richard Ellmen (Oxford: Oxford University Press, 1965), 248.
47. Rancière, "Politique de la littérature," 29.
48. Erich Auerbach, *Mimesis*, trans. Willard R. Trask (Princeton: Princeton University Press, 2003), 468.
49. Auerbach, *Mimesis*, 472.
50. Auerbach, *Mimesis*, 473.
51. Auerbach, *Mimesis*, 473, 497.
52. Rancière, "Politique de la littérature," 31.
53. Honoré de Balzac, *Le Père Goriot* (Paris: Gallimard, 1971), 34.
54. Georg Lukács, *The Historical Novel*, trans. Hannah Mitchell and Stanley Mitchell (Lincoln: University of Nebraska Press, 1962), 141.
55. Lukács, "Realism in the Balance," in Theodor Adorno et al., *Aesthetics and Politics* (London: Verso, 2007), 32–33.
56. Theodor Adorno, "Reconciliation under Duress," in Theodor Adorno et al., *Aesthetics and Politics* (London: Verso, 2007), 153. Adorno mourns the disappearance of the Lukács of the *Theory of the Novel* (1916), in which the latter presents the novel as "the epic of a world that has been abandoned by God." By this Lukács means that the novel, as a product of the modern-capitalist era, is intrinsically expressive and thereby also redemptive of modern man's state of alienation. See Georg Lukács, *The Theory of the Novel: A Historico-Philosophical Essay on the Forms of Great Epic Literature*, trans. Anna Bostock (Cambridge: MIT Press, 1971), 88.
57. Adorno, "Reconciliation under Duress," 163.
58. See: Angelo Restivo, *The Cinema of Economic Miracles: Visuality and Modernization in the Italian Art Film* (Durham: Duke University Press, 2002), 9–10.
59. Dudley Andrew, *What Cinema Is!* (Oxford: Wiley-Blackwell, 2010), 60.
60. Cited in Jean-Michel Frodon, "Bazin en Asie," *Cahiers du Cinéma* 640 (2008): 77.
61. Scott, "In Toronto, Sampling Realism's Resurgence."
62. *Rosetta*'s camera feel also inspired Darren Aranofsky for *The Wrestler* (2008).
63. Cited in Cécile Lagesse, "*Still Life* de Jia Zhang-ke: le réalisme à l'âge numérique," *Cahiers du cinéma* 640 (2008): 80.

64. Cited in Mariane Schouler, "Contraintes du tournage et choix techniques," http://entre-les-murs-laurent-cantet.blogspot.com/2009/04/contraintes-du-tournage-et-choix.html (accessed February 10, 2013).

65. Here it is worth mentioning that the Dardennes' production company Les Films du fleuve coproduced Christian Mungiu's *Dupa dealuri / Beyond the hills* (2012, RO/FR/BE).

66. Fredric Jameson, "Reflections in Conclusion," in Theodor Adorno et al., *Aesthetics and Politics* (London: Verso, 2007), 212–213.

67. Fredric Jameson, *The Geopolitical Aesthetic: Cinema and Space in the World System* (Bloomington: Indiana University Press, 1995), 82.

68. Jameson, *The Geopolitical Aesthetic*, 4.

69. Martin O'Shaughnessy, "Eloquent Fragments: French Fiction Film and Globalization," *French Politics, Culture and Society* 23, no. 3 (2005): 75.

70. Berlant, *Cruel Optimism*, 194–195.

71. Berlant, *Cruel Optimism*, 201–202.

72. Paolo Virno, *A Grammar of the Multitude: For an Analysis of Contemporary Forms of Life* (Los Angeles: Semiotext(e), 2004), 98, emphasis in original.

73. Alessia Ricciardi, "Immanent Miracles: From De Sica to Hardt and Negri," *Modern Language Notes* 122 (2007): 1157.

74. Ricciardi, "Immanent Miracles," 1158.

75. Michael Hardt and Antonio Negri, *Empire* (London: Harvard University Press, 2000), 413.

76. Hardt and Negri, *Empire*, 91.

77. Dudley Andrew, "A Binocular Preface," in *Opening Bazin: Postwar Film Theory and its Afterlife*, ed. Dudley Andrew and Hervé Joubert-Laurencin (Oxford: Oxford University Press, 2011), xv.

78. Deleuze, *Cinema 2*, 131.

79. Deleuze, *Cinema 1*, 217–218.

80. Rodowick, *Reading the Figural*, 187–188.

81. Michel Foucault, *The Order of Things: An Archaeology of the Human Sciences* (New York: Vintage Books, 1994), 315.

82. We here have the interpretant's instantaneous flash of self-recognition, ruled out by Peirce, where the interpretant becomes the object of an indexical relation with itself.

83. Deleuze, *Cinema 1*, 217–218.

84. Gilles Deleuze, *Foucault*, trans. Seán Hand (Minneapolis: University of Minnesota Press, 1988), 132.

85. This critic is Michel Mourlet, who wrote: "Le cinéma est un regard qui se substitue au nôtre pour nous donner un monde qui s'accorde à nos désirs." Michel Morlet, "Sur un art ignoré," *Cahiers du Cinéma* 98 (1959): 34.

86. This line, that "cinema is truth 24 frames per second," has often been cited as if it were Godard's own aphorism about cinema. Maybe it was indeed at the time he made *Le Pétit soldat*, and maybe it has always been in a way, even after his digital turn of *Film socialisme* (2010) and *Adieu and langage* (2014). After all "cinema" and "truth" are very malleable concepts. The point is, though, that

it is not Godard, but Michel who speaks these words. Michael Haneke has put it nicely: "My perspective on that, my article of faith, is that I've adapted Godard's observation to read, 'Film is a lie at twenty-four frames per second in the service of truth.' Film is an artificial construct. It pretends to construct reality. But it doesn't do that—it's a manipulative form. It's a lie that can reveal the truth. But if a film isn't a work of art, it's just complicit with the process of manipulation." Cited in Richard Porton, "Collective Guilt and Individual Responsibility: An Interview with Michael Haneke," *Cinéaste* 31, no. 1 (2005): 51.

87. Deleuze, *Cinema 1*, 218–219.

88. Deleuze, *Cinema 2*, 79, emphasis in original. Deleuze also writes: "The crystal is expression. Expression moves from the mirror to the seed" (72). This passage resonates with one from *Expressionism in Philosophy* (*Spinoza et le problème de l'expression*), the other place that Deleuze's expressive turn finds its clearest formulation: "Expressionist philosophy brings with it two traditional metaphors: that of a mirror which reflects or reflects upon an image, and that of a seed which 'expresses' the tree as a whole." Gilles Deleuze, *Expressionism in Philosophy: Spinoza*, trans. Martin Joughin (New York: Zone Books, 1992), 80.

89. Deleuze, *Cinema 1*, xi.

90. Deleuze, *Cinema 2*, 7.

91. Gilles Deleuze and Félix Guattari, *What Is Philosophy?*, trans. Hugh Tomlinson and Graham Burchell (New York: Columbia University Press, 1994), 36.

92. Deleuze and Guattari, *What Is Philosophy?*, 41.

93. Deleuze, *Cinema 1*, xix.

94. Deleuze, *Cinema 1*, 215.

95. Deleuze, *Cinema 2*, 40.

96. *Cinema 1*, 210. The first sentence actually reads: "People continue to make SAS and ASA films." Here "S" refers to "situation" and "A" to "action." "SAS" and "ASA" indicate the respective logics structuring the large and small form of the action image.

97 Deleuze, *Cinema 2*, 189.

98. Deleuze, *Cinema 2*, 185, 189–190.

99. Deleuze, *Cinema 2*, 185.

100. Philippe Lubac, "Maurice Pialat and John Cassavetes," trans. Inge Pruks, *Senses of Cinema* 35 (2005), http://sensesofcinema.com/2005/feature-articles/pialat_and_cassavetes/ (accessed March 1, 2013), emphases in original.

101. Kent Jones, "Lightning in a Bottle: Maurice Pialat Profile," *Film Comment* 40, no. 3 (2004): 32.

102. Jones, "Lightning in a Bottle," 32.

103. Alain Bergala, "Maurice Pialat: un marginal du centre," *Cahiers du cinéma* 354 (1983): 21.

104. See Ginette Vincendeau, "Therapeutic Realism: Maurice Pialat's *A nos amours*," in *French Film: Texts and Contexts*, ed. Ginette Vincendeau and Susan Hayward (London: Routledge, 1990), 262.

105. Pialat's rendering of this on-screen attack is not entirely fair game, not only because he had not given Fieschi the opportunity to prepare himself for his attack, but also because in the shot–reverse shot cutting back and forth between

them only Fieschi was actually recorded "live," whereas Pialat, necessitated by the demands of continuity editing, was recorded later, which makes his attack doubly rehearsed. See Vincendeau, "Therapeutic Realism."

106. Alain Badiou, *Deleuze: The Clamor of Being*, trans. Louise Burchill (Minneapolis: University of Minnesota Press, 2000), 96.

107. Benedict de Spinoza, *Ethics*, trans. G. H. R. Parkinson (Oxford: Oxford University Press, 2000), 5p36s.

108. Alain Badiou, *Saint Paul: The Foundation of Universalism*, trans. Ray Brassier (Stanford: Stanford University Press, 2003), 76–77, italics his.

109. Brian Price, *Neither God nor Master: Robert Bresson and Radical Politics* (Minneapolis: University of Minnesota Press, 2011), 13.

110. Godard and Delahaye, "The Question," 476–477.

111. Godard and Delahaye, "The Question," 482–483.

112. Godard and Delahaye, "The Question," 472.

113. Daniel Morgan, *Late Godard and the Possibilities of Cinema* (Berkeley: University of California Press, 2013), 235.

114. Morgan, *Late Godard*, 114.

115. Morgan, *Late Godard*, 115.

116. "'Metteur-au-scène ou directeur: il ne s'agit pas de diriger quelqu'un mais de se diriger soi-même.' Et ça: 'sois sûr d'avoir épuisé tout ce qui se communiqué pas immobilité et la silence.' Et ça: 'Que se soit les sentiments qui amènent les événements, non l'invers.'"

117. Jonathan Rosenbaum, "Trailer for Godard's *Histoire(s) du cinema*," *Vertigo* 1.7 (1997), http://www.closeupfilmcentre.com/vertigo_magazine/volume-1-issue-7-autumn-1997/trailer-for-godard-s-histoire-s-du-cinema/.

118. Alain Badiou and Nicolas Truong, *Éloge de l'amour* (Paris: Flammarion, 2009), 40.

119. Morgan, *Late Godard*, 25.

120. Colin MacCabe, *Godard: A Portrait of the Artist at Seventy* (New York: Farrar, Straus and Giroux, 2003), 241. "Godard told Gorin that he had always thought of himself as an essayist and that the figure he most identified with, the person he most wanted to emulate, was Montaigne."

121. In an interview, Godard talks about Badiou's lecture, which was actually given on the *Costa Concordia* on which the first movement was shot: "Badiou's lecture didn't interest the tourists on the cruise ship. We had announced that there would be a lecture on Husserl but nobody came. When we took Badiou to this empty room, he was very pleased. He said: 'Finally, I speak in front of nobody.'" "Le droit d'auteur? Un auteur n'a que des devoirs," interview with Jean-Luc Godard, Cannes 2010, *Les Inrocks* (blog), May 18, 2010, http://blogs.lesinrocks.com/cannes2010/2010/05/18/le-droit-dauteur-un-auteur-na-que-des-devoirs-jean-luc-godard/.

122. Sarah Cooper, "Mortal Ethics: Reading Levinas with the Dardenne Brothers," *Film Philosophy* 11, no. 2 (2007): 66. In this essay, Cooper discusses the influence of the philosophy of Emmanuel Levinas on the Dardennes' representation of the face-to-face on which all their early films end. Moreover, in his journal Luc Dardenne himself writes: "Emmanuel Levinas has died during our filming [of *The Promise*]. The film owes a lot to the reading of his books. . . . Without

these readings, would we have been able to imagine the scenes of Roger and Igor in the garage, of Assita and Igor in the garage's office and in the station's stairways? The entire film can be seen as an attempt to ultimately arrive at the face-to-face." Dardenne, *Au dos de nos images*, 56.

123. Dardenne, *Au dos de nos images*, 161.

Epilogue

1. Gilles Deleuze, *Negotiations 1972–1990*, trans. Martin Joughin (New York: Columbia University Press, 1995), 180.
2. Braidotti, *The Posthuman*, 23.
3. Rosi Braidotti, *Nomadic Subjects: Embodiment and Sexual Difference in Contemporary Feminist Theory* (New York: Columbia University Press, 2011), 17.
4. Deleuze, *Cinema 2*, 164–166.
5. Deleuze, *Cinema 2*, 167.
6. Berlant, *Cruel Optimism*, 201.
7. Berlant, *Cruel Optimism*, 171.
8. Gilles Deleuze, *Pure Immanence: Essays on a Life*, trans. Anne Boyman (New York: Zone Books, 2001), 28.
9. Deleuze, *Pure Immanence*, 28–29.
10. Michael Hardt, "The Power to Be Affected," *International Journal of Politics, Culture, and Society* 28, no. 3 (2015): 222.
11. Hardt, "Power to Be Affected," 215.
12. Hardt, "Power to Be Affected," 222.
13. Lauren Berlant, "A Momentary Anesthesia of the Heart," *International Journal of Politics, Culture, and Society* 28, no. 3 (2015): 275.
14. Spinoza, *Ethics*, 5p36, translation modified.
15. Spinoza, *Ethics*, 5p36s.
16. Spinoza, *Ethics*, 5p23s.
17. Deleuze, *Expressionism in Philosophy*, 137, emphasis in original.
18. "Just as light manifests both itself and the darkness, so truth is the standard both of itself and of falsity." *Ethics*, 2p43s.
19. Some of these reflections on Spinoza also appear in my essay "Miraculous Realism: Spinoza, Deleuze, and Carlos Reygadas's *Stellet Licht*" that was published in *Discourse: Journal for Theoretical Studies in Media and Culture* 33, no. 1 (2011): 27–54.

Films Referenced
(by director)

Akerman, Chantal. *Jeanne Dielman: 23 Quai du Commerce, 1080 Bruxelles*. 1975. Belgium / France.
Allégret, Yves. *Germinal*. 1963. France / Italy / Hungary.
Almodóvar, Pedro. *Todo sobre mi madre*. 1999. Spain / France.
Amalric, Mathieu. *Mange ta soupe*. 1997. France.
Amelio, Gianni. *Il Ladro di bambini*. 1992. Italy / France / Switzerland.
Andrien, Jean-Jacques. *Australia*. 1989. France / Belgium.
———. *Le Grand paysage d'Alexis Droeven*. 1981. Belgium.
Antonioni, Michelangelo. *Cronaca di un amore*. 1950. Italy.
———. *L'Eclisse*. 1962. Italy.
Arbi, Adil el, and Bilall Fallah. *Black*. 2015. Belgium.
Assayas, Olivier. *La Page blanche*. 1994. France.
———. *L'Eau froide*. 1994. France.
———. *Fin août, début septembre*. 1998. France.
Baily, Edwin. *Faut-il aimer Mathilde?* 1993. France / Belgium.
Baker, Sean. *The Florida Project*. 2017. United States.
Balteau, Bernard. *John Cockerill, toute une histoire*. 2017. Belgium.
Beauvois, Xavier. *Nord*. 1991. France.
Beineix, Jean-Jacques. *Diva*. 1981. France / United States.
Belvaux, Lucas. *Chez nous*. 2017. France / Belgium.
———. *La Raison du plus faible*. 2006. Belgium / France.
Belvaux, Rémy, André Bonzel, and Benoît Poelvoorde. *C'est arrivé près de chez vous*. 1992. Belgium.
Bercot, Emmanuelle. *La Tête haute*. 2015. France.
Berliner, Alain. *Le Mur*. 1998. Belgium / France.
———. *Ma vie en rose*. 1997. France / Belgium / United Kingdom.
Berri, Claude. *Germinal*. 1993. France / Belgium / Italy.
Bertolucci, Bernardo. *The Dreamers*. United Kingdom / France / Italy.
Besson, Luc. *Subway*. 1985. France.
Blain, Gérard. *Pierre et Djemila*. 1987. France.

Bonmariage, Manu. *Du beurre dans les tartines*. 1980. Belgium.
———. *Hay Po l'jou*. 1982. Belgium.
Bontzolakis, Bruno. *Chacun pour soi*. 1998. France / Belgium.
Boon, Dany. *Bienvenu chez les Ch'tis*. 2008. France.
———. *Rien à déclarer*. 2010. France.
Bresson, Robert. *Au Hasard Balthazar*. 1966. France / Sweden.
———. *Un condamné à mort s'est échappé*. 1956. France.
———. *Les Dames du Bois de Boulogne*. 1945. France.
———. *Journal d'un curé de campagne*. 1951. France.
———. *Mouchette*. 1967. France.
———. *Pickpocket*. 1959. France.
Buyens, Frans. *Vechten voor Onze Rechten*. 1962. Belgium.
Cabrera, Dominique. *Nadia et les hippopotames*. 1999. France.
Cameron, James. *Titanic*. 1997. United States.
Cantet, Laurent. *Entre les murs*. 2008. France.
———. *L'Emploi du temps*. 2001. France.
———. *Ressources humaines*. 1999. France / United Kingdom.
Capellani, André. *Germinal*. 1913. France.
———. *Les Misérables*. 1912. France.
Carion, Christian. *Joyeux Noël*. 2005. France / Germany / United Kingdom / Belgium / Romania / Norway.
Carrière, Christine. *Rosine*. 1994. France.
Cassenti, Frank. *L'Affiche rouge*. 1976. France.
Cauvin, André. *Bongolo*. 1952. Belgium.
Chabrol, Claude. *Les Cousins*. 1959. France.
Christiaens, Isabelle. *L'Homme au harpon*. 2015. Belgium.
Coninx, Stijn. *Daens*. 1992. Belgium / France / the Netherlands.
Couvelard, Michel. *Inséparables*. 1999. France.
Daquin, Louis. *Le Point du jour*. 1949. France.
Dardenne, Jean-Pierre, and Luc Dardenne. *Le Chant du rossignol*. 1978. Belgium.
———. *Deux jours, une nuit*. 2014. Belgium / Italy / France.
———. *L'Enfant*. 2005. Belgium / France.
———. *La Fille inconnue*. 2016. Belgium / France.
———. *Le Fils*. 2002. Belgium / France.
———. *Le Gamin au vélo*. 2011. Belgium / France / Italy.
———. *Le Jeune Ahmed*. 2019. Belgium / France.
———. *Lorsque le bateau de Léon M. descendit la Meuse pour la première fois*. 1979. Belgium.
———. *Pour que la guerre s'achève, les murs devaient s'écrouter*. 1980. Belgium.
———. *La Promesse*. 1996. Belgium / France / Luxembourg / Tunisia.
———. *Rosetta*. 1999. France / Belgium.
———. *Le Silence de Lorna*. 2008. Belgium / France / Italy / Germany.
Dekeukeleire, Charles. *Impatience*. 1928. Belgium.
———. *Visions de Lourdes*. 1932. Belgium.
Delvaux, André. *Belle*. 1973. Belgium / France.

———. *De Man die Zijn Haar Kort Liet Knippen.* 1965. Belgium.
———. *Vrouw tussen Hond en Wolf.* 1972. Belgium / France.
Denis, Claire. *Beau Travail.* 1999. France.
Desplechin, Arnaud. *Un conte de Noël.* 2008. France.
———. *Ester Kahn.* 2000. France / United Kingdom.
Dormael, Jaco van. *Toto le héros.* 1991. Belgium / France / Germany.
Dumont, Bruno. *Camille Claudel, 1915.* 2013. France.
———. *Coincoin et les z'inhumains* (TV mini-series). 2019. France.
———. *Flandres.* 2006. France.
———. *Hadewijch.* 2009. France.
———. *Hors Satan.* 2011. France.
———. *L'humanité.* 1999. France.
———. *Jeanne.* 2019. France.
———. *Jeannette, l'enfance de Jeanne d'Arc.* 2017. France.
———. *Ma Loute.* 2016. France / Germany / Belgium.
———. *Twentynine Palms.* 2003. France / Germany / United States.
———. *P'tit Quinquin* (TV miniseries). 2014. France.
———. *La Vie de Jésus.* 1997. France.
Egoyan, Atom. *Felicia's Journey.* 1999. Canada / United Kingdom.
Essiyedali, Youssef, and Louisette Faréniaux. *Au pays des mille et un puits.* 1991. France.
Eustache, Jean. *La Maman et la putain.* 1973. France.
Fellini, Federico. *Le Notti di Cabiria.* 1957. Italy / France.
Ferran, Pascale. *Petits arrangements avec les morts.* 1993. France.
Feyder, Jacques. *La Kermesse héroïque.* 1935. France / Germany.
Fontaine, Anne. *Entre ses mains.* 2005. France / Belgium.
Fonteyne, Frédéric. *Une liaison pornographique.* 1999. Belgium / France / Switzerland / Luxembourg.
Garrone, Matteo. *Gomorrah.* 2008. Italy.
Gheerbrant, Denis. *Et la vie.* 1991. France.
Godard, Jean-Luc. *A bout de souffle.* 1960. France.
———. *Adieu au langage.* 2014. Switzerland.
———. *Les Carabiniers.* 1963. France / Italy.
———. *Éloge de l'amour.* 2001. France / Switzerland.
———. *Film socialisme.* 2010. Switzerland / France.
———. *Histoire(s) du cinéma 3A: La Monnaie de l'absolue.* 1998. France.
———. *Je vous salue, Marie.* 1985. France / Switzerland / United Kingdom.
———. *King Lear.* 1987. United Stated / Bahamas / France / Switzerland.
———. *Le Livre d'image.* 2018. Switzerland / France.
———. *Masculin Féminin.* 1966. France / Sweden.
———. *Le Mépris.* 1963. France / Italy.
———. *Nouvelle vague.* 1990. Switzerland / France.
———. *Le Petit soldat.* 1963. France.
———. Trailer for *Mouchette* (dir. Robert Bresson). 1967. France.
Godard, Jean-Luc, and Jean-Pierre Gorin. *Tout va bien.* 1972. France / Italy.

———. *Le Vent d'est*. 1969. Italy / France / West Germany.
Godard, Jean-Luc, Jean-Pierre Gorin, and Anne-Marie Miéville. *Ici et ailleurs*. 1976. France.
Guesnier, Alain. *Va Petite!* 2002. Belgium / France / Morocco.
Guiraudie, Alain. *L'Inconnu du lac*. 2013. France.
Haneke, Michael. *Caché*. 2005. France / Austria / Germany / Italy / United States.
———. *Code inconnu: récit incomplet de divers voyages*. 2000. France / Germany / Romania.
———. *Happy End*. 2017. France / Austria / Germany.
Hänsel, Marion. *Between the Devil and the Deep Blue Sea*. 1995. Belgium / France / United Kingdom.
———. *Sur la terre comme au ciel*. 1992. Belgium / France / Spain / the Netherlands.
Hausner, Jessica. *Lovely Rita*. 2001. Austria.
Heusch, Luc de. *Jeudi on chantera comme dimanche*. 1967. France / Belgium.
Iñárritu, Alejandro González. *Babel*. 2006. France / United States / Mexico.
Ivens, Joris, and Henri Storck. *Misère au Borinage* (original title: *Borinage*). 1933. Belgium.
Jarmusch, Jim. *Ghost Dog: The Way of the Samurai*. 1999. France / Germany / United States / Japan.
Jean, Patric. *Les Enfants du Borinage: lettre à Henri Storck*. 1999. Belgium.
Jia Zhangke. *Gōng gòng cháng sŭo / In Public*. 2001. China.
———. *Sanxia haoren / Still Life*. 2006. China / Hong Kong.
———. *Shijie / The World*. 2004. China / Japan / France.
———. *Xiao Wu / Pickpocket*. 1998. Hong Kong / China.
Kassovitz, Mathieu. *La Haine*. 1995. France.
Kechiche, Abdellatif. *La Vie d'Adèle*. 2013. France.
Kelly, Richard. *Donnie Darko*. 2001. United States.
Khleifi, Michel. *La Mémoire fertile*. 1980. Belgium / the Netherlands / Palestine / Germany.
———. *L'Ordre du jour*. 1993. France / Belgium / Luxembourg.
———. *Urs al-jalil / Noce en Galilée*. 1987. Palestine / France / Belgium.
Khleifi, Michel, and Eyal Sivan. *Route 181: Fragments of a Journey in Israel-Palestine*. 2003. Belgium / French / United Kingdom / Germany.
Kiarostami, Abbas. *Dah / Ten*. 2002. Iran / France.
Kuypers, Rik, Ivo Michiels, and Ronald Verhavert. *Meeuwen Sterven in de Haven*. 1955. Belgium.
Lafosse, Joachim. *Ça rend heureux*. 2006. Belgium.
———. *Nue propriété*. 2006. Luxembourg / Belgium / France.
Lampin, Georges. *La Maison dans la dune*. 1951. France.
Lanners, Bouli. *Eldorado*. 2008. Belgium / France.
———. *Les Géants*. 2011. France / Belgium / Luxembourg.
———. *Les Premiers, les derniers*. 2016. France / Belgium.
———. *Travellinckx*. 1999. Belgium.
———. *Ultranova*. 2005. Belgium.
Lioret, Philippe. *Welcome*. 2009. France.

Lvovsky, Noémie. *La Vie ne me fait pas peur*. 1999. France / Switzerland.
Lynch, David. *The Straight Story*. 1999. France / United Kingdom / United States.
Mariage, Benoît. *Les Convoyeurs attendent*. 1999. France / Belgium / Switzerland.
Masset-Depasse, Olivier. *Cages*. 2006. Belgium / France.
———. *Dans l'ombre*. 2004. Belgium / France / Switzerland.
———. *Illégal*. 2010. Belgium / Luxembourg / France.
Masson, Laetitia. *En avoir (ou pas)*. 1995. France.
Mattar, Walid. *Vent du Nord*. 2017. France / Tunisia / Belgium.
Mazuy, Patricia. *Peaux de vache*. 1989. France.
Meier, Ursula. *Home*. 2008. Switzerland / France / Belgium.
Meyer, Paul. *Déjà s'envole la fleur maigre*. 1960. Belgium.
———. *L'Herbe sous les pieds*. 1977. Belgium.
———. *Klinkaart*. 1955. Belgium.
Meyst, E. G. de. *Les Filles des fraudeurs*. 1962. Belgium.
———. *Passeurs d'or*. 1948. Belgium.
Michel, Thierry. *Chronique des saisons d'acier*. 1982. Belgium.
———. *Hiver 60*. 1983. Belgium.
———. *Pays noir, pays rouge*. 1975. Belgium.
———. *Métamorphose d'une gare*. 2010. Belgium.
Michel, Thierry, and Pascal Colson. *Enfants du hasard*. 2017. Belgium.
Minnelli, Vincente, and George Cukor. *Lust for Life*. 1956. United States.
Moguy, Léonide. *L'Empreinte du dieu*. 1940. France.
Moreau, Yolande, and Gilles Porte. *Quand la mer monte . . .* 2004. Belgium / France.
Mungiu, Christian. *4 Luni, 3 saptamâni si 2 zile / 4 Months, 3 Weeks, 2 Days*. 2007. Romania / Belgium.
———. *Dupa dealuri / Beyond the hills*. 2012. Romania / France / Belgium.
Nolan, Christopher. *Memento*. 2000. United States.
Olivier, Richard. *Au fond Dutroux*. 1996. Belgium.
———. *Marchienne de vie*. 1994. Belgium.
Pabst, Georg Wilhelm. *Kameradschaft / La Tragédie de la mine*. 1931. Germany / France.
Panahi, Jafar. *Dayereh / The Circle*. 2000. Iran / Italy / Switzerland.
Pasolini, Pier Paolo. *Accattone*. 1961. Italy.
———. *Mamma Roma*. 1962. Italy.
Philibert, Nicholas. *Être et avoir*. 2002. France.
Pialat, Maurice. *A nos amours*. 1983. France.
———. *L'Enfance nue*. 1968. France.
———. *La Gueule ouverte*. 1974. France.
———. *Passe ton bac d'abord*. 1978. France / Canada.
———. *Sous le soleil de Satan*. 1987. France.
———. *Van Gogh*. 1991. France.
Puiu, Cristi. *Moartea domnului Lazarescu / The Death of Mr. Lazarescu*. 2005. Romania.
Rappeneau, Jean-Paul. *Cyrano de Bergerac*. 1990. France.
Reichardt, Kelly. *Wendy and Lucy*. 2008. United States.

Renard, Jacques. *Blanche et Marie*. 1985. France.
———. *Mémoires de la mine*. 1979–1981. France.
Renoir, Jean. *Le Crime de Monsieur Lange*. 1936. France.
———. *La Grande illusion*. 1937. France.
Resnais, Alain. *L'Année dernière à Marienbad*. 1961. France / Italy.
———. *Hiroshima mon amour*. 1959. France / Japan.
Riquita. *Le Maboul du quartier*. 1991. France.
Rivette, Jacques. *Paris nous appartient*. 1961. France.
Rohmer, Eric. *Ma nuit chez Maud*. 1969. France.
Rossellini, Roberto. *Europa '51*. 1952. Italy.
———. *Francesco giullare di Dio*. 1950. Italy.
———. *Germanio anno zero*. 1948. France.
———. *Giovanna d'Arco al rogo*. 1954. Italy / France.
———. *Roma: città aperta*. 1945. Italy.
———. *Viaggio in Italia*. 1954. Italy / France.
Schnabel, Julian. *Le Scaphandre et le papillon*. 2007. France / United States.
Sciamma, Céline. *Bande de filles*. 2014. France.
Seidl, Ulrich. *Import/Export*. 2007. Austria / France / Germany.
Sellani, Djamel. *Une vie de chacal*. 1994. France.
Serreau, Coline. *Mais qu'est-ce qu'elles veulent?* 1977. France.
Sica, Vittorio de. *Ladri di biciclette*. 1948. Italy.
———. *Miracolo a Milano*. 1951. Italy.
———. *Umberto D*. 1952. Italy.
Sidney, George. *The Three Musketeers*. 1948. United States.
Siodmak, Robert. *Mollenard*. 1938. France.
Spielberg, Steven. *Jurassic Park*. 1993. United States.
Storck, Henri. *Le Banquet des fraudeurs*. 1952. Belgium / Germany.
———. *Boerensymphonie*. 1942–1944. Belgium.
———. *Les Fêtes de Belgique*. 1972. Belgium.
Tavernier, Bertrand. *Ça commence aujourd'hui*. 1999. France.
Terme, Louis. *La Fille de la route*. 1962. France.
Truffaut, François. *Les 400 coups*. 1959. France.
———. *Tirez sur le pianiste*. 1960. France.
Varda, Agnès. *Cléo de 5 à 7*. 1962. France.
———. *Les Glaneurs et la glaneuse*. 2000. France.
———. *Les Plages d'Agnès*. 2008. France.
———. *Sans toit ni loi*. 1985. France.
———. *Visages, villages*. 2017. France.
Vernoux, Marion. *Rien à faire*. 1999. France.
Veysset, Sandrine. *Y'aura-t'il de la neige à Noël?* 1996. France.
Vincent, Christian. *Sauve-moi*. 2000. France.
Vincent, Thomas. *Karnaval*. 1999. France.
Virk, Manjinder. *With Love from Calais*. 2016. United Kingdom.
Visconti, Luchino. *Rocco e i suoi fratelli*. 1960. Italy / France.
Wachowski, Lana, and Lily Wachowski. *The Matrix*. 1999. United States.

Wang Xiaoshuai. *Shí qī suì de dān chē / Beijing Bicycle*. 2001. France / Taiwan / China.
Zonca, Erick. *Le Petit voleur*. 2000. France.
———. *La Vie rêvée des anges*. 1998. France.

Bibliography

7 *sur* 7. "'Ne dites pas 'Federatie Wallonië-Brussel' sur la VRT." (September 29, 2011), http://www.7sur7.be/7s7/fr/3007/Bruxelles/article/detail/1326587/2011/09/29/Ne-dites-pas-Federatie-Wallonie-Brussel-sur-la-VRT.dhtml.

25 Ans de films en Communauté Française de Belgique: 1967–1992 [special issue of *Pour le cinéma belge*]. "La Commission de sélection a 25 ans." 1993.

"Accord Canal+ 2005." http://www.larp.fr/dossiers/?p=631.

Adorno, Theodor, Walter Benjamin, Ernst Bloch, Bertolt Brecht, and Georg Lukács. *Aesthetics and Politics*. London: Verso, 2007.

Agamben, Giorgio. *Means without End: Notes on Politics*. Translated by Vincenzo Binetti and Cesare Casarino. Minneapolis: University of Minnesota Press, 2000.

———. *The Open: Man and Animal*. Translated by Kevin Attell. Palo Alto: Stanford University Press, 2004.

Agence Régionale du Centre pour le Livre, l'Image et la Culture Numérique, L' (CICLIC). "[Production Guide]." CICLIC, n.d.

Andersen, Thorn. "Against the Grain: Adding a Touch of Noir, the Dardenne Brothers Rethink Neorealism in *Lorna's Silence*." *Film Society of Lincoln Center*. 2009. http://www.filmlinc.com/fcm/ja09/lorna.htm.

Andrew, Dudley. "An Atlas of World Cinema." In *Remapping World Cinema: Identity, Culture and Politics in Film*, edited by Stephanie Dennison, Song Hwee Lim, 19–29. London: Wallflower, 2006.

———. "Time Zones and Jetlag: The Flows and Phases of World Cinema." In *World Cinemas, Transnational Perspectives*, edited by Nataša Ďurovičová and Kathleen Newman, 59–89. New York: Routledge, 2010.

———. *What Cinema Is!* Oxford: Wiley-Blackwell, 2010.

Andrew, Dudley, and Hervé Joubert-Laurencin, eds. *Opening Bazin: Postwar Film Theory and Its Afterlife*. Oxford: Oxford University Press, 2011.

Antenne 2. "Palme d'Or à Maurice Pialat pour son film Sous le soleil de Satan." Video. May 20, 1987. http://www.ina.fr/cannes/1978-1996/video/CAB87019039/palme-d-or-a-maurice-pialat-pour-son-film-sous-le-soleil-de-satan.fr.html.

Assemblée Nationale. "Le Ministre et le Parlement." http://www.assemblee-nationale.fr/histoire/andre-malraux/ministre_et_parlement.asp.

Association Jean Mitry, L', ed. *Le Nord et le cinéma: contributions à l'histoire du cinéma dans le Nord-Pas-de-Calais*. Pantin: Le Temps des cerises, 1998.

Astier, Henri. "How France's National Front Captured Henin-Beaumont." BBC News. May 14, 2014. http://www.bbc.com/news/world-europe-27387204. Accessed June 15, 2017.

Atelier de Production Centre Val-de-Loire. *Politiques territoriales de soutien à la production cinématographique et audiovisuelle: guide: mode d'emploi*. Château-Renault: APCVL, 2001.

Auerbach, Erich. *Mimesis*. Translated by Willard R. Trask. Princeton: Princeton University Press, 2003.

Austin, Guy. "The Amateur Actors of Cannes 1999: A Shock to the (Star) System." *French Cultural Studies* 15 (2004): 251–263.

———. *Contemporary French Cinema*. 2nd ed. Manchester: Manchester University Press, 2009.

Badiou, Alain. *Deleuze: The Clamor of Being*. Translated by Louise Burchill. Minneapolis: University of Minnesota Press, 2000.

———. *Saint Paul: The Foundation of Universalism*. Translated by Ray Brassier. Stanford: Stanford University Press, 2003.

Badt, Karin. "The Dardenne Brothers at Cannes: 'We Want to Make It Live.'" *Film-Criticism* 30, no. 1 (2005): 70.

Bairoch, Paul. "Niveaux de développement économique de 1810 à 1910." *Annales: économies, sociétés, civilisations* 20, no. 6 (1965): 1091–117.

Balzac, Honoré de. *Le Père Goriot*. Paris: Gallimard, 1971.

———. "Society as Historical Organism." In *The Modern Tradition: Backgrounds of Modern Literature*, edited by Richard Ellmen. Oxford: Oxford University Press, 1965.

Barthes, Roland. *The Reality Effect*. Translated by Richard Howard. Oxford: Blackwell, 1986.

Batz, Jean-Claude. *Colloque sur "Le problème de la production de films en Belgique": rapport sur le sous-développement et l'assistance financière et administrative de l'état*. Bruxelles: Institut de Sociologie de l'Université Libre de Bruxelles, 1963.

Bazin, André. *Qu'est-ce que le cinéma (édition définitive)*. Paris: Éditions du Cerf, 1975.

Benjamin, Walter. *Selected Writings, Volume 4: 1938–1940*. Translated by Edmund Jephcott et al., edited by Michael Jennings and Howard Eiland. Cambridge: The Belknap Press of Harvard University Press, 2006.

Benoliel, Bernard, and Serge Toubiana. "'Il faut être dans le cul des choses.'" *Cahiers du cinéma* 539 (1999): 47–53.

Bergala, Alain. "Maurice Pialat: un marginal du centre." *Cahiers du cinéma* 354 (1983): 20–21.

Berlant, Lauren. *Cruel Optimism*. Durham: Duke University Press, 2011.

———. "A Momentary Anesthesia of the Heart." *International Journal of Politics, Cultural, and Society* 28, no. 3 (2015): 274–281.

———. "Nearly Utopian, Nearly Normal: Post-Fordist Affect in *La Promesse* and *Rosetta*." *Public Culture* 19, no. 2 (2007): 272–301.

Bernanos, Georges. *Nouvelle histoire de Mouchette*. Bordeaux: Le Castor Astral, 2009.
Beugnet, Martine. *Cinema and Sensation: French Film and the Art of Transgression*. Edinburgh: Edinburgh University Press, 2007.
———. "Y'aura-t'il de la neige à Noël? / Will It Snow for Christmas?" In *The Cinema of France*, edited by Phil Powrie, 247–254. London: Wallflower Press, 2006.
Blankenship, Janelle, and Tobias Nagl. "Introduction: Towards a Politics of Scale." In *European Visions: Small Cinemas in Transition*, edited by Janelle Blankenship and Tobias Nagl 15–48. Bielefeld: Transcript Verlag, 2015.
Boni, Marc de. "*Chez Nous*: malgré 8 jours de polémiques, personne au FN n'a vu le film." *Le Figaro*. January 8, 2017. http://www.lefigaro.fr/elections/presidentielles/2017/01/08/35003-20170108ARTFIG00151—chez-nous-malgre-8-jours-de-polemiques-personne-au-fn-n-a-vu-le-film.php.
Bouras, Dimitra. "Dan Cukier, président de la Commission de sélection." *Cinérgie.be: Webzine*, no. 149 (2010), http://www.cinergie.be/webzine/wallimage.
Bouras, Dimitra, and Jean-Michel Vlaeminckx. "Tax Shelter, quatre ans d'existence: le point avec Patrick Quinet et Luc Jabon." *Cinérgie.be: Webzine*, no. 118 (2007), http://www.cinergie.be/webzine/tax_shelter_quatre_ans_d_existence_le_point_avec_patrick_quinet_et_luc_jabon.
Braidotti, Rosi. *Nomadic Subjects: Embodiment and Sexual Difference in Contemporary Feminist Theory*. New York: Columbia University Press, 2011.
———. *The Posthuman*. Cambridge: Polity Press, 2013.
Bresson, Robert. *Notes sur le cinématographe*. Paris: Gallimard, 1975.
Buache, Freddy. *Vingt-cinq ans de cinéma français: parcours croisés: 1979–2003*. Lausanne: L'Age d'homme, 2005.
Butler, Judith. "Bodies and Power Revisited." In *Feminism and the Final Foucault*, edited by Dianna Taylor and Karen Vintges, 183–194. Urbana: University of Illinois Press, 2004.
Cardullo, Bert. "Rosetta Stone: A Consideration of the Dardenne Brothers' *Rosetta*." *Journal of Religion and Film* 6, no. 1 (2002), https://www.unomaha.edu/jrf/rosetta.htm.
Cardullo, Bert, ed. *Committed Cinema: The Films of Jean-Pierre and Luc Dardenne; Essays and Interviews*. Cambridge: Cambridge Scholars, 2009.
Caruana, John, and Mark Cauchi. "What Is Postsecular Cinema? An Introduction." In *Immanent Frames: Postsecular Cinema between Malick and Von Trier*, 1–26. Albany: State University of New York Press, 2018.
Centre du Cinéma et de l'Audiovisuel. *Bilan 2015: Production, promotion et diffusion cinématographiques et audiovisuelles*. Brussels: Fédération Wallonie-Bruxelles, 2016.
Centre du Cinéma et de l'Audiovisuel de la Fédération Wallonie-Bruxelles. *Production, promotion et diffusion cinématographiques et audiovisuelles: le bilan 2011*. Brussels: Centre du Cinéma, 2012.
Centre National du cinéma et de l'Image Animée (CNC). *Bulletin officiel du Centre National du Cinéma et de l'Image Animée: accords de coproductions*. Paris: CNC, 2011.

———. *La Production cinématographique en 2011: bilan statistique des films agréés en 2011*. Paris: CNC, 2012.
———. *La Production cinématographique en 2015*. Paris: CNC, 2016.
———. *La Production cinématographique en 2018*. Paris: CNC, 2019.
Centre Régional de Ressources Audiovisuelles du Nord-Pas-de-Calais (CRRAV). *Rapport d'activités 2010*. Tourcoing: CRRAV, 2011.
Cinérgie.be: Webzine. "Tax Shelter: le monstre du Loch Ness du cinéma belge sort la tête de l'eau." No. 64 (2002), http://www.cinergie.be/webzine/tax_shelter.
Cine-regio. "'Cages' by Olivier Masset-Depasse." http://www.cine-regio.org/co-production/case-studies/cages/.
Clout, Hugh. *The Franco-Belgian Border Region*. London: Oxford University Press, 1975.
Club des 13, Le. *Le milieu n'est plus un pont mais une faille*. Paris: Éditions Stock, 2008.
Codaccioni, Félix. "Une puissance industrielle arrivée à maturité." In *Histoire du Nord-Pas-de-Calais: de 1900 à nos jours*, edited by Yves-Marie Hilaire. Toulouse: Éditions Privat, 1982.
Comediennes.org. "Marie-Christine Barrault: Eric Rohmer [Film Ma nuit chez Maud]." http://comediennes.org/video/marie-christine-barrault-rohmer-maud.
Commission Nationale du Film France. *Les Collectivités territoriales et la production cinématographique & audiovisuelle: compte-rendu, quatre tables rondes en région*. Paris: Commission Nationale du Film France, 2001.
Cooper, Sarah. "Mortal Ethics: Reading Levinas with the Dardenne Brothers." *Film Philosophy* 11, no. 2 (2007): 66–87.
Council of Europe. "European Convention on Cinematographic Co-production [ETS no. 147]." 1992.
Courtel, Anne. "Le CRRAV et le Pôle Images se marient . . . pour le meilleur de l'image." *La Voix du Nord*. January 18, 2012. http://www.lavoixdunord.fr/region/le-crrav-et-le-pole-images-se-marient-pour-le-meilleur-de-l-image-ia26b0n241279.
Dabashi, Hamid, ed. *Dreams of a Nation: On Palestinian Cinema*. London: Verso, 2006.
Dardenne, Luc. *Au dos de nos image (1991–2005), suivi de* Le Fils *et* L'Enfant *par Jean-Pierre et Luc Dardenne*. Paris: Éditions du Seuil, 2005.
Dardenne, Luc, and Jean-Pierre Dardenne. *Scénarios:* Rosetta, *suivi de* La Promesse. Paris: Cahiers du cinéma, 1999.
Darré, Yann. *Histoire sociale du cinéma français*. Paris: La Decouverte, 2000.
Delbar, Catherine. "Rosetta Plan Launched to Boost Youth Employment." *Eironline*. November 28, 1999. http://www.eurofound.europa.eu/eiro/1999/11/feature/be9911307f.htm.
Deleuze, Gilles. *Cinema 1: The Movement-Image*. Translated by Hugh Tomlinson and Barbara Habberjam. London: Continuum, 2005.
———. *Cinema 2: The Time-Image*. Translated by Hugh Tomlinson and Robert Galeta. London: Continuum, 2005.
———. *Cinéma 2: l'image-temps*. Paris: Éditions Minuit, 1985.

———. *Expressionism in Philosophy: Spinoza*. Translated by Martin Joughin. New York: Zone Books, 1992.
———. *Foucault*. Minneapolis: University of Minnesota Press, 1988.
———. *Negotiations 1972–1980*. Translated by Martin Joughin. New York: Columbia University Press, 1995.
———. *Pure Immanence: Essays on a Life*. Translated by Anne Boyman. New York: Zone Books, 2001.
Deleuze, Gilles, and Félix Guattari. *Anti-Oedipus: Capitalism and Schizophrenia*. Minneapolis: University of Minnesota Press, 1983.
———. *What Is Philosophy?* New York: Columbia University Press, 1994.
Delorme, Stéphane, and Mathias Lavin. "Nouveaux arrangements avec le jeune cinéma français." *Balthazar* 4 (1998): 2–10.
Demoulin, Bruno, and Jean-Louis Kupper, ed. *Histoire de la Wallonie: de la préhistoire au XXIe siècle*. Toulouse: Éditions Privat, 2004.
Depétris, Frédéric. *L'Etat et le cinéma en France: le moment de l'exception culturelle*. Paris: L'Harmattan, 2008.
De Standaard. "De BHV-Quiz." 2012. http://www.standaard.be/extra/bhvquiz/.
———. "Overzicht: Hoe Wordt BHV Gesplitst?" September 15, 2011. http://www.standaard.be/artikel/detail.aspx?artikelid=DMF20110914_184.
Dhainaut, Alexandrine. "Le Nord au cinéma, victime de ses clichés?" *Il était une fois le cinéma*. 2008. http://www.iletaitunefoislecinema.com/chronique/1802/le-nord-au-cinema-victime-de-ses-cliches.
Doane, Mary Ann. "The Indexical and the Concept of Medium Specificity." *differences: a journal of feminist cultural studies* 18, no. 1 (2007): 129–152.
Domenach, Elise. "Entretien avec Joachim Lafosse." *Positif* 576 (2009): 98–102.
Dubois, Guy, and Jean-Marie Minot. *Histoire des mines du Nord et du Pas-de-Calais: des origines à 1939–45*. 1991.
Dubois, Philippe, and Edouard Arnoldy, eds. *Ça tourne depuis cent ans: une histoire de cinéma francophone de Belgique*. Bruxelles: Communauté Française de Belgique/Wallonie-Bruxelles, 1995.
Dumont, Bruno. "*L'Humanité*—écrit pour un scénario." http://www.brunodumont.com/index.php?option=com_k2&view=item&id=20:sc%C3%A9narios&Itemid=54&lang=en.
Dupont, Joan. "Two Belgian Brothers' Working-Class Heroes." In *Committed Cinema: The Films of Jean-Pierre and Luc Dardenne; Essays and Interviews*, edited by Bert Cardullo, 85–88. Cambridge: Cambridge Scholars, 2009.
Ďurovičová, Nataša, and Kathleen Newman, eds. *World Cinemas, Transnational Perspectives*. New York: Routledge, 2010.
Elsaesser, Thomas. "The Mind-Game Film." In *Puzzle Films: Complex Storytelling in Contemporary Cinema*. Edited by Warren Buckland, 13–41. Chichester: Wiley-Blackwell, 2009.
Europa.eu. "Cohesion Policy 2007–2013." (2007), http://ec.europa.eu/regional_policy/atlas2007/belgium/index_en.htm.
Equipe technique INTERREG Nord-Pas-de-Calais. "Regards transfontaliers INTERREG 2, Hainaut, Nord-Pas de Calais, Picardie." INTERREG Hainaut, Nord-Pas de Calais, Picardie, 1998.

Fabre, Clarisse. "Des techniciens racontent le tournage difficile de 'La Vie d'Adèle.'" *Le Monde*. May 24, 2013. http://www.lemonde.fr/festival-de-cannes/article/2013/05/24/des-techniciens-racontent-le-tournage-de-la-vie-d-adele_3417150_766360.html.

Fonteyn, Guido. *Afscheid van Magritte: Over het Oude en Nieuwe Wallonië*. Antwerp: De Bezige Bij, 2011.

Foucault, Michel. *The Order of Things: An Archaeology of the Human Sciences*. New York: Vintage Books, 1994.

———. "The Subject and Power." In *Beyond Structuralism and Hermeneutics*, 208–226. Chicago: University of Chicago Press, 1983.

France 2. "Ouverture du festival." Video. May 12, 1999. http://fresques.ina.fr/festival-de-cannes-fr/fiche-media/Cannes00335/ouverture-du-festival-1999.

Frodon, Jean-Michel. "Bazin en Asie." *Cahiers du Cinéma* 640 (2008): 77.

———. "Le jury du 52e Festival décroche la palme de l'exigence." *Le Monde*. May 25, 1999.

Génie Culturel. "Benoît Dervaux, cadreur." http://genieculturel.siep.be/metiers/metiers/metiers-techniques-et-de-l-ombre-2/interviews/105/.

Gysseling, Maurits, and Jules Herbillon. "La Genèse de la frontière linguistique dans le Nord de la Gaulle." *Revue du Nord* 44, no. 173 (1962): 5–37.

Godard, Jean-Luc. "Exclu l'an dernier du Festival Truffaut représentera la France à Cannes avec *Les 400 coups*." *Arts* 719 (1959): 5.

Godard, Jean-Luc Godard, and Michel Delahaye. "The Question." In *Robert Bresson*, edited by James Quandt, 453–483. Toronto: Toronto International Film Festival Group, 1998.

Gogh, Vincent van. "[Letter to Theo van Gogh. Wasmes, Thursday, 26 December 1878]." http://vangoghletters.org/vg/letters/let149/letter.html.

Gorin, François. "Une journée au Nord." *Télérama*, http://www.brunodumont.com/index.php?option=com_k2&view=item&id=12:a-propos-de-lhumanit%C3%A9&Itemid=53&lang=fr.

Granval, Daniel. *Les Tournages de films dans le Nord et le Pas-de-Calais*. Bouvignies: Éditions Nord, 2008.

Grassin, Sophie. "Le Nord fait son cinéma." *L'Express*. October 21, 1999. http://www.lexpress.fr/informations/le-nord-fait-son-cinema_635346.html.

Gunning, Tom. "Moving Away from the Index." *differences: a journal of feminist cultural studies* 18, no. 1 (2007): 29–52.

Habermas, Jürgen. *Europe: The Faltering Project*. Translated by Ciaran Cronin. Cambridge: Polity, 2009.

Hardt, Michael. "The Power to Be Affected." *International Journal of Politics, Culture, and Society* 28, no. 3 (2015): 215–222.

Hardt, Michael, and Antonio Negri. *Empire*. London: Harvard University Press, 2000.

Hasquin, Hervé. "La Wallonie: d'où vient-elle?" In *Wallonie: atouts et références d'une région*, edited by Freddy Joris and Natalie Archambeau, 15–33. Mons: Gouvernement Wallon, 1995.

Hayward, Susan. *French National Cinema*. Second edition. London: Routledge, 2005.

———. "State, Culture and the Cinema: Jack Lang's Strategies for the French Film Industry 1981–93." *Screen* 34, no. 4 (1993): 380–391.

Higson, Andrew. "The Concept of National Cinema." *Screen* 30, no. 4 (1989): 36–46.
———. "The Limiting Imagination of National Cinema." In *Cinema and Nation*, edited by Mette Hjort and Scott MacKenzie, 63–74. London: Routledge, 2000.
Hjort, Mette. *Small Nation, Global Cinema: The New Danish Cinema*. Minneapolis: University of Minnesota Press, 2005.
Hjort, Mette, and Duncan Petrie, eds. *The Cinema of Small Nations*. Bloomington: Indiana University Press, 2007.
Hoeij, Boyd van, ed. *10/10*. Brussels: Ministère de la Communauté Française de Belgique / Wallonie Bruxelles International / Wallonie Bruxelles Images, 2010.
Honorez, Luc. "La Palme de 'Rosetta' remplit de fierté le cinéma belge." *Le Soir*. May 25, 1999.
Hugo, Victor. *Oeuvres complètes de Victor Hugo. Poésie IV. Les Chatiments*. Paris: J. Hetzel & Cie; A. Quantin & Cie, 1882.
Institut National de la Statistique et des Études Économiques. "Nord-Pas-de-Calais." 2010. http://www.insee.fr/fr/regions/nord-pas-de-calais/default.asp?page=faitsetchiffres/presentation/presentation.htm.
International Organization for Standardization. "FAQs—Answers to Questions Relating to Codes and Names of Specific Countries." http://www.iso.org/iso/country_codes/iso_3166-faqs/iso_3166_faqs_specific.htm.
Ivens, Joris. *The Camera and I*. New York / Berlin: International Publishers / Seven Seas Books, 1969.
Jameson, Fredric. *The Geopolitical Aesthetic: Cinema and Space in the World System*. Bloomington: Indiana University Press, 1995.
Jennotte, Alain. "Le Cinéma belge, c'est bon pour l'économie." *Le Soir*. February 3, 2010.
Jones, Kent. "L'humanité." *Film Comment* 36, no. 3 (2000): 73.
———. "Lightning in a Bottle: Maurice Pialat Profile." *Film Comment* 40, no. 3 (2004): 32.
Joris, Freddy, and Natalie Archambeau, eds. *La Wallonie: atouts et références d'une region*. Mons: Gouvernement Wallon, 1995.
Jousse, Thierry, Nicolas Saada, Frédéric Strauss, Camille Taboulay, and Vincent Vatrican. "Dix places pour le jeune cinéma." *Cahiers du cinéma* 473 (1993): 28–30.
Jungblut, Guy, Patrick Leboutte, and Dominique Païni. *Une encyclopédie des cinémas de Belgique*. Paris / Crisnée: Musee d'Art Moderne de la Ville de Paris / Yellow Now, 1990.
Kock, Ivo. "Bienvenu Chez les Français: Franse Films op Zoek naar een Vlaams Publiek." *Filmmagie* 590 (2008): 46–47.
Kracauer, Siegfried. *Theory of Film: The Redemption of Physical Reality*. London: Oxford University Press, 1960.
Lagesse, Cécile. "*Still Life* de Jia Zhang-ke: le réalisme à l'âge numérique." *Cahiers du cinéma* 640 (2008): 79–81.
Latil, Loredana. "Une métaphore du cinéma français: les sélections du festival de Cannes et la prime à la qualité." http://www.cg06.fr/document/?f=decouvrir-les-am/fr/rr168-cinema.pdf.

Lauretis, Teresa de. *Alice Doesn't: Feminism, Semiotics, Cinema*. Bloomington: Indiana University Press, 1984.
Laurin, Maryline. "Il était une fois le cinéma belge (4/4): le verdict!" *Cinevox*. March 11, 2012. http://www.cinevox.be/il-etait-une-fois-le-cinema-belge-44-sans-pretention.
Lavin, Mathias, and Stéphane Delorme. "Petits arrangements avec le jeune cinéma français." *Balthazar* 3 (1998): 24–32.
La Voix du Nord. "Vent du nord." May 25, 1999.
Leclerq, Florent. "A quoi rêvent les Lillois." *L'Express*. March 4, 1993. http://www.lexpress.fr/informations/a-quoi-revent-les-lillois_593598.html.
Lecomte, Olivier. "Nos cinéastes sont-ils heureux? Berliner, Lafosse, Lannoo, Malandrin, Renders, Sojcher répondent à Olivier Lecomte." *Cinérgie: Webzine*, no. 109 (2006), http://www.cinergie.be/webzine/nos_cineastes_sont_ils_heureux_berliner_lafosse_lannoo_malandrin_renders_sojcher_repondent_a_olivier_lecomte.
Le Monde. "59 réalisateurs appellent à 'désobeir.'" February 12, 1997.
———. "A Rosetta, pour L'Humanité." May 25, 1999.
Lentacker, Firmin. *La Frontière franco-belge: étude géographique des effets d'une frontière internationale sur la vie de relations*. Lille: Presses Universitaires du Septentrion, 1974.
Les Inrocks. "Le droit d'auteur? Un auteur n'a que des devoirs" (interview with Jean-Luc Godard, Cannes 2010). May 18, 2010. http://blogs.lesinrocks.com/cannes2010/2010/05/18/le-droit-dauteur-un-auteur-na-que-des-devoirs-jean-luc-godard/.
Lottin, Alain, and Eric Bussière, eds. *Deux mille ans du "Nord-Pas-de-Calais": Tome II: de la révolution au XXIe siècle*. Lille: La Voix du Nord, 2002.
Lubac, Philippe. "Maurice Pialat and John Cassavetes." *Senses of Cinema*, no. 35 (2005), http://sensesofcinema.com/2005/feature-articles/pialat_and_cassavetes/.
Lukács, Georg. *The Historical Novel*. Translated by Hannah Mitchell and Stanley Mitchell. Lincoln: University of Nebraska Press, 1962.
———. *The Theory of the Novel: A Historico-Philosophical Essay on the Forms of Great Epic Literature*. Translated by Anna Bostock. Cambridge: MIT Press, 1971.
Lumière Database on Admissions of Films Released in Europe. "Identification of Films in the Lumière Database." lumiere.obs.coe.int/web/sources/astuces.html.
Lumley, Henry de. "De la fête à l'identité." In *Géants et dragons: mythes et traditions à Bruxelles, en Wallonie, dans le nord de la France et en Europe*, edited by Jean-Pierre Ducastelle. Tournai: Casterman, 1996.
MacCabe, Colin. *Godard: A Portrait of the Artist at Seventy*. New York: Farrar, Straus and Giroux, 2003.
Mai, Joseph. "Corps-caméra: The Evocation of Touch in the Dardennes' *La Promesse* (1996)." *L'Esprit Créateur* 47, no. 3 (2007): 133–144.
———. *Jean-Pierre and Luc Dardenne*. Urbana: University of Illinois Press, 2010.
Malcolm, Derek. "Belgian Film's Surprise Cannes Victory." *The Guardian*. May 24, 1999.

Manovich, Lev. "What Is Digital Cinema?" In *The Digital Dialectic: New Essays on New Media*, edited by Peter Lunenfeld, 172–192. Cambridge: MIT Press, 2000.

Marie, Michel, ed. *Le Jeune cinéma français*. Paris: Nathan, 1998.

Marks, Laura. *The Skin of the Film: Intercultural Cinema, Embodiment, and the Senses*. Durham: Duke University Press, 2000.

Meersch, Maxence van der. *Quand les sirènes se taisent*. Douai: L'Imprimerie Nationale, 1960.

Merleau-Ponty, Maurice. *The Visible and the Invisible [Followed by Working Notes]*. Translated by Alphonso Lingis. Edited by Claude Lefort. Evanston: Northwestern University Press, 1968.

Metz, Christian. *The Imaginary Signifier: Psychoanalysis and the Cinema*. Translated by Celia Britton et al. Bloomington: Indiana University Press, 1982.

Michaux, Léon, ed. *Images et cinéma de Wallonie: une société en mutation*. Bruxelles: La Médiathèque de la Communauté Française de Belgique, 2000.

Morgan, Daniel. *Late Godard and the Possibilities of Cinema*. Berkeley: University of California Press, 2013.

———. "Rethinking Bazin: Ontology and Realist Aesthetics." *Critical Inquiry* 32, no. 3 (2006): 443–481.

Mosley, Philip. *Responsible Realism: The Cinema of the Dardenne Brothers*. New York: Wallflower Press, 2013.

———. *Split Screen: Belgian Cinema and Cultural Identity*. Albany: State University of New York Press, 2001.

Mottet, Jean. "Mardi 28 novembre 2006: Bruno Dumont." In *La direction d'acteur: carnation, incarnation*, edited by Frédéric Sojcher, 171–210. Paris: Éditions du Rocher, 2008.

Mourlet, Michel. "Sur un art ignoré." *Cahiers du Cinéma* 98 (1959): 23–37.

Mulvey, Laura. "Visual Pleasure and Narrative Cinema." *Screen* 6, no. 18 (1975): 6–18.

Nacache, Jacqueline. "Was There a Young French Cinema?" In *A Companion to Contemporary French Cinema*, edited by Alistair Fox, Michel Marie, Raphaëlle Moine, and Hilary Radner, 184–204. Malden: Wiley-Blackwell, 2005.

Niessen, Niels. "Lives of Cinema: Against Its 'Death.'" *Screen* 52, no. 3 (2011): 307–323.

———. "Miraculous Realism: Spinoza, Deleuze, and Carlos Reygadas's *Stellet Licht*." *Discourse* 33, no. 1 (2011): 27–54.

O'Shaughnessy, Martin. "Eloquent Fragments: French Fiction Film and Globalization." *French Politics, Culture & Society* 23, no. 3 (2005): 75–88.

———. *The New Face of Political Cinema: Commitment in French Film since 1995*. New York: Berghahn Books, 2007.

Overbey, David, ed. *Springtime in Italy: A Reader on Neo-Realism*. Hamden: Archon Books, 1978.

Parlement Wallon (session 2011–2012). "Budgets des recettes et des dépenses de la Région wallonne pour l'année budgéttaire 2012: exposé général: deuxième partie [4-III a/4-III bcd]." November 21, 2011.

Pascal, Blaise. *Pascal's Pensées with an Introduction by T. S. Eliot*. Translated by W. F. Trotter. New York: E.P. Dutton & Co., 1958.

Peirce, C. S. *The Essential Peirce: Selected Philosophical Writings Volume 1 (1867–1893)*. Edited by Nathan Houser and Christian Kloesel. Bloomington: Indiana University Press, 1992.

———. *The Essential Peirce: Selected Philosophical Writings Volume 2 (1893–1913)*. Edited by Peirce Edition Project. Bloomington: Indiana University Press, 1998.

———. *Peirce on Signs: Writings on Semiotic*. Edited by James Hoopes. Chapel Hill: University of North Carolina Press, 1991.

Pierrard, Pierre. *Histoire du Nord: Flandre, Artois, Hainaut, Picardie*. Paris: Hachette, 1992.

Pirotte, Jean. "Une image floue." *Louvain* 133 (2002): 26–28.

Polet, Jacques. "Un enracinement porteur d'universalité." *Louvain* 133 (2002): 23–25.

Popelier, Jean-Pierre. *Belges et Français du Nord: une histoire partagée*. Lille: La Voix Editions, 2010.

Porton, Richard. "Collective Guilt and Individual Responsibility: An Interview with Michael Haneke." *Cinéaste* 31, no. 1 (2005): 50–51.

Pouille, André-Jean, Danielle Sarlet, Jean-Louis Helary, and Jean-Jacques Malpot. *Atlas transfontalier: Tome 3: activités économiques*. Région Nord-Pas de Calais: Direction Régionale de l'Equipement du Nord-Pas-de-Calais / Direction Régionale de l'INSEE Nord-Pas-de-Calais, 2005.

———. *Atlas transfontalier: Tome 4: emploi-formation*. Région Nord-Pas de Calais: Direction Régionale de l'Equipement du Nord-Pas-de-Calais / Direction Régionale de l'INSEE Nord-Pas-de-Calais, 2006.

Powrie, Phil. "Heritage, History, and 'New Realism': French Cinema in the 1990s." In *French Cinema in the 1990s: Continuity and Difference*, edited by Phil Powrie, 1–21. Oxford: Oxford University Press, 1999.

Prédal, René. *Le Cinéma français des années 1990: une génération de transition*. Paris: Armand Colin, 2008.

———. *Le jeune cinéma français*. Paris: Nathan, 2002.

Price, Brian. *Neither God nor Master: Robert Bresson and Radical Politics*. Minneapolis: University of Minnesota Press, 2011.

Quasimodo, Salvatore. *Tutte le poesie*. Milan: Arnoldo Mondadori Editore, 1960.

Rancière, Jacques. "Le Bruit du peuple, l'image de l'art: à propos de *Rosetta* et de *L'Humanité*." *Cahiers du cinéma* 540 (1999): 110–112.

———. *Future of the Image*. London: Verso, 2009.

———. *Politique de la littérature*. Paris: Galilée, 2007.

Rayns, Tony. "*L'humanité*." *Sight and Sound*. October 2000. http://old.bfi.org.uk/sightandsound/review/433.

Restivo, Angelo. *The Cinema of Economic Miracles: Visuality and Modernization in the Italian Art Film*. Durham: Duke University Press, 2002.

Ricciardi, Alessia. "Immanent Miracles: From De Sica to Hardt and Negri." *Modern Language Notes* 122 (2007): 1138–1165.

Rodowick, David. *Reading the Figural, or, Philosophy after the New Media*. Durham: Duke University Press, 2001.
Roekens, Anne, and Axel Tixhon, eds. *Cinéma et crise(s) économique(s)*. Crisnée / Namur: Yellow Now / Presses universitaires de Namur, 2011.
Saintghislain, Valéry. "Un partenariat Hainaut-Nord-Pas de Calais consuire une 'eurorégion' du cinéma et de l'audiovisuel." *Le Soir*. April 11, 2003.
Schouler, Mariane. "Contraintes du tournage et choix techniques." http://entre-les-murs-laurent-cantet.blogspot.com/2009/04/contraintes-du-tournage-et-choix.html.
"Schuman Declaration—9 May 1950, The." *European Union*. http://europa.eu/about-eu/basic-information/symbols/europe-day/schuman-declaration/index_en.htm. Accessed May 19, 2015.
Scott, A. O. "In Toronto, Sampling Realism's Resurgence." *New York Times*. September 10, 2008. http://www.nytimes.com/2008/09/11/movies/11fest.html. Accessed March 10, 2013.
Serceau, Daniel. *Symptômes du jeune cinéma français*. Paris: Cerf-corlet, 2008.
Shaviro, Steven. *The Cinematic Body*. Minneapolis: University of Minnesota Press, 1993.
Sica, Vittorio de. "How I Direct My Films." Preface to the English edition of the screenplay of *Miracle in Milan*, 1–9. New York: Orion Press, 1989.
Sklar, Robert. "The Terrible Lightness of Social Marginality: An Interview with Jean-Pierre and Luc Dardenne." *Cineaste* 31, no. 2 (2006): 19–21.
Smeets, Marcel. "L'Apport wallon au cinéma." In *La Wallonie, le pays et les hommes: Tome 4: compléments*, 417–424. Brussels: La Renaissance du livre, 1981.
Société de l'Industrie Minérale, ed. *Gestion des anciens sites de carbochimie en Europe: synthèse du programma II Ocasicha*. Douai: Les Fascicules de l'Industrie Minérale, 2001.
Soir 3/Canal Plus. "Palmarès festival de Cannes dont Palme d'Or aux frères Dardenne pour 'Rosetta.'" Video. May 23, 1999. http://www.ina.fr/video/CAC99022160/palmares-festival-de-cannes-dont-palme-d-or-aux-freres-dardenne-pour-rosetta-video.html.
Sojcher, Frédéric. *La Kermesse héroïque du cinéma belge: Tome I: 1896–1965: des documentaires et des farces*. Paris: Harmattan, 1999.
———. *La Kermesse héroïque du cinéma belge: Tome II: 1965–1988: le miroir déformant des identités culturelles*. Paris: Harmattan, 1999.
———. *La Kermesse héroïque du cinéma belge: Tome III: 1988–1996: le carrousel européen*. Paris: Harmattan, 1999.
———. *Pratiques du cinéma*. Paris: Klincksieck, 2011.
Solanas, Fernando, and Octavio Getino. "Toward a Third Cinema: Notes and Experience for the Development of a Cinema of Liberation in the Third World." In *Twenty-Five Years of the New Latin American Cinema*, edited by Michael Chanan, 17–27. London: BFI / Channel Four, 1983.
Souppouris, Aaron. "Jean-Luc Godard Will Produce New Film, 'Adieu au langage,' in 3D." *The Verge*. http://www.theverge.com/2012/5/11/3013768/jean-luc-godard-adieu-au-language-goodbye-to-language-3d.

Spinoza, Benedict de. *The Chief Works of Spinoza:* A Theologico-Political Treatise *and* A Political Treatise. Translated by R. H. M. Elwes. New York: Dover Publications, 1951.

———. *Ethics.* Translated by G. H. R. Parkinson. Oxford: Oxford University Press, 2000.

Sporck, J. A. "L'Organisation de l'espace dans la métropole liégoise." *Travaux Géographiques de Liège* 159 (1972): 355–383.

Sublon, Romain. "[cinéphilies:] Bruno Dumont et Julie Sokolowski." *Cut* (2009), cutlarevue.fr/2009/11/26/cinephilies-bruno-dumont-et-julie-sokolowski/.

Taylor, Charles. *A Secular Age.* Cambridge: The Belknap Press of Harvard University Press, 2007.

Technologies Wallonnes de l'Image, du Son et du Texte. "Launch of the Nord-Pas de Calais Image Pole." http://www.twist-cluster.com/cms/en/news/market-news/248-la . . .

Thabourey, Vincent. "Les Nouvelles saisons du cinéma belge." *Positif* 576 (2009): 92–93.

Thys, Marianne, and René Michelems. *Belgian Cinema / Le Cinéma Belge / De Belgische Film.* Brussels / Ghent / Paris: Royal Belgian Film Archive / Ludion / Flammarion, 1999.

Tobin, Yann. "Entretien avec Yolande Moreau: on n'a rien a perdre." *Positif* 576 (2009): 108–109.

Toubiana, Serge. "Le Cinéma retrouvé." *Cahiers du cinéma* 536 (1999): 22–23.

Trémois, C. M. *Les Enfants de la liberté: le jeune cinéma français des années 90.* Paris: Seuil, 1997.

Truffaut, François. "Une certaine tendance du cinéma français." *Cahiers du cinéma* 31 (1954): 15–29.

Vandenberghe, Dirk. "Vier Vragen en Antwoorden over 'BHV.'" *NRC Handelsblad.* September 24, 2009. http://vorige.nrc.nl/buitenland/article2421833.ece/Vier_vragen_en_antwoorden_over_BHV.

Verbeken, Pascal. *Arm Wallonië: Een Reis door het Beloofde Land.* Antwerp / Amsterdam: Meulenhoff / Manteau, 2007.

Vincendeau, Ginette. "Therapeutic Realism: Maurice Pialat's *A nos amours.*" In *French Film: Texts and Contexts,* edited by Ginette Vincendeau and Susan Hayward, 258–268. London: Routledge, 1990.

Virno, Paolo. *A Grammar of the Multitude: For an Analysis of Contemporary Forms of Life.* Los Angeles: Semiotext(e), 2004.

Vlaams Audiovisueel Fonds. *Jaarverslag 2011.* Brussels: Vlaams Audiovisueel Fonds, 2012.

Vlaeminckx, Jean-Michel. "Wallimage." *Cinérgie.be: Webzine,* no. 48 (2001), http://www.cinergie.be/webzine/wallimage.

W'allons-nous. *Cinéma Wallonie Bruxelles: du documentaire social au film de fiction.* Virton: W'allons-nous, 1989.

Wallimage. "Casper, the Friendly Animated Project." October 16, 2009. http://www.wallimage.be/newsfile.php?lang=uk&id=173.

———. "The Pôle Image de Liège Grows with Wallimage Entreprises." December 20, 2010. http://www.wallimage.be/newsfile.php?lang=uk&id=382.

Wallimage Coproductions. "Regulations." 2010. http://www.wallimage.be/downloads. php?lang=uk.
Williams, James S. *Space and Being in Contemporary French Cinema*. Manchester: Manchester University Press, 2013.
Wollen, Peter. *Signs and Meaning in the Cinema*. Bloomington: Indiana University Press, 1972.
Wrigley, E. A. *Industrial Growth and Population Change: A Regional Study of the Coalfield Areas of Northwest Europe in the Later Nineteenth Century*. London: Cambridge University Press, 1961.
Zavattini, Cesare. "Some Ideas on the Cinema." In *Film: A Montage of Theories*, edited by Richard Dyer McCann, 216–228. New York: Plume, 1966.

Index

4 Months, 3 Weeks, 2 Days. See under Mungiu, Christian
400 coups, Les. See under Truffaut, François

Aachen, 72, 75
A bout de souffle. See under Godard, Jean-Luc, works of
Accattone. See under Pasolini, Pier Paolo Pasolini
acting (in cinema): and Agamben, 46; and Bresson, 35–36; and Cassavetes, 218–19; and Dardennes, 36–42, 46–47, 101, 207, 234; and Deleuze, 217–18, 222; and Dumont, 36, 42–47, 207, 234; and Godard, 35–36, 229; and new realism, 204; and Pialat, 216–22; and prizes at Cannes 1999, 1–3, 6; and Varda, 223. *See also* acting/acted image
acting/acted image, 6, 46, 62 194, 207, 216–24 passim, 234, 244
Adieu au langage. See under Godard, Jean-Luc, works of
Adorno, Theodor, 202, 207, 276n56
aesthetics: and Cinéma du Nord; 11, 70, 106, 111, 123; and Dardennes and Dumont, 6, 30, 41–42, 46, 56; and realism, 17, 192–207 passim, 211–12, 233, 274n14

affect: cinematic, 19, 42, 154, 222; concept of, 240–44. *See also* Marks, Laura: on tactile vision
Affiche rouge, L'. See under Cassenti, Frank
Agamben, Giorgio, 46
Akerman, Chantal, 135, 144, 218; *Jeanne Dielman*, 16, 97, 218
Allégret, Yves, 110; *Germinal*, 107–108, 122
Almodóvar, Pedro: *Todo sobre mi madre*, 3
Amalric, Mathieu: *Mange ta soupe*, 191
Amelio, Gianni: *Il ladro di bambini*, 204
Andrew, Dudley: on Bazin and realism, 204, 211–12, 274n14; on national cinema, 10
Andrien, Jean-Jacques, 135; *Australia*, 106, 260n78; *Grand paysage d'Alexis Droeven*, 105–107, 158
angels, vi, 19, 47–48, 53, 123, 125, 233, 240
animated cinema, 146, 164, 204, 262–63n105, 270n97
Année dernière à Marienbad, L'. See under Resnais, Alain
A nos amours. See under Pialat, Maurice
Antonioni, Michelangelo, 97; *Cronaca di un amore*, 203; *Eclisse*, 203

Arbi, Aidl el and Bilall Fallah: *Black*, 97, 154
ARTE (Association Relative à la Télévision Européenne), 132, 160, 163, 167; and *jeune cinema français*, 144–45
Assayas, Olivier, 143–44, 189, 192; *Eau froide*, 144; *Fin août, début septembre*, 192; *Page blanche*, 144
Au fond Dutroux. See under Olivier, Richard
Au Hasard Balthazar. See under Bresson, Robert, works of
Au pays des mille et un puits. See under Essiyedali, Youssef and Louisette Faréniaux
Australia. See under Andrien, Jean-Jacques
Austrasian field (geophysical), 75
auteur cinema: and (francophone) Belgian cinema, 97–98, 150, 153–54, 156, 159–60; and French New Wave discourse of, 110, 137–40, 220; and *jeune cinema français*, 143–45, 189, 191, 217–18; and northern French cinema, 123
avance sur recettes (advance on receipts regulation), 138, 140–41, 153, 160

Babel. See under Iñárritu, Alejandro González
Badiou, Alain, 5, 18, 224–25, 229, 244
Baily, Edwin, 147; *Faut-il aimer Mathilde?*, 113
Baker, Sean: *Florida Project*, 204
Balteau, Bernard: *John Cockerill, toute une histoire*, 76–77, 95
Bande des filles. See under Sciamma, Céline
Banquet des fraudeurs, Le. See under Storck, Henri
Bazin, André: and francophone-European film and philosophy, 5, 18; and French New Wave, 192, 211–15, 227; and Bresson, 54–55, 110, 195, 197–98, 227; and realism, 105, 192–211 passim, 222, 234, 274nn14–15, 275n30
Beau Travail. See under Denis, Claire
Beauvois, Xavier, 109, 143, 192; *Nord*, 12, 122
Beijing Bicycle. See under Wang Xiaoshuai
Beineix, Jean-Jacques: *Diva*, 141
Belgian national cinema, 150–54, 156
Belgium: and cinematic production, 3, 113, 121, 130, 134–36, 147–65 passim; and folklore, 123–24; history of 78–79, 82, 86, 92, 94, 103; and state organization, 70–74, 100–101, 107, 150. See also Belgian national cinema
Belle. See under Delvaux, André
Belvaux, Lucas, 25, *Chez nous*, 119, 189; *Raison du plus faible*, 100, 106, 190
Belvaux, Rémy, André Bonzel, and Benoît Poelvoorde, *C'est arrivé près de chez vous*, 155
Benjamin, Walter, 15, 84, 256n38
Bercot, Emmanuelle: *Tête haute*, 147
Berlant, Lauren, 5; and cinema of precarity, 17, 29, 208–209, 238–39; and discussion with Hardt, 240–42
Berliner, Alain: *Ma vie en rose*, 155; *Mur*, 107
Bernanos, Georges: and francophone-European film and philosophy, 18; *Journal d'un curé de campagne*, 6, 23, 47, 224; *Nouvelle histoire du Mouchette*, 6, 23, 47, 49; *Sous le soleil de Satan*, 6, 23, 47
Berri, Claude, 147; *Germinal*, 110, 140, 146
Besson, Luc: *Subway*, 141
Bête humaine, la. See under Zola, Emile
Between the Devil and the Deep Blue Sea. See under Hänsel, Marion
Beyond the Hills. See under Mungiu, Christian
Bienvenu chez les Ch'tis. See under Boon, Dany

Blain, Gérard: *Pierre et Djemila*, 113, 267n59
Black. *See under* Arbi, Adil el, and Bilall Fallah
Blanche et Marie. *See under* Renard, Jacques
Boerensymphonie. *See under* Storck, Henri
Boltanski, Christian (exhibition in MACs), 171
Bongolo. *See under* Cauvin, André
Bonmariage, Many: *Du beurre dans les tartines*, 105; *Hay Po l'jou*, 87
Boon, Dany: *Bienvenu chez les Ch'tis*, 15, 67–68, 70, 95, 107, 122, 146, 160, 261n92; *Rien à declarer*, 107
Bontzolakis, Bruno: *Chacun pour soi*, 113
border, French-Belgian: and analysis of Cinéma du Nord, 12, 15, 65, 135; and cinematic production and coproduction, 148, 161, 163–68; history of, 69–75, 92–93, 254n15; and northern French cinema, 122–24; and Walloon cinema, 107, 261n83. *See also* Nord, French-Walloon
border region, French-Belgian. *See* Nord, French-Belgian
border: concept of, 11, 175, 245; Flemish-Walloon, 107, 160, 268n70; French-German, 111; German-Dutch-Belgian, 261n83; Palestinian-Israeli, 134. *See also* border, French-Belgian
Borinage (documentary). *See Misère au Borinage*
Borinage: and cinema, 96; and Google, 89, 167–68; and MACs exhibition, 171; and mining and industry, 77, 84, 89, 100; and migration, 79, 97–98; photos of, 175, 176–79, 187f, 248; and Van Gogh, 79–80, 82, 84. *See also* Storck, Henri and Joris Ivens: *Misère au Borinage*
Bresson, Robert: and francophone-European film and philosophy, 5, 18; and Bazin, 54, 195, 198; and Christianity, 48, 54–55, 197–98, 224–25; and Dardennes and Dumont, 7, 18–19, 23, 44, 47–55, 230, 234, 238; and Deleuze, 217; and film funding, 138; and French New Wave, 192–93, 211; and Godard, 18–19, 35–36, 48, 226–30; and Paul Meyer, 97; and Pialat, 18, 47, 50–55, 113. *See also* Bresson, Robert, works of
Bresson, Robert, works of: *Au hazard Balthazar*, 43, 190, 227; *Dames du Bois de Boulogne*, 228; *Journal d'un curé de campagne*, 6, 23, 43, 47–55 passim, 59, 95, 97–98, 110, 112, 193–98 passim, 224, 230, 238; *Mouchette*, 6, 23, 47–55 passim, 234; *Pickpocket*, 204, 217, 227–28, 230, 275n38; *Un condamné à mort s'est échappé*, 138
Brexit, 8
Brussels (city): and Belgian state organization, 72, 74; and cinema, 13, 16, 77, 82, 84, 97, 103, 134, 147, 151–52, 158, 269n89; and cultural tension, 12; and Europe and EU, 5, 89, 168; and folklore, 123. *See also* Brussels-Capital (region)
Brussels-Capital (region), 16, 70, 72, 257–58n51, 268n70. *See also* Brussels (city)
Butler, Judith: on Foucault, 28–29
Buyens, Frans: *Vechten voor onze Rechten*, 101

Cabrera, Dominique: *Nadia et les hippopotames*, 145, 192
Caché. *See under* Haneke, Michael
Ça commence aujourd'hui. *See under* Tavernier, Bertrand
Cages. *See under* Masset-Depasse, Olivier
Cahiers du cinema: and Cannes 1999, 3, 6, 23; and French New Wave,

Cahiers du cinema (continued) 137, 211, 215; and *jeune cinema français*, 143; and realism, 97, 192, 204, 220
Calais encampment (the "jungle"), 8, 117
Cameron, James: *Titanic*, 68, 266n34
Camille Claudel, 1915. See under Dumont, Bruno, works of
Canal Plus, 130, 132, 141, 144, 160, 163, 267n55
Cannes International Film Festival, 160; (of 1955), 152; (of 1959), 137–38; (of 1963), 97; (of 1987), 1, 134; (of 1991), 156; (of 1997), 145; (of 1999), vi, 1–3, 6, 9, 12–13, 65, 129–30, 233; (of 2001), 158; (of 2004), 161; (of 2010), 147
Cantet, Laurent: *Emploi du temps*; *Entre les murs*, 19; and new realism, 19, 25, 206–207, 209; *Ressources humaines*, 145, 190, 192, 208
Capellani, André: *Germinal*, 13, 107, 110, 112, 121–22, 146; *Misérables*, 110, 261n92
capitalism, 17, 28–29, 84–85, 202–203, 208, 235, 244, 276n56
Carabiniers, Les. See under Godard, Jean-Luc, works of
Ça rend heureux. See under Lafosse, Joachim
carnival, 67, 116, 123–24, 170. See also *Karnaval*; *La Kermesse héroique*
Carion, Christian: *Joyeux Noël*, 146
Carrière, Christine: *Rosine*, 107, 113–14, 125
Cassavetes, John, 218
Cassenti, Frank: *Affiche rouge*, 263
Catholicism: and Bazin, 54, 198–99; and Bresson and Bernanos, 6, 50, 198–99, 225–26; and Dardennes and Dumont, 35, 41, 45, 59, 115, 230, 234; and Deleuze, 18, 199, 225, 237–38; and Godard, 226, 228; and neorealism, 210; and society 73–74, 86, 96, 103, 124, 259n69. See also Christianity; grace
Cauvin, André: *Bongolo*, 151
CGI, 203
C'est arrivé près de chez vous. See under Belvaux, Remy, André Bonzel, and Benoît Poelvoorde
Ch'ti culture and language, 15, 44, 68–70, 170, 261n92. See also *Bienvenu chez les Ch'tis*
Chabrol, Claude: *Cousins*, 138; on De Gaulle, 139; and realism, 211, 217; and French New Wave, 112, 137
Chacun pour soi. See under Bontzolakis, Bruno
Channel, The. See Pas-de-Calais (The Channel)
Chant du rossignol, Le. See under Dardenne, Jean-Pierre and Luc Dardenne, works of
Charleroi: and cinema, 101–103, 106, 260n75, 261n82; and cultural tension, 8, 120; and Magritte, 96; and mining and industry, 76–77, 79, 87; photos of, 175, 180, 186
Chez nous. See under Belvaux, Lucas
christ (with lowercase *c*), 19, 61–62, 230, 239
Christiaens, Isabelle: *Homme au harpoon*, 167
Christianity: and Bazin, 54–55, 222; and Bresson and Bernanos, 19, 36, 48, 54–55, 225, 238; and Dardennes and Dumont, 7, 9, 14–15, 19, 60, 62, 65, 125, 232–33, 239; and Deleuze, 237; and Easter egg, 14, 60; and Foucault, 27–28; and Godard, 36, 228, 237–38; and Hardt and Negri, 210; and Khleifi, 134; and Maxence van der Meersch, 82; and realism, 203, 211; and society, 88. See also Catholicism; grace
Chronique des saisons d'acier. See under Michel, Thierry

Cinéma du Nord: as cinematic movement, 11–12, 15, 17, 75, 92, 95, 119–27 passim, 171, 189; as critical fairy tale, 5, 19, 235; and debates in cinema studies, 10–11; and Dardennes and Dumont, 3, 8, 65; and French-Belgian border, 70, 107; as industry of film production, 12, 16, 132–36, 147, 162–64, 167; method of analysis and definition of, vi, 3, 5, 9, 11–13, 18–19, 68–70, 175, 216, 224; and new realism, 210
cinema of life, 103, 190–94 passim, 215–19, 234
Cinemascope, 30, 214
Cinematek, 13, 270n94
Cinémathèque Française, 3, 13, 148, 256n34
Circle, The. See under Panahi, Jafar
Cléo de 5 à 7. See under Varda, Agnès
climate catastrophe, 235
clouds, 3, 245
Club des 13, 143
CNC (Centre National du Cinéma et de l'Image Animée): and French national cinema, 137–38, 140, 142, 160; and *humanité*, 132; and regional cinema, 146; and *Rosetta*, 130; and Walloon cinema, 163
coal and coal mining: and Cinéma du Nord, 15–16; and French North and northern French cinema, 15–16, 47, 68, 77–92 passim, 108, 110; and Wallonia and Walloon cinema, 5, 8, 15–16, 75–92 passim, 100, 171, 254–55n17, 256n28; and Zola, 110
Cockerill (company), 76, 88, 101–102. See also *John Cockerill, toute une histoire*
Code inconnu: récit incomplet de divers voyages. See under Haneke, Michael
Coincoin et les z'inhumains. See under Dumont, Bruno, works of
colonialism and cinema, 150–51
computer game, 62, 167
Coninx, Stijn: *Daens*, 96
Convoyeurs attendant, Les. See under Mariage, Benoît
coproduction between Flanders and Wallonia, cinematic, 154, 270n97
coproduction, international cinematic: analysis of, 133; and Cinéma du Nord, 12, 163–65, 277n65; and francophone Belgian cinema, 16, 74, 119, 129–65 passim, 263n3, 271n115, 277n65; and French cinema, 113, 119, 129–65 passim, 264n10; and Palestinian cinema, 134, 265n14
Communauté Française de Belgique. See French Belgian Community
Cousins, Les. See under Chabrol, Claude
Couvelard, Michel: *Inséparables*, 267n59
Crime de Monsieur Lange, Le. See under Renoir, Jean
Cronaca di un amore. See under Antonioni, Michelangelo
CRRAV (Centre Régional de Ressources Audiovisuelles), 12, 129, 131–32, 136, 146–47, 160, 163–65, 264n10, 271n121. See also Pictanovo
Cyrano de Bergerac. See under Rappeneau, Jean-Paul

Daens. See under Coninx, Stijn
Dames du Bois de Boulogne, Les. See under Bresson, Robert, works of
Dans l'ombre. See under Masset-Depasse, Olivier
Daquin, Louis: *Point du jour*, 111–12
Dardenne, Jean-Pierre and Luc Dardenne: and Bresson, 18–19, 193, 224; Berlant on, 17, 29, 209, 238–39; and Dumont, 6–9, 18–19, 1–63 passim, 193, 220, 224, 230, 232–34, 238; and film production,

Dardenne, Jean-Pierre and Luc
  Dardenne (continued)
  129–30, 148, 158, 259n72, 277n65;
  and francophone Belgian cinema,
  129, 135, 148; and francophone-
  European film and philosophy, 5,
  18, 55, 193; and Godard, 18–19;
  Rancière on, 6, 23, 55–56, 62;
  and "Rosetta" Law, 65–67. See also
  Dardenne, Jean-Pierre and Luc
  Dardenne, works of; Dardenne,
  Luc: Au dos de nos images
Dardenne, Jean-Pierre and Luc
  Dardenne, works of: Chant du
  rossignol, 259n72; Deux jours, une
  nuit, 26, 36, 40, 232; Enfant,
  26–27, 36, 155, 204, 210, 230;
  Fils, 230; Gamin au vélo, 36, 156,
  233; Jeune Ahmed, 121; Lorsque le
  bateau de Léon M., 101–102; Pour
  que la guerre s'achève, 95, 101–102;
  Promesse, 26, 100, 190, 233,
  279–80n122; Rosetta, 1–67 passim,
  70, 92, 105, 129–30, 148, 155, 158,
  192, 207, 210, 233–34, 238, 247,
  251n1, 267n55; Silence de Lorna, 26,
  40, 106, 232–33
Dardenne, Luc: Au dos de nos images,
  40, 61, 279–80n122
Death of Mr. Lazarescu, The. See under
  Puiu, Cristi
Déjà s'envole la fleur maigre. See under
  Meyer, Paul
Dekeukeleire, Charles, 151;
  Impatience, 151; Visions de Lourdes,
  151
Deleuze, Gilles and Félix Guattari,
  41, 216
Deleuze, Gilles: on cinema, 17–18,
  50, 56, 194, 199–225 passim,
  237–40; and francophone-European
  film and philosophy, 5, 18; on
  immanence, 200, 240–43; on
  posthuman life and control society,
  236–37

Delvaux, André, 153–55; Belle, 154;
  Man die Zijn Haar Kort Liet
  Knippen, 153
Denis, Claire, 144; Beau travail, 145
Desplechin, Arnaud, 143, 147, 189,
  192; Ester Kahn, 192; Un conte de
  Noël, 147
Deux jours, une nuit. See under
  Dardenne, Jean-Pierre and Luc
  Dardenne, works of
digital cinema, 132, 194, 204,
  206–208, 223, 243
direct sound, 21, 30, 206, 233
Diva. See under Beineix, Jean-Jacques
documentary cinema: and Bouli
  Lanners, 260n75; and Dardennes,
  41–42, 62, 102–103; and
  Dekeukeleire, 151; and Khleifi,
  135; and new realist aesthetics,
  17, 190, 204, 222; and northern
  French cinema, 111, 117, 121,
  123, 262–63n105; online, 117, 167;
  and Richard Olivier, 260n75; and
  Storck (and Ivens), 15, 83, 103,
  151, 261n83; and Thierry Michel,
  90f, 101, 103, 259n71; and Varda,
  217; and Wallonia, 15–16, 69–70,
  76, 96, 105, 121, 123, 167, 258n58
Donnie Darko. See under Kelly, Richard
Dormael, Jaco van: Toto le héros,
  155–56
dragons, 19, 124–25
Du beurre dans les tartines. See under
  Bonmariage, Manu
Dumas, Alexandre: Trois mousquetaires,
  110, 262n93
Dumont, Bruno: and Bresson, 5,
  18, 35, 43; and Dardennes, 1–65
  passim, 193, 220, 224, 230, 232–34,
  238; and francophone-European
  film and philosophy, 5, 18, 55,
  193; and jeune cinema français, 143,
  145; and northern French cinema,
  121–22, 146–47; Rancière on, 6,
  23, 30, 42, 55–56, 59–60, 62; and

screen-acting, 36, 43–46. *See also* Dumont, Bruno, works of
Dumont, Bruno, works of: *Camille Claudel*, 44; *Coincoin*, 45, 113–14, 233; *Flandres*, 113–14, 190, 233; *Hadewijch*, 45, 113–16, 164, 210, 233, 264n10; *Hors Satan*, 45, 210, 233, 264n10; *humanité*, 1–65 passim, 70, 89–90, 92, 109, 113–16, 125, 129, 132–33, 148, 192, 204, 207, 210, 230, 233, 238–39, 251–52n14, 267n55; *Jeanne*, 175; *Jeannette, l'enfance de Jeanne d'Arc*, 45, 175; *Ma Loute*, 44, 113–14, 184f, 233; *P'tit Quinquin*, 113–15, 116, 207, 233; *Twentynine Palms*, 233, 264n10; *Vie de Jésus*, 35, 43–45, 113–14, 145, 191, 210, 233

Easter egg: in Christianity/cinema/computing, 13–14, 60; in *l'humanité*, 23, 60; in *Rosetta*, 23, 38–39, 60, 233
Eau froide, L'. *See under* Assayas, Olivier
Eclisse, L. *See under* Antonioni, Michelangelo
Egoyan, Atom: *Felicia's Journey*, 3
Eldorado. *See under* Lanners, Bouli
Eloge de l'amour. *See under* Godard, Jean-Luc, works of
Emploi du temps, L'. *See under* Cantet, Laurent
Empreinte du dieu, L'. *See under* Moguy, Léonide
En avoir (ou pas). *See under* Masson, Laetitia
Enfance nue, L'. *See under* Pialat, Maurice
Enfant, L'. *See under* Dardenne, Jean-Pierre and Luc Dardenne, works of
Enfants du Borinage: lettre à Henri Storck, Les. *See under* Jean, Patricean
Enfants du Hasard. *See under* Michel, Thierry and Pascal Colson

Entre les murs. *See under* Cantet, Laurent
Entre ses mains. *See under* Fontaine, Anne
Essiyedali, Youssef and Louisette Faréniaux: *Au pays des mille et un puits*, 263n105
Ester Kahn. *See under* Desplechin, Arnaud
Et la vie. *See under* Gheerbrant, Denis
ethics: and Bazin, 198, 200; and Cinéma du Nord, 123; and Deleuze, 225; and methodology, 19; and new realism, 17, 193, 238; and parochial power, 28; and Spinoza, 241–43
Eurimages, 11, 156, 270n104
Europa '51. *See under* Rossellini, Roberto
Europe, 208, 236, 258n57, 263n5, 270n105. *See also* European Union
European Coal and Steel Community (ESCS), 86
European Regional Development Fund (ERDF), 91, 258
European Union, 5, 8, 86–87, 91, 133
Euroregion across French-Belgian border, 10, 74–75, 91–92; and cinema, 16, 129, 163–66, 171
Euroregion, cross-Channel, 257–58n51
Euroregion: notion of, 91
Eustache, Jean, 193, 218; *Maman et la putain*, 218
everyday life. *See under* life
expression (as in difference from representation), 213, 215, 217, 237, 242, 244, 278n88

fairy tale: Cinéma du Nord as critical, 5, 19, 122–23, 235; cinematic examples of, 16, 18, 63, 157, 238; "happily ever after," 234; "once upon a time," 1
Faut-il aimer Mathilde? See under Baily, Edwin

Felicia's Journey. See under Egoyan, Atom
Fellini, Federico, 200; *Notti di Cabiria*, 57
Ferran, Pascale, 143, 189, 192; *Petits arrangements avec les morts*, 190
Fêtes de Belgiques, Les. See under Storck, Henri
Feyder, Jacques: *Kermesse héroïque*, 150
fiction cinema: and acting, 36, 45, 234, 244; and Cinéma du Nord, 16, 65, 121, 123, 135–36; and cinematic production, 11, 98, 146, 162, 270n97; and documentary, 65, 96–97, 103, 121, 217, 222, 275n35; and French North, 117, 146, 262–63n105; and Wallonia, 16, 96–98, 103, 105–106, 158, 259n72
Fille de la route, La. See under Terme, Louis
Filles des fraudeurs, Les. See under Meyst, E. G. de
Film socialisme. See under Godard, Jean-Luc, works of
Fils, Le. See under Dardenne, Jean-Pierre and Luc Dardenne, works of
Fin août, début septembre. See under Assayas, Olivier
Flanders: and Belgian history, 72, 74–75, 78–79, 135, 257n51, 259n69; and cinema, 96, 107, 150, 154, 160, 258n52; and folklore, 123–24; and migration to Wallonia, 8, 78, 88; and tension with Wallonia, 121, 149. *See also* French Flanders
Flandres. See under Dumont, Bruno, works of
Flaubert, Gustave, 201, 203; *Madame Bovary*, 55
Flemish cinema. *See* Flanders: and cinema
Flemish Community (Vlaamse Gemeenschap), 71–72, 149
Flemish Region. *See* Flanders
Florida Project, The. See under Baker, Sean

Fontaine, Anne: *Entre ses mains*, 147, 164
Fonteyne, Frédéric: *Une liaison pornographique*, 155
Francesco giullare di Dio. See under Rossellini, Roberto
francophone Belgium. *See* French Community of Belgium
French Community of Belgium (Communauté Française de Belgique): and Belgian state organization, 72, 159; cinema of, 135; and cinematic production and funding, 130, 153, 159–60, 163; and coproduction agreements, 160–61, 271n115. *See also* Wallonie-Bruxelles, Fédération
French Flanders, 68, 71–72, 115, 145, 254n6, 255n23
French national cinema: decentralization of, 121, 140, 145, 190; and francophone Belgian cinema, 16, 136, 150, 160, 162; northern French cinema within, 16, 108–109, 112, 125, 135–48 passim
French New Wave. *See* New Wave, French
French North: cinema of, 1, 15–16, 51, 53, 61, 67–70, 106–25 passim, 145, 156, 166, 189–90, 223, 261n85, 261–62n92, 262–63n105; and cinematic production and funding, 10–12, 130–37, 146–47, 160, 163–65, 171, 263n2, 264n10; and coal and industry, 75–78, 86–87, 89–91, 255–56n27; culture of, 44, 68, 70, 122–24, 169, 254n6, 261–62n92; and Dumont, 23, 32, 35, 45, 47, 50, 145; and economy and society, 92, 94–95, 257n40, 258n52, 258n55, 258n57; and French-Walloon Nord, 5; and literature, 32, 35, 82–83, 111, 261n85, 261–62n92; and Louvre-Lens museum, 169; and migration, 8, 117–21; photos of, 175, 181–85,

187; and Pialat, 23, 51, 109, 112, 114–15, 147; regional history of, 5, 70–75, 254n15, 257n51; and Varda, 223. *See also* Hauts-de-France, Nord-Pas-de-Calais
Front National, 8, 189
funding (in cinema), 11–12, 69, 131–66 passim

Gamin au vélo, Le. See under Dardenne, Jean-Pierre and Luc Dardenne, works of
Garrone, Matteo: *Gomorrah*, 17, 204
Gaul (region), 72
Gaulle, Charles de, 138–40, 170, 229
Géants, Les. See under Lanners, Bouli
Germanophone Community of Belgium, 72, 257–58n51, 270n94
Germanio anno zero. See under Rossellini, Roberto
Germinal (André Capellani). *See under* Capellani, André
Germinal (Claude Berri). *See under* Berri, Claude
Germinal (Emile Zola). *See under* Zola, Emile
Germinal (Yves Allégret). *See under* Allégret, Yves
gesture: Agamben on, 46; and Dardennes, 36–38, 46, 56, 102, 209; Deleuze on, 218, 220
Gheerbrant, Denis: *Et la vie*, 106, 262n105
Ghost Dog: The Way of the Samurai. See under Jarmush, Jim
giants, 19, 79, 100, 116–17, 123–25, 145, 167, 170–71, 223, 263n107. *See also* Lanners, Bouli: *Géants*
Giovanna d'Arco al rogo. See under Rossellini, Roberto
Glâneur et la glaneuse, Le. See under Varda, Agnès
globalization, 10, 193, 208–209, 211
God: and absence of, 7, 9, 23, 50, 53–55, 61, 125, 230, 233, 238–39; and *Nouvelle histoire de Mouchette*

(Bernanos), 47; and human, 213; and Adorno, 276n56; and Spinoza, 196, 224, 242
Godard, Jean-Luc, 5, 18; and Bresson, 18, 35–36, 226–27, 238; and Dumont and Dardennes, 18–19, 102, 238; and New Wave, 112, 137, 192–93, 211, 222, 237; and Varda, 223. *See also* Godard, Jean-Luc, works of
Godard, Jean-Luc, works of: *A bout de souffle*, 222, 237; *Adieu au langage*, 227, 229–30, 238; *Carabiniers*, 192, 212, 214, 260; *Éloge de l'amour*, 228–31; *Film socialisme*, 229–31, 277–78n86; *Histoire(s) du cinema*, 228; *Je vous salue, Marie*, 227, 230, 237–38; *King Lear*, 227; *Livre d'image*, 230; *Masculin féminin*, 237; *Mépris*, 214–15, 227, 260; *Mouchette* (trailer for), 48; *Nouvelle vague*, 227–28, 231f *Petit soldat*, 215, 277–78n86
Godard, Jean-Luc and Jean-Pierre Gorin, 102; *Vent d'Est*, 259–60n73; *Tout va bien*, 259–60n73
Godard, Jean-Luc, Jean-Pierre Gorin, and Anne-Marie Miéville, 102; *Ici et ailleurs*, 259–60n73
Gogh, Vincent van: 12, 84, 99; *Aardappeleters*, 79–80; life in Borinage, 17, 80, 167–68, 175, 178
Gomorrah. See under Garrone, Matteo
Google, 17, 57, 69, 89, 93, 167–68
grace: and Bazin, 53, 198, 222; and Bresson, 50–51, 53–55, 224–25, 238; and Dardennes and Dumont, 9, 19, 53–55, 60, 62, 230, 238; and Godard, 19, 224–25, 230, 238; and Pascal, 55; and posthuman renouncement of longing for, 244
Grand paysage d'Alexis Droeven, Le. See under Andrien, Jean-Jacques
Grande illusion, La. See under Renoir, Jean

Gueule ouverte, La. See under Pialat, Maurice
Guesnier, Alain: *Va Petite!*, 271n122
Guiraudie, Alain: *Inconnu du lac*, 147

Habermas, Jürgen, 18
Hadewijch. See under Dumont, Bruno, works of
Hainaut, 68, 72, 76, 78, 91, 258n57, and cinema, 163–64
Haine, La. See under Kassovitz, Matthieu
handheld shooting, 21, 30, 113, 192
Haneke, Michael: *Caché*, 14; *Code inconnu*, 208, 219; on Godard, 278n86; *Happy end*, 113, 117, 147
Hänsel, Marion: *Between the Devil and the Deep Blue Sea*, 154–55; *Sur la terre comme au ciel*, 154
Happy End. See under Haneke, Michael
Hardt, Michael, 5; and discussion with Berlant, 240–42
Hardt, Michel, and Antonio Hardt: *Empire*, 18, 209–10, 238
Hausner, Jessica: *Lovely Rita*, 204
Hauts-de-France, 5, 70–75, 117, 136, 145. See also Nord-Pas-de-Calais; Picardy
Hay Po l'jou. See under Bonmariage, Manu
Heusch, Luc de: *Jeudi on chantera comme Dimanche*, 100, 105, 158
Herbe sous les pieds, L'. See under Meyer, Paul
Hiroshima mon amour. See under Resnais, Alain
Histoire(s) du cinema. See under Godard, Jean-Luc, works of
Hitchcock, Alfred, 137
Hiver 60. See under Michel, Thierry
Hollywood, 97, 156; Classical, 194, 199, 212, 237
Home. See under Meier, Ursula
Homme au harpon, L'. See under Christiaens, Isabelle

Hors Satan. See under Dumont, Bruno, works of
Hugo, Victor: "Happy Life" (poem), 79; *Misérables*, 110, 261n92
humanism: and acting/acted image, 222; and Bazin, 197–99, 203; and Dardennes and Dumont, 15, 63, 193, 233; definitions of, 17; minimal, 17, 23; and neorealism, 198–99; and new realism, 17, 19, 211, 216–17; and northern French cinema, 111, 113; and posthumanism, 18, 210, 235, 237–40, 245; and Walloon cinema, 103
humanité, L'. See under Dumont, Bruno, works of

Ici et ailleurs. See under Godard, Jean-Luc, Jean-Pierre Gorin, and Anne-Marie Miéville
Ile-de-France: and cinematic production and funding, 264n10, 267n58, 108, 145; and French-Walloon Nord, 79, 86
Illégal. See under Masset-Depasse, Olivier
immanence: and approach of Nord and Cinéma du Nord, 11–12, 19, 75, 124; and causality, 215–16; and cinematic plot space, 47, 60, 199–200; and Dardennes and Dumont, 26, 233; of global networks, 208; and Hardt & Negri, 18, 209–10; plane of, 216; and postsecular turn, 18–19; and Spinoza and Deleuze, 224–25, 239–44
Impatience. See under Dekeukeleire, Charles
Import/Export. See under Seidl, Ulrich
Inconnu du lac, L'. See under Guiraudie, Alain
indexicality: and cinema, 194–97, 216, 274n15, 274–75n22, 277n82. See also monster: *monstrum*
Industrial Revolution, First, 5, 74, 255n17

In Public. See under Jia Zhangke
Inséparables. See under Couvelard, Michel
Interreg program cycles, European Union's, 65, 91–92, 163, 257n50, 258n52, 258n57
interregional: and Cinéma du Nord, 3, 12, 122, 163; and Nord, 70. *See also* border and border region, French-Belgian; Cinéma du Nord; Interreg; Nord, French-Walloon
intuition, 219; posthuman, 242–43
Iñárritu, Alejandro González: *Babel*, 208
Italian neorealism. *See under* neorealism
Ivens, Joris, 84. *See also under* Storck, Henri and Joris Ivens

Jameson, Fredric; on realism, 207–208
Jansen, Cornelius, 50. *See also* Jansenism
Jansenism, 50, 226
Jarmusch, Jim: *Ghost Dog: The Way of the Samurai*, 3
Jean, Patric: *Enfants du Borinage: lettre à Henri Storck*, 106
Jeanne. See under Dumont, Bruno, works of
Jeanne Dielman: 23 Quai du Commerce, 1080 Bruxelles. See under Akerman, Chantal
Jeannette, l'enfance de Jeanne d'Arc. See under Dumont, Bruno, works of
Jeudi on chantera comme Dimanche. See under Heusch, Luc de
Jeune Ahmed, Le. See under Dardenne, Jean-Pierre and Luc Dardenne, works of
jeune cinéma français: and *Cahiers du cinema*, 143; critiques of, 190–93; definitions of, 143–45, 189; and new realism, 204, 206, 211, 213, 216–17
Je vous salue, Marie. See under Godard, Jean-Luc, works of

Jia Zhangke, 204, 207–208; *In Public*, 206; *Pickpocket*, 204; *Still Life*, 17, 19, 204–205; *World*, 204–205, 208
John Cockerill, toute une histoire. See under Balteau, Bernard
Journal d'un curé de campagne (Georges Bernanos). *See under* Bernanos, Georges
Journal d'un curé de campagne (Robert Bresson). *See under* Bresson, Robert, works of
Joyeux Noël. See under Carion, Christian
"jungle," the. *See* Calais encampment (the "jungle")
Jurassic Park. See under Spielberg, Steven

Kameradschaft/La Tragédie de la mine. See under Pabst, Georg Wilhelm
Karnaval. See under Vincent, Thomas
Kassovitz, Matthieu: *Haine*, 190
Kechiche, Abdellatif: *Vie d'Adèle, La*, 147
Kelly, Richard: *Donnie Darko*, 62
Kempen, De (region), 79
Kermesse héroïque, La. See under Feyder, Jacques
Khleifi, Michel, 134–35, 265n17; *Mémoire fertile*, 135; *Noce en Galilée*, 134; *Ordre du jour*, 134. *See also under* Khleifi, Michel and Eyal Sivan
Khleifi, Michel and Eyal Sivan: *Route 181: Fragments of a Journey in Israel-Palestine*, 134
Kiarostami, Abbas: *Ten*, 204
King Lear. See under Godard, Jean-Luc, works of
Klinkaart. See under Meyer, Paul
Kracauer, Siegfried, 10, 275n35
Kuypers, Rik, Ivo Michiels, and Ronald Verhavert: *Meeuwen Sterven in de Haven*, 152

labor movement: and (northern) France, 84, 262–63n105; and

labor movement *(continued)*
subjectivity, 8; and Wallonia and Belgium, 77, 84, 86, 100, 102, 259n70
Ladri di biciclette. See under Sica, Vittorio de
Ladro di bambini, Il. See under Amelio, Gianni Amelio
Lafosse, Joachim, 159; *Ça rend heureux*, 155; *Nue propriété*, 155, 260n78
Lampin, Georges: *Maison dans la dune*, 107, 110, 261n85
Lang, Fritz, 214
Lang, Jack (French Minister of Culture), 140, 141, 144, 146
Lanners, Bouli, 155–59, 261n82; *Eldorado*, 106, 155–57, 270n105; *Géants*, 155–57; *Premiers, les derniers*, 156–57; *Travellinckx*, 260n75; *Ultranova*, 100
Lens: in cinema, 113, 119; and coal mining and industry, 111, 168; and French-Walloon Nord, 76; photos of, 175, 181. *See also* Louvre-Lens, museum of
Liège (city): in cinema, 100, 106; and cinematic production, 130, 158, 165; and coal mining and industry, 76–78, 88; and Dardennes, 5, 24, 37, 101, 130; and French-Walloon Nord, 72, 75–76; Liège-Guillemins railway station, 12, 89–90, 95, 174–75; photos of, 175–76, 187, 248; and tension around migration, 8, 120
Liège (province), 72, 257n51
Liévin, 111, 113; photos of, 175, 182–83
life: and Badiou, 225; and Berlant, 29, 208, 241–42; and Deleuze, 18, 215, 237, 240; everyday life, 5, 8, 119, 200, 202–203, 243; and hardship, 68, 79, 101, 103, 105, 111; and Jansenism, 50; life narrative, 244; notion of "human" life, 17, 21, 25, 27, 56, 103, 123, 206–207, 209, 211, 222, 240, 245; notion of "normal" life, 6, 23–41 passim, 56, 67, 125, 167, 230, 239; and power, 28–30, 57, 125; and precarity, 25, 29; and screen acting, 44, 46–47; and Spinoza, 242–43; struggle for "better" life, 105, 125, 156, 200. *See also* cinema of life, intuition, love
Lille: and Dumont, 6, 32, 35, 43; and cinema, 54, 67, 111, 113, 123, 125, 136, 146–47, 164; and economy and industry, 32, 78; and folklore, 124; and French-Walloon Nord, 71, 92–93; 89; and Lille-Europe railway station, 12, 89–90; Victor Hugo on, 79
Limburg, Belgian, 51, 74
Limburg, Dutch, 75, 79, 175, 255–56n27, 261n83
Lioret, Philippe: *Welcome*, 113, 117, 147, 189–91
Lynch, David: *Straight Story*, 3
literature: and archive of analysis, 12; and adaptations of French cinema, 110; and Bazin's ideal of realism, 54, 193; and realism in, 200–202, 207
Livre d'image. See under Godard, Jean-Luc, works of
location shooting: and Cinéma du Nord, 163–65; and cinematic realism, 190, 200, 204, 214; and Dumont, 184; and northern French cinema, 108, 111, 134, 146; and Walloon cinema, 96, 103, 135
Lorsque le bateau de Léon M. descendit la Meuse pour la première fois. See *under* Dardenne, Jean-Pierre and Luc Dardenne, works of
Louvre-Lens, museum of, 17, 69, 167–70
love, 18, 37, 83, 98, 105, 107, 113, 117–18, 147, 175, 187, 197–98,

202–203, 208, 215, 218–30, 234–48.
  See also life
Lovely Rita. See under Hausner, Jessica
Lukács, Georg, 202, 207, 276n56
Lust for Life. See under Minnelli,
  Vincente and George Cukor
Lvovsky, Noémi: Vie ne me fait pas
  peur, 192

Maastricht Treaty on European
  Union, The, 5, 87, 140
Maastricht, 72, 248
Maboul du quartier, Le. See under
  Riquita
Macron, Emmanuel, 119
MACs (museum), 171
Madame Bovary. See under Flaubert,
  Gustave
Magritte, René, 12, 42, 96; Chambre
  d'écoute, 33
Mais qu'est-ce qu'elles veulent? See
  under Serreau, Coline
Maison dans la dune, La. See under
  Lampin, Georges
Maison dans la lune, La (George
  Lampin). See under Lampin,
  George
male gaze, 35, 45, 147
Ma Loute. See under Dumont, Bruno,
  works of
Malraux, André, 138–40, 170
Maman et la putain, La. See under
  Eustache, Jean
Mamma Roma. See under Pasolini,
  Pier Paolo
Man die Zijn Haar Kort Liet Knippen,
  De. See under Delvaux, André
Mange ta soupe. See under Amalric,
  Mathieu
Ma nuit chez Maud. See under
  Rohmer, Eric
Marchienne de vie. See under Olivier,
  Richard
Marcinelle: 1956 mine catastrophe of,
  79; photo of, 180

Mariage, Benoît, 25; Convoyeurs
  attendent, 100, 106, 155–56, 261n82,
  270n105
Marks, Laura: on tactile vision
Marseille, 98; and cinema, 108, 122,
  145
Marx, Karl, and Marxism, 84–85,
  209
Masculin, féminin. See under Godard,
  Jean-Luc, works of
Masset-Depasse, Olivier, 147,
  271n111; Cages, 163; Dans l'ombre,
  163; Illégal, 106, 270n105
Masson, Laetitia: En avoir (ou pas),
  122
Matrix, The. See under Wachowski,
  Lana, and Lily Wachowski
Ma vie en rose. See under Berliner,
  Alain
Mazuy, Patricia: Peaux de vache,
  267n59
MEDIA program (European Union),
  11, 133, 156
Meersch, Maxence van der: Maison
  dans la dune, 107, 110, 261n85;
  Quand les sirènes se taisent, 82–83
Meeuwen Sterven in de Haven. See
  under Kuypers, Rik, Ivo Michiels,
  and Ronald Verhavert
Meier, Ursula, 271n111; Home, 155
Memento. See under Nolan, Christopher
Mémoire fertile, La. See under Khleifi,
  Michel
Mémoires de la mine. See under
  Renard, Jacques, 262–63n105
Mépris, Le. See under Godard, Jean-
  Luc, works of
Métamorphose d'une gare. See under
  Michel, Thierry
Meyer, Paul: Déjà s'envole la fleur
  maigre, 16, 97–105, 123, 125, 152,
  155–56, 158, 259n68; Herbe sous les
  pieds, 259n68; Klinkaart, 97
Meyst, E. G: Filles des fraudeurs,
  261n84

Michel, Thierry: *Chronique des saisons d'acier*, 259n71; *Hiver 60*, 100–101, 158; *Métamorphose d'une gare*, 90; *Pays noir, pays rouge*, 100–101. See also under Michel, Thierry and Pascal Colson

Michel, Thierry and Pascal Colson: *Enfants du Hasard*, 103–104

migration: and French North and northern French cinema, 8, 113, 116–17, 119–20, 190, 255n23; and *jeune cinema français*, 189–90; and Jia's *The World*, 208; and Wallonia and Walloon cinema, 8, 40, 78–79, 97–98, 102–103, 106, 255n24, 262–63n105. See also Calais encampment; xenophobia

mimesis, 191, 193, 195, 200–201, 204, 212, 217

mind-game film, 14, 62

Minnelli, Vincente and George Cukor: *Lust for Life*, 80–81

miracle: and Badiou's notion of event, 229; concept of, 9, 209–10; and Dardennes, 62–63, 233–34; and Dumont, 53, 55, 60, 62–63, 115, 234; Italy's economic, 203; and *Journal d'un curé de campagne*, 54; and late Godard, 227; notion of immanent, 209, 224–25, 233, 238, 243. See also *Miracolo a Milano*; miraculous realism

Miracolo a Milano. See under Sica, Vittorio de

miraculous realism, 3, 175, 204, 230, 238, 245

Misérables, Les (André Capellani). See under Capellani, André

Misérables, Les (Victor Hugo). See under Hugo, Victor

Mitterand, François, 140

modern: cinema, 112, 127, 154, 193–94, 199, 204, 211–18 passim, 222, 237–38, 259–60n73; literature, 110, 276n56; subject and society, 8, 18, 27–28, 41, 57, 77, 201–203, 236, 243–44

Moguy, Léonide: *Empreinte du dieu*, 261n85

Mollenard. See under Siodmak, Robert

Mons: and French-Walloon Nord, 76–78; and Google, 17, 89, 167–68; photos of, 178, 180; and society, 84, 123

monster: bête humaine, 35; of Loch Ness, 159; *monstrum*, 216; and *Rosetta*, 193

montage, 101, 192; and Godard, 19, 223, 227, 229–30, 234, 238; Russian, 84

Moreau, Yolanda and Gilles Porte: *Quand la mer monte*, 16, 123, 146, 149, 155

Mouchette. See under Bresson, Robert, works of

Mouchette (trailer). See under Godard, Jean-Luc, works of

Mulvey, Laura: on pensive spectator, 62

Mungiu, Christian: *4 Months, 3 Weeks, 2 Days*, 17, 204; *Beyond the Hills*, 277n65

Mur, Le. See under Berliner, Alain

Nadia et les hippopotames. See under Cabrera, Dominique

national cinema, 10–12, 16. See also Belgian national cinema, French national cinema

Negri, Antonio, 5. See also Hardt, Michael, and Antonio Negri: *Empire*

neorealism: and Bazin, 105, 198–216 passim; and Deleuze, 212, 215–17, 222; and French New Wave, 212, 214–17; Italian, 26–27, 97, 193, 198–216 passim, 232–33, 237–38, 275n35; and new realism, 17, 204, 206–208, 211; and northern French cinema, 110, 112; and Walloon cinema, 16, 96, 98, 103, 105

Netherlands, The: and ECSC, 86; and French-Walloon Nord, 72, 74, 76, 79, 92, 94; and Van Gogh, 80

new realism: Berlant on, 17, 208–209, 238; and Cinéma du Nord, 127, 210, 233, 235, 239; ethics and aesthetics of, 17, 19, 25, 193–94, 204–17 passim, 233; Jameson on, 207–208; and *jeune cinema français*, 190, 211, 216; after modern cinema, 17, 127, 211, 216–17; of modern cinema, 212–13

New Wave, French, 112, 138, 143, 211

Noce en Galilée. See under Khleifi, Michel

Nolan, Christopher: *Memento*, 62

Nord, the French-Walloon: and cinematic production, 16, 136, 164, 166, 171; definition and approach of, 5, 9, 11–13, 75; and expression in cinema, 15–16, 23, 68–70, 79, 82, 95, 98, 121–24, 136, 189, 233–34; history of, 5, 8, 73–95 passim, 167, 236; photos of, 17, 175–87. *See also* Cinéma du Nord

Nord (department), 71, 78, 86, 257n39. *See also* Hauts-de-France, Nord-Pas-de-Calais

Nord (film). *See under* Beauvois, Xavier

Nord-Pas-de-Calais: and 1982 Decentralization Law, 74–75, 145; merger with Picardy into Hauts-de-France, 71, 131. *See also* French North; Hauts-de-France

Normandie, 223

north wind, 1, 8, 11; as miracle in *Rosetta*, 38–39, 55, 61

northern France. *See* French North

Notti di Cabiria, Le. *See under* Fellini, Federico

Nouvelle histoire du Mouchette. *See under* Bernanos, Georges

Nouvelle vague. *See under* Godard, Jean-Luc, works of

Nue propriété. *See under* Lafosse, Joachim

Olivier, Richard: *Au fond Dutroux*, 260n75; *Marchienne de vie*, 100, 102–103

Ordre du jour, L'. *See under* Khleifi, Michel

outdoor shooting. *See* location shooting

Pabst, Georg Wilhelm: *Kameradschaft/La Tragédie de la mine*, 111; *Passeurs d'or*, 261n84

Page blanche, La. *See under* Assayas, Olivier

painting: and approach of Nord and Cinéma du Nord, 12; and Dumont, 42–43; and *Kermesse héroique*, 150; and *Convoyeurs attendent*, 261n82. *See also* Magritte, René; Gogh, Vincent van

Palestine, 259–60n73; and cinema, 134–35, 265n14

Panahi, Jafar: *Circle*, 204

Paris nous appartient. *See under* Rivette, Jacques

Paris: and Balzac, 202; and centralization of French culture, 138–39, 168–70; and cinema archives, 13, 175; and cinematic production and infrastructure, 97, 145; and francophone Belgian cinema, 148–50, 153, 160; and French New Wave, 112, 212, 217, 222; and relation to French North, 67, 89, 107–109, 114, 121, 136; and *jeune cinema français*, 189–90, 202; representations of and references to, 35–36, 98, 115, 164

Paris basin (geophysical), 75

parochial power: crisis of 19, 56, 62, 235, 243; Foucault on, 27

Parti Socialiste (France), 117

Parti Socialiste (Wallonia), 120, 268n70
Pascal, Blaise, 5, 18, 50, 55, 224–27
Pas-de-Calais (department): and Bernanos, 47; and cinema, 111, 117, 119; and coal mining, 78, 257n39; and French state organization, 71, 73. *See also* Hauts-de-France, Nord-Pas-de-Calais
Pas-de-Calais (The Channel), 70, 117
Pasolini, Pier Paolo: *Accattone*, 203, 232; *Mamma Roma*, 203
Passe ton bac d'abord. *See under* Pialat, Maurice
Passeurs d'or. *See under* Meyst, E. G.
patriarchy, 18–19, 34, 44–45, 63, 238, 245. *See also* male gaze
Pays noir, pays rouge. *See under* Michel, Thierry
Peaux de vache. *See under* Mazuy, Patricia
Pen, Marine le, 8, 117, 119
Petit soldat, Le. *See under* Godard, Jean-Luc, works of
Petit voleur, Le. *See under* Zonca, Erick
Petits arrangements avec les morts. *See under* Ferran, Pascale
photography: aerial 92; and Cartier-Bresson, 261n82; and Christian Boltanski, 171; and cinema's ontology, 194–98, 214; and the French-Walloon Nord, 171, 175–87, 214, 223; and *Visages villages*, 223
Pialat, Maurice: *A nos amours*, 216, 218–21, 278–79n105; and Cannes 1987, 1; *Enfance nue*, 112–15, 217–18, 222; and francophone-European film and philosophy, 5, 18, 55, 193; and French New Wave, 112, 217; and French North, 109, 112; *Gueule ouverte*, 218; *Passe ton bac d'abord*, 112–13; *Sous le soleil de Satan*, 1, 6, 23, 47, 50–55, 95, 112–13, 147, 210; *Van Gogh*, 219

Picard, 44, 48, 68, 72, 254n6. *See also* Ch'ti culture and language
Picardy, 5, 68, 70–71, 75, 117, 131, 136, 145. *See also* Hauts-de-France
Picasso, Pablo, 151, 227–29
Pickpocket (Robert Bresson). *See under* Bresson, Robert, works of
Pickpocket/Xiao Wu. *See under* Jia Zhangke
Pictanovo, 12, 131, 146–47, 163, 165–66. *See also* CRRAV
Pierre et Djemila. *See under* Blain, Gérard
Plages d'Agnès, Les. *See under* Varda, Agnès
plot-space (in cinema), 14, 63, 199, 207
Point du jour, Le. *See under* Daquin, Louis
Poirier, Manuel, 145
posthuman, 17–18, 210, 215–17, 222, 225, 235–44 passim
postindustrial, 8, 25, 27, 29, 89 194
postmodern and postmodernism, 18–19, 208
postsecular, 14, 18–19, 63, 244
Pour que la guerre s'achève, les murs devaient s'écrouter. *See under* Dardenne, Jean-Pierre and Luc Dardenne, works of
precarity: cinema of, 17, 26, 41, 208–209, 236, 238–39; and postindustrial economy, 8–9, 92, 194; and subjectivity, 56, 222, 240
Premiers, les derniers, Les. *See under* Lanners, Bouli
Promesse, La. *See under* Dardenne, Jean-Pierre and Luc Dardenne, works of
P'tit Quinquin. *See under* Dumont, Bruno, works of
Puiu, Cristi: *Death of Mr. Lazarescu*, 204

Quand la mer monte. *See under* Moreau, Yolande and Gilles Porte

Quand les sirens se taisent (Maxence van der Meersch). *See under* Meersch, Maxence van der
Question, The, 19, 35, 55, 224–30 passim, 238

Raison du plus faible, La. See under Belvaux, Lucas
Rancière, Jacques, 5, 200–202; on *Rosetta* and *humanité*, 6, 23, 30, 42, 55–63, 239
Rappeneau, Jean-Paul: *Cyrano de Bergerac*, 108
realism: and Bazin, 54, 193–98, 204, 211–12, 274n14; classical, 125, 212; and Dardennes, 21, 26, 30, 102; and Dumont, 35, 42, 44, 60, 233; and literature, 110, 201–202; magic, 155; and northern French cinema, 109–10, 123; and philosophy, 241; and Pialat, 220–22; social, 84, 124; and Walloon cinema, 105, 123, 155–56. *See also* miraculous realism; neorealism; new realism
region: concept of, 216; and posthuman, 236. *See also* border and border region, French-Belgian; Borinage; Brussels-Capital (region); Euroregio, notion of; Flanders; Gaul; Hainaut; Hauts-de-France; Limburg, Belgian; Limburg, Dutch; Nord, French-Walloon; Nord-Pas-de-Calais; Picardie; regional cinema; Wallonia
regional cinema: notion of, vi, 10–12. *See also* northern French cinema; Walloon cinema
Reichardt, Kelly: *Wendy and Lucy*, 17, 204
Renard, Jacques: *Blanche et Marie*, 262–63n105; *Mémoires de la mine*, 262–63n105
Renoir, Jean, 195, 220; *Crime de Monsieur Lange*, 107, 110; *Grande illusion*, 150

representation: and Bazin, 197–98, 200; crisis and modern critiques of, 19, 125, 127, 193, 211, 214, 230, 235; and Deleuze, 200, 213, 237; and democracy, 236, 244; and Godard, 214–15, 230, 259–60n73; and indexicality in cinema, 274–75n22; and new realist belief in, 17, 127, 211, 279n122; and Rancière, 200–201. *See also* expression
Resnais, Alain, 138; *Année dernière à Marienbad*, 192; *Hiroshima mon amour*, 138
Ressources humaines. See under Cantet, Laurent
Reynaert, Phillipe, 130–31, 263–64n5
Rien à declarer. See under Boon, Dany
Rien à faire. See under Vernoux, Marion
Riquita: *Maboul du quartier*, 262–63n105
Rivette, Jacques, 137; *Paris nous appartient*, 212
Rocco e i suoi Fratelli. See under Visconti, Luchino
Rohmer, Eric, 138–39, 192, 211; *Ma nuit chez Maud*, 138
Roma: città aperta. See under Rossellini, Roberto
Rosetta. See under Dardenne, Jean-Pierre and Luc Dardenne, works of
Rosine. See under Carrière, Christine
Rossellini, Roberto: Deleuze on, 237; *Europa '51*, 203; *Francesco giullare di Dio*, 210; *Germanio anno zero*, 100; *Giovanna d'Arco al rogo*, 237; and Godard 214; and neorealism, 198, 200, 210–11; *Roma: città aperta*, 203, 275n35; *Viaggio in Italia*, 203, 214
Roubaix: and cinema, 45, 147; and politics and society, 67, 78, 82, 255n23, 257n40; and textile industry, 136, 262–63n105
Route 181: Fragments of a Journey in Israel-Palestine. See Khleifi, Michel and Eyal Sivan

RTBF (Radio Télévision Belge Francophone), 72, 76, 102–103, 130, 164, 167, 254n9, 259n68, 260n74
Ruhr (region), 75, 77, 79, 255–56n27
Rupo, Elio di, 268n70

Sans toit ni loi. See under Varda, Agnès
Sauve-moi. See under Vincent, Christian
Scaphandre et le papillon, Le. See under Schnabel, Julian
Schnabel, Julian: *Scaphandre et le papillon*, 147
Schuman Declaration, 86
Sciammi, Céline: *Bande des filles*, 190
screen acting. See acting (in cinema)
Seidl, Ulrich: *Import/Export*, 204
Sellani, Djamel: *Une vie de chacal*, 262–63n105
Seraing, 5–6, 24, 76, 88, 259n71
Serreau, Coline: *Mais qu'est-ce qu'elles veulent?*, 262–63n105
Sica, Vittorio de, vi, 97, 200, 237–38; *Ladri di biciclette*, 193, 199, 202–204, 219, 233, 275n35; *Miracolo a Milano*, vi, 18, 156, 203–205, 209–10, 233, 238–40; *Umberto D*, 49, 203
Sidney, George: *Three Musketeers*, 262n93
Silence de Lorna, La. See under Dardenne, Jean-Pierre and Luc Dardenne, works of
Siodmak, Robert: *Mollenard*, 110
sky, 30, 32, 51, 92, 102, 107, 198, 233, 247
Sous le soleil de Satan (Georges Bernanos). See *under* Bernanos, Georges
Sous le soleil de Satan (Maurice Pialat). See *under* Pialat, Maurice
Spielberg, Steven: *Jurassic Park*, 140
Spinoza, Baruch: and Deleuze, 215, 222, 224, 240–41, 278n88; *Ethics* of, 196, 242–44, 280n19; on inclination, 29; on miracles, 9; on right and power, 11; on wonder, 9, 235
steel industry: in French North, 78, 87, 188; in Wallonia, 77, 86, 88–89, 150, 256n28, 259n71
Still Life. See under Jia Zhangke
Storck, Henri and Joris Ivens: *Misère au Borinage*, 15, 38, 83–85, 95, 97, 100–101, 123, 151, 256n34
Storck, Henri, 97, 102–103, 135, 151–52, 268–69n80, 270n95; *Banquet des fraudeurs*, 106; *Boerensymphonie*, 151; *Fêtes de Belgique*, 123, 154. See also under Storck, Henri and Joris Ivens
Straight Story, The. See under Lynch, David
strike: Borinage 1932, 84, 86; and *Germinal*, 107; and *humanité*, 34; Roubaix 1931, 82; Wallonia 1960–1961 ("strike of the century"), 95, 100–101, 105, 259n69
Strip-Tease (television series), 260n74
subjectivity: acting/acted image, 207; Adorno on, 202; Badiou on, 224–25; Foucault on, 27–29, 213, 237; and humanism, 210; and Lacan, 197; and modernity, 213, 215–16, 219; posthuman, 235–45 passim; and precarity, 209, 217, 222; and *Rosetta* and *l'humanité*, 23–30 passim, 44–45, 57
Subway. See under Besson, Luc
Sur la terre comme au ciel. See under Hänsel, Marion

Tarkovsky, Andrei, 218
Tax Shelter (France), 141
Tax Shelter (French Community of Belgium), 159–61, 165, 266n41
Tavernier, Bertrand: *Ça commence aujourd'hui*, 113, 146, 190
television: Flemish VRT, 72; and francophone Belgium, 72, 130, 134, 152, 160, 165, 258n58, 259n68,

260n74; Canal Plus, 130, 132; and French cinema, 139–41, 144–46; and *jeune cinema français*, 144; and new realism, 194. See also ARTE; RTBF
Ten. See under Kiarostami, Abbas
Terme, Louis: *Fille de la route*, 262–63n105
terril, 84, 98, 100–101, 106, 123, 167, 169, 171, 173f, 175–77
Tête haute, La. See under Bercot, Emmanuelle
textile industry: in French North, 32, 78, 136, 263n105; in Wallonia, 76–77
Three Musketeers (George Sidney). See under Sidney, George
Tirez sur le pianiste. See under Truffaut, François
Titanic. See under Cameron, James
Todo sobre mi madre. See under Almodóvar, Pedro
Toto le héros. See under Dormael, Jaco van
Tout va bien. See under Godard, Jean-Luc, and Jean-Pierre Gorin
transnational cinema, 10–11, 69, 135
Travellinckx. See under Lanners, Bouli
Truffaut, François: *400 coups*, 112–15, 137–38, 211, 217, 222; and francophone-European film and philosophy, 5; *Tirez sur le pianiste*, 212; "Une certaine tendance du cinéma français," 109–10, 137
Twentynine Palms. See under Dumont, Bruno, works of

UK. See United Kingdom
Ultranova. See under Lanners, Bouli
Umberto D. See under Sica, Vittorio de
Un condamné à mort s'est échappé. See under Bresson, Robert, works of
Un conte de Noël. See under Desplechin, Arnaud
Une liaison pornographique. See under Fonteyne, Frédéric
Une vie de chacal. See under Sellani, Djamel
United Kingdom, 8, 25, 117, 254–55n17

Va Petite! See under Guesnier, Alain
Valenciennes: and cinema, 130, 132, 263n2, 264n7; and coal and industry, 76, 78, 87; photo made in, 187
Van der Meersch, Maxence. See under Meersch, Maxence van der
Van Gogh, Vincent. See Gogh, Vincent van
Van Gogh (film). See under Pialat, Maurice
Varda, Agnès: *Cléo de 5 à 7*, 222; and francophone-European film and philosophy, 5; *Glâneur et la glaneuse*, 223; *Plages d'Agnès*, 223; *Sans toit ni loi*, 190, 217; *Visages villages*, 223
Vaucluse, 47, 223
Vechten voor onze Rechten. See under Buyens, Frans
Vent d'est, Le. See under Godard, Jean-Luc, and Jean-Pierre Gorin
Vent du Nord. See under Walid, Mattar
Vernoux, Marion: *Rien à faire*, 113
Veysset, Sandrine, 143; *Y'aura-t'il de la neige à Noël?*, 190–91
Viaggio in Italia. See under Rossellini, Roberto
Vie d'Adèle, La. See under Kechiche, Abdellatif
Vie de Jésus, La. See under Dumont, Bruno, works of
Vie ne me fait pas peur, La. See under Lvovsky, Noémi
Vie rêvée des anges, La. See under Zonca, Erick
Vincent, Christian, 143; *Sauve-moi*, 113
Vincent, Thomas: *Karnaval*, 113, 116, 122–23

Virk, Manjinder: *With Love from Calais*, 117–18
Virno, Paolo: *Grammar of the Multitude*, 209
Visages villages. See under Varda, Agnès
Visconti, Luchino, 97, 200; *Rocco e i suoi Fratelli*, 98
Visions de Lourdes. See under Dekeukeleire, Charles
Vlaamse Gemeenschap. See Flemish Community
Voix du Nord, La, 1–2, 146
Vrouw tussen Hond en Wolf. See under Delvaux, André
Wachowski, Lana, and Lily Wachowski: *The Matrix*, 14–15, 62
Walid, Mattar: *Vent du Nord*, 113, 165
Wallimage, 12, 130–31, 158, 160, 163–66, 263n2
Wallonia: and cinema, 6, 8, 10–12, 16, 25, 65, 83–87, 96–107, 129–32, 148–49, 156–66 passim; and culture, 17, 102, 123–24; and economy, 24, 65–67, 75–95 passim, 100–103, 171, 257–58nn51–2, 258n55, 258n57, 259n69; and migration, 8, 40, 78–79, 119–21; and regional history, 68, 70, 72–75, 149, 254n12, 254n15. *See also* Nord, French-Walloon; Walloon cinema
Wallonie-Bruxelles, Fédération: discussions about name change of the francophone Belgian community into, 72, 159, 171, 254n9. *See also* French Community of Belgium; MACs (museum)
Walloon popular movement, 74, 259n70
Wang Xiaoshuai: *Beijing Bicycle*, 204
Welcome. See under Lioret, Philippe
Wendy and Lucy. See under Reichardt, Kelly
With Love from Calais. See under Virk, Manjinder
wonder, 9, 40, 96, 235, 244
World War I, 32, 74, 78–79
World War II: and Belgium, 8, 74, 254n11; and coal mining and industry following, 78–79, 86; and France, 74; and cinema, 137, 151, 214, 217, 222
World, The. See under Jia Zhangke

xenophobia: and cinematic engagement with, 8, 102, 117; and French North, 117, 119–21; and Wallonia, 102

Y'aura-t'il de la neige à Noël? See under Veysset, Sandrine
young French cinema. See *jeune cinema français*

Zola, Emile, 82; *Germinal*, 12, 32, 110; *Bête humaine*, 35
Zonca, Erick: *Petit voleur*, 145; *Vie rêvée des anges*, 113, 125–26, 146–47, 190–91

THE SUNY SERIES

HORIZONS OF CINEMA

MURRAY POMERANCE | EDITOR

Also in the series

William Rothman, editor, *Cavell on Film*

J. David Slocum, editor, *Rebel Without a Cause*

Joe McElhaney, *The Death of Classical Cinema*

Kirsten Moana Thompson, *Apocalyptic Dread*

Frances Gateward, editor, *Seoul Searching*

Michael Atkinson, editor, *Exile Cinema*

Paul S. Moore, *Now Playing*

Robin L. Murray and Joseph K. Heumann, *Ecology and Popular Film*

William Rothman, editor, *Three Documentary Filmmakers*

Sean Griffin, editor, *Hetero*

Jean-Michel Frodon, editor, *Cinema and the Shoah*

Carolyn Jess-Cooke and Constantine Verevis, editors, *Second Takes*

Matthew Solomon, editor, *Fantastic Voyages of the Cinematic Imagination*

R. Barton Palmer and David Boyd, editors, *Hitchcock at the Source*

William Rothman, *Hitchcock: The Murderous Gaze, Second Edition*

Joanna Hearne, *Native Recognition*

Marc Raymond, *Hollywood's New Yorker*

Steven Rybin and Will Scheibel, editors, *Lonely Places, Dangerous Ground*

Claire Perkins and Constantine Verevis, editors, *B Is for Bad Cinema*

Dominic Lennard, *Bad Seeds and Holy Terrors*

Rosie Thomas, *Bombay before Bollywood*

Scott M. MacDonald, *Binghamton Babylon*

Sudhir Mahadevan, *A Very Old Machine*

David Greven, *Ghost Faces*

James S. Williams, *Encounters with Godard*

William H. Epstein and R. Barton Palmer, editors, *Invented Lives, Imagined Communities*

Lee Carruthers, *Doing Time*

Rebecca Meyers, William Rothman, and Charles Warren, editors, *Looking with Robert Gardner*

Belinda Smaill, *Regarding Life*

Douglas McFarland and Wesley King, editors, *John Huston as Adaptor*
R. Barton Palmer, Homer B. Pettey, and Steven M. Sanders, editors, *Hitchcock's Moral Gaze*
Nenad Jovanovic, *Brechtian Cinemas*
Will Scheibel, *American Stranger*
Amy Rust, *Passionate Detachments*
Steven Rybin, *Gestures of Love*
Seth Friedman, *Are You Watching Closely?*
Roger Rawlings, *Ripping England!*
Michael DeAngelis, *Rx Hollywood*
Ricardo E. Zulueta, *Queer Art Camp Superstar*
John Caruana and Mark Cauchi, editors, *Immanent Frames*
Nathan Holmes, *Welcome to Fear City*
Homer B. Pettey and R. Barton Palmer, editors, *Rule, Britannia!*
Milo Sweedler, *Rumble and Crash*
Ken Windrum, *From El Dorado to Lost Horizons*
Matthew Lau, *Sounds Like Helicopters*
Dominic Lennard, *Brute Force*
William Rothman, *Tuitions and Intuitions*
Michael Hammond, *The Great War in Hollywood Memory, 1918–1939*
Burke Hilsabeck, *The Slapstick Camera*

www.ingramcontent.com/pod-product-compliance
Lightning Source LLC
Chambersburg PA
CBHW030009240426
43672CB00007B/878